VENICE
AN ODYSSEY

15-8-22

To Daniel
for your next
visit to
Venezia.
Neil

NEAL E. ROBBINS

VENICE
AN ODYSSEY

Hope, anger and the future of cities

with the testimony of 150 Venetians, 3 maps and 21 illustrations

First published in Local Secrets edition in July 2020

Second revised Local Secrets edition November 2020

First La Toletta edition 2021

ISBN 9788885455290

Cover image: Giudecca Canal, photo by Neal E Robbins

PHOTOS: (salon, p. 9) by Giovanni Keller; (rowing, p. 31) by Sofia Bareato; (Nuovo Trionfo, p. 80) by Daniele Resini, used with permission; (lagoon erosion, p. 115) courtesy of Dr. Luigi D'Alpaos; (forcole, p. 118) reproduced with permission from "la voga veneta" published by the City of Venice; (Artisans, p. 121) by Fabio Macaluso; (Nono painting, p. 123) courtesy of Serena Nono; (pointing to marsh, p. 166) by Silvio Testa; (Acqua alta, St. Mark's, p. 188) by Ihor Serdyukov/ Shutterstock; (Mose, p. 194) by Naeblys; (Fondaco dei Turchi now, p. 263) by Didier Descouens CC BY-SA 4.0; (M9 museum, p. 296), courtesy of M9 by Alessandra Chemollo; (grosso, p. 321), by CNG - CNG, CC BY-SA 3.0, https://commons.wikimedia.org/w/index.php?curid=4310909. All other photography is by Neal E Robbins.

TEXTS: p. 145–6, "As in the Arsenal of the Venetians..." Ciaran Carson, *The Inferno of Dante Alighieri,* a new translation, p. 140. Quoted with permission from Head of Zeus Ltd, and the Susijn Agency, London; p. 352, "Le erbe matte di Venezia: piccola storia di resistenza vegetale e umana," used with permission of Tiziana Plebani and the translator, Daniele Pio Buenza.

FOREWORD
TO THE THIRD EDITION

This is a book of multiple voices. I wanted the many Venetians I've interviewed to speak for their city.

That said, as a journalist originally from Chicago and now living in Cambridge, England, who has had the good fortune of getting to know Venice intimately during his lifetime, I will be the reader's main guide. This is a non-fiction work based on my own life and my explorations of Venice and its lagoon. I draw on the scholarship on Venice to deepen the investigation. But, by and large, the book is a conduit for the thoughts, observations and feelings of the 150-plus ordinary and extraordinary Venetians I interviewed during 2018 and 2019. In over 200 hours of taped interviews, I asked them to help me unravel the enigma that is *La Serenissima*.

I have quoted these sources in the chapters, but have also given some a platform in between chapters in a passage I call an intermezzo. The sources speak in their own words, which I have translated from Italian and edited for conciseness and clarity of expression. All the people mentioned are real and identified with their real names. In a few cases I have chosen not to use the names at all of real individuals. There are no composite characters.

I continued to update the book into 2021.

PREFACE

A nonfiction essay? A guide? A historical text? An autobiographical story?

There's a bit of everything in this accurate, interesting, original work created by a writer who has lived in Venice and worked and studied all over the world.

As an adolescent Neal Robbins attended a classical high school in the city for a year hosted by a beautiful Venetian family — father, mother and three children — that after 50 years he still considers his own parents and siblings. Neal is an American who became Venetian and he will never forget his own hometown even even though he left the United States to make a home in Great Britain.

I apologize to those who believe in *jus soli* and also for those followers of *jus sanguinis*, but I believe I am not wrong in affirming that (as always) *one becomes Venetian*.

It is not important where you are born or which culture you belong to: if a person understands this city he or she is Venetian. It's a way of being, a way of existing, a way of perceiving the benefits of a city built on the water, a city that lives on the water, made its fortune and its myths on the water, and has always and will always share these benefits with whoever lives there or appreciates it when they go there.

It's a sort of permanent humanism favored by the surrounding natural environment, by the absence of automobiles, a paradigm of modernity, by the freedom to walk and talk without annoying noises, while surrounded by beautiful architecture of every age, and with the invigorating element — water — accompanying you in every moment through the sestieri, among the many islands of the lagoon, well-known or and less known, inhabited or temporarily abandoned.

The lagoon water is special, being salty and a mixture of fresh from the rivers and salty water from the sea.

Neal Robbins is the Venetian Ulysses, and as a Venetian he gives everyone the chance to better understand this special city that is spoken of around the world, but perhaps little known for its historic, modern, humanistic and future potential, one that is considering and wishing for a new Renaissance.

The picture in the book of Neal Robbins is symbolic and authentically realistic, showing him at the stern of a typical Venetian vessel, a sandolo, in a Venetian canal, rowing in the Venetian style.

Neal's experience in the lagoon started in the 1970s when the urban center of the city was living perhaps its last moments of normality before the uncontrolled invasion of the so-called *mordi e fuggi*, "eat and run," tourists (or rather an invasion controlled by the powers that be, local and international, with a precise business strategy).

For personal reasons, I have often reflected about the objectives of the two professions: journalist and historian, often grouped with another noun; writer. Deep down, the journalist is a historian of the present and a historian is a journalist of the past.

I think this because Neal Robbins embodies and interprets magnificently these two intellectual professions, always maintaining the sole objective of "cracking the puzzle that is La Serenissima," answering simple questions with the support of Venetians, and bringing the additional fundamental element, passion.

Understanding and making others understand, sharing in and sharing with, loving and bringing love, Neal involves the inhabitants of the lagoon, both from the islands and the *terraferma*, and he interviews them. It is a heterogeneous group from every cultural and professional level, including his old school friends, and he brings in many and varied authoritative quotes from scholars of history of La Serenissima and famous writers of the present and the past.

With wisdom and judiciousness, Neal confronts the fundamental themes, historic, social and environmental, in an attempt to overcome the clichés, the invented traditions and prejudices (relevant to the life and conservation of the lagoon) that have marked part of the dominant culture — probably influenced by myths surrounding the not-too-distant history of Italian unity achieved after centuries — due to legendary facts about the Italian Resurgence brought out by the Saubada monarchy, which had no intention of giving value to the memories and experiences of many important regional realities linked too closely to established republican policies, even if secular.

With 28 chapters with fine titles, an original coda ending, 11 intermezzi focused on extraordinary contributions of the 150 Venetians involved in the narrative, the book succinctly sums up what the sociologists say are the important pillars of a modern community: Culture, economics and politics (in alphabetical order).

The common wish is for a future for the city, because, as Joseph Brodskij, another great Venetian said, "A work of art has only two choices: to illuminate the heart of men or be destroyed."

The hope, with this precious contribution that needs to be read carefully and shared around, is that Venice continues in the future to illuminate the hearts of all.

Giorgio Crovato,

Academic Director, Ateneo Veneto

CONTENTS

"What is the city but the people?"

—SICINIUS, FROM ACT 3, SCENE 1

OF WILLIAM SHAKESPEARE'S TRAGEDY, *CORIOLANUS*

Venice
1 2 3 4 5 6 7 8 9
A B C D E F G H I
N
W
E
S
500 m
1000 feet
Campo Sant'Alvise
Baia del Re (Sacca San Girolamo)
Fondamenta delle Cappuccine
Palazzo Rizzo-Patarol
Fondamenta degli Ormesini
Madonna de l'Orto
Fondamenta di Cannaregio
Ghetto
Arzanà
Cannaregio
Ca' Vendramin Calergi
Tronchetto (parking)
Fondaco dei Turchi
Ca' Tron
Strada Nuo
Santa Lucia Train Station
Scalzi bridge
Ca' Corner della Regina
Palazzo Soranzo Cappello
Campo San Giacomo dell'Orio
Ponte delle Tette
Pescaria
Stazione marittima (maritime terminal)
Campo San Giacon
Calatrava Bridge
Rialt
Piazzale Roma
Rio Noio
San Polo
Scuola Grande di San Rocco
Basilica dei Frari
Ca' Farsetti
Santa Croce
Palazzo Pisani Moretta
Canal Grande
Campo Santa Margherita
Campo San Pantalon
Palazzo Nani-Bernardo
Campo Santo Stefano
Ateneo Veneto
La Fenice
Palazzo Grassi
Ca' Rezzonico
Ponte dei Pugni
Teatro de l'Avogaria
Palazzo Malipiero Barnabò
Liceo Classico Marco Polo
San Moisè
Teatro Ca' Foscari
Ponte dell'Accademia
Palazzo Barbaro
Gallerie dell'Accademia
Palazzo Contarini
Dorsoduro
Basilic della Salu
Zattere
Giudecca Canal
Sacca San Biagio
Redentore
Giudecca

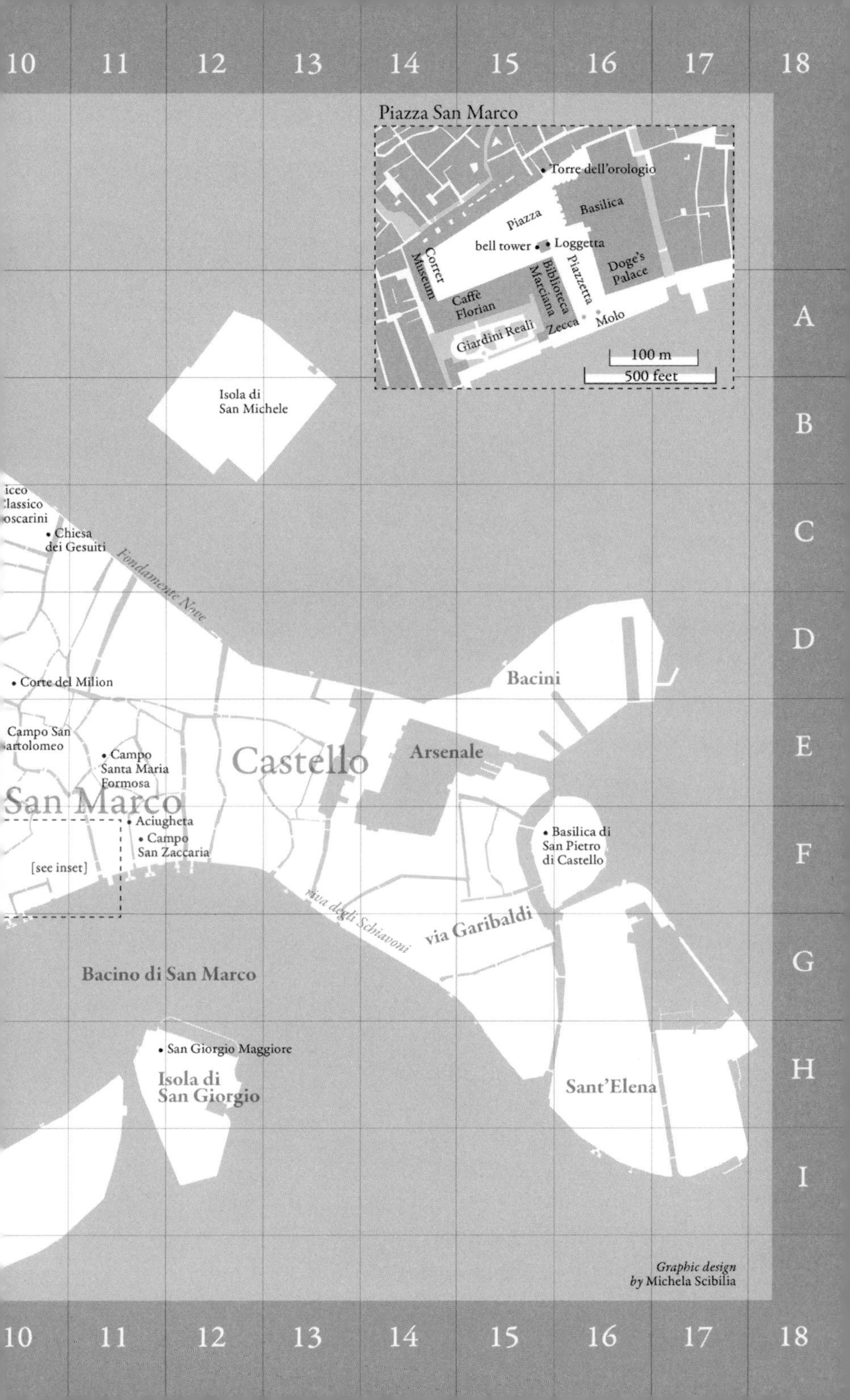

10 11 12 13 14 15 16 17 18
A B C D E F G H I
Piazza San Marco
Torre dell'orologio
Basilica
Piazza
bell tower
Loggetta
Correr Museum
Biblioteca Marciana
Piazzetta
Doge's Palace
Caffè Florian
Giardini Reali
Zecca
Molo
100 m
500 feet
Isola di San Michele
Chiesa dei Gesuiti
Fondamente Nove
Corte del Milion
Campo San
Campo Santa Maria Formosa
San Marco
Castello
Arsenale
Bacini
Aciugheta
Campo San Zaccaria
[see inset]
Basilica di San Pietro di Castello
riva degli Schiavoni
via Garibaldi
Bacino di San Marco
San Giorgio Maggiore
Isola di San Giorgio
Sant'Elena
Graphic design by Michela Scibilia

Venice lagoon and *terraferma*

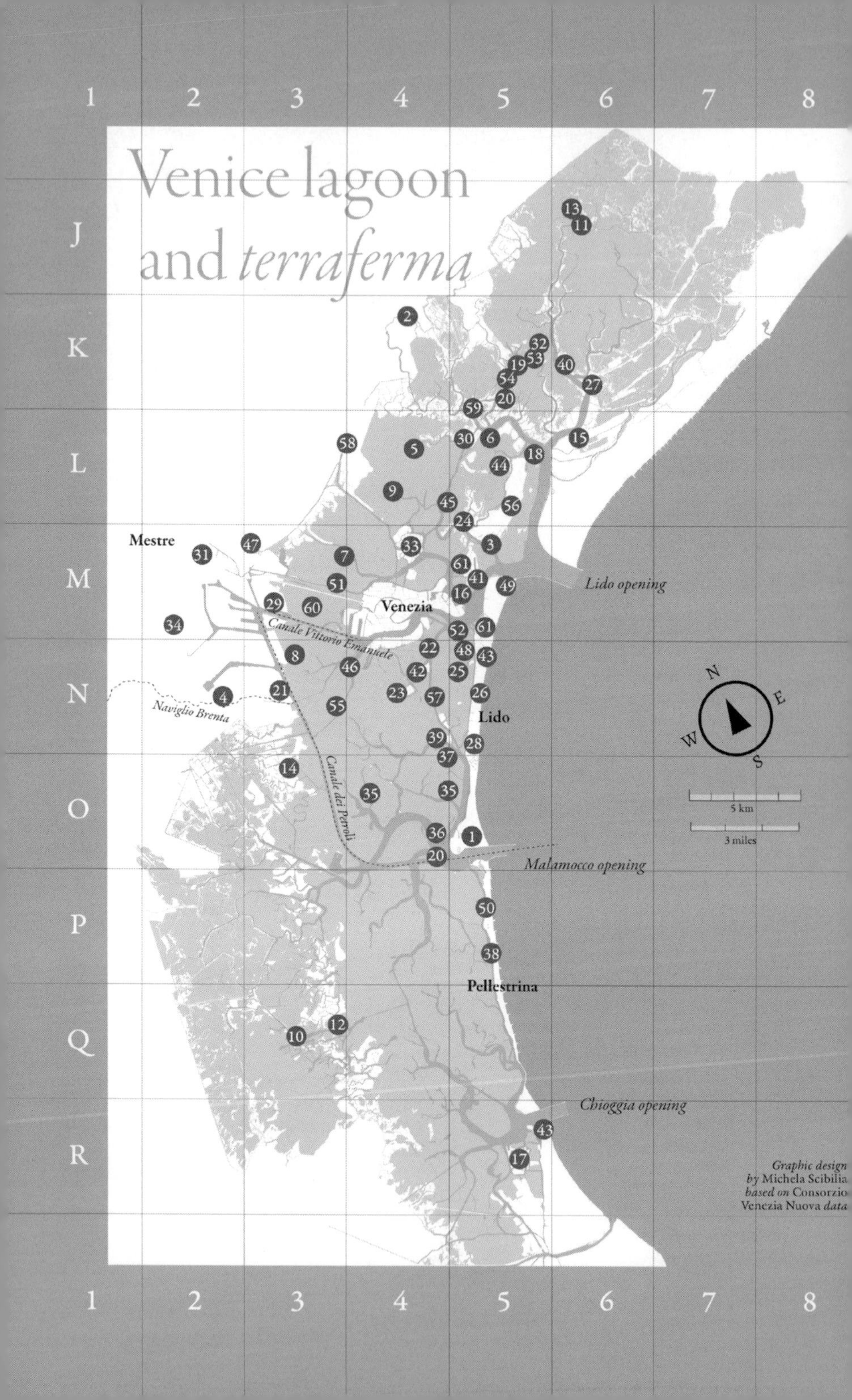

Graphic design by Michela Scibilia *based on* Consorzio Venezia Nuova *data*

LAGOON MAP KEY

1 Alberoni
2 Altino
3 bacàn, il (beach)
4 Brenta (Naviglio)
5 Buel del Lovo
6 Burano
7 Campalto
8 Canale dei Petroli (canal)
9 Carbonera
10 Cason Millecampi
11 Cason da Pesca Val Dogà
12 Cason dei Sette Morti (vanished)
13 Cason Montiron
14 Cassa di Colmata (landfill area)
15 Cavallino-Treporti (town)
16 Certosa
17 Chioggia (town)
18 Crevan
19 Cura, La
20 Faro Spignon (lighthouse)
21 Fusina
22 Grazia, La
23 Isola delle Rose (Sacca Sessola)
24 Lazzaretto Nuovo
25 Lazzaretto Vecchio
26 Lido
27 Lio Piccolo
28 Malamocco
29 Marghera (city)
30 Mazzorbo
31 Mestre (city)
32 Motta dei Cunicci
33 Murano
34 Nave de Vero (shopping mall)
35 Ottagono Abbandonato
36 Ottagano Alberoni
37 Ottagono Poveglia
38 Pellestrina
39 Poveglia
40 Saline, le
41 Sant'Andrea (fort)
42 San Clemente
43 San Felice (fort)
44 San Francesco del Deserto
45 San Giacomo in Paludo
46 San Giorgio in Alga
47 San Giuliano (town)
48 San Lazzaro degli Armeni
49 San Nicolò (fort)
50 San Pietro in Volta
51 San Secondo
52 San Servolo
53 Santa Cristina
54 Sant'Adrian
55 Sant'Angelo della Polvere
56 Sant'Erasmo
57 Santo Spirito
58 Tessera (town)
59 Torcello
60 Vittorio Emanuele (canal)
61 Vignole

PROLOGUE
ORIGINS OF AN ODYSSEY

I borrowed a little Venetian boat, a *sandolo*. My friend's mamma watched from her window over the canal, perhaps a bit apprehensively, as I rowed by in the slender vessel, silently gliding over the glassy waterways that crisscross Venice. I looked up at her and smiled. I was making my way through the medieval-scale city and heading out into the lagoon, the surrounding 552-square kilometer body of water. I aimed to begin that very day my own extended exploration of the scores of ancient islands scattered over these Adriatic coastal shallows.

It was June 1976, the summer after college; I was a twenty-two-year-old American from Chicagoland and I had no idea exactly what I would encounter or how long I might be away. Having organized the expedition rather on the spur of the moment, I would just row, and I would write about whatever happened. I had brought my portable typewriter and sleeping bag with me, for I imagined myself to be an explorer and had long been a writer, having edited my school and college newspapers. I felt sure my fearless journalistic spirit would be sufficient for any exigency.

I rowed in the Venetian style, standing up, looking forward, oar grasped with both hands, like a gondolier. I was in Venice on a return visit to look up Italian friends whom I had met when I attended my last year of secondary school there, five years earlier, at which time I had also learned to row like a Venetian. I had come back fired up with adventurous ambitions that were indulged but apparently not infectious. Most of my school friends had better things to do. Going to the beach was big. But I was never a beach person. I quickly tired of beaches and had declared I wanted to climb mountains because they were there; I wanted to explore wild and difficult places and pen stories about them in gripping prose.

So, I was rowing off by myself, with the still cool morning air soothing my cheeks. I rowed for a couple of hours, aiming to reach a nondescript island within view whose name I never discovered, and I arrived by mid-morning just as the sun began to bear down. I pulled the wooden craft up, securing it to a post on the muddy shore and clambered up the bank to the shade of a tree to wait for the heat of the day to pass. Sitting on a little rise, I looked back at *La Serenissima*, the "most serene" city of legend, with stories on every street, every doorway and every nook, a place where I had first discovered the brotherhood of man by living among the Italians, where I had learned to speak the language and where I had found lifelong friends.

I pulled out my typewriter and bashed away at the keys until I had exhausted what words came. Perhaps I nibbled a bit of cheese and bread. I had a book. I cracked it open. The day grew steadily hotter; the sultry, mid-summer sun made me itch, even in the shade. I soon realized I would be stuck on this islet for hours more if I wanted to avoid the intense midday sun. The cooler evening seemed ages away. It was then that boredom struck. That was all it took to break my resolve.

I gathered up my stuff, returned to my sandolo and, oblivious to the sun beating down, headed back to Venice. Young enough, strong enough and, as foolish as the mad dogs and Englishmen, I seemed to have survived the return journey. I tied up the boat at its mooring on the canal where I had found it and thanked the lender. I made my way back to the *palazzo* of the Italian family I had stayed with when I spent that year in Venice, pressed the buzzer outside the courtyard door and climbed the marble stairs back to their floor of the palazzo. I had returned to their kitchen by late afternoon. My Italian hosts, generously putting me up for this return visit, smiled at the brevity of my escapade. Because I'd left with little fuss, with a scope and commitment to the mission unclear then even to myself, my reappearance hardly raised an eyebrow. Fickleness comes with youth.

With time on my hands and Italian friends who liked to travel around their own land even more than the foreign tourists did, I was soon swept up in a plan to visit a music festival. But somehow my curiosity towards the lagoon that had propelled me to make that first abbreviated foray never faded. What had begun as zeal for adventure would, in the fullness of time, also become a sublime odyssey of the heart and of the mind — a rediscovery of old friendships, a forging of new ones and most of all, a dispelling of the fog of my own ignorance long obscuring the real Venice.

1

LETTERS

A CRITIQUE OF MY SEVENTEEN-YEAR-OLD SELF

> *"At 45°14′N., 12°18′E., the navigator, sailing up the Adriatic coast of Italy, discovers an opening in the long low line of the shore: and turning westward, with the race of the tide, he enters a lagoon."*
>
> —OPENING LINE OF *THE WORLD OF VENICE*, BY JAMES [JAN] MORRIS

I got a minor celebrity send-off when I first went to Venice in 1971. I still have the clipping from the suburban Chicago newspaper reporting on my imminent departure as my town's "envoy" to Venice. The grainy black-and-white photo shows a tousle-headed me seated next to the mayor of my hometown, Highland Park. He is leaning over my shoulder, signing a letter of greeting to the mayor of Venice that I would take with me.

The article, in describing why a seventeen-year-old high school junior would be flying to Venice in a few days, included my expectations: "I've heard Venice is a very beautiful city, that it's very unusual and that no other place is like it," I said. "I know I'll have to adjust [my] concept of age. There, something isn't considered old until it's 1,000 years old. Here, we put something in a museum when it's seventy-five years old." That's an overstatement, but from my vantage point in the postwar New World, Venetian history was awe-inspiring.

In my youth, "old" happened at the edges of living memory. My father built our ranch-style single-family home on prairie land in the year I was born, 1954. We found flint arrowheads in the backyard as the lot had been part of the homelands of the native American Potawatomi until the early 1800s. Highland Park is one of the sprawling suburbs that spun off from the original 1837 frontier settlement of Chicago, which itself had rapidly filled with waves of immigrants — at first Germans, Irish and Scandinavians and then Czechs, Poles, Italians, and Jews, the last of which included my own antecedents. But relative to Venice, in Chicago, and especially its suburbs, more or less everything was new.

Now I was going back to Europe. The Old Continent. When the letter came saying that I had been selected for a study abroad scholarship for "*Venezia*," we panicked. Where was "Venezia"? My mother and I ran for a map, and soon realized that "Venezia" was "Venice" in Italian. I was going to Venice! I was dazzled for quite some time, as my destination could have been anywhere abroad. In this program for secondary school students, selection was based on whether the candidate was expected to thrive. You were "adopted" by a family with children of your age, attended school and stayed for up to a school year, not to see the world so much as to break through cultural barriers, while your host family learned about your culture from you.

I was super excited to be going, and my host family, who had applied, like me, to participate in the exchange, had sent me pictures of themselves. But I was unable to get much of a feeling for Venice in the few weeks

The Keller family residence was on the top floor of the palazzo with the balcony. My 'bedroom' window was top-most left.

I had before leaving. In 1971 the city was only beginning to be the mega-popular destination it would become. I knew no one who had been there. International travel was then still a considerable privilege, not a middle-class staple. So, apart from reading the dry entry in the encyclopedia and having my mom make pasta, in terms of preparation, I can only recall sitting in the kitchen of a nice Italian lady who tried to teach me to say *grazie* and *ciao*, polite words I then found terribly hard to pronounce.

After a flight with a couple of hundred other exchange students and a bit of orientation from the sponsoring organization, I arrived at Venezia–Santa Lucia train station. I wrote home:

> *12 September 1971: I got off the train the first day in Venezia and walked right past* [my host family] *who were waiting. But, after a moment, we got straightened out and found each other. I guess they looked like their pictures, but they were bad pictures. They took me home on the "bus" (a ferryboat). My initial impression of Venice, I must admit, was not positive... The buildings at first looked quite decrepit. The plaster was falling off, they were dirty.*

Oddly this first reaction, I was to learn, was not unusual. Questions like this multiplied during my stay. For instance, why did my Italian brother play basketball in a magnificent fourteenth-century building (I had always thought it was a church) that had been converted into a sports hall? How could the Venetians use such a fabulous old monument for basketball? Had a glut of the history led to devaluation? Why did Venice look so run-down? I knew it was old, but why didn't they smarten it up a bit? In fact, in that first letter I wrote, confusedly:

> *I began to feel that this was not a real place. It must have been set up for tourists... but the difference was [sic] that Venice is a real living, working city! Meant to be lived in. This is somewhat difficult to adjust to.*

Extreme reactions to Venice from travelers arriving in the city have long been commonplace. Even in the Middle Ages and Renaissance, visitors struggled to take in the place. When Friar Felix Fabri approached Venice by boat in the mid-fifteenth century, he and his companions were "astonished" at the very sight of this "famous, great and wealthy city... standing in wondrous fashion in the midst of waters, with lofty towers, great churches, splendid houses and palaces." Later in 1765, Edward Gibbon, author of *The History of the Decline and Fall of the Roman Empire*, reported feeling, "momentary surprise which gives way to satiety and disgust. Old and in general ill-built houses, ruined pictures and stinking ditches dignified with the pompous designation of Canals; a fine bridge spoilt by two rows of houses upon it, a large square decorated with the worst architectures I have ever yet saw." In 1844, Charles Dickens said Venice was "beyond the fancy of the wildest dreamer. Opium couldn't build such a place...."

In the last century, somehow hitting the modern zeitgeist squarely on the head, American humorist Robert Benchley stepped out of the train station in Venice to find before him the Grand Canal. He telegraphed his editor in New York: "Streets Full of Water. Please Advise."

So there I was, at seventeen, an American from bland suburbs built up mostly in the 1950s staying with a family that lived in a fifteenth-century palazzo, a building that the father, ophthalmologist Walter Keller, had inherited from his father, a coal merchant originally from Switzerland who served as the honorary Swiss consul general in Venice. We — Walter, his wife Maria, son Giovanni, and daughters Marta, Ursula, and Anna, plus Aunt Giuliana who lived in an adjoining apartment — lived four flights up. It took ninety-eight long steps to reach the *piano nobile*, or main floor, with its high-ceilinged portego, which was the large central ballroom with big windows overlooking a canal. Any big, old structure in Italy is called a "palazzo," but in Venice they tend to be former homes of the Venetian nobility built in a particular style. Over the centuries this one, like many, had been modernized and divided into flats inhabited by various branches of the same family.

The main room — as long as a tennis court and half as wide, with fine fabrics on the walls, oil paintings and a frescoed ceiling — was rarely used. These formal entertainment spaces don't quite fit into modern life. The family lived in rooms flanking the portego, where a modern kitchen, bedrooms and a study had been installed. The only other remaining formal reception room on the other side of the portego was used to store spare furniture — and while I was there it served as my bedroom. I used to pass the time lying on my bed looking up at the cherubs and angels in the ceiling frescoes or looking out the window over the canal at the sea of red-tiled roofs.

I recall that I used to sit at an antique, dark wooden desk illuminated by a shaded lamp that stood in one corner. There I wrote letters home on onion-skin airmail paper. Re-reading them now reminds me of how I saw the world and provides glimpses of the city I encountered.

> *12 September 1971: We went to hear an orchestra play in the theater near the house. The inside was something like Chicago's opera house, but 10 times more ornate. It's hard to describe but a room scultured [sic] and gilded from the 15th century...*[In fact, the theater I saw dated to 1836.]

I vividly remember that evening of my first theater visit. The Kellers led me through Venice's maze of crevasse-like alleyways and mystifying angles until they opened out into a square where the columned façade of the famous La Fenice theater rose with classical flourish. I climbed the

The salon which served as my bedroom. Note the frescoed ceiling.

steps and entered the great theater, where the seating boxes were (and still are) arrayed in a horseshoe around a stage framed in gold. I can't remember what music we heard, but I was thoroughly bewitched by the sounds, the opulence and the idea that famous operas had premiered there. We went to the theater quite regularly, but what makes Venice, Venice, is the water.

> *19 or 20 September 1971: A few days ago my Italian brother Giovanni took us fishing in the lagoon. We caught about 10 squid... I ate and enjoyed the little critters. My Italian is progressing.... The worst thing is sitting around the dinner table and not being able to understand what everyone is saying....*

From the very start of my stay I loved getting out on small wooden boats in the lagoon. With the sights, the smells of the water, the sounds of the wind, the senses took over. Everyone relaxed. The activities were always very physical and hands on, requiring only minimum communication which was most welcome when I all too often found myself suddenly wordless and speechless, reduced to infantility amid fluent speakers of another language. Later, when school started, I learned the language in part by surreptitiously reading Italian Donald Duck comic books in class, painstakingly looking up every word in a dictionary, as, anyway, at first I could not follow what the teacher was saying.

As late summer drew to a close, I got into the routines of school and daily life.

> *31 Sept – Oct 1 1971: School begins tomorrow and all the kids are sort of depressed.... Everything in the family is fine. Yesterday I accidentally chipped the corner of a 15th or 16th century mirror and my father was a bit angry. However, it can be repaired....*

Every school day began in the high-ceilinged kitchen in the palazzo,

My Italian father, Dr. Walter Keller, left, taking me and my siblings on a outing into the lagoon with a fisherman friend in 1971.

with its rows of pots and pans hanging from a suspended rack next to the hearth and stove. This was where we ate all our family meals. Breakfast, however, was strictly a rolling repast, with a big cup of *caffè* with warmed whole milk, big spoonfuls of sugar, and biscuits to soak in the drink. With no time to linger, I would gather up my things, climb back down the stairs, cross the potted plant-filled courtyard and, closing the heavy wooden doors carefully behind me, step out onto the street. I proceeded across Campo Santo Stefano, the nearest square, and over the Grand Canal via the gently arched Ponte dell'Accademia, past the white marble Gallerie dell'Accademia art museum and then over a little bridge to my new school, Liceo Classico Marco Polo. Coming from a 2,500-student-strong American high school built in 1959 that was surrounded by sports fields, streamed students by ability, allowed subject choices and sizzled with the full panoply of American teenage rituals (ranging from yearly prom dances to printing the school newspaper and other after-school activities), I found this new school a shock.

It had no sports, no activities, no social program and no choice. You came there to learn the given classical syllabus. It was housed in a sixteenth-century palazzo that had been the home of Venetian nobles, had 250 students and a curriculum that emphasized the humanities, including Latin and Greek. I was ushered into the second-year class, section B, where the students sat in rows of two-seater desks that were bolted to the floor. I was given a well-worn wooden seat adjacent to the windows overlooking the canal next to a cheerful girl who was full of fun. We never lacked for something to chat about, which was a good thing as we had to sit together all year long. We went to school six days a week, 8 a.m. to 1 p.m. Pupils were assigned to their permanent seat for the entire three years of *liceo*, while the teachers rotated through the classrooms lecturing for one hour at a time from behind a plain wooden desk on a raised podium at the front. Boys could wear whatever, but girls had to don black smocks over their clothing and when the teacher entered, everyone stood up.

Meanwhile, it didn't take long to get to know my host family, as we were all curious about one another.

> *10 October 1971: La mamma is a housewife and very much takes care of the family. I can never walk out without her reminding*

> *me to put on my coat... Il papà... is very jovial and intelligent. Marta, the seventeen-year-old girl is easiest to talk to... Giovanni... is interested in politics. Ursula, the twelve-year-old should be about fourteen the way she carries herself. She doesn't act like a silly twelve-year-old, but a girl of two or three years more. Anna, nine, is quiet and never naughty like her sister Ursula.... La zia* [the aunt], *Walter's sister, is very devoted to Catholicism. The family were interested in my slides of Chicago, especially of Negroes* [a word unacceptable today but common then] *and the ghetto there. There are few blacks* [black people] *here.*

Getting used to living in another family took some doing. As a seventeen-year-old, still mostly a child myself, I never chafed at the regimes of family life, nor, with so much going on, did I feel homesick. But I had little sense of how much I needed to learn. Was there more to know about Europeans other than that they ate with a fork differently to the way I had always been taught? I soon found there was. My Italian family liked to hear about my life, too. They were fascinated with my pictures of a long series of stoplights in Chicago. Venice has no stoplights. I had shots of poor, black neighborhoods on Chicago's South Side, but tended to trail off as I tried to explain the civil rights movement. What did I know? I was from a suburb where the only black people we saw commuted in from downtown to do the cleaning.

Alongside school work, I found some books that helped me understand Venice and on October 25, I wrote:

> *I read* The World of Venice *by James Morris. I think you might enjoy it.... I am finding Italian schools more demanding than those in the US... I have to learn 10 or 12 lines of poetry by heart every week.*

The Morris book, based initially on the author's experience in the US military in the 1950s, made a big impression on me as the only book I had read so far that attempted to describe the Venetians in the context of their history. Literally hundreds of books are written about Venice every year, but very few attempt to pull together these strands as Morris did in this first 1960 edition. It alerted me to the way a place could have many dimensions. And as for school, moan as I did about memorization of poetry, including the opening lines of poet Dante Alighieri's *Purgatorio*, part of his epic work, the *Divine Comedy*, I learned more than I can say, and I can still recite a few of the lines.

That didn't stop me from complaining, however.

> *3 November 1971: The schools are very traditional and very irrelevant, if you ask me. For example Greek and Latin are useless.... And the method of teaching is also rather poor.... For young Venetians Venice is a very dull city. There are absolutely no sports, a couple of movie theaters and that's all.*

It was hard to move away from thinking that the way we did things in America was better. When I had an upset stomach the Italian doctor suggested I eat bananas. At home in America they always had a pill for things. Bananas as a cure for an upset tummy was hard to accept, as were medicines administered by means of suppositories. They didn't have those in America either. Italian food I got along well with — though whole, marinated mini-octopus was a hurdle at first. The fact is I was just attached to the familiar, driven by a stubborn insistence that whatever was done in America had to be better.

Yet my mind was being wrenched open daily by the new and unfamiliar territory I found around me and by school friends who wanted to share their lives with me, while at home with my hosts, life had a decidedly elevated air.

> *20 November 1971: The Kellers are putting on a* [Carlo] *Goldoni play. I get a bit part... walking on the stage, saying, "Patrona, magneremo sti confetti?" ("Signora, will we eat the wedding candy?")*

From left: Anna, Giovanni and Marta Keller in the countryside of Venice in 1971 or 1972.

In the palazzo's big ballroom, the portego, we rehearsed and later put on the play *Sior Todero Brontolon* to raise money for the restoration of Santa Maria Gloriosa dei Frari, a massive church nearby. The Kellers happened to be a family who took great pride in the city. With a network of friends, they put together a professional-quality performance of this eighteenth-century Venetian comedy, complete with homemade period costumes. Later we performed it again for a Venice Society in Switzerland. My role was that of a servant and I came on stage at the very end of the last scene, delivering my line in Venetian, but with my unavoidably American accent, it got some laughs.

In contrast, Italian life around us felt rather like a cauldron and my host father, Walter, would share his frustration about the state of Italy at the dinner table. It was a turmoil you could not avoid.

> *24 November 1971: Today I didn't go to school because there was a strike by the teachers.... Everybody's striking around here! ... there is a law that will, if passed, give Venice the money to restore itself. But this is a political football* [hot topic]....

Teachers, students, janitors, everyone, it seemed, went on strike in turns and with my still rudimentary Italian, I hardly grasped what they were striking about. But when this happened, one had to take sides. I found that a matter of great anguish. What was the right thing to do? My friends were divided. I could go to school, as many did, or stay away. I don't recall what I decided. The Venice of the early 1970s was in a whirlwind of change within a vortex that was Italian politics, which itself was struggling with the legacies of the Second World War, the Italian economic boom, the role of the Catholic Church and the aftershocks of the 1968 student movements. But I took on board the sheer emotion of it, the shouting and the seriousness.

Venice's own battles arose in part from the devastating floods of 1966 that had threatened its survival and brought the decay of its heritage to global attention. At that time, people were debating new laws that would help Venice. They would also fire up a debate that rages still today. People over the world worried that Venice might be dying. When an Italian journalist asked me what I thought, this is what I said:

> *29 January, 1972: Venice is dying, not dead. And at this moment its beauty and nobility are most strongly felt.*

Poetic as that may be, I now feel dissatisfied with that kind of response. What exactly is dying when we speak about a city? When is it dead? High thoughts seemed so easy at seventeen. I was just taking it all in, and learning about new worlds.

In my April 3 letter, I recorded that I had asked a Jewish friend if I could:

> *...spend Passover with her family in the Ghetto. We went to the Orthodox service, men on one side, women on the other. At the Seder the food and the manner of chanting the prayers were different* [based on Sephardic traditions, of Spain and Portugal, whereas I was familiar with those of the Ashkenazi of my Germanic forebears]. *In every Italian community they have a different way. They don't eat matzos and chicken soup. There are other local foods.* [My friend's family was] *here, in Venice... for centuries and... had to leave, escaping the Nazis. The mother of the family pointed out to me that, "In that building there they came and took away all the old people."*

I remember two things about that dinner. First, the mother later reported that except for the way I chomped on a banana at dessert, my behavior had been acceptable. The other was the emotion in her voice when she described the roundup of 200 Jews. I felt something in the pit of my stomach. It had happened during the Nazi domination of Italy in 1943–45, with the support of the Italian Fascists. Actually, few Jews lived — or live now — in the Ghetto. They haven't been compelled to reside there since Napoleon liberated the Ghetto in 1797. The small Venetian Jewish community lives, to this day, all over the city.

Soon after the Passover meal, my American aunt and uncle were to visit. I wrote to my parents:

> *25 April 1972: Would you tell them the best things... to bring are: a bottle of maple syrup, a jar of peanut butter and a "Jiffy Pop" popcorn. These are things that they don't eat here that I want the Kellers to try.*

The foods duly arrived and were sampled with interest by my Italian family. I tried to make them pancakes to go with the maple syrup, but unfortunately, not having much experience in cooking, I mixed up the salt and sugar, adding a cup of the former and tablespoon of the latter. The first batch of pancakes were disgusting. I had to do it over.

Cooking, of course, was only a passing part of my re-education, as politics remained ever in the foreground.

> *17 May 1972: From here the latest events in the US really look grave. All this trouble in Vietnam and now* [Governor George] *Wallace being shot.... In Italy elections took place....The city was covered with banners... there are about 20 parties from Maoist to socialist to Catholic Democratic and fascist parties....*

Italian high school students marched in protest and fought over the elections just like the adults, and these were not fun days out but angry demonstrations. It was almost unheard of for American school kids to engage in politics in that era; even Vietnam War activism started mainly in college. In Italy teens got involved because they were already so politicized. Now, it seems climate change has mobilized teens all over the world.

The year ended. I could speak passable Italian and, later, back home, I was deemed to have graduated high school. In June I took the 10.46 train from Venezia–Santa Lucia and left a bit of my heart in Venice. I picked up from where I had left off in the United States.

Having watched Alfred Hitchcock's 1940 film, *Foreign Correspondent*, I was determined to become a foreign correspondent, to go abroad again to explore foreign lands, meet with intrigue and write stories at the cutting edge of history. At university, I studied Chinese language and later journalism, and eventually stepped onto the job ladder as an intern, landing a post in 1979 on the "desk" at a news agency in Hong Kong.

The job was not at all like the movie. We mostly sat in a windowless skyscraper office, working in shifts including midnight to 8 a.m., rewriting news releases that spilled out of a row of buzzing printers. But we could also write feature stories of our own that went out on the "wire," as our communications system was known during this time when journalism still recalled its ties to the telegraph. That made it all worthwhile for me.

After a few years I moved on, joining the agency's news bureaus in India and Washington, DC, and then teaching journalism in Taiwan and Chicago. Traveling the world suited me. But, as my Venetian friend Emiliano Simon once told me, "Travel is a way to learn that everything you really need is already at home." Suffice to say that after twenty years of moving around the world, I found myself working as a foreign correspondent in London and felt that the time had come to settle down. That was made amply clear when my six-year-old daughter, who on learning that we would be moving again — but hopefully for the last time — asked her mother, "Can I make friends now?"

When my wife got a job teaching in Cambridge, England, we moved there and before I knew it, two more decades of family life passed as I engaged in more mundane endeavors in internet publishing.

Although I had corresponded with friends and family in Italy for years after leaving Venice, as time rolled by, letter writing mostly dwindled to Christmas card writing and then faded away entirely — with one exception. I stayed in touch with my Italian sister, Marta, who had, as it happens, moved to Barcelona in the 1980s, but still had friends and her family in Venice.

With all the kerfuffle about Venice of late, with the startling images of tourist crowds, floods in Piazza San Marco (St. Mark's Square), and oversized cruise ships blocking the views, I began to think about the city again. I returned to the book *The World of Venice*, which had since been renamed *Venice* and updated, most recently in 1993. The author, who became Jan Morris in 1964, still eloquently captures Venice. But she remarks on how much Venice and the world had moved on.

My own book is inspired by Morris' classic. Like her, I try to see Venice as it is and as it was, but my book looks at Venice through a slightly different prism. I also want to see how it is part of the wider world, how it reflects the political, economic and environmental trends shaping lives everywhere today. In short, not just how Venice is different — but how it faces the same challenges as everywhere else.

That year I spent with the Keller family still serves as my reference point, my door into Venice and an emotional focus. But my first exposure to Venice as a seventeen-year-old left me with abiding questions. Although once since my return trip I visited briefly as a tourist, I had never had the opportunity to try to understand Venice in depth until one day, not long ago, I found my children had grown up and a long-nurtured internet publication I had set up came to an end. I was free to return to see what difference all that time had made to the city. And so I did.

2

FRIENDS

THE JOY OF UNEXPECTED REUNIONS

What will be, will be
who knows what my life will be?
I know how to do everything or perhaps nothing,
we'll see from tomorrow
and what will be, will be.

—JOSÉ FELICIANO'S CHORUS OF "CHE SARÀ," SUNG AT THE SANREMO FESTIVAL, 1971, A SONG I HAVE BEEN SINGING EVER SINCE I WENT TO VENICE.

It's early September 2018. I step off the train at Venezia– Santa Lucia. I am coming back after nearly fifty years. A boiling sun is beating down. A torrent of humanity streams towards the station along the platform; we have to gather ourselves quickly as lingering with our luggage would cause a jam.

Rather than a family waiting for me, this time I find Sofia Bareato. A recent graduate of Venice University, she has shoulder-length brown hair and is wearing jeans and a blue striped T-shirt. She will be my research assistant. Sofia cheerfully helps my wife Susan and me lug our suitcases through the crowd to the square in front of the station — where the humorist Benchley did his double take, as do many who emerge to find canals instead of streets.

As we make our way by foot through the tourist throngs I make quick mental notes of what I see as we exit the station: apart from the fact that there are ever-increasing numbers of people — now all with a smartphone on a selfie-stick — and a lot more graffiti on the aging buildings, Venice looks much the same. But is it? Over the coming months, I am determined to look behind the scenes.

If you fly in to Venice's Marco Polo Airport on a clear day, you can get a good overview of the lagoon, and the sixty or so islands dotted over it. Clearly visible is the way the land spoons the crescent-shaped lagoon at the rounded end of the upper Adriatic Sea. The terrain below you itself tells the story of how 4,000 to 6,000 years ago Ice Age wind, waves and subsidence gouged the lagoon out from detritus left when the glaciers retreated from the river deltas converging there. Sediments flowing down the Alpine rivers formed the scattered islands and, combined with waves, shaped the long, thin coastal islands of Lido and Pellestrina that trace the inner curve of the crescent. The outflow of river water from the lagoon keeps three gaps open to the Adriatic. On the *terraferma* side — the mainland, as it is known — the Alpine sediments left extensive salt marshes that from the air look like the cross section of the human lungs ventilated by sinuous, vein-like channels with larger arteries snaking into the open water at the heart of the crescent.

Venice, the city itself, at the midpoint of the watery crescent, resembles a fish in profile — more a shortish sole or perch than a lanky sturgeon or barracuda — with its head pointing west and its tail to the east. The city is organized into districts, or *sestieri*, three on each side of the Grand Canal, which splits Venice in half like a leaning, mirror-written letter "∾." Above the reversed letter, find San Marco, with Piazza San Marco at its heart; Castello is the "tail" and lower back; and Cannaregio the "forehead and upper back." On the lower side, one finds San Polo, with Santa Croce, at the "mouth"; Dorsoduro in the belly, and the skinny Giudecca wrapped close below it.

My pied-à-terre for this extended visit sits just above the fish eye in Cannaregio, in Sacca San Girolamo, facing the wind and rain from the northern lagoon, which is what Venetians know as Baia del Re, nicknamed after the location of the frostbitten base set up by Italian North Pole researchers in Norway in 1928. Baia del Re would make a peaceful retreat. Rough, poor and crumbling until the 1980s, it has been given a facelift with a cubist-inspired re-development into squat, pastel-hued apartment blocks set around little squares with leafy trees and red wood-slatted benches. Here, retirees bring out folding chairs and form little chatting circles on warm days. On the benches, book readers look out over the water, couples find solitude, and, on a clear day, the Alps are visible in the distance.

With the help of Sofia and a friend who was loaning me the flat while she was away, we made our way up two flights of stairs and settled in. My wife stayed with me for a couple of days, long enough to share an overpriced meal at a canal-side restaurant and get to know the area. I felt happier, somehow, knowing that she had seen the flat. But, with my thoughts on how I would miss her, we said goodbye and then she was off, back to her own work in Cambridge. I am on my own.

I have my first moment to take a breath, and feel I am on a new journey, continuing the one by the younger me to explore the lagoon. Take journeys we must, and sometimes we reach the place we aimed for, sometimes we find a new beginning, and sometimes we end up far from what we thought of as our goal. I think of my taxi ride to the airport in 1979 on my way to Hong Kong for my first job, when the New York taxi driver gave me his card, which I still have, saying: *Success is a journey, not a destination*.

Sofia has a tireless attitude towards work and a sharp mind. Sometimes she would come along with me to an interview or on tours. But mostly she would spend her days transcribing the 150 or so interviews in Italian — about 200 hours of recordings in all — that I would carry out over the months ahead.

With Sofia ready to go, my plan was to begin re-contacting old friends, whom my Italian sister, Marta, had helped me find. Although I could see them in my memory at age seventeen, when we last had met, I had no idea what they would be like now, when, like me, they were about sixty-five years of age. I wanted to hear from them how life had changed in La Serenissima since the 1970s.

I wait anxiously at the water fountain in Campo Santa Maria Formosa where Alessandra Schiavon had told me to meet her. No Venetian believes a non-Venetian can actually find the right residential door in the city's labyrinth of streets, so a rendezvous almost always starts at a more easily discoverable place — if not by a fountain, then on a bridge or under a statue in the nearest *campo*, the Venetian name for a square.

I approach the stubby, forged-iron spout at the very moment Alessandra, "Ale" to her friends, arrived from the opposite direction, and I recognize immediately the girl I had once known in the slender woman, with a grinning, tanned face and sparkling eyes framed in a mass of unruly curls, hardly looking my age. She greets me with a hug and leads me through the narrow streets to a table outside her favorite haunt, Aciugheta. We begin to catch up over white wine and delicate mini-pizzas as big as the palm of my hand.

Talking comes easily, although I sometimes struggle for the right word in Italian. But we have so much to say! Somehow, as Ale commented later, it was as if no time at all had passed. We feel as if we were picking up where we had left off, recalling memories and learning about each other's current lives with enthusiasm. "What happiness!" she messaged later, "that life gifts such encounters! After so many years!"

We talk of the old days. Ale tells me I was remembered as the funny American who amused the class when he recited a "contrasto" by Cielo d'Alcamo, one of the finest types of thirteenth-century Italian poetry, in incongruously American-accented Italian. Ale fills me in on the current whereabouts of my old classmates. "And my *compagna di banco*?" I ask about the desk-mate who had sat next to me. I loved her above all others; she had been extremely kind to me, warmly taking me under her wing in an alien world.

"You don't know?" she says uneasily. "Some years ago she contracted Alzheimer's disease." Ale was not sure she would recognize me.

That hit me hard. Later, I called her husband and arranged to visit. The three of us walked along the water's edge for an hour, and my friend seemed cheerful and well cared for by her loving companion, but blank. Alzheimer's cruelly saps the individual from the mind.

❦

I meet my former classmate Laura Mangini not long after at another fountain, this one a stone pillar with a brass faucet, situated in Campo Santa Margherita, a broad, open space with kids running around it, bells chiming, big trees, students celebrating and moms with strollers. We go to have a glass of white wine and find ourselves chatting as if it were just another day after school. Now a bright, confident professional who teaches secondary school English and lives in nearby Treviso, Laura says I had not lost my "aplomb." We catch up on family and friends, and some weeks later meet again, which is when she sets out for me her recollections of school politics and life in the turbulent year in Italy that had so bewildered me:

> Our class was assigned a group of very traditional teachers. As a teacher now myself I understand that for them teaching was

a routine that they had been doing for years with little interest. Teaching methods were old, obsolete and out of synch with the times. The teachers wanted you to learn everything by rote. That is to say, the questions we now ask, like 'What did you learn from this poetry?' or 'What does this image suggest to you?' didn't exist. In those days, we learned a canto of Dante's *Divina Commedia* by heart without any involvement in the meaning of the work. In 1970 a great flood hit Bangladesh, killing lots of people, and a big concert was organized to collect contributions — even George Harrison took part. That morning when the teacher walked into class we were all talking about it. We were upset and would have liked to discuss it with him. 'We are at school. We don't talk about that here. Open your books for the lesson on Dante,' is what he said. He could have said, 'Boys and girls, let's talk about it.' Something, but no. Life and reality were outside. But we were the generation that wanted more.

1968 had just passed and we joined the movement. I remember we called a meeting in the school, calling for free textbooks, the end of academic taxes and support for economically disadvantaged students, and we called on everyone to go on strike to fight for the cause. The irony is that, except for a few of us, we were all from rather well-off, comfortable families. But at that time all of Italy was up in arms. Almost everybody at school took part in the strikes.

With the benefit of hindsight, I can now see that there was a lot of politics behind things. We got very strong guidance from a number of left-wing political groups and parties, and there were representatives elected by each school who tried to persuade us to participate. They took advantage of the idealistic aspects of things, but that was typical of the age. 'Are you for or against school for everyone?' In favor! 'Do you agree that the school should be democratic?' Certainly! It was very ideological.

On another day I am at lunch with my Italian brother, Giovanni Keller, who has always lived in Venice. When I stayed with his family here in the 1970s, he had his own circle of friends. Outside school I hung out with my coetaneous Italian sister Marta and her friends, so now to be sitting across a table packed with plates of vegetable risotto, fried shrimp, whitebait and cuttlefish, plus glasses of white wine, felt like winning respect from my big brother. A big guy with a grey beard, he greets me at Campo San Giacomo, a square tucked behind the Rialto Bridge, with a hearty, hairy kiss on both cheeks. A man with three sisters appreciates having a brother around — and we had missed each other greatly.

We used to take trips together through the canals or out into the lagoon in *Helvetia*, Giovanni's *topa*, an open-topped Venetian boat. I fell in love with the lagoon during these outings. We piled into the station wagon-sized boat powered by a small outboard or oars and set off, without adults, to anywhere the water would take us, carefree masters of our day.

I ask him whether he had any ideas as to how I might find a boat for my planned lagoon exploration, a relaunch of the aborted trip he had kidded me about so many years ago. I had in mind returning to Venice in the spring to take a journey that would be as much as possible by oar and sail. He would not be up to the trip, he says, and then tells me that *Helvetia* had long ago been retired, as Venetian boats are, by being taken on one last journey into the lagoon, where it was beached on a remote bank and left to be reclaimed by time and tide.

So I would have to keep looking for a boat. We talk about other things that had changed. Giovanni, for years a publisher of books on Venice, took a long view, remembering well how things used to be half a century ago. He expounds on global trends impacting the city, on how political battles had rolled out and how some things had gone awry — like tourism — while others, like housing, had improved. "Venice is just the tip of an iceberg," he says, suggesting global trends seem to be expressed there more sharply than elsewhere in the world.

Most notably, he tells me that the canals now stink less than they used to. This was startling. People have been lamenting the smelly canals of Venice for centuries. Over the decades, however, the city had made it a requirement that new and renovated buildings install sewage processing tanks. Now, only half the city's raw waste flows directly into the canals. Agricultural runoff from the mainland that has fed the algae in the lagoon for decades has been curbed. Swimming in the canals is still forbidden as the bacterial levels exceed safety margins, but what smells bad is relative. I was intrigued and made a note to find out more.

When I met Francesco "Checco" Turio-Bohm, it had taken a moment for us to recognize each other. He had attended school with Marta. We last saw one another on a 1976 hitch-hiking trip around Italy, when both of us sported beards. Now, we are both clean-shaven. However, I recognized him by the good-humored eyes and jet-black hair. We hug in greeting under the trees in Campo Santi Apostoli, then walk and talk. Later, while we are sitting at an outside café table, Checco, a professional art photographer, started reminiscing:

> I remember the beautiful little boat we had when I was fourteen or fifteen. It belonged to my friends. It was the sort of boat you could row and it had a little outboard motor. We would organize short trips through the canals and into the lagoon. It was a beautiful way to see the city, and very different from seeing it on foot. This always fascinated me. It still does.

Boats seemed the natural way to get around. "Even as a boy, you get to know the water and feel free to take your boat there to explore it," he said.

> I never felt closed in in this space. It's always been a natural thing. I have never felt privileged or unfortunate because I lived here. I am aware that I am a bit special, that my life is different from other people's. I would like to preserve and maintain the place because it's given me so much pleasure; for example, when I look over the water and can see the mountains in the distance, perhaps covered with snow. It's like when I took a flight through the desert and over the Grand Canyon in the USA, and then all in a moment below you, you see this magical thing. I would like Venice's magic to continue in some way, so everyone can live and appreciate it. That's how I feel.

With those last words he starts to sob but soon regains his composure. This surprised me at first, then made sense when I recalled that he spends his days taking pictures of Venetian art, especially church paintings and sculpture on location, often taking images of every object in extended conservation projects. To him, the threats to Venice are personal.

A few weeks later I find myself climbing the stairs to the flat of my 1971–72 mentor, Andrea Pavanini, then a college student. I am pleased to find on arrival that dinner is nearly ready, with appetizing platters already set out on a checkered cloth over the rectangular table in the warm, bright kitchen: mild, sliced sausage; preserved meat; soft cheeses, including two kinds of mozzarella-like *burrata* and a soft, nearly liquid, pure white *stracciatella*, a cheese from Puglia; artichoke hearts trimmed into doughnut-sized disks — a Venetian specialty — along with bread rolls typical of the lagoon town of Chioggia.

As we sit down, Andrea's wife, Francesca Paruzzolo, in one sweeping movement, gives the pot a stir and doles out five portions, placing bowls of fragrant, hot mushroom-and-sausage risotto before the wide-eyed diners, including Andrea's twenty-eight-year-old daughter, Fosca, and a friend. Further flavorsome courses are prepared and cleared with this impressive efficiency, and the meal concludes with buttery-rich chocolate "salami" slices, rich ricotta cheese tort and the red, brown and white button-sized *fave dei morti*, the biscuits made to commemorate All Saints' Day. We drink a dark-red Cabernet del Tocco from the family's own vineyard, followed by prosecco from Treviso and a sweet liqueur from the Marche region.

Local food means so much to Italians. I recall that when I was in Venice at age seventeen, Andrea and his younger brother Piero took us to their pocket-sized vineyard outside Venice. We spent the day gathering grapes, then, mainly for fun, dumped some of them in a huge hot tub-like vat, rolled up our trousers, rinsed off our feet and stepped into the container to stamp the juices out of the fruit to make wine. On hearing the story now, Andrea's daughter, Fosca, is incredulous. "Did you really?"

"Yes," her studious and stubble-bearded father assures her, with a bit of a mischievous smile. The past is a foreign country, is it not?

Several weeks before, I had interviewed Andrea at his law firm's glass-walled offices in Rio Novo, a concrete 1960s building of a type rarely found in Venice. He came round from the vast expanse of his desk to greet me warmly. I am writing about Venice, all about the city, its past, the present and future, I explained, including how it has changed.

"We are changed, not just Venice," he responded.

PRIEST

NOW IS NOT A GREAT MOMENT IN TIME
DON FAUSTO BONINI

I could think of no one better to put his finger on the pulse of the city in comparison with the past than Don Fausto Bonini, whom I had first met in the 1970s. We met in the book-lined, sun-lit study of his residence in Mestre.

Life has moved a long way in Venice since 1971, mostly for the worse, Don Fausto Bonini, a priest since 1962, explains to me when I drop by. “I found a beautiful picture of those years,” he says, brightly showing off a photo in fading colors of long-haired teenagers standing on a platform in the church center with electric guitars in hand. They were university and secondary school students supercharged with idealism who gathered weekly at Catholic youth groups.

“The church was packed with youngsters, perhaps 400 or 500, and it was really crowded, and that is when the famous ‘beat mass’ began,” says Bonini, recalling how on weekends from 1968 through to 1974, the students would gather, bringing their new music and their new ideas into spaces where only years before Mass had been read only in Latin.

The youth groups he organized were “not for religious devotion, but places where people could share their choices and organize things, so as to participate in life... a living community... gathered for debates, discussions, prayers and reflection,” he says.

I had met Don Fausto when, on Saturdays, my classmates sometimes brought me along to such Catholic youth gatherings — a calmer part of the bigger swirl of protests, conflict and change after 1968 and into the 1970s. A slender, modest man, he is balding with a little grey hair remaining, and wears reading glasses on a cord around his neck.

“That was when the occupations of the university started, along the lines of similar actions in the United States, France, England and so forth,” he says. “They said, ‘The university is ours.’ I remember at one time all the students were seated on the steps of the university. Along came the rector, who is the supreme authority, and he wanted to get past. He got mad when the students would not let him get to his office. When he got mad the students said, ‘Who are you?’ He said, ‘I am the rector.’ They replied, ‘Sorry, we can’t let you in’. It was a real protest against authority.”

In those years the young “grew aware and decided to make a difference,” he says. But in the intervening years, the world has lost its way, according to the priest.

“Now, not only in religious life, but also in society and politics, you see an indifference to commitment. Even if there are many youngsters who are activists, there’s a retreat to private life, so everyone thinks first of themselves, with less awareness of any need to do something for society or take part in politics. It’s someone else’s problem,” says Don Fausto. “So, from a social perspective we’ve gone backwards and from a religious one even more so. There’s such lack of interest. The churches of Venice are closing because fewer and fewer people attend, but that is a general trend, also in England, France and America.” Church attendance, once at 80 percent, is down to 18 to 20 percent all over Italy.

He still runs youth groups in Mestre, where he moved to as a priest in 2002, but these are pale affairs in comparison. They attract young people coming from all over Italy and abroad who want to rediscover their faith. “I say ‘rediscover’ because many of them have abandoned their beliefs, but want to understand a bit more.” But now they also have to face drug dealers who are “destroying the young world.... Rather than activism you find an interest in drink and having a wild time.”

Now Venice seems angry and disillusioned to me. Back in 1971 it seemed different, I say.

“No, unlike today, it was a city awakening,” says Don Fausto. “Today no one cares. Whoever is able to, deals drugs. Venice is at an historical turning point. An existential turning point...” involving environmental and political challenges. “Because we are moving towards putting value only on money instead of ideals, and letting money take charge. This is sad." As I leave, he asks me what religion I have, and I don't even have time to answer before he continues. "What is missing, overall, is a religious inspiration reminding us that we are all brothers and sisters and there's a need to wish one another well and help one another. This is what is lacking, not just among Catholics, but in religion in general. This is not a great moment in time."

SCENES

3

POINTING A CAMERA AT KEY QUESTIONS

"The public couldn't care less about understanding what Venice is. They want to see Venice."

—CARLO MONTANARO, FILM HISTORIAN OF VENICE, 2018 INTERVIEW

"You look like you're acting! Act natural," yells the director. "Let's do it again."

Never having appeared in a documentary or a film, I am puzzled. How do actors "act natural"? It is obviously harder than it looks.

I turn around and walk back down the canal towards the camera in a quiet section of Cannaregio, and try again, self-consciously but less extravagantly taking in Venice on this warm spring day. Four tries later, we do it again from another angle. And again in the other direction. It is just the beginning of what would be a long day shooting a visual trailer for this book.

It is April of 2019 and I have returned to Venice again after the first months-long sojourn there to continue the investigation by taking a rowing trip through the Grand Canal and out into the lagoon. The film of this leg would provide an introduction to my Venice story, a way of explaining what I had understood through the hours of interviews, the observations and a week-long exploration of the lagoon I had recently completed. These provide the basis for this book, and by recounting the scenes of the video preview I am also laying out what lies ahead in this story, the menu for the feast, so to speak.

One of our first stops in making the film that day was for a scene on a bridge with the white stone sculptures of saints on the fourteenth-century Madonna dell'Orto church façade in the background. People who walk by eye us oddly, their expressions revealing either curiosity — *Who is that guy and what film is this?* — or annoyance — *Why are they getting in the way?* I get on with my narration, explaining to the camera: "The world has changed, but attitudes to an iconic place like Venice seem unchanged, so it's time to look again at what makes Venice tick."

As the camera crew films from the quay, I step down into our boat, the narrow, 9-meter vessel, *Gigeta*, an emerald-green sandolo. *Gigeta* is one of the last boats of this type constructed with the wooden hull curving to the left to streamline rowing, giving it a smooth and fast contour. I am rowing at the stern and my rowing partner, Emiliano Simon, thirty-one, slender and nautical down to his tattooed arms, is in the bow, as we rhythmically push the long oars, each one almost twice as tall as a man, levering the boat forward through the water *alla veneta*, Venetian style. The film crew follow in a motorized launch.

I say my lines about when settlers arrived in the lagoon over a thousand years ago, they found a wild river delta that spilled into a great lagoon dotted with islands. They learned to row standing up in order to see what was ahead of them in the shallow, shifting waters where the fresh water mingled with the saltwater tides of the Adriatic Sea. They invented myriad types of specialized, flat-bottomed boats — canal boats like ours, boats for the open sea, for fishing or hunting or cargoes, as well as the famed black gondola — and they discovered new technologies to collect water and to make possible building on soft mud invaded by tides. They created a new way of life based on trading the salt they produced and fish they caught for goods from overseas. It was a community of close social ties that empowered women and enabled Venetians to work together for the common good.

Traditional history surrounding these beginnings early in the first millennium is based on self-serving origin stories touting alleged Roman origins. These tales invented in the eleventh and twelfth centuries often still hold sway. I found that recent archaeology tells us a very different story; Venice was in reality a less Roman and a more pirate nation than many like to admit.

We row through choppy waters — turbulence caused by the intense motorboat traffic — to San Michele, the square cemetery island where brown sargassum seaweed, an invasive species alien to the lagoon, drags on our oars, slowing progress.

There I do a piece to the camera to address the misconceived ideas that everyone everywhere who has ever heard of Venice seems to believe: that Venice is sinking fast or dying or about to disappear. The reality is even more surprising.

We row clockwise around Venice from the Cannaregio district toward its eastern end, where castle-like red brick walls as tall as a three-story house enclose the Arsenal, the starting point for the story of Venetian wealth, power and empire, a David and Goliath story of a little city that became a giant.

How? Taking up a ninth of the area of Venice, I say, the Arsenal powered the economic engine that drove the Venetian Republic from the close of the first millennium through its decline in the seventeenth and eighteenth centuries. There, 2,000 or 3,000 workers built and maintained a fleet of as many as a hundred merchant and war galleys on the water at any one time that enabled it to conquer markets in the Mediterranean and beyond.

The author rowing the canals of Venice in preparation for his journey around the lagoon in the following months.

The wooden ships, over twice as long as a big bus and powered by sail or by up to 400 men on fifty or sixty oars, lumbered across the seas at close to 10 kilometers per hour. Astonishingly, by the twelfth century Arsenal workers built galleys production-line style — 800 years before Henry Ford reinvented the system to build identical automobiles one after another. The Arsenal boasted of being able to build galleys in as little as a day by the sixteenth century, after having apparently demonstrated the feat to visiting Henry III, the king of France.

While partner Emiliano and I bob on the waves, director Giovanni Pellegrini leaps into our rowboat from the bigger launch, camera in hand, so I will appear to speak to the viewers as if they were on board. I recount how the fourteenth-century poet Dante used scenes of toxic boiling pitch, leaking hulks and noises of hammering from inside the Arsenal to evoke Hell in his work, *La Divina Commedia*. Yet, in many ways, those passages evoke scenes of industry we recognize in the modern world. What can we learn from that?

We stop for lunch. The rowing and the presence of the lurking camera were both exhausting. But we take an hour or so for provolone and prosciutto sandwiches. Chomping my bread roll, I overhear the intriguing theories about modern music being expounded by our soundman, and this sets me to thinking about how Venice's culture fits in. Where does this treasure trove of medieval and Renaissance art and architecture belong in a digital, fast-paced world? How can the long traditions of the people who live in Venice today be maintained? It's a lot harder than it looks.

We push on, following the profile of Venice round to the *bacino*, the inner port where the trading vessels of yore unloaded and loaded goods, and where we pass close to the Adriatic Sea. Its tides push up the lagoon water levels twice a day. Sometimes they rise too far, causing *acque alte* — flooding caused by the tides — which are becoming ever more frequent due to climate change and rising sea levels.

On November 4, 1966, such floods inundated the entire city. Waist-high, stinking, muddy, oily water destroyed housing, shops, goods and art treasures on all the islands and lagoon shorelines. The catastrophe sparked an international uproar and triggered efforts to save Venice. Recognizing the critical role of the lagoon — a place with scores of other islands, many abandoned, with ancient island communities living in semi-seclusion and rare wetlands full of fish and birds — and the overwhelming need to preserve its equilibrium with the city, the authorities planned the Mose project, which were gigantic dams to be constructed at the openings where the lagoon meets the sea. But, after decades of fraught deliberation, the hopelessly out-of-date and over-budget barriers were to be completed in 2021.

People wonder how well the dams will work. Even if they do the job in the short term, climate change may force Venice to face unimaginably hard choices, between saving the world-heritage city and saving the lagoon. But this raises scary unknowns. I ask my documentary team: How can you pull apart nature and man thoroughly intertwined for so many centuries without destroying them?

We approach the gateway to Venice, with the exalted Doge's Palace and the great columns in the square outside, the Piazzetta, visible from the water, along with the adjacent Byzantine-style St. Mark's Basilica and the stately Piazza San Marco. These monuments, the ultimate statement of power and wealth during the Venetian Republic, are the architectural legacy of a state that survived tenaciously for 900 years until its final humiliating demise in 1797. But its greatest legacies are unseen.

The Venetian Republic was not only the greatest expression of early democratic forms since the height of the Greek and Roman empires, but it also endured far, far longer than any other government, anywhere, past or present. What was it about a certain murder in the Doge's Palace on May 27, 1172 that gave shape to this outlier centuries before the rest of the world rediscovered democracy? Why did it last so long? To my surprise, these musings would brighten a tired historian I cornered at the end of a long day of teaching. "Those are the million-dollar questions!" she exclaimed.

From the bacino, we row on to the Grand Canal, at the point where it begins its reverse "∾" through the heart of the city. The crew in the launch drive off to approach the Piazzetta to take shots of sunlight glinting on the water, of the tourist crowds at the water's edge and of the gulls that have recently laid siege to Venice. In the last few decades, drawn by food waste and pushed by global habitat loss, the birds have left their natural homes on the open seas to invade Venice and other cities. But La Serenissima has learned to live in peace with these animals — and a menagerie of others.

Meanwhile, we move our little boat to the opposite bank and to La Salute church, topped by a white dome decorated with classical columns and a swirly, Baroque ornamentation punctuated by the statues of saints. We stop to film a scene to acknowledge this monument to the Virgin Mary, built in gratitude for the end of the 1630 outbreak of the Black Death, the bubonic plague, that killed a third of the city's population of 140,000.

Something strangely similar is happening today. Venice is suffering a drastic decline in population. There's been a steady exodus of Venetians over recent decades that has reduced the number from 174,000 in the 1950s to 52,000 by 2020. The trend has various causes, but of late the main one is the rise of mass tourism. The surplus of tourists has unbalanced the economy, with souvenir shops, holiday rentals and hotels pushing residents out. UNESCO, the UN body that supports and protects world heritage, is now worried about Venice's safety. There is an enormous depth of feeling among Venetians about excessive tourism, but surprisingly, it's not mainly the tourists who are at fault. It's all bound up with the political struggle going on in Venice — a matter of international finance, speculation and of people fighting to preserve a way of life.

To show that the beauty of Venice has long attracted artists and writers, we rowed to the Academia Bridge, where I stand before the camera and point to the Palazzo Barbaro, where the nineteenth-century novelist Henry James stayed, and then over to the other side, to Palazzo Contarini, where Proust and Stravinsky lodged. From Byron to Wordsworth and from Wagner to Petrarch, Venice has provided inspiration. The city continues to thrive as a locus for art, music and writing, despite all the changes. But why? One city resident, Spanish novelist Eugenia Rico, told me: "Writing about Venice is like writing about love. Every important writer has to write about love." I also asked internationally renowned crime thriller writer Donna Leon, prize-winning novelist Tiziano Scarpa and many others: "What is it about Venice?"

Between shots, our soundman — Enrico Lenarduzzi — rides in the rowboat, his box of recording machines on his lap. So we get to talking. He happens to know the only Italian folk song that I can remember, "La Valsugana," a bittersweet tune from the Tyrolean Alps about going home and lost love.

La mamma, la sta bene,	Mother is well,
il papà è ammalato.	Father is sick.
Il mio bel partì soldato,	My love went soldiering,
chi sa quando tornerà.	Who knows when he will return.

So we sing it while rowing along, an enjoyable moment that brings to mind that the Venetian Empire was never just the city. It encompassed at times expanses of northern Italy, including the Tyrol, and much of the eastern Mediterranean, Cyprus and Crete, making Venice the most cosmopolitan city of its age. Nowhere else in the world would so many Muslim Turks, Jews and Levantines of all types mix with Christian Italians and other Europeans; nowhere else would one find such a profusion of markets selling goods from all corners of the continent — furs from Russia, silver from Germany and wool from England — as well as silk, spices and, not least, slaves, from the East.

That happened nowhere more than on the Rialto, the old market and trading center where the iconic Rialto Bridge crosses the Grand Canal. I explain that from the thirteenth to the fifteenth century the Rialto acted as a global crossroads of trade, where goods from all over Europe, the Middle East and as far away as China were bought and sold. What's more, it served as the financial heart of commerce — the Wall Street of the world. Banking was practically invented in Venice and some people even think the city was the birthplace of capitalism.

Venice's mercantile blossoming produced a form of government that is often likened nowadays to a corporate board — rule by merchants. That legacy shaped today's global economics in ways that are still being felt, not least through something called "double-entry bookkeeping," a system perfected in Venice and still fundamental to business accounting today. This bookkeeping system is often blamed for blind spots of business for things like the cost of pollution. And, in a great irony, in as much as Venice and its lagoon are endangered by out-of-control market capitalism, Venice is at the receiving end of the same system it helped create. I will describe how this came about later.

We row our boat over into a side canal for an hour and chat while the film crew in the launch heads round to the other side of Venice to catch the departure from the maritime terminal of tourists on board one of the gigantic cruise ships. The ship's scale makes Venice look like a Lego-built mini-city. These cruise ship giants not only cause erosion and pollution, but when they passed close to the city as they moved through the Giudecca Canal and past Piazza San Marco, they risked accidents like the one off Tuscany in 2012, when a cruise ship ventured too near the coast, overturning and killing people. A minor accident also occurred in Venice in June 2019. A long-running protest by city inhabitants aims to distance the ships from the lagoon.

This controversy is really part of a larger environmental story of how the lagoon has been encroached upon by modern industry. The terraferma development has been disastrous for the fragile lagoon environment, leaving mountains of industrial poisons that still seep into the water.

This toxic legacy is threatening the city because the lagoon and Venice are symbiotic — one cannot live without the other. The remarkable story to be told in this book of the centuries-old relationship between city and the water, of a détente that lasted until the early ninteenth century, but has since increasingly fallen away, deserves to be more widely known. The age of environmentalism, I tell my video audience, is only a remembering of what we already knew but have willfully forgotten in the hubris of science and technology.

Our journey and our filmmaking are coming to an end for the day, and so we head towards the abandoned island of San Secondo, once the site of a thriving monastery. It's now a shrunken green dot thick with bramble. We now enter the wider lagoon, and I say that this body of water is critical — more than just for Venice. Its fate will be a test for mankind as it strives to save the environment, preserve heritage and assure its own economic well-being. Venice is more delicate than other cities, so, like the caged canary in the mine, whose sensitivity warns miners of poison gas, its fate may be a warning for us all.

But before I follow up on these matters in coming chapters, now let us wind the clock back several months to my return visit to Venice after such a long absence, to the tale of what I saw with my own eyes in the city that lives on despite rumors (and forces) to the contrary.

4

LIVING

LIFE AT A PACE SET BY WALKING

> *"... the Venetian was bound to develop into a new kind of creature, and that is why, too, Venice can only be compared to itself."*
>
> —J.W. GOETHE, ITALIAN JOURNEY, 1786–88

The scene in Campo Santa Maria Formosa one sunny October morning has all the signs of the aftermath of a disaster, with brick, rubble and trash strewn over the square, water flooding the stone paving and fruit sellers' stalls knocked over onto the stone slabs. In fact, it is going to *be* a disaster — or at least a disaster *scene* staged for a superhero movie.

For on the far side of the square, film crews, extras and technicians stand around cameras under tents. Guards in orange vests keep bystanders back, explaining that as soon as the sun moves into the right position they would film a scene from the movie *Spider-Man: Far From Home*. In the computer-enhanced action, the fifteenth-century bell tower that looms over the square would collapse as the hero battled to save the world. Again.

Signs posted at entrances to the football field-sized square warn: "By walking through this area, you automatically and irrevocably consent to being filmed... if you do not want to be filmed, photographed and/or recorded, please do not enter... this area. We apologize for any inconvenience...."

Though irksome for those whose passage is blocked, such orders are not infrequently issued for films made in Venice. Yet despite this and the constant pressures of mass tourism, for the most part, life goes on as normal. As long as residents have some space — behind the scenes, you might say — they go to work, attend school and make time for play. It remains a city of car-less, bus-less, even bicycle-less streets, where, perforce, people live at a pace set by walking and adapt accordingly.

Life in the lagoon city — Venice including Murano, Burano, Lido, Pellestrina and other islands — shares a common characteristic. In these places, all the heavy traffic, the public transport and the gondolas, use canals running typically along the streets and under the bridges. People walk above or apart, so motion around the city has separate levels which makes Venice, one of the oldest living cities, also one that is studied for its futuristic features.

"Venice is a cutting-edge laboratory of modernity," says Iuav University urban planning expert Laura Fregolent as we sat in a classroom of Ca' Tron with sunlight filtering in from a window high above the adjacent garden courtyard.* Following Venice's lead, Oslo will soon be pedestrianized, except for electric cars and public transport, and Berlin is going the same way. "They show that quality of life in a city is about pedestrianization... Venice has always been that way, with a rhythm much slower than other Italian and European cities," which are distinguished from many of the American counterparts by this triumph of public over private space, she adds.

After Fregolent takes her leave, I gaze through the window. Outside, it is blissfully quiet. After a moment, the bell tower opposite rings with a deep sonorous resonance, wafting its clear tones over the red clay roofs of Venice. Both the sound and the silence are full of beauty. Such pure peacefulness makes Venice special. At midday, I found I could hear the distinct footsteps of an approaching man on a side street. I treasured waking up in my urban flat to hear only the coos and caws of pigeons and gulls, sometimes mixed with human voices, mostly of moms pushing strollers and trailing kids on the street below.

There are many quiet neighborhoods in Venice, but noise is encroaching.

On the side of my flat facing the open lagoon, I keep the window shut. While on the internal canals that cut across the main body of Venice speed limits dampen the noise of motorized boats, out there in the lagoon, beyond our courtyard, barges loaded with hotel laundry, massive white box freezers full of fish, stacks of lumber and bags of cement, all rumble past. *Vaporetti*, the ferries, churn by and yellow ambulance boats race by, along with water taxis and motorboats that emit a pretty constant buzz BUZZ, buzz BUZZ as they cut through the waves. Even on many of the city's busier internal streets, these

* Iuav is the Instituto Universitario di Architettura di Venezia.

days, especially in daytime, the watery chug of boats moving steadily along at jogging speed grinds constantly in the background.

In the nineteenth century, when lagoon traffic moved only by oar, before the invention of the oversized 40-horsepower outboard engine, Henry James, in his book *Italian Hours*, could remark of Venice:

> There is no noise there save distinctly human noise; no rumbling; no vague uproar, no rattle of wheels or hoofs. It is all articulate and vocal and personal. One may say indeed that Venice is emphatically the city of conversation; people talk all over the place because there is nothing to interfere with its being caught by the ear....

He compared Piazza San Marco to "an enormous salon."

But for leading contemporary Venetian novelist Tiziano Scarpa, author of *Venice is a Fish*, it is as if the urban environment has become rural. He describes walking the streets without traffic as like taking "a path through the countryside or the woods" because you can "disconnect from the city" and be lost to your own thoughts.

Venice remains a city of conversation. People lean out of upper-floor windows to chat with neighbors on the street; they hail an acquaintance on the opposite side of the canal or chat on bridges, mid-street or in the squares. There seems every reason to talk to people around you — in fact, Venetians expect it. Bumping into friends along the way is what they love most.

"You are less isolated than in other cities because being on foot, and not being enclosed in a car, helps you recognize others and communicate," Venetian artist Serena Nono remarks. "You move about and have no option but to meet other people; you get to talking, even with people you don't know. It happens to me all the time. I believe in some way you feel closer to others."

In Venice you just have to s-l-o-w d-o-w-n.

Until the end of the Republic in 1797, time in Venice was measured by the 24-hour clock, with the day beginning at sunset. Time still moves at a different pace for residents because amongst other things, Venice is not big. You can walk end to end in about an hour.

The city has no fast option. Water taxis are pricey and unsuitable for routine getting around. The incredibly on-time vaporetti, even with their handy timetables on the *CheBateo?* app, cut walking time but tend to be slower (unless traveling to the islands, of course). Walking is usually faster, and you can take a shared *traghetto*, gondola passenger ferry, to cut distances. There used to be thirteen Grand Canal crossing points on traghetti. Now only three survive, costing €2 each for tourists or 0.70 for residents to have two gondoliers row up to ten or so standing passengers across.

You get used to walking. Admittedly, it works less well for the disabled people and those with luggage. Mothers with baby buggies face extra work on the steps of bridges, but there are compensations. Quite apart from the health benefits of going on foot (I lost 4 kilos), walking is less programmed than car travel. Without traffic, you always know how long it takes to get from place to place and can relax instead of staying alert to traffic dangers. You can dip into a shop, pause to look around or stop to chat with friends over a caffè or wine without worry about parking or driving under the influence. The favorite is a *spritz* — prosecco with sparkling water, a mix introduced in the nineteenth century by Venice's Austrian occupiers, and later the Italians added red, bitter Campari or Aperol liqueur. Or you can pop into one of the city's hundreds of traditional *osterie*, like Bacaro da Fiore, near Campo Santo Stefano, where customers mostly stand or perch on bar stools, talking animatedly in the wood-beamed rooms that are only a few paces wide. The mustachioed barman officiates from behind a U-shaped bar, proudly doling out red or white local wines and a tempting array of *cicchetti*, the traditional tapas savories placed on slices of baguette, along with triangles of white and yellow grilled polenta, *fritto misto* (battered fried fish), stewed mini-octopuses and cold, spiced eggplant. Going places becomes a pleasure.

The maze of Venice can be very disorienting. I often found myself staring down at a map and up at the painted black-and-white lettering on the building corners, called nizioleti, which showed Italian street names not on the map or sometimes slightly different names in Venetian dialect. I found myself relying, as many do nowadays, on smartphone maps — or trying to. In the deep brick-sided canyons of the Venetian labyrinth, the signal often fails, sending the "you are here" dot drifting off wildly. Wandering, something even many Venetians enjoy, is recommended as a way to discover the city.

"There's a place in Castello where you get this sensation of not knowing where you are," says my Venetian friend Checco Turio-Bohm, the professional photographer. "So you think, how's that possible? This is my city. Is it right or left? But then it doesn't matter. Either way you exit. Yet in that moment of disorientation you experience an extraordinary, extremely beautiful sensation. I would like to feel it every day, ten times a day, because it is in these moments that Venice expresses its fascination and mystery to me."

❧

As you observe people on the streets, especially off-season when the tourist crowds have thinned, you notice something. Venetian society is more equal than others; everyone has to get out and walk. That levels differences. People of all backgrounds, rich and poor, gondolier and entrepreneur, meet and talk. Even so, without cars in which to process down the streets — though cars are a material good that Italians love and own more than other Europeans — Venetians still show off their status by dressing especially well. Gentlemen often wear long coats or trendy jackets. Women come out in dresses, with jewelry. They bring along their dogs on a leash, in a buggy or a backpack, often decked out with coats too.

❧

To say, as many do, that the streets of Venice are like open-air living theaters, risks giving a one-dimensional picture of life. Beneath the surface, community ties run deep.

One day, I step into Mario Tagliapietra's barbershop for a haircut. I tell him about my work. "Have you spoken to Alberto Vitucci, the *Nuova Venezia* newspaper journalist who writes about the dam?" he asks. "Yes." He then lists several other journalists, all of whom I was in touch with. Perhaps they would hear about me next time they sat in his chair. News travels fast here, for Venice for its residents is a small town within a huge cultural bazaar.

I had walked with Vitucci along the canal down to a bridge next to the magnificent fourteenth-century Scuola Grande della Misericordia. We watched as a lone rower in a wooden *sanpieròta* boat fought her way up the waterway against the churn of one rumbling water taxi after another. A crocodile of tourists, plugged into special earphones transmitting the patter of the guide, marched by over the bridge. The enervating noise and bustle displeased him.

"This place used to be quiet. I would play here as a boy," said the lanky, bearded sixty-something journalist. "Now it's crowded with tourists and restaurants." He has steadfastly stayed with his newspaper job. Why? It was important, he said, because he wanted to do something for the under-siege community, and his in-depth reporting on the environment has led the way in energizing social action.

On November 21 every year at the Festa della Salute, crowds of Venetians cross a specially constructed pontoon bridge over the Grand Canal to commemorate the end of the 1630–31 plague. They file up the steps of La Salute church, stopping just inside the doors of the huge domed chamber to hand over slender white candles to volunteers behind a rope barrier. The hundreds of votive offerings are lit and planted one by one in a little forest of light on a banquet-sized table as a special mass is conducted at the altar opposite. Thousands more candles are handed over all day, while the marginally burnt ones are removed by the armful to make way for more.

After this outpouring of feeling and prayer to the Virgin Mary, to whom the church is dedicated, the crowd files through the adjacent alleyway, where stalls sell balloons, sweets, pastries and always *castradina*, the mutton, onion and cabbage soup eaten during the festival.

Celebrations like this testify to the still vigorous commitment of Venetians to their embattled traditions. Even as population numbers have declined, Venetians have hung on to their festivals.

Venice savors memories of how things used to be.

The 1950 black-and-white documentary *I Nua* (*They Swim*) depicts a sweltering Venetian summer. Now a treasured artifact, the ten-minute film shows gangs of boys joyfully throwing themselves into the canals and paddling around as the women and girls, who could only dip a foot in, looked on. Canal swimming is now both outlawed and risky, but remains part of living memory.

Venetians light up when you ask about the old days. School let out at midday and the children would return home for lunch with their families. In those days all the shops closed for lunch, whereas today unbroken morning-to-evening commerce meets the demands of the tourists.

Out on the campos, children played games "including one that used the heel of an old shoe, and one game that was a sort of street baseball; another was a pile-on game called "rotten bread, hard bread." Soccer — football to the non-American world — was not allowed in these constrained squares as kids got underfoot and balls smashed into windows and upset café tables. But it was constantly played anyway. Whenever police caught kids playing football they would confiscate the ball — which probably added to the daring of the game.

The campo life used to have a leveling influence on Venetian life. The offspring of doctors and barkeepers, teachers and gondoliers played together. When journalist Silvio Testa grew up in the 1950s and '60s, he remembers, "There were no rich zones or poor zones. We youngsters were all equal, no matter what kind of family we came from. No one took any notice of class." But as the lower-income groups and young families leave Venice, more individualistic, cosmopolitan living is taking over.

Campo San Giacomo dell'Orio is one of the few squares where the locals come out for a walk or a chat, and where children still come out to play. Bounded by a church, a palazzo, a supermarket and the four- and five-story flats, the stone-paved expanse shaded by trees was bursting with youthful energy when, one sunny day, I meet an acquaintance there. He had brought along his granddaughter, who quickly shoots off on her bright pink-and-blue roller skates to join a score of other kids — some as young as five and others budding teenagers. My acquaintance keeps an eye on the nine-year-old in his care while we talk over tall glasses of spritz. Soon, still breathless, the little girl winds her way back to our ring-side seats for an ice cream.

A few places in Venice feature something new: a student nightlife.

Young Venetians of past decades spent their evenings, as elsewhere in Italy, with a gentle *passeggiata*, a walk. In earlier generations, local society would make the rounds of Piazza San Marco. As it became more touristy, meetings shifted to Campo San Bartolomeo, near the Rialto Bridge. At around 6 p.m. people congregated there, smoked cigarettes and drank a little wine, and everyone headed home for a family supper by 8:30 p.m. Friends went out for a pizza perhaps once a month. When they went to college, many commuted. Not anymore.

Those older than school age go out on the town at night. Due to the growth in tourism and the universities, which now draw some 25,000 students annually, the city has sprouted a heavy-drinking nightlife. Big, loud student bars have opened in student areas.

"As you will have seen," says Francesca Paruzzolo, who grew up in the 1960s and '70s, "youngsters get drunk, properly drunk. When we were kids I don't recall ever having seen a friend drunk." Another Venetian mother, Michela Scibilia, remarks that the problems begin in adolescence. "At thirteen or fourteen they want to stay out late, and there are lots and lots of drugs. So much of it!"

The life of younger Italians has changed in lots of other ways. They marry less and later while local job opportunities, already scarce with 30 percent youth unemployment, have become even rarer as Venice has lost most of its non-tourism based industries, such as insurance, manufacturing and artisanal work.

Some traditional markets and local shops hold out despite being superseded by supermarkets. Some Venetians go out to Mestre on the terraferma to shop, but some also try to stay in Venice to support small traders. "I have decided to do all my shopping in Venice," says Stefania Senigaglia, a midwife among my friends from the 1970s. She spotted me without difficulty when we met again. I recognize the diminutive girl I had known, and I see that age had given her something more — a face glowing with gentle kindness. We sit at a popular canal-side wine bar where she ordered big glasses of white wine that glistened in the setting sun.

"I try to keep the few shops that are left from dying. Nearby to home I have a fruit seller, and I get my vegetables from the weekly boat from Sant'Erasmo," which is Venice's own garden island. "There's an excellent bread shop and butcher close where I live, and they both know me when I visit!" She misses only a good local bookshop and the recently closed Coin department store, with its day-to-day wear and household goods, which leaves only the luxury stores catering to tourists.

The ancient covered market at Rialto, the *pescaria*, where fish and vegetables have been sold for hundreds of years, still functions, though it is much reduced from its heyday. Shoppers can still buy seafood displayed on crushed ice; mounds of fresh shrimp, crabs, and all manner of lagoon and Adriatic sea bass, bream, mullet, sole, turbot and brill, along with swordfish, lobsters, octopus and cuttlefish. Shops in the area sell artisanal wines, big loaves of bread and pungent cornucopias of cheeses, while stalls display the colorful cucumbers, tomatoes and artichokes from Sant'Erasmo and elsewhere.

In the alleys behind the market, the bars and osterie fill quickly, especially on Saturdays when friends meet for wine and cicchetti, including white *baccalà* — ground salted cod in milk, peanut oil and spices. The customers spill into the street, conversing animatedly, some with two-wheeled shopping trollies, a necessity for carrying heavy groceries home — and doubtless they will return home with their shopping in tow, still tipsy.

To hear what is special about Venetian life for children, I met up with Teresa Sartore, who was on a break from her job at a nearby office. She had grown up in Venice, but left for some years to work in Brussels and Germany, returning to raise her child in Venice out of "beautiful memories of the Venetian way of life, particularly for children — and the great freedom they enjoy." She remembers playing in the square with neighborhood kids:

> Now and again someone would keep an eye out for you from a window, and say, 'How is everything?' Playing outside in the square we would jump onto the boats moored along the canal to chase after a ball that fell in the water. It was wonderful. Then, as I grew up a bit, at, say nine or ten, I recall walking with my friends elsewhere in the city — you can get anywhere on foot. Venice has always been a fairly secure place compared to other big cities, which have cars obviously. Water can be a danger up to a point, but unlike the danger of cars, you are in control as long as you pay attention.

Now she is raising her four-year-old Zoe, who enjoys going to Rialto with her for Saturday shopping. While the adults share glasses of white wine, the children play in Campo San Giacomo, at the back of the market. If the weather permits on weekends, the family might go to the beach on Lido or in spring, motor into the lagoon. "We use our boat a lot, and having a boat adds to our quality of life. Whether or not you have your own boat to use every day, living in Venice is beautiful," she says, describing how she loved to travel to school by ferry in her own school days:

> I don't know if Zoe has the same feeling, maybe she does. In a boat the feeling is more personal than on public transport. I see she has freedom; she runs about in the square and adores going by boat and suffers a lot when we go by car on a trip.
>
> She seems happy to me. She said something to me recently when we were going to Rome to see my husband's parents. It made me smile. One day when we were waiting for the family motorboat to go to school [used on days when they miss the ferry], and she knew we were going to Rome, she said to me, 'Mamma, when we go to Rome, can we bring Venice?' and I said, 'In what sense? You want to bring the city?' 'Yes, please, let's bring Venice to Rome.' So I took her to mean the tie to the city. Then recently when we were on a trip, she got a bit nostalgic. 'We will go back to Venice, won't we?' she said, and I felt she had a strong feeling of belonging to Venice.

When asked what is different about the Venetian way of life, people who have always lived in the city draw a blank. Life is normal, of course, they say. People live their lives. It takes someone who has also lived elsewhere to attempt an answer. "Everyone who lives in a place that is a bit exotic faces this paradox. What's strange to others is normal to them," says novelist Tiziano Scarpa when we talk at a café. Yet many Venetians admit to feeling a bit special, living as they do. "Doesn't the world come to Venice and tell them, 'What a beautiful place. How lucky you are to live here!'"

For some, the difference all comes down to the water. Children who clamber over boats to retrieve a ball from a canal enter the world of water. Everyone has a boat or a friend with a boat. Giovanni Montanaro, a novelist from a family that has been established in Venice for generations, has a strong sense that water transforms the space and the way people interact. This is how he describes life:

> Water is fundamental. We feel it in the sky and hear it outside the window.... We don't have tsunamis or tornadoes, but we are constantly battling water. We defend our houses and entry doors from water. It's humid; mould invades the house. If you're only here for short periods, the power of nature in our city is not something you would perceive. Sometimes I believe I have understood that water is the city's greatness. Water gives this sense of disquiet, that nothing stays fixed or is given forever and everything wears out. It has a lot to do with restlessness, with the unresolved, getting on and talking about things. I definitely think water is fundamental.

Some Venetians feel deeply pessimistic about what is happening to Venice. Forty-three-year-old art entrepreneur Mara Sartore, Teresa's older sister, is not among them.

As we sit at one of the open-air tables in front of Vino Vero, she emphatically describes Venice as the best place for her family. With her sunglasses perched on her head, stopping now and again to send messages on her phone, Mara says she is fed up with the gloom that has settled over Venice. She loves the city for its beauty, even its decay, for its peace, for the car-less streets where her family and friends live close by and where her children can run free — just as she did when growing up in Venice.

"If Venice is not to become a postcard, the city needs people to live here," she insists. Yes, admittedly, some people are leaving, but mainly for reasons of lack of suitable employment. She knows lots of others returning to make a life in the city and many foreigners who have found Venice an ideal place — especially creative types who can locate themselves wherever they like to do their work. She herself, as a publisher of art books, finds Venice puts her at the center of the art world with the annual Biennale international art shows attracting the best and most avant-garde art and artists.

Venice may be a village inhabited by mostly privileged people — and who knows, it may be underwater in a few decades due to sea level rise, she tells me with a frown — but the solution, in her view, lies not in lamenting short-sighted government but in changing the way we live, using less petroleum, making a better world, making a positive contribution. For her, the real problems Venice faces are air and water pollution and toxins leaked from the refineries on the mainland, which have led to a high incidence of cancer. Venice has unbeatable lifestyle, beauty and a human pace, she says, adding, "People don't appreciate how good they have it."

5

DYING
BEYOND DEATH IN VENICE

One day, perhaps, it will end this way,
this legend made of water and rock.
Swallowed up by mud and soft
sands, she will lie beneath a transparent sheet
of greenish crystal: she who was
the glory of the world,
an enchanting mirage
in the restless desert of the sea,
now sweetly dead,
supine in the light
of all the gold and flaming gems
time dressed her in,
a gleaming basilissa, too beautiful
to last through time,
created to be dead.

—FROM LINES BY DIEGO VALERI (TRANSLATED BY MICHAEL PALMA)

To live in Venice is also to live among constant reminders of past lives, and nowhere more so than behind the long, red brick wall backed by spikes of cypress trees and punctuated by solemn neo-Gothic gates and towers that rises from the lagoon ahead of my ferry. This boundary with white Istrian stone trim encloses the cemetery of San Michele, an island formed into a square just beyond the northern edges of the city. I have come to this tightly packed landscape of graves and funerary monuments that takes all of five minutes to cross to try to make sense of the perennial ideas linking Venice and death.

These words are most often seen together as *Death in Venice*, which is the translated title of a 1912 novel *Der Tod in Venedig* by German author Thomas Mann. In his book, the character Gustav von Aschenbach dies of cholera at the swanky Hotel des Bains in Lido, after suffering unrequited homosexual love. The novel is about discipline and freedom, repressed desire and forbidden love. At heart, it is not really a story about Venice at all. Mann, who arrived among the droves of well-heeled tourists visiting in the early twentieth century, found that Italy and, in particular, Venice, caught the sense of darkness that hung over Europe in the pre-World War I era in which he lived. He used the city as a symbol of decay and death.

The 1971 film by Luchino Visconti brought *Death in Venice* to a wider audience, as did the opera by Benjamin Britten and endless other ruminations and variations on the topic. Innumerable other books and films have used Venice as a background for decay, death, doomed love affairs and mysterious darkness, not to mention retelling the stories of famous lives that have ended in the city.

Especially since the 1966 flooding of Venice — a sort of near-death experience for the devastation it wrought on residents' livelihoods and the city's heritage — the idea that Venice is dying has had added virulence. That event spread fears that Venice was sinking and by extension seemed to encompass threats ranging from rising sea levels and mass tourism to depopulation. The concerns have been stoked by UNESCO's announcing in 2014 that Venice, a World Heritage site, was to be considered for the watchlist of endangered sites, along with many African wildlife parks and Bamiyan in Afghanistan, where the Taliban blew up Buddhist statues.

The association of death with Venice also goes back to the demise of the Republic, and its slow degeneration before 1797, and encompasses the Black Death, first carried to the city in 1348 by rats who scurried off ships, killing half the city and later over half of Europe in the course of a decade and returning again and again from then into the seventeenth century.

For people who live in Venice, its death is a real concern. Some regard it as a foregone, but deeply regretted, conclusion. Others fear it may be too late for Venice, but they cling to hopes for change that will salvage the future. For yet others, the present represents a sort of challenging transition, and the talk of death is just a marketing ploy to exploit its future "demise" for profit as Venice is turned increasingly into a "Disneyland."

All through the year, posters dot the pillars along Venetian streets with funeral announcements, each a single white page giving the name and age of the deceased along with a picture of the departed and an invitation to attend the service. But the day of my arrival on the island of San Michele, November 1 — Ognissanti, All Saints' Day — has coincided with a bout of acqua alta, with the high tides spilling over onto the streets, discouraging visitors; only a few souls are taking the short journey on the frequent ferries from the Fondamente Nuove. Normally, flocks of families and relatives make the trip, especially on the next day, Giorno dei Morti, All Souls' Day.

From the ferry landing on San Michele, the cemetery opens into a matrix of some twenty-five interconnected sections varying in size, with the largest no bigger than a football field. Mourners and visitors wander among the graves, some built into the outer brick walls and stone-paved walkways, some perched within what look like giant, elongated, multi-drawer marble filing cabinets, with cremation urns behind each meter-square door bearing the deceased's name and cameo picture.

In the tree-shaded burial sections, row after row of marble headstones and wood crosses stand over displays of bright bunches of flowers in vases. Spigots and watering cans on neat hooks are provided at nearby stations. Scattered among individual plots stand marble, garden shed-sized mausoleums belonging to the wealthier families, some with glassed-in doorways revealing the decorated coffins stacked on shelves inside. Some of the shelves are empty, awaiting the arrival of future residents.

San Michele first became a cemetery in 1807 after Napoleon's expanding empire gobbled up Venice, imposing modernizations, which included the requirement that all burials take place outside the city. This gave many Italian cities beautiful, out-of-town cemeteries.

Earlier I had visited the storefront offices of Funebre Pagliarin, a firm of funeral directors founded in 1849 and run by a series of families for five generations. Director Andrea Savoldello understands the Venetian style of passage. "For those of us who run funerals professionally, it's a routine, even if this routine helps us understand and appreciate life much more," says the soft-spoken undertaker. "Living with death, you come to value life much more."

Due to the population decline, fewer people die in Venice each year. In 2009, when the population first dipped below 60,000, a campaigning group held a mock funeral declaring that the city had been reduced to a village. Funebre Pagliarin, which carries out burials of residents as well as those of tourists or visitors who pass away while in Venice, customarily completed 900 funerals a year in the 1980s compared to an average of just 300 today.

In the past, the deceased would be rowed out to San Michele in traditional black-draped funeral gondolas, but this practice has become extremely rare. Nowadays, mourners arrive by ferry. An electronic lift on a hearse-boat transfers the coffin onto a trolley on the dock and then it is taken to the fifteenth-century church of the former Franciscan monastery or, increasingly, to a secular refectory.

Occasionally, the Pagliarin funeral directors also deal with curious deaths.

"In recent years, we find people have come to Venice specifically to die," says Andrea Savoldello in an interview. "We have arranged funerals for non-residents and even foreigners. In talking to the widows we often learn that their husbands came to Venice when terminally ill, so that they could die here." He also knows of cases where these deaths were evidently suicides.

Foreign deaths in Venice are legion. In 1894, American writer Constance Fenimore Woolson fell or threw herself out of a fourth-story window onto the street, perhaps out of frustrated love for Henry James, the American-British turn-of-the-nineteenth-century author of *The Wings of the Dove*, the story of a ravishingly beautiful, terminally ill woman who breathes her last in Venice. German composer Richard Wagner, who wrote part of his opera and romantic tragedy *Tristan und Isolde* in Venice — having been inspired in part by the mournful singing of a gondolier — died in Venice of a heart attack at sixty-nine in 1883 while staying at Ca' Vendramin Calergi on the Grand Canal. His death became a potent symbol for later writers, not least Mann, and would "make death in Venice a virtual expectation in the next century," wrote historian Margaret Plant in her exhaustive review of post-Republican Venice.

Many notables died in Venice or chose to be buried on San Michele. The grave of American poet Ezra Pound, who found refuge in Venice after flirting with the Fascist Party, lies under a tombstone near those of Russians including composer Igor Stravinsky, ballet impresario Sergei Diaghilev and poet Joseph Brodsky. Pairs of ballet shoes left by admirers are stacked on the grave of Diaghilev, founder of Les Ballets Russes, while flowers amply deck the graves of Brodsky and Stravinsky, both of whom had many ties to Venice. On this particular Ognissanti, I watch as a young Russian woman next to Brodsky's grave attracts an audience as she recites "Pilgrims", the 1987 Nobel Prize winner's poem about disillusionment and faith. Beside her a friend records it all on a smartphone.

In visits to the other burial grounds of Venice, I was touched by the care of graves and rituals. The tiny graveyard on Sant'Erasmo island has even become a focus of the aging rural community, where relatives socialize as well as pay their respects. The ancient Jewish cemetery on Lido has found supporters who maintain and protect the once neglected tree-shaded grounds. Similar attention was noticed by Henry James, who called the city "the most beautiful of tombs. Nowhere else," he wrote, "has the past been laid to rest with such tenderness, such a sadness of resignation and remembrance."

Lots of literati have imagined Venice darkly. In the nineteenth century, the poet Lord Byron envisioned Venice sinking; for Charles Dickens, the city was "a place of ruin"; for Friedrich Nietzsche, it was a mirror for human melancholy. Among the most influential observers of Venice must be English critic John Ruskin, known for his meticulous analysis of the city's architecture. He believed, as he put it in 1846, using a homely metaphor, that: "The rate at which Venice is going is about that of a lump of sugar in hot tea."

In the twentieth century, Jean-Paul Sartre described Venice as "The surpassing-all-or-nothings embodiment of that 'absolute ambiguity' which is in indeed radiant life containing certain death," while Ernest Hemingway's postwar novel sited in Venice, *Across the River and into the Trees*, deals with the aging and mortality of a soldier. Later, an endless stream of thrillers would associate Venice with crime, corruption and death, ranging from Daphne du Maurier's 1970 story "Don't Look Now", which also became a cult film, to the fine *Dead Lagoon* by Michael Dibden published in 1994, and books by the likes of Dan Brown, Jason Goodwin, Donna Leon and French writer Paul Morand.

Non-fiction is no less forgiving. The 1976 book on industrial pollution and corruption, *The Death of Venice*, declared, "Venice is dying and there is no hope of saving her," and Jan Morris in her review that year heartily agreed, saying, "There is no saving Venice." In 2013, Anna Somers Cocks wrote an article entitled, "The Coming Death of Venice" for the *New York Review of Books*. Even Peter Ackroyd's profile *Venice: Pure City* mixes exaltations of the city's mystery and beauty with attacks on Venetians for everything from corruption to impetuousness. The dark metaphors are enduring.

I asked Venetians what they thought. The answers were heartfelt.

"If you speak to ten Venetians now, almost ten out of ten or at least nine out of ten, but I am convinced it is ten out of ten, will tell you that Venice is already dead," says undertaker Savoldello's colleague, the white-haired Michele de Monino.

> That's because the Venice that used to be was the true Venice, where daily life let one breathe and where you'd meet on the streets.... Here I meet a person and I socialize; it is a better kind of social encounter, like you used to have, over a glass of wine, where you could really talk about everything. That was the true Venetianness.... The pulsing heart of this city was the people who lived in it. I have always defined Venice as a theater and the people as its actors, but Venice is an empty theater now, only good for spectators, like the ruins of the Colosseum in Rome.

I often heard such views, especially from older Venetians, but what people mean by "death" can vary. Attorney Andrea Pavanini had this to say: "Venice is not dying. Absolutely not. The point at which a city dies is when it loses its memory.... Today, among those who live in Venice, I believe a small minority retain that historical memory.... What's important is that someone lives here, that they work here, have children and die here, but above all that the city is worth living in." He sees no threat in the fact that people move and populations change. What's important is that the city continues to serve its residents, but this is being threatened by a shift in government towards serving tourist needs.

For philosopher and playwright Alberto Madricardo, of the citizens' lobbying group Venezia Cambia, the death of Venice means its "definitive disaggregation" — the scattering of the parts — "of the social fabric and the almost total expulsion of the citizens." In short, it's the "metamorphosis of the living city into the mummy of a dead city," a sort of ghost Disneyland.

So at what point is Venice dead? That depends on our choices, he says. The emptying of the historic center continues because of lack of political will to reverse the trend, but the growing movement to reject this outcome extends beyond Venice. Venice is but a leading example; what's at stake is the future of all cities.

For Venetian author Tiziano Scarpa, Venice is like the Italian language, which is at least 1,000 years old. It is a living tongue, but one with historical baggage including dying words and structures from the past. Similarly, "Venice is already dead, but it is among the living dead.... That is, Venice is a living corpse, in the sense that it obviously has buildings and form. It has people who move and live there, so, in other words, the city lives as a zombie. In this sense, Venice and the idea of death go together," he explains. "You might say, 'But in this church they still say Mass,' but the Catholicism, the Christianity we see, is dead. It is no longer Christianity, but yet they say Mass. Or, 'this canal is no longer the way used to transport merchandise and people in our world'; nonetheless, they transport packets from Amazon."

Entirely independently, Pieralvise Zorzi, scion of one of the twenty-four founding noble families of Venice, also used the z-word (for zombie). I bump into him at a book launch, where the noble, wearing jeans and a sport coat, spoke out for the need to save Venice from tourism. For Zorzi, whose family dates back to the nineth century in Venice and gave Venice a doge and many other officials, "Venice is not dying, it is just living in the wrong dimension... it's sort of a suspended life. It's like a beautiful zombie." But Zorzi's zombie is a victim of political failure to deal with tourism. "Venice is an open-air museum and an amusement park but everybody refuses to call it that," says this son of a noted historian of Venice. "It would be better run by the Disney Corporation.... If Venice was run like an open-air museum and you had to pay a ticket and the inhabitants were paid to appear in certain places and run shops and do things they normally do, the place would have more regulations and rules and more police probably because everybody would be paid for it."

Can this zombie return to life? Yes, "but only with very strong action" which he doubts is likely, not from any city government in the next ten years nor from Italy, where nobody in power "gives a damn about traditions." In the meantime, the government allows the tourists to run riot, not cracking down on disrespectful behavior and other harmful effects of tourism, says Zorzi.

Venice as Disneyland became a topic of public discussion mainly after an August 2017 headline in the *New York Times*: "Venice, Invaded by Tourists, Risks Becoming 'Disneyland on the Sea.'" But the Disneyland trope has been around since at least the 1990s and as far back as 1968, when Robert Sheckley used it in a novel.

In reality the thought of actually running Venice like Disneyland provokes real anger among many residents. It has propelled street protests, such as against Mayor Luigi Brugnaro's 2018 attempt to impose turnstiles at entry points to the city at peak times. It conjures up visions of Venetians wandering around in the period dress of the 1700s. Requiring an entry ticket could be seen to mean that tourists would expect to be treated as customers instead of guests in someone else's home, killing off any vestige of humanity in the relationship. "That is the death of Venice: deciding, in order to avoid having too many tourists, to become a closed city. When it becomes a closed city, Venice dies. It has finished developing. It looks only backward," says publisher Giovanni Keller.

This poses a key paradox, one I will deal with later: How can Venice retain its integrity as a city and yet take action to control the ever-growing excessive crowds that are both the root of degradation of residential life and an engine of the economy and key source of employment?

Venetian psychoanalyst Antonio Alberto Semi dismisses the talk of death of Venice in his book on the subject. He sees it as a feature of the commercial culture. Since 1500 or so, when the Venetian Empire began to decline, Venetians sold whatever they could to survive, including symbols and ideas. Now they sell the death of Venice.

"This symbol [of death] has been very profitable!" he says in a midday break from his schedule of seeing patients. Looking a bit like Freud himself with his pure white head of hair and beard, he works in a high-ceilinged, bookshelf-wrapped room over a quiet canal. "The city has continued to make money based on, 'Come to see Venice before it disappears, before it dies,'" he comments, referring especially to the marketing pitch after the devastating 1966 floods that triggered a global "save Venice" movement. "Although the city no longer produces anything, it can still produce symbols, and this is part of a long tradition in Venice, which has always sought to sell pictures of itself."

Venetian doges had to swear to promote the "honor and profit" of Venice. The eighteenth-century entrepreneurial artist Giovanni Antonio Canal, known as "Canaletto," produced city scenes on what was virtually an industrial scale for sale to northern European tourists. Venice also sells the Republic of Venice as the ideal state, or alternatively, as the infernal state, one of intrigues, assassins and spies, notes Semi. "Venice constructs a myth and then sells it all over the place. The idea of selling symbols is already part of Venetian tradition. You see, they can even earn from death!"

Surely, I ask, there is more to it than marketing. Depopulation is a reality.

That's true, he agrees. The population has shrunk and now most residents are old, so it's difficult to see how it can bounce back. "That's a pessimistic note. But there's an optimistic view," he adds. There's the possibility that the city can win new residents, who become Venetian, taking on local culture. "That can happen. As an example, my children used to play in the square with all the other Venetian children twenty years ago. The Chinese immigrant children spoke Italian very poorly, without good grammar or structure, but they spoke Venetian dialect well. This is interesting because just by being with other children, they were learning, becoming part of the culture and integrating." In fact, the Venetian dialect has unexpectedly maintained its vitality in the face of population changes.

I sit in the Great Hall of the sixteenth-century building now housing the Ateneo Veneto, a venerable cultural institution created in 1812, with historian Giorgio Crovato, its academic director, who gives death and Venice short shrift. "Thomas Mann and others have used literature to create the myth of death, haven't they? Which has been exploited by Venetians, who use it to attract visitors, with the line, 'Venice is dying, so come quickly to spend your money because we don't know what future it faces.'" He, however, looks to the past and finds Venice is resilient. "On many occasions Venice could have died due to the water, if they had failed to look after the lagoon, or due to natural causes or disease or invasion; the city has always bounced back. This is our hope for the future," he says.

But Crovato still has concerns. "Our ancestors always took great care of the lagoon and the city. If the idea of conservation fades, the future will be sad," he says. Without intervention, conservation and the necessary political support, the city has no future. Why? "Because everything is collapsing." The corruption scandals and the continuing failure to control lagoon erosion are eating away the city's foundations. "This is a moment of pessimism" and if the "cosmic ignorance" about these challenges and of the "fragility of Venice" is not lifted, the actual death of Venice is a possibility, he says.

During my months in Venice, I asked everyone I could about the fate of Venice, and, as if to avoid thinking about what they fear, more than one person answered by talking about utopian futures.

"Well, by now that's all that's left," my poet friend, Isabella Panfido, says of such seemingly utopian ideas when I pointed out that the hopes she described for a brighter future had been suggested to me before. Having lost faith in local politics, she dreams of putting Venice under the rule of a council of sages, that is, an economist, an urbanologist and an ecologist — anyone not associated with the miasma of Italian politics. She hopes for the realization of an idea that has been put forward and discussed a number of times since the 1960s, that of "giving Venice back a minimum of dignity in life by transforming it into the capital of Europe." She explains: "Europe, which is now falling apart, does not have a real capital. Brussels is an administrative center. Maastricht is the legal seat, but a real, moral home, that Europe recognizes, is missing. That would be the salvation of the city. Because the city would repopulate with people who lived and worked here, the palazzos would be the offices of Europe, and all the people who work there, all the functionaries, would need to live in the city, and so the stores would be reborn to serve the residents and not the tourists. There would be a real prospect of real life, of daily life — and not life under the closed sphere of *The Truman Show*."

But when I asked how far things have really gone, she just looks forlorn. "You could say that we have already gone past the line of no return. But, I want — since I have children — to be positive, and think, instead, 'No, there are prospects for a future.'"

6

CITIES

CITIZENS IN THE AGE OF CONSUMERS

> *"Every time I describe a city I am saying something about Venice."*
>
> —ITALO CALVINO, AUTHOR OF *INVISIBLE CITIES**

The exact moment of the minor calamity is still crystal clear in my memory. I was working on my laptop while tucking into a plate of pasta with shrimp when I knocked a whole glass of water onto my keyboard. I gave a sharp intake of breath, whipped up the laptop by the still-glowing screen to slosh away the spill and patted the keys with a napkin. But I was already losing hope. Indeed that night it failed to restart.

I made my way the next day to a repair shop in Mestre, just across the bridge on the terraferma. The technician shook his head gravely, so I made my way to the Apple store in Mestre to buy a new computer. As everywhere, the brand has installed itself in the smartest spot in town — and here in Venice that means the metal, glass and marble colossus that calls itself "Venice's shopping mall," Nave de Vero.

After walking from the parking lot through the massive trellis of steel at the entrance designed to resemble a ship's bow, I pass along the rows of more than 115 shops — from Al Girasole to Zara to the *Space Odyssey* white neon and gray of the Apple outlet — and my heart drops. After a month in Venice — just long enough to have begun to enjoy living life as if I were in a different era — looking around me I could have been anywhere; I could have been back in Cambridge or Chicago. The Apple shop at Nave de Vero is in fact identical to the ones in those places — except that the assistants speak Italian and the keyboards come with à, è, ò, ì and ù keys built in. The Venice I had been enjoying so much seemed suddenly like a fragile dream; everywhere you go, these days, cities are all so much alike.

Nowhere looks like Venice, though. Well, not the real Venice.

* *Invisible Cities*, the 1972 novel by Italo Calvino, imagines how Venetian merchant Marco Polo might have described cities he visited to the Chinese emperor, Kublai Khan. The book is seen as a parable of human experience and imagination.

Lots of places think of themselves as like Venice. For instance, there are at least ten locations in the United States called Venice, along with one each in Zimbabwe and Canada. Venezuela, translated from Spanish, means "little Venice." Scores of places are nicknamed "Venice of the East," from Basra in Iraq to Srinagar in India and Kyoto in Japan, or "Venice of the North"— Amsterdam in Holland and Birmingham in England, for instance. Venice has come to refer to anywhere with canals.

Most bizarre, perhaps, are scale models of Venice, such as the one in the Las Vegas casino resort which features phantasmagorical facsimiles of Piazza San Marco, the bell tower and the Doge's Palace — with a shopping mall inside. Similar amusing imitations are found in China, while Cambridge and Oxford each have a Bridge of Sighs, fashioned after the iconic passageway from the real Doge's Palace to its dreary jail next door.

But here I was, actually in the hinterland of Venice, in Mestre, which looks much like thousands of other places with shopping streets, office parks, residential areas and industrial zones. Yet even historic, central Venice grows more like a typical city over time; in the nineteenth century, the French and Austrian occupiers of Venice began to reshape the city in their own image of a metropolis. Of late, blandness has invaded Venice in the form of McDonald's, Burger King and other ubiquitous cloned brands.

This is globalization and it has been underway for centuries, as goods, people and ideas have spread around the world. When I was a child the McDonald's hamburger was born near my home in Chicago. Today, you can eat their burgers in 119 countries.

"If Mestre has turned into Chicago, why should I bother to go?" historian-journalist and scion of an ancient Venetian family Alberto Toso Fei asks when we talk. A tall man in his fifties in a stylish jacket with neatly cut hair, he is author of some twenty books on Venice. While I had focused on how globalization undermines culture and local character, he reminds me that the process also has its upsides.

In today's world "we are all connected. This is obviously a beautiful thing," says Toso Fei. "But none of us can ignore one's individuality and originality. Why do we fall in love with one person and not another? If we were all equal, or if we all became equal, the world would be extremely boring!" he says. "Instead, everybody has their own story. The stories belong to the person. My Venetianness is made up of thousands of years of stories, and I live inside that Venetianness in a profound way, but it is not just mine, because, with my books and talks, I share this Venetianness with others."

Toso Fei thinks we need to balance the gains from learning from each other's differences against the erosion of individuality. "We must be able to exchange our specificity and in doing so we both become more wealthy." That's the ideal — but it does not always work out.

Venice has "a communication problem," that arises in part from the problems of managing the torrent of tourism, says Toso Fei. "We are all bending ourselves out of shape to accommodate the tourists — where they need to sleep, eat, buy things and so forth. On one hand, our attraction for centuries has been our differences, our 'Venetianness,' in some manner... but we are less and less able to deliver this. We can't explain to visitors that they can go to McDonald's ... but if you go to a typical locale and eat a traditional cicchetto, you experience Venice more deeply.... These millions of visitors just come and go too quickly, faster than we can possibly assimilate them. We need to communicate who we are to get people to participate more when they visit; someone you know acts differently, looks for different things, and shows more respect than a stranger does."

Venice is still unlike any other place, any imitation, any other city — but is also under pressure to lose its distinctiveness. Where does that pressure come from? In part, from a loss of culture that took place at the end of the Republic when colonial powers were imposed on Venice. I ask historian Giorgio Crovato about this and he tells me about the Venetian "culture of water" — the way of life on the lagoon, which consisted both of attitudes in human relations and towards the natural environment. This mindset managed to keep the lagoon functioning, productive and alive for centuries, creating a widely admired equilibrium between man and nature.

The French and then the Austrians who ruled from 1797 until Venice became part of Italy in 1866 in particular lacked an appreciation for these aspects of Venetian culture; that is, its balanced relationship with nature and the benefits of organizing the city around water. The French, with grandiose ideas for Venice, filled in canals to make the wide boulevard-like Via Garibaldi, while the Austrians, and later the Italian government, built bridges to the terraferma and knocked down a lot of buildings for the city's only wide, straight-ish street, Strada Nuova, as part of a strategy to integrate wheeled traffic one day. It would have gone much further had they continued. "That was blocked, thank goodness, and the city maintained its characteristics," says Crovato, who believes the colonists and their Italian successors would have buried the lagoon marshes bit by bit, given the chance.

"Even today everyone thinks mobility must be with a tram, a train, automobile" or the underground rail system proposed at the turn of the millennium for Venice. "'Why not link Venice directly with Fusina, San Giuliano, Tessera?' they suggested," he says, referring to points on the mainland and the international airport. They want these routes because getting to these places from Venice is said to be "inconvenient." But these faster links would also cause congestion in Venice. "The problem is not that 70,000 people come to Venice daily for tourism and other reasons, adding to the 50,000 residents.... The city used to be inhabited by 120,000 people. It can manage. The problem is that all these people go to the same places... because modernity — the automobile, trains — have forced them to come to the city" only through these points. With water transport, anyone could reach any point in the inside of the city more easily and the arrivals would be better dispersed.

When the French and Austrian administrations began, "the first thing they thought, in good faith, was that the city ought to be made more like other modern cities," says Crovato. "But luckily, they did not succeed. The city has always maintained its characteristic style; it still looks ancient, and yet, in certain ways, it has shown itself to be modern and future-focused. Think of pedestrianization," which has only fairly recently been introduced in many cities. "Venice had this feature from its very origins."

The economic challenges Venice faces today grow from capitalism, which first took root in northern Italy and in particular in Venice. Traders in the Middle Ages, encouraged to accumulate wealth by the Church in its drive to conquer Jerusalem for Christianity, created modern banking and, critically, the system we know today as "double-entry bookkeeping."

This brilliant — but from our contemporary perspective, flawed — system was perfected by Venetian merchants and was known as bookkeeping *el modo de Vinegia*, Venetian style. Making use of the 1, 2, 3, 4 of Hindu-Arabic numbers we know today, instead of the I, II, III, IV of Roman numerals used in commerce previously (and possibly drawing from a concept of "bahi-khata" already used by Indian traders for possibly thousands of years), the Venetians by the 1430s "had perfected a system of double-entry account-keeping in two columns.... It is this Venetian method that, through its extraordinary resilience and mutability, has come down to us today, transformed over several centuries from a rudimentary business tool into an efficient calculating machine," writes economist Jane Gleeson-White. A Renaissance monk who lived on Giudecca, Luca Bartolomeo de Pacioli, known as the father of modern accounting, developed the algebra that underpins the system — and with the establishment of printing houses in Venice, his discoveries spread around Europe.

The story of double-entry bookkeeping is "one of history's best-kept secrets and most important untold tales" according to Gleeson-White. These arcane procedures of business arguably "made possible the wealth and cultural efflorescence that was the Renaissance," enabling capitalism to flourish. Over centuries, bookkeeping "grew into a sophisticated system of numbers which in the twenty-first century governs the global economy. This medieval artefact is still in daily use around the world." Most significantly, it now has the potential to make or break the planet. "Because accounting reduces everything to its monetary value, it has allowed us to value least that apparently free source of life itself: the planet. Through this logic we have let the planet go to ruin — and through its logic we now have a chance to avert that ruin." In other words, as the environmental crisis advances, it may be accountants who have the key to valuing the resources we have squandered by overcoming the tendency to see things purely in terms of profit.

Ironically, Venice's bequest to accounting is responsible for undervaluing its own environment, the lagoon — on which the city's existence depends. Since the eighteenth century, in particular industrialists and agriculturalists, led by politicians, used the lagoon "for free," acting in a way that left it severely poisoned and eroded. The "culture of water," fundamental to Venice's survival, has been lost.

But more than a narrow focus on the bottom line explains Venice's problems today.

These issues are the pawns of politics — many levels above the accounting offices — and an outgrowth of an ideology attributed to a twentieth-century economist from Vienna by the name of Friedrich Hayek, winner of the Nobel Prize in 1974. His theories, and those of others like Milton Friedman, gave an air of authority to attitudes in those years that aimed to do away with restrictions imposed on economies after the crash of 1929. That event sparked the years of economic depression and led governments to create laws based on the view that the market was too capricious to be left to business and consumers. At heart, the concept amounts to the veneration of the logic of the market, to the point of ceding political authority to the market and allowing decisions involving human values to be determined by profitability.

One of the stories of Venice: A grotesque carved head said to dispel evil spirits is on an arch at the base of the bell tower in Campo Santa Maria Formosa. John Ruskin, the English critic, hated this sculpture, insisting it was characteristic of the later years of the Republic, that it symbolized the "evil spirit" that lead to Venice's final decline. I thought it made a nice contrast with Nave de Vero. The gargoyle is said to depict someone probably suffering from fibromatosis or von Recklinghausen's disease.

The ideology, called neoliberalism, spread from purely economic problems to all social issues, seeing humans as profit and loss calculators, rather than individuals with inalienable rights and duties, and reducing the environment to a matter of business, rather than something vital to the survival of all life. Putting a price on everything has played into the hands of the powerful as wealth is increasingly concentrated in the hands of the few. Today a single minibus full of the world's billionaires, just twenty-six people, own as much as half of the planet's population, while average workers' salaries if paid at the same rate as in the 1970s would be a fifth higher.

Hayek's thinking energized left and right from the late 1970s. On the right, it was taken up by British Prime Minister Margaret Thatcher, US President Ronald Reagan and later in Italy, Prime Minister Silvio Berlusconi and the increasingly powerful League and Five Star parties. Recent adherents include American leader Donald Trump and Viktor Orbán of Hungary. On the left, meanwhile, it was adopted by US Democrats under Bill Clinton, the Labour Party of Tony Blair in the UK, the center-left Democratic Party in Italy, and by mayors in Venice from the 1990s and, not least, since his election in 2015 and re-election in 2020, the entrepreneur-basketball team owner-mayor, Luigi Brugnaro.

In Italy, which already bears a heavy burden through a culture of organized crime, tax evasion and unwieldy decision-making, this supremacy is troubling. Never in politics is action tied to one factor — but in the context of Venice, a city unlike any other in its delicacy, the advent of neoliberalism and emphasis on profit over heritage, environment and community life has potentially dire consequences. The tug-of-war over the myriad challenges of managing a medieval city in a lagoon, the draining away of population under the pressure of tourism and the demands of speculators and developers have put Venice's survival on a knife edge.

This reality was brought home to me on another evening in the hallowed great hall of the Ateneo Veneto. I had taken a seat surrounded by the oil paintings on the walls and ceiling depicting Bible stories, where we heard that all this, indeed all of Venice, could die. Cities do die. That is the firm view of our speaker that evening, art historian and archaeologist Salvatore Settis, whose book *If Venice Dies* has been read by thousands all over the world

He starts from the view of the city as the quintessential form of human community, embodied not only in buildings but also in institutions, governing practices, and in the relationship between the city and its countryside. Cities contain the city that they once were and the cities that they could have been; a city is a physical entity, but its soul, the "invisible city," is its inhabitants and culture.

Cities can be destroyed physically — as in war or by volcanic eruptions — but they can also just forget who they are.

Could Venice become an empty shell? The real and present danger for Venice is that the diminishing population will reach a point at which the collective memory of its past, the skills, the very love that protects its buildings and natural environment, will be lost. That is the kind of death Venetians fear today.

Settis identifies the source of pressure on heritage cities as coming particularly from the new idea of the city as a megalopolis. Examples of this new phenomenon are Chongqing with 34 million people and Sao Paolo with 11.3 million, where the rich live in gated communities and skyscrapers, the poor in slums and squalid tower blocks. The megalopolis model turns the city into a "productive machine," rather than as a source of well-being for its "citizens" and the provider of a sustainable balance with nature. The new city is for "consumers."

Venice is being pulled in the same direction. Proposals have been put forward not only for an underground system under the lagoon but also for skyscrapers on the land around it, while property speculation has already sharpened the divisions between the rich and the poor. The horizontal skyscrapers of the sea — the huge cruise ships, dwarfing the city's scale and endangering the lagoon — are seen by many as an assault on the survival of the city. This puts Venice under pressure to pursue a path of rapid growth that is in line with its larger modern counterparts.

Settis asks some good questions. "Do we really want the megalopolis to supplant all other urban forms or do we want to keep other growth alternatives when we think of the city of the future?" "Do we wish to nurture or destroy the multiplicity of diversity of urban forms?" That's exactly what some parts of our society want, he says. The "unacknowledged but obvious goal [is] to erase diversity, to homogenize cities, substituting civil conversation as created spaces with machines for production and consumption of goods."

A thought just like that resonated as I stepped out of a taxi on returning to Venice from the Nave de Vero (literally "ship of glass") shopping mall with my new laptop in hand. I was relieved to be back in the city where people moved around at a human pace on foot and by boat, where along every alleyway the gaze falls upon carved stones set in the brickwork, the human tales of which have been lost in time, where every day is an endless discovery of the present and the past keeps boredom at bay.

I GIUDECCHINI
PAST AND PRESENT
PAOLO VIANELLO AND SERENA NONO

One place that exemplifies how homogeneity and diversity are threatened in Venice is Giudecca and, to appreciate what has changed there, I have paired the comments of Paolo Vianello, an engineer who lived on Giudecca from 1950 to 1987 (now he lives in Treviso), and afterwards of a current resident, Serena Nono.

"I was born on the Giudecca in 1950. The island was where the working class lived. It was a community of simple people and it was fundamentally a very cohesive community. But, as is perhaps the custom in Italy, the island was divided into what were little districts within a district, with petty rivalries among the boys of each one, but then they all went to the same school! Beyond these differences, the Giudecchini [residents of Giudecca] felt very united. This was particularly true after the war, because until the economic boom in the 1960s and '70s, there was real poverty.

"My father worked at the Junghans, the watch factory, so we were among the better off, and we had enough to eat. At least we had a shower, even if just for cold water. But in other parts of the Giudecca, some really didn't have enough. The new generation on Giudecca today has probably never lived through the hardship that we lived through, something that cemented our friendships and the feeling of belonging. Not much remains of the spirit we shared. I believe it will disappear with us as we pass away over the years. Like the rest of Venice, the island is depopulated. Back then there were many inhabitants and important companies. Junghans was a German firm that made watches and bomb fuses in the war. There was a shipyard for vessels of modest sizes, a beer brewery and the Stucky flour mill, and they all required a lot of workers. Some came daily by the ferry from the Zattere, having traveled from other parts of Venice or the terraferma.

"My family lived in a block of flats among a number within a walled-in compound built for company dependents. Each house had a garden of some 200 or 300 square meters where the families put out the washing and some had swings. Our garden had an orchard of fig trees, two white and one black. I never loved figs. We also grew eggplants, peppers, tomatoes, greens for salad and marvelous tiny strawberries. My mother was a housewife. She cooked. My father and oldest brother looked after the garden, which was a lot of work.

"Some kids went swimming for fun. I never learned to swim but my brothers did. They learned on their own. They either threw you in and you swam, sometimes with a rope tied around you, or you learned holding onto a washing board. Some learned with little balloons tied to them. Some kids were really good at swimming and could swim across the canal from the Giudecca to the Zattere in Venice, and then back again, which was extremely dangerous. Ships used to pass through that canal! But nothing ever happened.

"I went back to my old house once, but found the gardens unkempt. People have lost the desire to keep them up. They all buy what they need at the supermarket now. Giudecca has become fashionable! People want to live there now. The Altanella was the restaurant for the biggies in the Communist Party. The composer Luigi Nono lived on Giudecca. François Mitterrand and Elton John had houses there. Now, every year, we old Giudecchini, who live in Mestre, Lido, and other distant places, have a reunion. One year 150 people came! It's a great pleasure to get together to see how everyone is doing. We have a dinner in the big banquet room at Cipriani's restaurant, which is a bit like a redemption — because when we were poor we saw the rich people go there. Now it's us who are dining at Cipriani!"

Artist Serena Nono grew up and currently lives on Giudecca.

"My aunt who lived on the Zattere [across from Giudecca] never sent my cousins to play here on the Giudecca because she said that it was a dangerous neighborhood! It's not true, but there was this attitude. In reality, it has always been a very lively place, very Venetian and very real, and it still is. It's changed a lot, too, as it now has a lot of hotels, bed and breakfast places and restaurants, all things that never used to be here.

"But Giudecca still has a spirit of resistance, in the sense that there are lots of artists and artists' studios, and people who live here support Giudecca's culture and social life: an exhibition, events, music and theater. It's a place with the feel of the countryside, where people feel in control. Everyone knows everyone else. We still resist [tourism], but I don't know for how long. There are people who live here from all over the world. It's probably the least touristy place in Venice. It seems to work, and it's a beautiful thing; this goes beyond Venetianness."

7

ROWING

DYNAMICS OF AN ENDURING TRADITION

THE BLONDE IN A GONDOLA

I went rowing the other night
with my blonde in a gondola:
Poor thing, such was her delight
that she fell asleep instantly
and in my arms she nestled
I woke her from time to time,
but the rocking of our vessel
soon sent her back to dreaming.

—POPULAR "BARCAROLA" BY ANTONIO LAMBERTI SUNG BY GONDOLIERS (TRANSLATED BY SHAUL BASSI AND PHILIP MORRE)

Holding an oar for the first time in decades, I try to remember how to row.

"The other side!" instructs Emiliano Simon, as I stand at the back of our topa, resting the oar on the sculpted wooden *forcola*, the oarlock, with the paddle in the water upside down. "The oar is asymmetrical. One side is flat and the other angular. The angular side is called the 'diamond.' Always keep the diamond up."

I roll the fat pole in my hands, set my stance with left foot forward, and then begin rowing — which is like standing at one end of a chest of drawers, pushing it forward over a carpet — twisting the oar slightly at the end of the stroke to keep the boat in line and then circling around again.

"Keep your wrists relaxed. That way you can push and add resistance. You need to do both to go straight," he advises, as I move the boat into the open canal. After a few strokes, rowing comes back to me. "Perfect! You see? You remember how to do it! It's like riding a bicycle, huh?"

Rowing *alla veneta*, is initially, maybe, like learning to ride a bike, but after a while is more like learning tennis. The basic moves can be acquired in hours, but a good rower takes months, even years to train, if he or she wants to become an expert.

Rowing, sailing and lagoon excursions have now gained popularity, but in the years just after the 1966 floods, it became clear that Venetians needed to get to know the lagoon better. So, Paolo Rosa Salva had an idea. Why not organize a marathon, a Venetian-style rowing race to get people out on the water? That met with a barrage of nay-saying.

"I don't know about that, Paolo. You need to talk with your uncle and cousin," his close friend Silvio Testa told him, sending him to the heads of the rowing and sports associations. "Are you crazy? We could never do that in Venice. It's impossible," the association heads said, dismissing the idea out of hand.

But the flood disaster — including the near collapse of the ancient *murazzi* walls on Pellestrina island, the loss of which could have spelled the end of Venice — had concentrated minds in its aftermath. It spawned an environmental movement, which went on to fight a long campaign that continues today.

"When fighting this battle, something became clear," Testa told me. "The authorities could do whatever they wanted in the lagoon because Venetians no longer went there. They had forgotten about it. They had lost touch with it." Traditional rowing and sail boating was by then seen as a relic of the bitter hard work of poverty-stricken old days, and all the associated artisanal trades were already at risk of dying out by the 1960s. Venetians "didn't know what happened when a channel was dredged out there. All the centuries of culture that had once been part of Venetian character had practically been lost. So, the environmentalists began to think, 'How can we get Venetians back into the lagoon?'" recalled the tall, sun-tanned Testa, now seventy, a senior journalist and author of a Venetian sail boating history, who never misses a chance to get on the water.

As it happened, Paolo was familiar with the popularity of long ski races in the Alps. He was also the son of architect Giuseppe "Pino" Rosa Salva, the man behind the campaign by the Front for the Defense of Venice and later head of Venice's Italia Nostra environmental group. Paolo persisted in pushing his race idea. He even had a name for it: Vogalonga, the long row. In the end, he settled for a regatta that went ahead on St. Martin's Day, 1974 with ten boats and twenty rowers. Testa came second to last, he recalled with a grin.

At their celebratory dinner afterwards, the initially reluctant rowing federation head, Paolo's uncle Toni, and others, relented, deciding to launch the marathon the next year. It has since grown into an annual event with over 2,000 boats and 8,000 rowers doing a 30-kilometer route reaching far into the northern lagoon, the more scenic half of the 50-kilometer long by 10- to 12-kilometer wide body of water. "The Vogalonga has gone on to fuel the blossoming of traditional sport and leisure boating in Venice," says Testa, who took part in the trial race and has participated in every Vogalonga since. Along with the undying demand for gondola rides among tourists, the Vogalonga has also helped sustain the livelihoods of artisans who produce the specialized boats, oars and the shapely wooden oarlocks.

There were just three rowing clubs in the 1970s; now, scores of amateur rowing and sailing associations dot the lagoon, with an estimated 10,000 alla veneta rowers in Venice and nearby communities. From April to September an estimated 370 traditional sailing vessels, most with colorful gaff-rigged sails, have lagoon races. More than 120 rowing events are held. The Canottieri Giudecca, among others, holds training programs for schools. Venetian-style rowing even has pockets of aficionados in England, the United States and Australia.

But, like so much in Venice, the race itself, as well as boating more broadly, has changed almost beyond recognition. Whereas Vogalonga was once something for Venetians, a bit of fun to encourage environmental awareness, it has become "a nice international celebration of rowing," says Testa, but "yet another manifestation of tourism" that has also lost its original purpose of safe-guarding the lagoon. Only a tenth or so of the participants now row Venetian style, with the majority pulling oars English style or scooting along in plastic kayaks. The number of Venetians taking part has also stagnated.

Meanwhile, out on the lagoon, the number of boats has exploded, some say tripled, but the increase is predominantly due to non-traditional day trippers in fiberglass boats with outboard motors or general traffic related to the growth of tourism. Even teenagers have their own boats. The wakes these boats cause, the excessive speeds and overcrowding, apart from interfering with traditional boating and adding to erosion of the ancient buildings, have created a lawless chaos on the water —

likened by Testa to a watery "Wild West." In August 2013 an accident between a gondola and a vaporetto killed a tourist. The crowding is such that even public transport can be dangerous.

Those who cleave to sail and oar often find themselves marginalized on the lagoon while demand for the cheaper, easier to maintain, plastic boats so outstrips demand for wooden ones that few boatyards still support wooden boats. The rich history of traditional boating continues to face threats, but the wide engagement with boating exemplifies the plight of so much of Venice's cultural wealth; it survives only in as much as people make it part of society.

In around 1962, at a lagoon *squero* (boatyard), a *varo*, or boat christening, is about to be celebrated. So special is this occasion that the boss's family

At a ceremony at a boathouse near the Bacini vaporetto stop, Mattia de Marchi christens Cocola, which he built in wood over four months.

is invited to attend. The visitors to the yard at San Pietro on Pellestrina gather round the newly built *burcio* held upright on the land by stilts and wedges, among the scores of other motorboats and vessels under repair or construction. Drinks are passed round and toasts are proposed as the audience examines the wooden vessel.

Slender with a large, open cargo hold, flat bottom and upturned bow, a burcio can be up to 30 meters long and, once upon a time, they would carry two masts that could be taken down to allow passage under bridges. Historically, they were towed by men or oxen along rivers feeding the lagoon. Building a cargo boat like a burcio would have been a big job, even for a sizeable boatyard like this one, which employed ninety men. The shipwrights would first have had to build up the skeleton in timber, then heat wet wooden planks with flames from burning reeds so the boards would bend, and then wrap them around the frame, caulk the seams and paint the hull. The finished burcio could be rowed, or it might have had an onboard engine. The driver guided the boat with a tiller connected to a house door-sized rudder at the end of the boat.

Building with wood was still standard in the 1960s. Wood for boats like this came mainly from oak trees in Istria, across the Adriatic, and the owner of the yard, Benedetto Schiavon, had always traveled over the sea himself to the Istrian forests to select the trees for his boats. When he found just the right tree, or a part of a tree with just the right shape, he would whack it with a special axe that would imprint his seal, "BS," on the trunk or branch so that when it was felled and shipped back to his yard in Venice for finishing he knew it was what he had selected.

When the moment comes to launch the newly built boat, Schiavon, who was then around eighty, must have been mightily proud. Having gone to sea at age nine in the 1890s, he had never learned to read or write, but he built up a business from nothing and started a family. One can only imagine the expression on his face as he stood with his family to watch the event.

His granddaughter Alessandra remembers the emotional moment of the launch. "My grandmother and the workers shouted *'Oh issa!'*" and with that cry they knocked away the wedges holding up the boat. "It slid into the lagoon, with the bow going down into the water! So, I shouted, 'Grandpa! The boat's sinking!'" Boats launched in that way bob up and right themselves, of course, so no doubt, Grandpa and the others had a good laugh.

Fast forward to 2018. Over half a century later, Alessandra Schiavon, now an archivist in Venice, takes part in a varo for a new sanpieròta, 6 meters long, typical of the sort built on San Pietro in the nineteenth century, when they were used for fishing. The red-painted wood hull, varnished and shiny on the open interior, rests on a trolley before the open door of a boathouse on a quay near the Arsenal, while fifty or so guests mill around with wineglasses and plates of potato chips and *pasta con fagioli*, pasta with beans.

The young artisan who single-handedly built the boat in four months, Mattia de Marchi, had, only moments before, explained to a beaming Alessandra that the boat was "a tribute to your grandfather because the sanpieròte that he built lasted fifty years." Named *Cocola*, which means "pretty" or "sweet," the new boat was commissioned for leisure sailing and rowing around the lagoon. De Marchi had built eight of them over the years, each selling for about the cost of a small car.

"I liked the idea of having a traditional boat," says the proud new owner, Roberto Rinaldo. "We could have bought a used one — there are lots on sale — but it seemed like such a beautiful opportunity to give someone who knows how to build the boats a chance to continue a Venetian tradition that would otherwise be slowly lost." The rate at which wooden boats are built today is hardly enough to replace the rate at which older wooden ones are fading away.

After the speeches, a hydraulic arm lifts the boat off the quay, placing it gently in the water as cheers burst out from onlookers.

Sandro Potenza, a tall, strong, retired doctor, aged seventy-two, who wears a fashionably cut coat and a neatly trimmed goatee beard, has been rowing all his life. We talked over a glass of white wine:

> I remember I had a little boat, a sandolo, when I was six and I would go round the canals. I would go from the side canals through the Giudecca Canal and beyond it to the lagoon. Back then, goods were transported in boats rowed with great fatigue because they were big and heavy. Rowing was a part of work. Even the police

> made their rounds by oar! But those who were passionate went rowing for fun or a day out or just to take in a bit of good air and sun.
>
> In 1973, I began working as a locum on Burano and Sant'Erasmo islands, where lots of rowers came from. These island people grew up with boats that were used back then for work — for fishing; maybe they fished with their dads or grandfathers. Maybe they carried fish from Burano to Venice, and they traveled over great distances by boat. So they had to understand how to row with the least possible effort. They had learned the secret, because rowing *alla Veneta*, Venetian style, is very technical and requires strength. The oars on each boat vary in length and you adjust the position using the oarlock, the part we call the forcola. In the regattas you have to adjust it very carefully because if it is positioned badly, either too high or low or at the wrong inclination, you get less force and the boat moves more slowly, even if you push hard on the oars. As a doctor on Burano I met all the regatta racers, the best ones, and by talking with them I got to be a passionate regatta rower myself.

The gondola, first mentioned in Venetian records in 1094, was the carriage of the aristocrats during the Republic and had a dozen variants before the twentieth century. An example, par excellence, of a boat made for hydrodynamic efficiency, it has an 11-meter, flat-bottomed hull that curves left to balance the force from the oar of a single rower at back. A gondolier rows with little more effort than walking, moving the boat forward at jogging pace. The version known today, along with many of its traditions, like the symbolism of the "S"-shaped metal prow — with six prongs, each representing one of the sestieri — dates from the nineteenth century.

Most of the old types of gondola have passed into history, but Venetian organizations like Arzanà, founded in 1992, work to preserve surviving examples. They have purchased about fifty row and sailboats made for the lagoon, restoring and preserving them in part at their museum, a chamber of nautical wonders, itself a fifteenth-century squero, active until the 1920s. Efforts have also started to recreate the magnificent two-tier palace-on-water, the *Bucintoro*, used for ceremonies for the doge until it was burned by Napoleon when Venice fell at the end of the eighteenth century.

Another association has saved the last working *trabaccolo* in the upper Adriatic, a merchant vessel used from the 1700s into the last century. *Il Nuovo Trionfo* (*The New Triumph*), the two-masted, bathtub-shaped cargo carrier, at 17 meters long and 5.5 meters wide, has a berth of distinction on the bacino, the inner harbor. Built in 1926, it was saved from oblivion by a hundred Venetians who paid €1000 to €5000 each to buy the boat and then, in a 2011–12 project that engaged carpenters, blacksmiths and other artisans, helped restore it to navigability. *Il Nuovo Trionfo* is "the historical memory of the city of water. Saving it means, in a certain way, saving the city of Venice," said the group's leader, Massimo Gin.

White-haired Dante Maestro, aged sixty-six, has rowed a gondola all his life. He first rowed one that ferried passengers over the Grand Canal, a traghetto, in the 1960s.

Il Nuovo Trionfo (The New Triumph), the last surviving trabaccolo, a merchant vessel, under sail. It was saved by Venetian volunteers.

The gondolas used to pick up tourists at the train station or Piazzale Roma, where cars and buses arrived, and take them to their hotels. In those days we would do a few trips a day, and quite often we worked for tourist families, English, American and German, mainly, who often hired us for five, ten or fifteen days, the whole period of their holiday. Italians from the south came to Venice on honeymoons. Once I took the actress Joan Collins around Venice. I have also rowed my gondola for films — *The Italian Job* and *Casanova*. I enjoy the work.

There were no organized gondola 'tours.' We would take the visitors everywhere, anywhere they wanted to go, to churches or museums, even over to San Giorgio, to Murano or even Burano! At Redentore, the celebration in July with fireworks, families used to hire gondolas to go out to watch. Maybe 300 or 400 gondolas would be out there in the bacino. Beautiful!

Venice used to be different. The gondoliers were respectful and courteous. There were maybe ten or fifteen taxis and many fewer motorboats. On the Grand Canal a vaporetto passed maybe once an hour. The water was calm and flat. Children used to swim in the canals. Now we have mass tourism. We used to wait four or five hours for a job. Now we have more work, but less quality. Being a gondolier is a year-round job. We have 350 water taxis on the canals and the vaporetti pass every few minutes. The motorboats make traffic dangerous. They can make waves over a meter high. The water's far too rough. You could lose your life! We couldn't take a trip to Murano if we wanted to. Only a few gondolas go out on Redentore. It's all yachts and motorboats. It's a mess.

Oars powered the lagoon until the mid-1950s when the first outboard motors liberated boaters from fatigue and the caprices of the wind and tides. Plastic came in the 1960s and the first to use it for Venetian boats was Agostino Amadi, member of a Burano boat-building family dating back to at least the 1700s. At eighty, he still runs the business in basketball court-sized sheds filled with boats on cradles, buzzing saws and sanding machines. The racket filters into his glass-enclosed office at back. This is what he tells me:

> I was the first to have the idea of building in fiberglass for boats carrying merchandise. The boats that we had had until then were constructed in wood. In Venice it seemed like a scandal. It was met with a wave of protest: 'Building boats in fiberglass in Venice is not right. If things continue like this next they'll be making gondolas in fiberglass!' they said.... But after a while the reality has proved right, because now they can do nothing without fiberglass — nobody wants boats in wood. When something is no longer useful, enough! Wooden boats are luxuries. Just for sport rowing. These convenient modern boats require less maintenance, are less delicate, more robust. They work better. With fiberglass, once the mold is made, the shape is complete. It still has a flat bottom, as suits canals and the lagoon, but is easier to construct, and I adapted it to propulsion with an engine.

Amadi, having built the first fiberglass boat — a motorized topo — in 1981, is looking ahead now. He has built Venice's first electric-hybrid boat. It's already working and ready.

On Giudecca, a 9.3-meter *caorlina*, a six-rower boat for the Regata Storica, is under construction at the old naval shipyards. Carpenter Francesco Stengel is on the shop floor, halfway into the two months needed to build the vessel, which rests like a truncated whale skeleton on benches. Like most of the Venetian boats built today, this one is being made using marine plywood instead of the old method of overlapping boards for the outer shell. Plywood is less costly, simpler and allows the boat to be stored out of water.

Stengel works deliberately, first measuring each of the twenty-nine ribs, then cutting a knuckle-deep groove on one side with a rotary saw and returning to repeat the entire operation on the other. He screws a guide strip onto the boat with a drill, and then moves on, occasionally stopping to light a cigarette. "As long as there are people who row, there will be wooden boats," he says, expressing his faith in wood, which can be custom built, while fiberglass boats are all the same.

Stengel is an employee of Gianfranco "Crea" Vianello, who sits upstairs at his dusty desk under an oil painting of himself as a blond young man with a full beard, muscles bulging under a red-striped shirt, Venice in the background. To one side of the portrait are all the rowing regatta trophies he won in the 1960s and '70s. The former all-time rowing champion, once a gondolier and fisherman, looks not all that different at seventy-two, still barrel-chested and determined. He has long been opposed to fiberglass for Venetian boats.

> We build mainly gondolas and do lots of repairs. There's a bit of return to wood, but there is hardly anyone left who builds in wood now. Fiberglass has ruined the culture and the art of the Venetian boat and the capacity to build them as needed for the environment and for different uses. You can't do that with fiberglass where boats come out of a mold. Wood is beautiful whereas fiberglass is cold. For boat building in Venice, it's been really deadly. It's destroying a profession, and hundreds of jobs have been lost. The fiberglass hulls have to be made on the terraferma due to the pollution they cause and they only get finished in Venice. In a city like Venice, artisans and boat building should not have been abandoned. But fiberglass needs less than half the maintenance of wood, so the artisans are starved of work.
>
> The city shouldn't have permitted this to happen. They should stop the exodus of artisans. If only there were a law to protect traditional boats as there is for gondolas; you can't make them in plastic. Artisans should be protected with lower taxes and fewer hassles. They should teach the young the profession. The boatyards would have workers. Now we have had three generations that no longer work in wood in Venice. Three generations! At this point, the government has destroyed something and it is a very difficult to turn back.

He is writing a book about his life in the lagoon and the struggle to keep artisanship alive. "I've been writing it for ten years. And every time I write something, when I get to this part of the story I want to cry. So, I stop.... But what I write is the truth that I have lived."

On a sunny Sunday, all of Venice takes to the water. With the sails of our yacht furled, six of us sit sprawled out in the cockpit and on the deck taking in the afternoon rays and grazing on savory tart, fried zucchini and marinated artichokes washed down with a good red wine. We have motored out to a quiet stretch of water near Lio Piccolo and anchored the boat. It's just like the ones I knew on Lake Michigan where I grew up, with its white fiberglass hull, keel and aluminum mast. On the open sea, these boats ride confidently, but in the shallow lagoon they can only navigate the main channels — which is quite enough on a lazy afternoon like this one.

Under the boat, the tide moves the water at pace, and we see a pale jellyfish as big as a bucket float by. Adriana Teot and I take a swim, and so fast is the flow that we can barely stay in place in the water. Similar boats are anchored along the channel, and now and again a motorboat or a big launch full of tourists zips by, but mostly peace reigns.

When we tire of lounging and the day is waning, we up anchor and motor by Torcello island, where a caravan of half a dozen open motorboats with outboards, each with a young driver seated next to a female companion, buzz by, one after another. "They're kids from Murano who are going out to a stilt house just over there where they smoke marijuana, drink beer and watch the sunset," says Teot. My face must have shown some surprise, but she reassures me. "They are fine. Just young."

As young as twelve, thirteen, or fourteen, these lagoon riders often have a boom box with music blaring as they push their engines to the max. The "Brube," the prevalent brand of fiberglass boat, has added a new element to the explosion of taxi and hotel traffic: their vessels for getting around the city on a daily basis are the equivalent of the private car. For the boys and girls, it's like having a motorcycle.

Traffic on the water has become treacherous, according to journalist Silvio Testa. "It's a 'Wild West' everywhere. It's dangerous. There are deaths, overturned boats or boats colliding with posts. Everything happens. And in this Wild West, there are the leisure motorboaters in ever-larger boats, in inflatables and kids in Brubes," he says. "It's a world of bullying, where the strong prevail over the weak. And what is sad is that even people who row, when they get on a motorboat, they're exactly like the others," says Testa. An attempt to reach a "*pax in aqua*", a peace agreement, between the rowing and sailing societies and the city of Venice in the 1990s came to naught.

Something magical happens when you row. You feel again that this uniquely Venetian way of living is inseparable from the water, which is how the Venetians used to experience their city most of the time — from the water — on a topa, sandolo, *mascareta* or gondola.

On one of my first rows, I took along my assistant Sofia, who had sat in the boat quietly taking it all in. Although she had long lived in Venice as a student, she had never before rowed through the canals. "Going from land to water you enter a different world," distinct from Venice at the bustling street level, she said later. "There is a sense of freedom. The tranquility of the city comes back."

Something even more profound happens when you first row down the Grand Canal. Somehow history seems to come alive. It happened to scholar and guide Cristina Gregorin. "I learned rowing alla veneta with an American friend ten years ago," she recalls. "When she took me onto the Grand Canal to row, after living in Venice for so many years, I started to cry because I understood that only in that moment had I become truly Venetian."

8

TOURISTS

TOO MUCH OF A GOOD THING

> *"Everyone wants to go to Venice once in their lifetime.... There will never be a moment in the existence of this planet when there will not be tourists who want to go to see Venice once in their lives."*
>
> —GIOVANNI BASTIONELLI, DIRECTOR OF ENIT, AGENZIA NATIONALE DEL TOURISMO (APRIL 30, 2018 DURING A RAI RADIO INTERVIEW)

In a flat overlooking a flowered courtyard garden, the mild-mannered Anna Ammirati will soon glow with recollections of how she loved Venice, its sounds, its smells and its art. But at first she wants to tell me about Venice today, and she is angry. Very angry.

> Venice is not a beautiful city anymore. People live in the wrong way. I cannot understand the spirit of the city. Everyone is always looking at the clock to see if it's time to leave. Venetians live badly. The crowding is oppressive; they live in this anxious way. They have lost their normal courtesy and kindness. Many are leaving and find themselves unable to properly restore any balance. The city has been horribly transformed. It's no longer the real Venice. You just need to get on a ferry to see the exasperation of the local Venetians. They are mad. They can't take it anymore.

Ammirati, aged sixty-six and a retired bank worker, is describing how she feels mass tourism has transformed Venice in the past few decades. She's a slender woman, who is blind; she and her partner, who has a disability, live in a flat in Cannaregio. She was born in Venice and used to love walking around on the arm of her sighted uncle to experience the city. Her disillusionment with the excessive numbers of tourists, many seemingly with little real interest in Venice, is as unequivocal as it is tinged with sadness and grief — and shared by many of the residents I spoke to.

"We have lost our liberty. We have lost our city," she concludes. "This is not the city we wanted."

Until 1990, fewer than 10 million tourists visited Venice annually, but with cheap air fares and growing global affluence, that figure doubled and then tripled in a few decades, increasing at an even faster rate after 2000. Except for 2020 and 2021, when tourists were excluded for months by the Covid-19 virus lockdowns, Venice typically accommodates some 30 million tourists annually, more than there are citizens of Australia. Worldwide tourism has been growing exponentially, and by 2030, the number of travelers is forecast to balloon from 1.5 to 1.8 billion, pouring visitors not just into Venice, but many of the similarly frail cities and landscapes of the world — from Barcelona and Amsterdam to the Isle of Skye, Mallorca, San Sebastian, Dubrovnik, Florence, Edinburgh, New Orleans and Thailand. But of them all, Venice is under the most agonizing pressure.

Small, concentrated and delicate, Venice exemplifies both the good that comes from tourism and its destructiveness when it is out of control. A perfect storm of badly managed economic deregulation combined with just too many *mordi e fuggi* (eat and run) tourists, has caused environmental degradation, evisceration of the community's way of life and accelerated runaway depopulation that at least halved the number of Venetian residents in the last fifty years. By the end of the 1990s a local newspaper columnist was already calling mass tourism a scourge in the history of Venice, unequalled by any previous pestilence or war.

Mass tourism enlightens and delights throngs from America, Europe and increasingly countries that are speedily growing richer, like India and China. It has become the largest employer on the planet, with one in every eleven people relying on the industry for work. It brings €50 billion worth of trade, property deals and employment to Venice annually — though much of that money flows right out again. But this tourism is reminiscent of the Greek legend of King Midas, who won the power to turn everything he touched into gold, only later to discover, to his horror, that his touch had turned his food and drink — and even his daughter — into gold. He begged the gods to take back his powers.

Venice is one of the world's oldest tourist destinations.

During the Crusades starting from 1095, after the pope galvanized Europe's warriors and sent them to fight for the Holy Land, Venice became a place of pilgrimage and a point of departure for Europeans journeying to Palestine on Venetian galleys. Arriving from France, Germany and England, the travelers required food and lodging while they awaited, often for months, for passage. They were like tourists. They did what tourists do. They created a "tourist trail" of places to visit in the city. They bought trinkets like crosses and glass beads as souvenirs; they made religious visits to the city's churches, attracted to them especially by the opportunity to see and touch many of the saintly relics inside. These visitors, over the centuries of the nine Crusades, generated a demand for guides, agents, translators and gondolas for hire. There was competition for their business and enterprising Venetians even adapted ceremonies during the April to June festival season — which became increasingly commercialized with theater and drama — to add to the city's attractiveness.

The pilgrims published many accounts of the city by the end of the fifteenth century, so many that the Milanese canon Pietro Casola complained that Venice was a place "about which so much has already been said and written... that it appears to me there is nothing left to say." He was among the first of a long line of commentators to say that.

In the mid-1500s, Venetian trade with the East collapsed, and at about the same time pilgrimages to the Holy Land dwindled, to be replaced by trips to the Vatican in Rome. But tourism made a comeback by the 1660s through the "Grand Tour," the custom made popular in Germany, Holland and France, but above all England, where it became customary to send men — at twenty-one typically — and very occasionally young women, to explore the art, culture and roots of Western civilization as part of year-long, aristocratic educational "field trips." This meant travel to Rome, Florence and, among other stops, Venice, which lacked many of the classical Roman artifacts these travelers particularly sought out, but was nonetheless of interest for its polity. A notable aspect of Venetian culture, especially for British and French in the seventeenth and eighteenth centuries, was its rather special form of government: a form of democratic rule by the nobles, without a monarch. The doge had very little power.

When the Grand Tour visitors arrived by rowboat from Fusina or Chioggia on the lagoon's banks, they marveled at the improbable city on water. They toured the churches, examined the artworks and purchased paintings of the Grand Canal to take home; they took in Piazza San Marco, then a place of social encounters, of evening walks and street theater. There were food stalls, preachers and, in the eighteenth century, coffee shops that were among the world's first, such as Caffè Florian, which is still flourishing today.

The travelers were particularly attracted by the city's pre-Lenten celebrations, *Carnevale*, the Carnival. In Venice it lasted longer than similar celebrations elsewhere and Venetians adopted the particular habit of going around in costume, some cross-dressing, others in Chinese dress and yet others in the get-up of harlequins from the *commedia dell'arte* stage. Most, however, wore a simple white mask over the eyes and nose. The Grand Tour visitors went to the opera, joined in pop-up gambling salons and availed themselves of what Venice was most noted for — courtesans and prostitutes.

With the fall of the Republic itself in 1797, Carnival ended unceremoniously and with it the party city lost its reputation. Venice became a pawn in the land grabs of the day. The French conqueror Napoleon Bonaparte himself visited in triumph in 1807, applying his Enlightenment ideas and looting Venice of its most precious treasures, following a shopping list drawn, apparently, from tourist guidebooks. When, in 1814, the Austrians took control, tourism gradually made a new start, especially after construction of the rail bridge in 1846. The link, at the time the longest bridge in the world, ended Venice's isolation, reducing the journey time from the mainland from an hour or more by boat to minutes by train. Rail lines connected to the growing European network, opening the gates to middle-class tourism, even as Venice's new overlords allowed the city to languish in poverty.

The new Italian state, which incorporated Venice in 1866, made efforts to address this dire situation. In 1873 came the ferry, the "vaporetto," a name arising from the boats' steam-driven power. The international art show, the Biennale, was launched in odd-numbered years from 1895. Tourism grew at pace, with annual visitor numbers soaring to 3.5 million in 1907. Pre-World War I tourists, including the well-heeled of Europe, came with their Belle Époque dreams and disillusion, filling up the Hotel Excelsior and the Grand Hotel des Bains on Lido where there was a new craze for bathing.

Turn-of-the-century novelists like Gabriele D'Annunzio puffed up the reputation of Venice as a sexy place of romance. When the First World

War interrupted the flow of tourists, causing the Venetians to suffer months of hunger, they came to realize that they needed the "foreigner industry" as it was then called. The film festival was launched in 1932. The Italian dictator Benito Mussolini built an automobile bridge in 1933 to boost access and new industry was introduced before and after the two world wars to alleviate the city's wretched economic state.

The tourists came back after the wars, and their numbers grew to 5 million annually in the 1950s, and were boosted again by the building in the 1960s of Marco Polo Airport, now Italy's third-biggest hub. From the 1960s onward, the Italian economy boomed but, at the same time, factories at Marghera on the mainland went into decline due to changes in demand. Big business once based in historic Venice left to find better housing stock and more modern buildings and facilities elsewhere. Tourism then became the single most dominant force, boosted by the 1979 relaunch of the Carnival and the phenomenal growth of the Biennale, which became annual and added architecture, dance and music to its repertoire in the 1990s.

The Pink Floyd concert on July 15, 1989 "was the first alarm bell that Venice could not support such huge numbers of people. It was the first time Venice realized what it means to have 200,000 visitors in the city all at the same time," says publisher Giovanni Keller. It was "a massive turning point. Everybody remembers the headline the day after: '*Mai Più Così*'" ('Never Again Like This'), over a picture of Piazza San Marco strewn with garbage in the aftermath."

"It marked a very significant change in the attitude toward the problem," he says. The concert, timed to coincide with the traditional Redentore celebration, marking the end of the 1575–77 plague, was performed on two huge pontoons floating on the bacino in the lagoon with seats on the platforms going for the equivalent of €200 each. Some 100,000 people viewed it on TV in twenty countries and the visitors watched from the waterfront around the bacino and on giant screens around the city. Nine charter flights delivered fans to Venice led by Woody Allen, Mia Farrow and their children.

Venice was totally unready for the onslaught. Traffic on access roads backed up for eight kilometers; the city's narrow streets were blocked up for hours with people trying to enter the city. Fans crawled onto buildings overlooking the lagoon and police were unable to call in reinforcements due to traffic jams. Extra toilets and other facilities for crowds had not been provided. Fans urinated all over the place, including on the doors of St. Mark's Basilica. The next day, concertgoers who could not get out of the city were left sleeping outside; hundreds of tons of rubbish covered the pavements and residents had to step around piles of excrement.

Concern grew over the commercialization of traditional festivals as people realized that the big numbers hid a more complex story.

At present, on any average day in normal times up to 70,000 to 80,000 tourists, or over 500 tourists per historic center resident, are in Venice, creating crowds which are swelled also by the 40,000 commuters, including many of the 25,000 seasonal university students. A study found that if the city were a stadium, it would contain twice as many people than is safe for an emergency exit. But security is just one of the problems. The mix of tourists matters. About 80 percent are day trippers and 20 percent stay over, while ideally Venice can sustain 40 percent day trippers and 60 percent who stay longer. This means the pressures on the city are even greater. Studies suggest Venice can sustain from 12 to 20 million tourists a year.

In Campo San Zaccaria a Chinese family sit down on a step near me — mother, father and teenage son — breaking off from a group tour herded into the glass showroom at one end of the square. I say a few words in my rusty Mandarin to spark up a conversation, and the son, who speaks good English, explains that they had come from Chongqing on their first trip abroad and were doing a ten-day tour of must-see places in Italy and Greece. We exchange smiles and say little more but the excited interest in their faces makes an impression. They seemed so genuinely thrilled to be in Venice, to witness its past and present, to be talking to a stranger. But, exhausted though they appear, it was off to the next stop, probably later that day.

On most group tours, the tourists don't get much chance to wander. They follow a leader who often holds high a flag or umbrella, while many of them have earphones plugged into orange boxes through which they receive the guide's spiel — sometimes of dubious accuracy — along the usual routes: Piazza San Marco, maybe a ride in a gondola for thirty minutes, a visit to gift showrooms or a department store and then a meal, probably just a sandwich, and then off again.

When we talked over her dining room table, the blind pensioner Ammirati remembered when tourists were mainly interested in the culture.

> People came to Venice... because they loved the art or going around the museums, showing respect for Venice and Venetians. These were people who wanted to get to know us, who would watch the children play in the squares for hours, and would speak discreetly and look around the old artisan shops, approaching the city with delicacy and intelligence. I met lots of young people who came here — Americans and French — with their parents to go to the museums and experience the slowness of the city.

Though Venice of late has positively blossomed with conferences and events, from the international, months-long art and history exhibitions to the Biennale festivals and the sophisticated La Fenice theater program, where opera seats go for astronomical prices, just 10 percent of tourists do something cultural. Those who do partake in these activities mostly attend performances of Antonio Vivaldi's *Four Seasons* and the *commedia dell'arte* plays by the eighteenth-century playwright Carlo Goldoni, which are re-run week after week for tourists. Overcrowding also detracts from the tourist experience. Ironically, while thousands of less iconic sights are mostly disregarded, tourists stand in long lines for "must-sees." Trying to take in the beauty of places like the St. Mark's Basilica, however, gets hard when you are funneled through as if on a conveyor belt, pushed along by the pace of the line. The average time spent inside is six minutes, hardly enough to take in its beauty.

But not all tourists are equal. "Japanese are the best tourists. Everyone adores them," says guide Pinella Trivisonno. Typically well educated, "They really engage with the city. They define our culture as 'one of stone,' contrasting Venice's 400-, 500- or 1,000-year-old palazzos with their own culture where buildings are made 'of wood.' Building in stone is unthinkable in Japan because all their buildings are continually reconstructed in wood. So the 'stone' cultures, that give testimony to the past and remain unchanging over the centuries, are what strikes them the most [about Venice]. You can see on their faces that they are thinking of how all these centuries have gone by, and yet the buildings are still here," says the Japanese-speaking Trivisonno.

For Venetian writer Tiziano Scarpa, we are all tourists at one level. He has no problem with "look at me" selfie tourism. "A city is an experience, not an intellectual lecture," he says. "Even if a person comes knowing nothing, even without them knowing the stories behind the birth of a church, a palazzo, the bridges or canals... the experience makes you grow."

When he moved to a new house in Venice recently, he saw a man and woman on the landing and thinking they were his new neighbors, introduced himself. They looked at him curiously.

"Today is my first day here," he explained.

They looked at each other. "Sorry?" they said in English.

It was only then that he realized that his neighbors were tourists, guests at a bed and breakfast in the flat opposite, staying a few days. "Without realizing it, I came to know the true lay of the land. They were the real inhabitants of the neighborhood, even if they were only staying in Venice for one weekend." For Scarpa, belonging to a place is not a matter of labels, of tourists versus residents; he also rejects the idea of being elite just by being born in Venice. Identity is a continuum. "I don't need to feel like the city is my property, just because I have lived here for thirty or fifty or seventy years. What does that mean? It's nothing compared to the duration of the city's entire history. I, too, am in a certain sense a tourist, here just in passing. The stones of the city are not mine; they are to be respected, to be handed on to those after us, and not allowed to fall into ruin. Venetians should learn from tourists, from their temporariness. Because we are tourists, too."

Of the decline in numbers of long-term Venetian residents he is accepting — or perhaps resigned. "We are dying out. We will soon disappear. The city prefers to be inhabited by someone else: not so much other categories of human beings, but by another way of being in the world." Thanks to tourists, he says, Venice "feels lighter, temporary and fleeting, like their passage; thin and two-dimensional like their photos," but he also thinks it might help if some just read about Venice in a book and avoided visiting.

Among the tourists in Venice for the Carnival in 2018, Californian Andrea Stryer came away impressed. It had been like "being in another world," she says, but she and her husband found the crowds oppressive.

She remembers heading to the opening evening's festivities. "The crush of people was so great that my husband and I could not walk side by side." After several attempts to reach the site they were heading to, they gave up and retreated to their hotel.

"Wherever we walked in town, we saw numbers of strolling, costumed people" dressed in gold, silver, white, black and bright colors of "velvet and silk... denim and rayon, all decorated with sequins, rhinestones, braid, feathers and lace." The merrymakers had fun "taking on new personas" and "posing for passersby and snapping cameras," she says.

In its early years the Carnival was mostly for, and run by, Venetians, but in recent decades the growing commercialization and crowding has kept many locals away. Events once dispersed throughout the city, encouraging local participation, have been dropped. Even so, most visitors are Italian and, in recent years, scores of cultural activities, dances and new festivities in Mestre have been added.

In 2018 a record was set for attendance, with 200,000 arriving on one day, triggering the closure of the car bridge. With daily attendance as high as 80,000 or 100,000, authorities have had to limit to 20,000 the number who can enter Piazza San Marco for the slick launch event paid for by corporate sponsorship and accompanied by TV coverage. During the gala, a "Maria," a young woman chosen as part of a revived tradition, floats down over the square from the bell tower, suspended by a wire and dressed in a billowing gown.

"The biggest problem now is to make tourism sustainable and manage the co-existence of inhabitants and tourists when so many people are concentrated in the city, in particular on the days of extraordinary peaks in numbers," says Marta Moretti, spokesperson for Vela, the public organization that has run the event since 2013. The thought of returning Carnival to being an event purely for Venetians is long past. It is now about money. "By the end of the 1980s... it had increasingly become a tourist medium... a way to make up for the low season."

As we sit on a park bench in the Sant'Elena neighborhood on a sunny day in October, I watch with my friend Alessandra Schiavon as a lumbering white behemoth moves slowly over the water on the horizon.

"You see that cruise ship?" Schiavon asks. "When it arrives here it will obscure the sun." The huge white ship is totally out of proportion with the scale of Venice. Carrying up to 4,000 passengers and 1,000 crew members, it was exiting the lagoon via the Giudecca Canal, being carefully maneuvered by tugboats, one at the front and one at the back, often within a stone's throw of the embankments. "Look how close it comes to the island of San Giorgio and the St. Mark's Basilica. If it makes an error in its maneuvers, or if something happens — when there is wind, the sides of the cruise ship are like sails — the force of the tugboats would not be enough to hold the ship back."

For Schiavon, like many Venetians, the 700 gleaming cruise ships typically entering and exiting Venice each year pose a serious threat. Each one, on average ten stories high, three times the length of an American football field, and twice as massive as the *Titanic*, is a floating resort city, with casinos, shopping centers, restaurants, night clubs, cinemas, gyms, theaters, ice skating rinks and running tracks. The boats carry some 1.6 million of Venice's tourists to the city each year, and, though Covid-19 has thrown a question mark over the future, the number of vessels arriving had been rising and may well go up again after the pandemic.

Tending to arrive on the busiest weekends, the liners can together pour as many as 35,000 passengers into Venice when it is at its most crowded. And as many as seven or eight cruise ships can be in port at the same time. They generate terrible air pollution, burning "bunker fuel" with extremely high levels of cancer-causing, land-and-water acidifying sulfur oxide. Even at dockside, each spews out fumes equivalent to thousands of cars. According to one study, the largest cruise ship fleet alone gives out ten times more sulfur oxide than all of Europe's automobiles. Venice, the third-most cruise-ship polluted port in Europe, additionally suffers from the erosion cruise ships cause. On entering and exiting they make waves that erode seawalls and foundations. Their propellers stir up and wash away lagoon sediments, turning the water brown.

After the capsizing of the *Costa Concordia* off the Tuscany coast on January 13, 2012, which killed thirty-two people, Italy passed a law forbidding the ships from coming closer than two miles from the coast — except in Venice. The government actually banned ships of over 40,000 tons from the Giudecca Canal, but then refused to enforce the ban, insisting that, for economic reasons, passage for such boats should continue until other arrangements can be made — and they were never made. This exception, allowing ships of more than twice that tonnage, sparked international furor, regular protests in Venice and expressions of concerns from UNESCO over the risk to Venice.

But the crisis unexpectedly moved toward resolution on March 25, 2021, when Rome finally enforced the ban and rerouted cruise ships around the back of the lagoon via the Canale dei Petroli commercial shipping channel. An outside port for cruise ships was broached, but temporarily passengers would disembark at Port Marghera, where a €61 million reception facility was to be constructed.

Since the mid-1990s, cruise ship tourism has been burgeoning, such that shipyards around the world are so confident of the future that they have an estimated 124 new ships with capacity over 5,000 passengers or more coming out in the next few years. Cruise ship passenger numbers worldwide have risen steadily and capacity is expected to reach 32 million in 2021. Despite Covid-19, bookings for 2021 and 2022 continued to rise.

To Filippo Olivetti, who manages Bassani shipping services from his offices in Marghera, the appeal is clear: "To take a voyage on board one of these cruise ships is to see three or four countries within a week without ever having to pack or unpack; you board, you put your suitcases in your cabin, and you have all the services you could want. It's effectively a tourist package without comparison."

The perception among many is that as the cruise tourists don't need hotels, or even to disembark, they bring little to Venice. But Olivetti contends Venice is a port where 90 percent are joining or leaving a cruise, not just transiting, and many stay over. His staff of fifty arrange travel, baggage transfers and all the local tours and stays. "This is mega-organized tourism," says Olivetti. Directly or indirectly creating some 5,000 jobs in the area, it includes the checking in and out of thousands of people, as at an airport. "To say this sector doesn't bring money to the territory, believe me, is the biggest lie ever made." He expects the next generation of ships to be more environmentally friendly, and new rules of fuel use in 2020 may reduce emissions.

Even so, the ships have become the most visible symbol of a new kind of tourism eating away the Venetian social and cultural fabric.

"When I have to pass through the hordes of tourists I hate Venice because there are such massive numbers of tourists that it makes you nervous," says Caterina Falomo, who lives in Lido and came back to live in the city after years in Rome. "On the ferry boats you see Venetians getting aggressive. They are not normally aggressive. Normally, Venetians are rather cool and collected, so seeing them get angry says a lot about what the city has become. Venice is treated badly, with tourists stopping to eat on the bridges and their suitcases clogging passageways a few meters wide, so that people who live there and need to get places can't do so. My father got so fed up that he bought a whistle to use in a street near home. When he blows the whistle people turn and look and move aside. My thin, small, aging grandmother got pushed over by people rushing by. It happens."

Tourism has overstayed its welcome.

Cristina Gregorin, novelist and guide who moved to Venice in 1990, remembers what Venice used to be like. "If you asked for information from a lady, she would start up a half-hour conversation, and tell you the story of her life. There were lots of friendships between Venetians and tourists," she says. "Many Venetians married tourists! Now, in the last few years, it's become so difficult with mass tourism; the interaction between tourist and Venetian no longer happens." She is also upset by the loss of privacy. "There are moments in daily life when people should show respect: for example, when people die. When there are funerals in churches, it's really sad to see tourists going up and taking pictures, or when groups of tourists get in the way of marriages and baptisms." Gregorin regrets what happens to popular restaurants, too. "When a restaurant becomes too famous with tourists, we can't get a seat anymore.... And when a restaurant gets famous, because it is in demand, it often goes downhill."

Others lament the loss of community on the streets. Restaurateur Adriana Teot used to bump into friends and chat on the walk home from the train station, but on a recent trip, to her shock, she met no one she knew. She used to enjoy the open market shopping at Rialto, where she'd meet friends, but she finds those social encounters happen less as the market has declined. Similarly, there's been a collapse in the sense of neighborliness in apartment buildings, as the residents now find adjacent flats are often occupied by tourists and booked online.

"A Venetian family with three sons told me they have an apartment above theirs which is filled with tourists, and four or five times a month the tourists throw parties," says Andrea Mehanna, the entrepreneur who created and runs the independent booking site Hostelsclub. "Obviously if you are on a holiday you want to drink and eat and laugh until three or four in the morning, but just in the flat below, they want to go to school and to work the next day. Yet, the visitors ring your bell at 11 p.m. or midnight to ask for oil or because they don't know which doorbell to ring. They take their garbage out at the wrong times. These are real problems."

Some Venetians lash out at tourists. Mehanna knows a seventy-five-year-old woman who deliberately gives wrong directions. He objected, saying this was wrong, but the woman angrily responded: "No, these people are taking away our houses!"

An ongoing "#EnjoyRespectVenezia" campaign encourages good tourism, but the list of "forbidden behaviors" gives a hint as to how badly behaved a minority of tourists can be. The campaign targets littering, graffiti and swimming in the sewage-filled canals, or worse, jumping off the bridges, with the danger of being hit by a boat. It bans pigeon feeding, riding bicycles, camping, street selling of contraband, snapping love-pact padlocks on bridge railings, picnicking in inappropriate places, wandering around in swimwear or shorts — especially when in churches — urinating on private doorways, skateboarding down bridges and finally, posing nude in public places for photographers.

Yet Venetians "know Venice has been sustained by tourism," providing something like 40 percent of employment. "They're not tourist-phobic and they don't hate tourists. There have never been episodes of clamorous protests against tourism per se," says Jan van der Borg, a University of Venice professor who specializes in tourism studies. The eerily empty streets during the 2020 virus lockdowns drove home the need for tourists, even as it restored a welcome serenity. But when the crowds return, attitudes that have been tested of late will be tested anew.

The atmosphere has been poisoned in other ways. Restaurants, once mostly family-run eateries, are becoming properties to be milked as cash cows. This has led to short-changing customers on ingredients or simply marking up prices for tourists. In one incident, a Japanese tourist was overcharged €1000 for a €100 meal by a restaurant, causing an uproar. Some immediately pointed to the increase in "foreign" owners. It came out that the restaurant was owned by a Venetian, who had rented to a Chinese person, who sublet to an Egyptian, who apparently was very hard pressed to meet the steep rents he had to pay.

The situation bothers restaurateur Gianni Bonaccorsi, whose city-center Ristorante Ridotto won a Michelin star in 2013. He wants to move to the periphery, out of the crowded, costly mass tourism-dominated city center. "Leave the center to the robbers," he says.

Leaving is what a lot of people do. With inexorable constancy, the loss of residents has continued at a rate of a thousand a year, mainly because of tourism-related pressures. Venetians watch nervously as the numbers descend on an electronic population countdown display in the pharmacy window in Campo San Bartolomeo. In 2019, 1,092 people had left the lagoon city — the historic center and eleven inhabited islands — reducing the population to 52,000 by 2020. It has been predicted that Venice will be without Venetians, that is, permanent residents, by 2030 or 2050.

SIGHTLESS WOMAN
PICTURES OF LA SERENISSIMA
ANNA AMMIRATI

When I heard the retired bank worker Anna Ammirati had served as a tour guide for a special project during a recent Biennale art exhibition, I wanted to know more. She is blind, but knows the city intimately through its sounds, feelings and smells.

"People are very curious about how I know the whole city without seeing it, and how I get around and know where things are. I am sixty-six, and from the time I was a child, I could see very little, but I have an uncle, now ninety-two, who showed me all of the city, describing it to me, and in as far as possible, getting me to touch it. I remember what it was like so well.

"For the Venetians, at that time, this was their city, the city of their parents. Nothing changed. Without cars, the rhythms of life never changed. We walked, even when it was crowded, and we knew more or less everyone, and we greeted one another on the street, even people we didn't know. Venetians have always been people who loved company, so when you met someone you knew you stopped for a chat. It was a slow life, but not slow because of laziness, slow because the dimensions of the city would not allow you to move more quickly. There were lots more inhabitants — around 120,000 or so, I believe — when I was a girl. We would go out with friends — there weren't so many bars as now — the osterie were popular with workers, mostly. After work they would drink an *ombra*, a glass of wine or a spritz. There were beautiful pastries. As youngsters, we went to exhibitions or sometimes museums or just walked around the city. And there were ever so many small children. The squares and streets were full of kids who played with balls and played old games. It was all on a human scale. We left the doors open.

"I can remember the voices of the children, of everyone speaking in Venetian dialect, the sounds of the steps — today you hear sounds of suitcases, pushcarts and guides who are talking into microphones. It was beautiful to hear the sounds of people all around. When people passed by, if they were food shopping, you could smell the odor of the vegetables or fish that they had in their bags. When you passed in front of the artisans' shops you could smell carpentry, wood polish and gilt for Venetian picture frames. For me, the odors — those of bread, meat and dried cod for sale — were what told me the location I was in. The city was full of sounds, odors and fragrances. In the spring many of the Venetian gardens had roses, and so, even if you could not see the flowers behind the walls, you could smell the fragrance of the flowers. In the summer almost all of the gardens of Venice grew figs, pomegranates, and magnolia trees, and passing under walls, you could smell them. 'Ah, here there's a garden,' I would say. Now you don't find them.

"These days you still sometimes sense morning a bit by the smell of bread, and Rialto by the odor of fish and smells of vegetables. But even at Rialto the fruit and vegetable stores have mostly disappeared. Hardly anything is left. There are those little stores that sell souvenirs now for tourists. You used to go there to do your food shopping! And the vendors would say, 'The cheese is delicious, buy some!' calling out the prices of goods with these shrill voices. I liked to hear my city around me.

"I love the museums of Venice. For example, when I go with someone they describe the pictures to me. Incredibly, I love paintings. I recall only vaguely the colors and styles; I love the old pictures of Venice. I particularly like those that portray scenes of life, like the paintings of Canaletto and Longhi. My uncle used to help me see with my powerful magnifying glass, saying, 'Look here,' and describing all the particulars and curiosities that people don't know. Like how in the pictures of Canaletto, he always includes, hidden somewhere little in a corner, a man urinating against a wall! And I like paintings of laundry hanging out, just like you see now over the canals and in the streets near me. The other day, there was a breeze and I went down to the end of the street, and there was laundry hanging between the houses and you could hear the sheets flapping and smell the fragrance of washing. It brought me back to my childhood, when they put out laundry like that.

"And sometimes we went into the lagoon in rowboats. When my father and brother had time, we used to go rowing once or twice a week when the weather was good, with one rowing in front and one at back. Even my mother could row. The sounds of the water, of the oars, are beautiful. The rower is one with the boat and the water, with our lagoon, this umbilical cord that never comes away! For me as a Venetian, and not only for me, I just need to get into a wooden boat, a boat in the old style, like a sandolo or sanpieròta; it is marvelous because I think that anyone who rows, in immersing the oar in water, becomes one — the boat, the oar, the man are one thing. And it's beautiful. Things change completely if you go out into the lagoon in the evening or the morning. The sounds change, the odors change. Now the motorized boat traffic is horrible, horrible! But if one goes into the south lagoon, there are still times when you can enjoy these moments, something that touches the heart."

9

LAGOON

ITS REMAKING AND UNMAKING

"The water 'beyond a limit established by nature and not by man, cannot be governed, but in some measure only listened to.'"

—RENZO FRANZIN

Amid the salt marshes of the southern lagoon, far from the bustling city center of Venice, I am on a journey of discovery in spring 2019 on the *Pevarina*, a two-masted *topo ciosoto*, making our way alongside the expanse of low, color-of-toast vegetation. Skipper Giampaolo Rinaldo lends me binoculars to look at the salt marsh as we tack west and back again along a channel marked by series of *bricole*, tripod-shaped channel markers, to try to locate the place linked to the most famous lagoon legend: "Cason dei Sette Morti," ("The House of Seven Dead Men"). This fisherman's hut is the subject of a story told and retold in many forms as far back as the 1500s:

> Seven fishermen out on the lagoon caught in their nets the body of a drowned man. As the weather on the lagoon was threatening a storm, they found shelter in a fishermen's hut in the lagoon and there found Zaneto, an orphan who was thin, forlorn and alone. When the boy saw the visitors he was crazy with joy. But the fishermen just ignored him.
>
> They set about cooking their dinner, a big pot of polenta, corn meal porridge. When it was ready, and they sat down to eat, Zaneto reached for a slice — but they grabbed his wrist. Wait, they said. You have to earn your slice. Making fun of him, they said to go out and call in their companion outside, the one lying under the tree — referring to the corpse. The boy went out into the night and poked its shoulder, but the body didn't move.
>
> Zaneto returned and told the others, but, laughing, they sent him back to try again. On the third trip, with the ridicule ringing in his ears, he kneeled and begged the corpse to wake because he was dying of hunger. Then the body slowly sat up, opened its eyes and

> looked at the boy with the kindness of a father. Let's go, he said. The boy walked ahead and said to the fishermen that the man was coming, so they burst out in laughter. But when the corpse walked in behind him, they turned cold because before them they saw Theodore, patron saint of Venice.
>
> He had come to judge them and with just a gesture he decided their fates. All seven instantly died, petrified as they sat around the table because, the legend says, he who shows no kindness to the innocent and has a heart of stone cannot find compassion or pardon.

The tale is typical of those told about the lagoon, which are often about fishermen, lost souls at sea, storms whipped up by witches and battles with evil. Some recount good spirits that help fishermen in difficulty. In churches in the fishing town of Chioggia on the other side of the lagoon, you can still see oil paintings depicting scenes of saints rescuing fishermen in boats tossed by tempests.

I had seen what looked like recent photographs of the ruins of Cason dei Sette Morti, showing a substantial set of red brick walls and a chimney standing amid the water of the lagoon. They resembled the jagged brick ruins we had seen ourselves nearby, those of Cason Barenon, where from 1943–45 fisherman Cèncio Fòfe Doria and his family hid Jews and resistance fighters from the Nazis. I was now anxious to see Cason dei Sette Morti for myself.

But through my binoculars I can see only the salt marsh, white birds and the occasional hunter's hide. "Cason dei Sette Morti has disappeared! What has happened?" I exclaim.

Rinaldo looks nonplussed. "That's the way the lagoon is. It will have been washed away."

Indeed, the ruins had been completely leveled, the bricks, the walls, all reclaimed by tides. The lagoon is ever-changing. Not only do the marshes move or vanish along with any structures built upon them, but whole lagoons, by their very nature, if left alone, disappear. Rivers over time bury them in sediment or they become part of the sea. The city of Ravenna, south of Venice, once sat at the water's edge, but is now kilometers from the coastline. The lagoon has survived in Venice because of massive human intervention under the Republic to manage the waters.

By traveling the lagoon, I am getting a feel for the challenge it poses. Just in the course of this trip, our wooden vessel gets stuck as the tides ebb on entering one of the *ghebi*, a creek going through the salt marshes. Fearing we might be there all night, as can happen, Rinaldo maneuvers urgently with the outboard, churning up the bottom and jerking the tiny motor up from the soft, sticky mud, as I man an oar to push the boat back into deeper water. This tiny incident serves as a place to begin, but to understand this body of water you need to look at it from another perspective. Look at the lagoon with the same lens we turn on our celestial neighbor: the red planet of Mars. Science fiction imagines our degraded environment will drive us to colonize Mars, that we will reshape it to suit our needs and that, in doing so, the harsh climate would also change its human interlopers.

Well before we envisioned these scenarios, the lagoon similarly provided refuge and opportunity, shaping the people who traveled to live there as they in turn reshaped it.

As early as the second century before Christ and then in waves in the middle of the first millennium, migrants settled in the lagoon. From the fifth century, tradition holds that they sought shelter from marauding armies, as the shifting channels and shoals made the lagoon unreachable without a boat and knowledge of its labyrinthine layout. But it's more likely that they simply sought to avail themselves of its enormous resources of fish, birds and salt and of its ready access to trade via the rivers and Roman-built waterways and over the Adriatic Sea and the Black Sea.

Yet in some ways the lagoon was a place as foreign as Mars, lacking drinking water, land to grow food and building materials. When settlement began, it was part of a 240 kilometer-long line of lagoons that stretched end-to-end all along the Adriatic coastline from Ravenna almost to Trieste.

This environment was, disconcertingly, in constant motion. Tides surged in and out twice daily. Rivers flowing down from the Alps deposited silt. The opposing flows eroded and reshaped the scores of mosquito-infested islets and shifted navigable channels unpredictably. Seasonal winds — the hot, dusty North African *scirocco* and gusty winter bora — bore down on the exposed, brackish waters bounded on the sea side by dunes and on the land side by marshes with gelatinous grey mud so soft that a man's foot sinks in up to the knee.

The migrants, like the spacemen of the imagined Mars fantasies, met the challenge with innovation. Adapting to their new world, they became a new society, ultimately the nerve center of an empire, creating in the process new technologies — from ways to collect rainwater to massive "terraforming" projects and other startlingly modern ideas. They created a republican government in an age of feudal kings, centuries before forms of democratic rule had taken root elsewhere, and became pioneers in establishing an equilibrium between human life and the environment's demands. As French historian Elisabeth Crouzet-Pavan wrote in a key study connecting Venice to its natural surroundings: "A political and social organization came to be built, at least in part in response to the challenge of the waters."

The settlers came to understand the rivers, the mud and reeds, the far-flung islands, the rhythmic tides and changeable climate, seeing them as a hostile, unstable unit over which, through constant labor, they could learn to assert mastery.

The conquest of the lagoon started with stabilization of the islands and then a steady wresting of further territory from the water along the muddy edges. In a laborious process, the settlers encircled the banks with closely set rows of wooden piles, or palisades, driving them one by one into the mud at the edges, and then filling in behind with rubble. Over time these walls were reinforced with brick and stone — thus beginning the creation of Venice itself.

Humble thatched houses first provided shelter for the common people; the powerful inhabited wooden fortresses. Each island community, organized around clans and families, probably had a wooden church. The islands typically had a common layout, with a field at the center that might be used for grazing, graveyards, vineyards or gardens. Houses lined the shore, where boats were tethered — much like pets on a leash, as one ancient chronicler observed.

A Roman official named Cassiodorus admired these lagoon settlements in AD 523, and wrote to the inhabitants in flattering tones to ask for cooperation in trade:

> Rich and poor live together in equality. The same food and similar houses are shared by all; wherefore they cannot envy each other's hearths, and they are free from vices that rule the world. All your energies center on the saltworks; instead of ploughs and scythes,

> you work rollers [used to break up the salt] whence comes all your gain. Upon your industry all other products depend; for, although there may be someone who does not seek gold, there never yet lived the man who does not desire salt, which makes every food more savory.

Cassiodorus may, for his own reasons, have overstated the egalitarianism of those early days, but he rightly focused on the importance of salt-making in the economy. Salt would power the Venetian expansion from the moment when the lagoon inhabitants learned that trading salt was even more profitable than making it in evaporation ponds.

As trade and population grew, by the Middle Ages, Venice had a population of over 100,000, putting it on par with Naples and Paris. The land and water were soon put to more dedicated uses. The little lakes that had dotted the archipelago of 118 central Rialto islands were drained and many of these central fields, over time, became *campi*, or squares. These became the heart of church parishes, of which Venice already had around sixty by the tenth or eleventh century, each with its own patron saint and local festivals. Gradually paved over with stone, the campi were a place for gossip and for children to play. In later centuries, the government used them to make pronouncements. An official crier read decrees and death sentences from a stone pulpit still standing in Campo San Giacomo di Rialto, for example. The Grand Canal of the eleventh century was flanked not by towering palazzos but by many farmed areas and with piers busy with workers loading and unloading merchant vessels. The *campanile*, the bell tower, of Piazza San Marco, was originally a watch tower and later a beacon for mariners. Its *Marangona* — meaning carpenters — bell sounded at the opening and end of each work day. Other bells pealed to announce midday, executions and meetings of the Grand Council or Senate.

The city grew as salt and silver was hauled overland by pack horse from northern countries to be exchanged for Oriental spices and textiles. Any beaten earth path leading in and out of the squares became one of the 2,650 or so streets, or *calli*. Those on embankments along canals were *fondamente*, and along major waterside routes, *rive*. The islets of Rialto were linked by wooden bridges, but by the fourteenth to sixteenth century they were replaced by brick and stone structures that were easier to maintain, and of which Venice now has 433. Until the eighteenth century, the Grand Canal had but one span at Rialto; initially in wood, it was replaced in 1591 by the ponderous, iconic stone design we know today.

The city's maze-like layout came from building and growth that traced the irregular contours of the archipelago of islets and reclaimed lands. In absence of any wheeled transport, no one needed to eliminate kinks or narrow streets, and a good number of these streets today are not even a man's arm span in width. Similarly, as pedestrians could always easily scuttle around corners, no one bothered to line up streets between islands, resulting in many bridge spans crossing canals at an angle. By the fifteenth century the historic center, with its 182 canals, had taken on the layout that is still recognizable today.

For administrative purposes, the city was divided into six sestieri, which served for policing and tax collection. They boosted local rivalry among popular factions known from about 1600 for their brutal free-for-all fisticuff games on the Ponte dei Pugni, the Bridge of Fists. Today the facing footprint outlines in the topmost centerpoint of the bridge still mark the starting positions for the opponents. But sestieri today are simply part of the city's address system. The first house in each sestiere is number one and then the numbering unwinds along unpredictable routes.

The divisions between noble and citizen grew. The wealthier residents, the emerging aristocrats, hardly used the streets. They almost always got around by boat, using the canal-facing grand gates where the family gondolier would be waiting. Even today to get to some palazzos by land you have to take the little narrow, dark streets that were used by the servants.

Wealth that flowed into the city over the centuries was channeled into the building of the grand palazzos, each the home of a merchant family, where on the ground floor goods were traded, warehoused and counted. They spent fortunes on building materials, obtaining brick from Mestre, Treviso, Padua or Ferrara; timber from the upland forests of Cadore and the Marca Trevigiana; stone from Istria, directly across the Adriatic Gulf; and marble from Greece, the Middle East, Tuscany and Brescia. But it wasn't easy to build on waterlogged ground.

Extraordinarily, the Venetians learned to support the canal banks and heavy buildings by driving millions of wooden piles deep into the mud. Hammered vertically into the soft ground in groupings recalling phalanxes of soldiers, the oak or larch trunks 2 to 10 meters in length and 0.1 to 0.3 meters thick supported a raft of planks nailed on top of them. Venice sits on "trunks...mineralized precisely because of the mud, which has wrapped them in a protective sheath, preventing them from rotting in contact with oxygen: breathless for centuries, the wood had been turned almost to stone. You're walking on a vast upside-down forest, strolling above an incredible inverted wood," wrote novelist Tiziano Scarpa. On the wooden supports the Venetians built thick brick walls, then added a layer of the hard, white Istrian limestone, then more bricks and, where the wall met the water flowing in the canal, other walls with damp-proofing layers and stone cladding to shield the surface from the corrosive saltwater tides.

On top of this structure they might lay a herringbone pattern with brick or *masègni*, slabs of pale grey Eugenean trachyte, used for walkway pavements or the walls, and they built great palazzos, cleverly spreading the weight over the whole structure and using flexible, soft lime mortar and bendy timber alternating with heavy terrazzo floors, which were made of compressed chipped marble. To reduce fire risk among the closely built structures — a major fire destroyed the Rialto district in 1514 — houses had chimneys with an ingenious cone-shaped pot allowing smoke but not cinders to escape.

Venetian houses of this time all had a terracotta plumbing system within the walls that flowed into covered channels under the pavements and then into the canals. The tides washed out the dirt and (mostly) replaced it with clean seawater — a better result than in other medieval cities where until the modern age, human waste and debris mostly flowed into the street or open sewers.

Walking through the squares of Venice today, you'll find in most what look like cylindrical stone stumps of white Istrian stone, often beautifully carved.

"Wells" is what they are called by Venetians, but a normal well dug in Venice would be useless, as the water table under the city is salty and undrinkable. These are Venetian "wells": cisterns designed to harvest rain, the wellhead being the outlet for underground collection basins several meters deep and often as wide as the square itself. The basins were sealed with waterproof clay, filled with sand and then covered with surface paving that has special slotted drains a few meters distant from the wellhead to receive rainwater falling on the ground and on neighboring buildings. The collected water, after impurities had been filtered out by the sand, seeped into the well shaft, a porous tube of brick that sits on a stone slab at the central point under the wellhead. Water would be hauled up by bucket through the wellhead, which was always protected by a locked iron cover.

Even so, water remained a scarce resource for centuries, with the amount available per person limited to around 5.5 liters a day (compare that to the 300 to 350 liters used today by each person in Venice). To maintain supplies, the government paid for communal wells in the squares. Some one hundred served the populace by 1500, and 4,000 more were dug privately for the use of extended aristocratic households. In dry periods, fresh water was also delivered by barge from the Brenta river and distributed in buckets, for the government was anxious to assure scarcity never reached a crisis point.

Like the imagined Mars settlers, Venetians not only invented these new technologies, they created new ways of thinking. The demands of the lagoon are linked to how Venetian society itself fostered collective discipline, how it ensured the subservience of private interests to the public good and imposed limitations on ostentatious displays of wealth. This social management was most clearly expressed in the city's relationship to the demanding lagoon environment. Everyone — from rich to poor, from noble to monk — was expected to respect nature's dynamics and the principles that represented what came to be called "the culture of water."

The lagoon was seen as a force to be guided and pushed, but not usurped; as something wild that could be trained if not tamed. Trial and error governed the inter-action with the lagoon. When digging canals, for example, unknown consequences were expected. The lagoon was seen as an organism — what today we might call an ecosystem — needing management, care and nutrition. The water itself was seen not as a division but as the tissue connecting islands to each other via watery streets prolonged by linking rivers and the sea.

Government imposed tough controls, such as on dumping of toxic waste by dyers and abattoirs. No effort was spared to ensure the security and navigability of the lagoon. Venetians knew how to redirect the lagoon flows with walls of reed mats to build islands or trap fish, but fishermen or private interests were not allowed to obstruct the waterways. To prevent the canals from silting up, they were dredged at state expense. From the 1500s, Magistrato alle Acque, the Water Ministry, conducted immense construction projects to build seawalls on Lido and Pellestrina and to reroute whole rivers — the Bacchiglione, Piave, Sile and Brenta — away from the lagoon to reduce and prevent silting up lagoon channels.

Even with this level of oversight, Venice was known as one of the most dangerous ports in Europe. Apart from requiring careful timing to avoid running aground at low tide, ships entering or leaving had to follow circuitous routes and fight currents. Many ended up as shipwrecks.

Today, if you stand before the former offices of the Water Ministry at the foot of the bridge in Rialto and look up, you will see an inscription etched in gold on black marble that reads:

aquis pro muro munitur

This means "defended as if by a wall of water." The words are followed by the caveat: "...anyone who dares in any way to damage the public waters should be considered an enemy of the motherland and punished." It shows that the importance of keeping the lagoon functioning was paramount because Venetians had learned through their own ordeals that it gave more than sustenance; the lagoon provided security that was far more reliable than any castle wall or moat. When besieged by enemies, once in AD 810 by Germanic Franks and then again in the fourteenth century when Venice was attacked by Genoese rivals, the defense of Venice depended on the lagoon. Both events are recalled with all the lore and color of great military victories, though the actual results were somewhat more mixed. Yet the fact remains that Venice's lagoon defenses were never breached. The forts built on the outer islands never fired a shot. And when Venice did fall in 1797, a moment to which we will return, it was a mortifying act of surrender.

"When the Venetians of antiquity understood that the lagoon continually transforms itself and that the conservation of the lagoon depended not only on nature but on human intervention, they dedicated all their resources to maintaining that space," remarks historian Giorgio Crovato. "They changed the course of rivers and built huge dykes, investing enormous amounts because if they did not, either the rivers or sea would prevail." The most sophisticated expression of this idea came from a sixteenth-century debate. Alvise Cornaro, reflecting on the aftermath of setbacks in Venice's ambitions to gain territory on the mainland, argued for a "culture of land" to make La Serenissima more like other European nations. Cornaro believed Venice's weakness was that she was not self-sufficient. "Let's let the rivers fill in the lagoon. It can become another field to cultivate," he said, according to Crovato.

On the other side, Crovato recounts, hydraulic engineer Cristoforo Sabbadino said, "On the contrary, we need to govern the water, and not allow the rivers to bury the lagoon." Over centuries, that is exactly what Venice did. It was an enormous undertaking — like building the Pyramids — but they felt it was matter of survival. "Sabbadino said, 'The source of our fortune is the water; it is the lagoon. We must conserve the lagoon,'" again according to Crovato.

The alterations extended the life of the lagoon, but this détente with nature, one that matured over the centuries, would be lost at the end of the Republic and neglected in our own age. After Venice lost its empire in 1797, the rules and administrative apparatus collapsed. The city tried to safeguard the lagoon, impressing on the various powers, with varying degrees of success, its fragility. But, driven by political agendas, the lagoon was overlooked.

Faced with periodical neglect and bereft of its economic foundations, Venice sank into poverty, sometimes including times of famine and epidemics. Those who came to Venice's aid in the nineteenth and most of the twentieth centuries focused on fortifying the city economically with new industries and employment. On a purely economic level, much was accomplished, bringing jobs with a big insurance company that planted its office in Piazza San Marco, the building of the Stucky flour mill on Giudecca and the establishment of two universities. In the twentieth century, a port and petrochemical industries at Marghera were constructed. A related economic transformation continues today with the development of tourism, which has by and large supplanted all the other industries. The flour mill is today a Hilton Hotel with a rooftop swimming pool.

But until the 1970s, much of the growth was realized at the expense of the lagoon's fragile balance. Land reclamation from the nineteenth century to 1973 cleared space for the port, refineries and airport, gobbling up a third of the lagoon — most of it rare natural habitat. The petrochemical plants have caused the worst damage and health hazards, dumping millions of tons of toxic waste into the lagoon for decades, including heavy metals and dioxin, and most of it remains spread around in the mud under the surface. In addition, modern-day industrial and agricultural runoff from the 1,615-square kilometer river basin of northern Italy adds to lagoon pollution. Since the 1970s better treatment facilities and a requirement for new buildings in Venice to install local septic tanks has improved water quality markedly, but the city still lacks a sewer system. Half of the buildings pour human waste, detergents and household chemicals directly into the canals.

But the most devastating damage is much harder to see.

To make way for bigger ships, the openings to the sea separating Lido and Pellestrina were deepened and the Canale dei Petroli was dredged in 1960–1969 down to 17 meters. Enlarging the openings and dredging of the new channel caused massive surges of tidal water that are washing away the silty lagoon bottom, and in the southern lagoon, they have gouged out an ever-widening crater and destroyed natural channels that feed the lagoon ecosystem. This, with the added erosion from boats, ships and illegal fishing, is fundamentally altering the lagoon, diminishing its prized wetlands and converting the lagoon into a sterile branch of the Adriatic Sea. A study has shown the digging of the channel in the '60s and the shaping of the lagoon openings for the Mose dams after 2003 appear to have contributed to increases in acqua alta flooding.

The true environmental costs only came to the attention of the public after the 1966 floods hit 1.94 meters, the highest in 200 years, triggering a total reset of attitudes toward the lagoon.

The event sparked an outcry that led the Italian government to pass a "special law" in 1973, protecting Venice's heritage and scenery. It officially recognized the inseparability of the fate of the lagoon and Venice. This legislation, intended to turn back the environmental devastation of the last centuries, promised the restoration of the lagoon's physical and ecological integrity, rescuing the salt marshes, ending land reclamations and curbing pollution. Later laws specified the "reversal of the process of lagoon degradation," the "elimination of causes" of degradation and the "restoration of the lagoon's equilibrium" and health.

Several decades after the laws came into effect, much has been accomplished, but the hopes they've raised have taken a battering in the face of inaction, reaction and inertia.

The progressive destruction of structure, or morphology, between 1901 to 2003, in the lagoon south of Venice due to erosion. (Depth shown on the scale at left.)

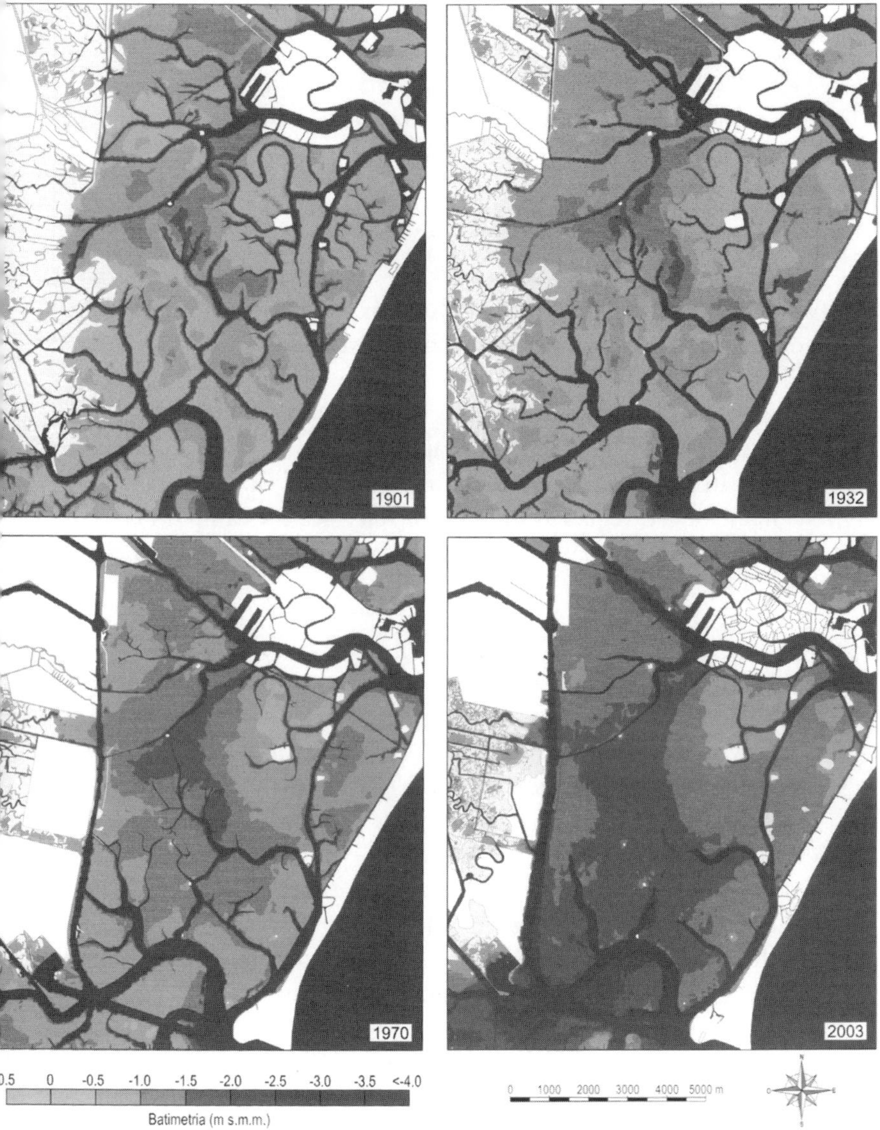

10

CREATIVITY
SOURCES OF ART AND ARTISTRY

> *"...the actual stillness — one never hears a carriage — is indispensable for me. I am now returning to* Tristan*, that it may speak to you of the profound art of resonant silence."*
>
> —COMPOSER RICHARD WAGNER DURING A STAY IN VENICE IN 1858 TO SEEK PEACE AND WRITE HIS OPERA *TRISTAN UND ISOLDE*

What is it that powers the artisans who make rough logs of cherry wood into useful, comely objects, artists who paint the watery scenery and photographers who seem to prefer to see Venice in black and white images, gardeners who grow roses and pomegranate flowers, chefs who delight our palates with new flavors, musicians who create symphonies mimicking insects, and filmmakers who, in the name of art, regularly gum up the city's calli e campi in creating fantastic on-screen pasts and futures? What makes Venice a city of art and artistry?

In his workshop facing a canal, Saverio Pastor leans over the arm-length block of walnut wood, carving it with a scraper chisel he drags with both hands, repeatedly shaping sinuous curves, slow waves and peaks. Occasionally, the sixty-year-old straightens up to sharpen the curved blade using an oiled whetstone, and then resumes, grabbing the tool's handles at both ends, rhythmically pulling and turning to create a forcola, the oarlock for a traditional Venetian boat. A standing, forward-facing rower will rest his oar on the semi-circular indentations in the forcola, using them as fulcrums for the long oars that move the boats through the water.

"This work is one of the most ancient labors in the city," says the leather-aproned Pastor while his colleague at the back noisily cuts out an oar. "When the first settlers arrived in the wild lagoon, someone made the oars. There's always been someone who made oars in Venice. The first artisans got together, set up rules and... were incorporated in 1307." The association lasted until Napoleon broke up the guilds and monasteries at the end of the Republic, "but he still needed oars!" says Pastor. "The real crisis came in the 1950s, with the arrival of motorized boats." The oar makers thought it might be all over, but then at the end of the 1950s a Swiss art critic wandered into the work-space of Pastor's maestro, Giuseppe Carli, and rediscovered these functional pieces made in cherry, walnut, pear or maple wood. He suggested they might be put on pedestals to become objects of beauty. Now, in addition to making *forcole* for rowing, they sell to collectors. A mounted gondola forcola goes for €1500 — but is it art?

Saverio Pastor in his workshop, carving out a forcola.

"In the Renaissance, in the sixteenth century, those we now consider artists," like Bellini, Veronese, Tintoretto and Tiziano, "were thought of as artisans. They were linked to art, but today art is something different, something that expresses emotions in a way that we artisans are not required to do," says Pastor, as he works on a stock of wood in a waist-high vice made of two beams pressed together with a giant wooden screw. "We seek to make things that are beautiful and functional — or rather functional and beautiful. Thus I'd say we are not artists. We are artisans."

Venice was the capital of artisanship. A dwindling cadre of artisans still carry forward ancient crafts of brickwork, restoration and metallurgy; in the palazzos they make the textiles on the walls and the

Forcole for gondolino (left), gondola (center) and pupparino (right); the upper row are for the stern rower and lower for the bow.

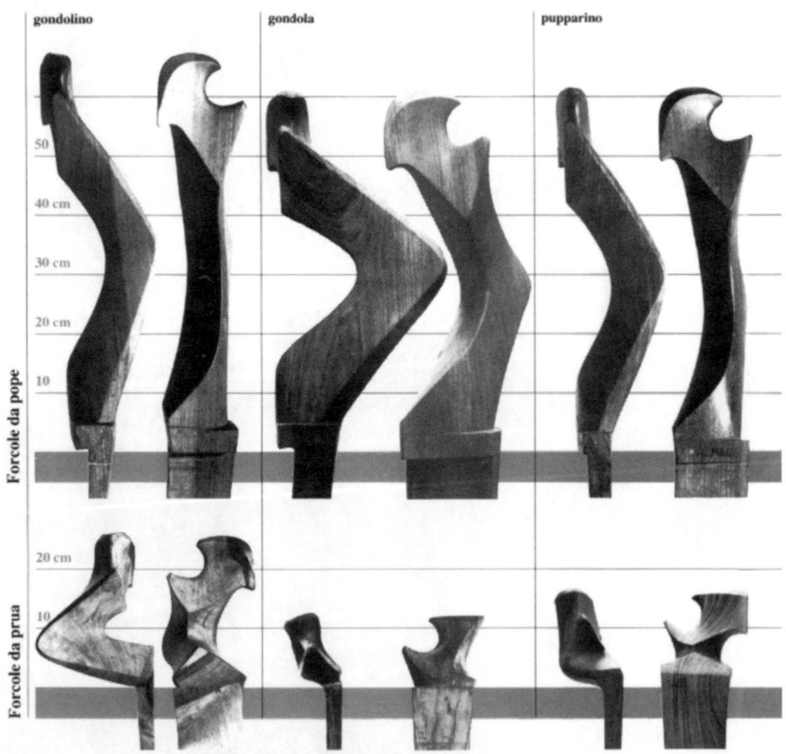

famous terrazzo floors. As recently as the 1970s, carpenters, marble carvers, textile workers, jewelers and those who worked in leather were found along every calle e campo. The glassmakers of Murano who for centuries produced goblets, beads, mosaics and mirrors for clients around the world, are now a much reduced industry, while Burano lacework, which similarly enjoyed a global reputation, survives only in a museum. Among the flashiest of artisans were the makers of picture frames, who would display gold-painted creations painstakingly chiseled with twirled vines and cherubs in front of their shops. They are rarely seen now. "Something has been lost," Pastor says, with an undertone of frustration. "No one buys carved, gilded frames for pictures they don't have. Today at home people put up posters with sticky tape, so nobody needs frames. They all go to IKEA to spend less."

A handful of wooden boat makers and a few oar and forcola makers have survived. They have been buoyed by the popularity of the gondola, by the minority of Venetians who use wooden boats and by the global growth of Venetian-style rowing. "The artisan still has a value for the city, because a city without artisans loses its cultural heritage," says Pastor. "In one way or another, we maintain the cultural heritage — also the intangible heritage, the knowing how to do things in a certain way. A city deprived of this heritage is a city that renounces its past and its future."

But the number of artisans rooted in history have plummeted from 2,600 in the 1970s to 1,087 today, with some categories dropping more precipitously than others, according to figures gathered by the Confartigianato, or small businesses' association. Its head, Gianni de Checchi, blamed "tourism that seeks low-value merchandise, typically bought in a hurry. This greatly lowers demand, and, in response, what's on offer declines. Some stick with producing excellence, but they are like solitary resisters on a sinking ship who have to work very hard to stay afloat in an ocean of people who want in reality an ice cream and a pizza, possibly bad ones, because they only buy what costs little."

He knows the world evolves, that tastes change and that some trades fail to adapt. Others do. There are examples of artisans who have made a transition — such as terrazzo makers, who are finding customers in Milan for brightly colored floors — but for most artisans their survival has a lot to do with the survival of Venice, which, unlike other historic centers, has fewer options, stranded as it is in the watery limits of the lagoon.

De Checchi's colleague Enrico Vettore has little good to say about how the property speculation-driven economy of Venice is pushing artisans out of their workshops. "It's not a healthy economy. It's an economy on drugs," he says. "Venice is no longer what is defined as a city, a place characterized by complexity" with diverse populations and work. "Venice is trivializing its identity.... We need to realize this: that Venice is becoming something else."

Many creative activities continue, but that "something else" has taken a toll on living arts and traditions. In areas ranging from the culinary scene to the care of gardens to theater, it undermines the city's ability to produce and support its own cultural life.

Yet these dynamics have not prevented the saving of Venice's historic buildings, which have been better supported nationally and internationally since the floods of 1966. From the great monuments in Piazza San Marco to the hundreds of churches and tens of thousands of precious objects in museums, they are tirelessly cared for by a small army of overseers, restorers and scholars. Venice provides endless examples of its historical magnificence.

Take the Scuola Grande di San Rocco, a building from the first half of the sixteenth century, and called one of the greatest decorative achievements of the entire Renaissance. Standing at the foot of the marble staircase of the cavernous main chamber, the Sala del Capitolo, looking up at the glimmering carved ceiling above, its paintings of biblical figures gazing out from on high, I am stunned. Something about this passageway, leading to this magnificent room, transfixes. I look upward to the room where every angle, every surface casts a spell as it tells stories that transport the visitor to another realm, another time, another way of looking at the world.

Stepping up into the great rectangular room above, with light pouring from the tall windows on either side and illumination boosted by carefully placed lamps, the panorama widens and the attention is drawn first to the faces on the ceiling, to canvases by Tintoretto of God and his ardent and determined disciples. The painter was called "the first film director of history" by Jean-Paul Sartre for depicting in oils the kind of drama and perspectives we now all take for granted with the ever-evolving technical magic of visual media in our times.

When my neck tires of gazing upward (platter-sized mirrors are provided for the stiff-necked), I find myself mystified by seventeenth-century walnut carvings of human figures by Francesco Pianta along the long wall, each a moral allegory moving between vice and virtue, with avarice as a man with a flowing beard, ledgers and money bags; ignorance as a figure of bestial ugliness; and science as a scholar with a lectern and a book. Each part of the room and the endless richness feels like a new universe. The Scuola Grande, a sort of mutual aid society in the age of the Republic, is one of those collective creations that inspires wonder: What is the source of this energy, this burst of creativity, this wealth? What kind of society could create it?

Venetian artisans and friends in the forcola workshop of Paolo Brandolisio. Back from left: Saverio Pastor, oar/forcola maker; Cristina Gregorin, tourist guide; Pinella Trivisonno, tourist guide; Ermanno Ervas, blacksmith; Vincenzo Casali, architect; the author; Elisabetta Mason, gold gilder; Marzio De Min, woodcarver; Alessandro Ervas, blacksmith; Erika Poberai, friend; Francesco Pavan, winemaker. Seated: Paolo Brandolisio, oar/forcola maker; Michela Scibilia, graphic artist; Piero Dri, oar/forcola maker; Giuseppe Amato, architect.

Renaissance ideals and resources came together here in a spectacular way at a moment and in a place when a rare balance of discipline, freedom and mental concentration prevailed, releasing a creative force that is always there — that is part of man's being — but only occasionally has the scope to fully express itself. In our day, it seems creativity sometimes has a much harder road to travel.

Painting remains a lively art and growing up with the colors of Venice has a lot to do with artists' work. Take the work of Serena Nono, who lives on Giudecca where she paints and where I found her in a ground-floor studio surrounded by a series of recent canvases, all in blues and subdued colors.

> My painting is mostly figurative. I think the English school has influenced my work [she trained at Kingston University in the 1980s], but also being Venetian has meant a lot, because my painting was formed through looking at Venetian painters from the time when I was little. In Venice it's inevitable that you see paintings from the time you are born because you see them in churches and in every corner of the city. In Venice you are confronted with art continually because, apart from seeing paintings, the whole city is beautiful and it has an important artistic and cultural story, not just from the 1500s, 1600s and 1700s but also into the 1960s. Maybe it ended in the 1980s. After that it declined — but that's another story. However, it's a city where you breathe in art, you live it, you see it. You feel the need to look for beauty. You grow up with this, perhaps unconsciously.
>
> I can give you examples of how this happens. I remember the first time I went to the Gallerie dell'Accademia [the foremost museum gallery of pre-nineteenth century art in Venice] when I was little, seeing original Venetian paintings at full size. I saw how large the canvases really were and the feeling of movement in the pictures. Take Tintoretto. He was the first to make everything move and to move the focus off center. Even if you aren't able to analyze what you are seeing artistically at the time, it still provides a meaningful experience.
>
> In front of these paintings, comparing the early ones with background in gold from the 1300s and 1400s to the ones from

the 1500s, you are overwhelmed by the revolution in Venetian art. Because you see, the Florentine artists are much more formal, while the Venetian artists break through the space with color, and they create movement and seek to do without a center in the picture. Tintoretto does a *Last Supper* where he puts a dog in the center, not Jesus.

One of the influences on artists has been the water, or rather the light on the water, in the sense that the types of light are so different in this city. If you go, say, to Tuscany, the light is completely different. The tones of dark grey, green and so forth are unique to Venice, and it is in constant motion because you don't have land. You have waves, water that is flowing, and this has an effect. I am not sure how it affects me, but it does, maybe unconsciously. But certainly you grow up with the colors of the city and you find them inside you.

Figura con fiore, 2018, oil on canvas, by Serena Nono. (The original is in color.)

Food traditions evolve as well. You can only get a dish like octopus, turnip tops, black garlic and lemon, at Il Ridotto, where every plate is a work of art, because chef Gianni Bonaccorsi's Michelin-star restaurant uses seasonal ingredients from the Venetian kitchen, but otherwise sets itself completely apart from the tradition.

"We work essentially on transformations that are fairly long," said the aproned Bonaccorsi, taking a break from cooking. "We ferment many things, using a lot of algae. A lot of things we mix, dry, burn, smoke, that is to say, each thing is taken in hand two or three times; they take different voyages. We use a lot of cooking in oil. Squid is cooked in oil at a low temperature, whelks in another. It's a whole different way of cooking — very different!" He's got nothing against Venetian cuisine, which he loves. "But we can't be a *trattoria*," where you get traditional Venetian dishes like *sarde in saor*, sardines with onions, and *baccalà mantecato*, spiced cod, or *bigoli in salsa,* a pasta with anchovy sauce. "Our restaurant has a distinct mission!"

Back in the 1960s, Venice and most of Italy had only traditional restaurants. Times have changed. The family trattoria is disappearing, while since the 1980s pioneers in chef-run restaurants have, in Bonaccorsi's view, reinvented Italian cuisine. Il Ridotto opened in 2006 following the trend at a time when tourism was driving an upsurge in restaurants, pushing the number in Venice to 1,400. But for Bonaccorsi, of those 1,400, only thirty or forty are any good, which is a lot by his standards.

Just as culinary attractions proliferate, nothing seems to get in the way of Venice as a movie location.

"And this, finally," proudly says our guide Carlo Montanaro, who has a mop of thick white hair and a mustache to match, "is *Pigeon dans le place San Marco*, the original of one of the first films ever made and projected in Venice." I have found him in his film history archive La Fabbrica del Vedere, the Factory of Seeing. He picks from a shelf a fat slice of film that would have fitted into a cinematograph, a wooden box film projector invented in the 1890s by the Lumière brothers. This title, shown for the first time on July 9, 1896 in the now defunct Teatro San

Moisè, was the first of a series of forty-five-second silent films they made in Venice.

It is among the thousands of priceless objects stored and stacked to the ceiling over the two upper floors of the archive, with 1,400 photographic films, projectors, videos, DVDs, photographs, books, daguerreotypes, magic lanterns, stereoscopes, cameras oscurae and old television sets.

Venice has played a key role in cinema, though it lacks a film industry of its own. Film got going in a big way in Venice in 1932, with the annual film festival. Giuseppe Volpi, the Conte di Misurata, the early twentieth-century entrepreneur behind industry and hotels on Lido, saw this new form as a way to stir up business for his interests on the upcoming beach resort, calling the event *Esposizione Internazionale d'Arte*. At that time, cinema was not yet widely seen as an art form, says Montanaro, who taught film at the city's Accademia di Belle Arti. So the idea "was to add art to cinema. This was the winning and extraordinary idea that occurred only in Venice," says Montanaro. The festival today acts as a great selector of movies, along with Cannes and the other awards festivals, and its teams of experts and judges work for months every year to showcase the best new films internationally.

Venice itself has been part of innumerable films, probably making it the most filmed city in the world, Montanaro believes. The activity has changed the very image of the city. Collectively these films depict it as "the city of romanticism and death," of love adventures, Gothic tales, of assassins and darkness, he says. "Very few films have tried to understand what Venice *is*."

The film *Death in Venice* has had the greatest impact on popular attitudes. Others that have been widely influential are the 1973 psychological thriller with Julie Christie and Donald Sutherland, *Don't Look Now*, and the Italian *The Anonymous Venetian*, a dark love story of 1970 with American actor Tony Musante and Brazilian actress Florinda Bolkan, a film noted for its extraordinary scenography.

For Montanaro the best film ever made in Venice has to be the historical melodrama *Senso*, made in 1954 by Visconti. He is also fond of the Italian comedy film *Giacomo Casanova: Childhood and Adolescence*, directed by Luigi Comencini, a vision of Venice that is rarely seen, and also *Bread and Tulips*, a 2000 Italian romantic comedy directed by Silvio Soldini, about a housewife who decides to start anew in Venice. Some

500 films have been set in the city, including seven versions of Othello and blockbusters including the Indiana Jones series, James Bond films, *Tomb Raider*, and 2019's *Spider-Man*.

Another of Venice's lively art forms is music and no other place has a musical story like it. Historian of music Franco Rossi, who runs La Fenice theater archive, outlined some highlights, beginning with the choral and instrumental music of St. Mark's Basilica:

> One of the mosaics on the ceiling records that when the body of Saint Mark was brought to Venice in 828, it was welcomed with sweet song — so, such music in the Basilica already existed even 900 years ago! Not even the Sistine Chapel can match that. Music made for the Basilica is special, because it is music written especially for the location. All those mosaics and all that marble change the duration of sounds; the echo is very long. It's been measured at five to six seconds, which is enormous! In a place like that I can't write music as I would, say, for a house. The sounds would overlap and no one could make any sense of it. So harmonies must be very simple, the music must have certain colors, contrast and blocks; the musicians must be placed carefully around. It has a flavor all its own. Claudio Monteverdi, Francesco Cavalli and Giovanni Legrenzi wrote music there in the 1600s.
>
> The owner of the Basilica was the doge. It was the church of the state! The music at St. Mark's had to be splendid because it gave grandeur to the Republic. It was once written that the most beautiful jewel of the doge wasn't sewn into his crown; it was the music in St. Mark's.
>
> The same goes for opera. European public theater began in Venice. It's true that opera originated in Florence, but it gained the structure it has today in over 400 years in Venice. Verdi came to Venice to write five operas for La Fenice theater, including *La Traviata* and *Rigoletto* — extraordinary operas. Then there's the invention of music printing with moveable type invented by Ottaviano Petrucci. What Guttenberg did for words, he did for music! It created a whole industry.
>
> Venice was also among the first to pick up on the new idea of the music conservatory, first conceived in France. A conservatory

> was set up here in 1876, to train musicians for La Fenice, the city and the St. Mark's choirs, continuing a tradition set by Venice's *ospedali* [forms of social assistance under the Republic]. Among the needy were infants abandoned on the steps of churches, who were sent to the ospedali. The boys were taught a trade and the girls learned music so they could play and sing to make money for the institution. Venice had four schools for orphans: Pietà, Mendicanti, Ospedaletto and the Incurabili from the mid-1600s to the end of the 1700s.
>
> Why did composer Antonio Vivaldi write so many concertos for so many instruments? [He became violin master at Ospedale della Pietà in 1703.] There are concertos he wrote for cello, flute, oboe, trumpet, bassoon, mandolin, lute and recorder. He had to teach all these girls, and he would write difficult music to challenge them to improve. They would perform behind a screen in church.

As to music in Venice today, Rossi declares it "pretty healthy," giving as evidence the Biennale of Music, which began in 1930, and its many extraordinary moments such as the first performance of *The Turn of the Screw* by Benjamin Britten. Lots of music continues to be written, such as Giovanni Mancuso's typical Venetian opera, *Il Ritorno dei Chironomidi*, after little insects that once invaded Venice.

But something bothers Rossi too: the behavior of the public.

"They have lost a sense of culture, even in little things," he says, exasperated. "At one time you got to the theater on time. If you got there late, you stayed outside. Today, they make you get up as if it were a cinema.... These are live performances. If you lose a note you never get it back." And a lot of music is put on just for tourists, especially of Vivaldi, and the groups must always play his *Four Seasons*. If they do anything else, even another Vivaldi piece, half as many people attend. The program stays boringly the same and "the tourists, who only know *The Four Seasons*, come and go. It's a big problem."

Just as it is for theater.

Four actors, still panting with effort, faces dripping with the sweat of exertion, line up for a bow with their musical accompanist after giving an athletically vigorous performance of *Arlecchino Furioso*, a comedy by Carlo Goldoni. In what happened to be the last performance of the tourist season, they had given the love-farce their all, making us laugh, smile and draw breath as the masked Arlecchino jumped, ran and somersaulted, while his love Isabella, won our hearts.

A door-and-window backdrop behind them had been constructed on the stage, but facing away from the seating in the eighteenth-century Goldoni Theater. The audience of about a hundred tourists sat packed onto temporary bleachers at the back of the stage, facing out towards the set and behind it, the empty auditorium. So when the lights came on again, the applause washed over the players and behind them, into the unoccupied red-plush seating of the cavernous main theater.

A tall, bespectacled man from the audience, who said he was from Salzburg, stood up to make a little speech to the actors, praising them for the performance and adding, "Theater is still alive, especially in Venice." And then we filed out into the lobby for a glass of wine. It was kind of the man to have expressed his appreciation, and indeed the show was extremely good, the actors exceptionally capable, but I wondered about the irony of his comment. This was a performance for tourists that the actors had been giving day after day for months and we could see behind them the emptiness of the embarrassingly large theater.

In the 1700s, Goldoni had risen to prominence writing satires about the aristocracy and the servants they employed, drawing on the local traditions of *commedia dell'arte*, a form dating from the fifteenth century that may have had its roots in the Venice Carnival. Troupes later toured Europe, probably influencing Shakespeare and Molière. The Goldoni comedy *Sior Todero Brontolon*, in which I had a walk-on part in 1972 when I lived with my Italian family, was part of the popular revival of theater that led to the re-launch of the Venice Carnival years later.

With Venice's depleted population, that kind of amateur dramatics happens infrequently now. Indeed, according to Paolo Puppa, playwright and retired professor of theater, out of the eight commercial theaters that existed in the glory days of the Republic, Venice is left with only La Fenice, which does mostly opera and music, and the Goldoni Theater, now given over to tourists for most of the year. "For at least 200 years Venice was the city where the world went to see theater. There was great vitality," he says. Today, "what's on has been reduced to a little flickering lamp, discontinuous, and poor," but theater these days has its moments too, he adds. Every two years the Biennale theater festival brings a burst of quality productions to the city from September to October. In addition, the university theater, Teatro Ca' Foscari, produces shows and the tiny independent Teatro a l'Avogaria keeps a regular presence, often of experimental performances.

In contrast to the theater, open to all, Venice's 500 gardens, like coy lovers, seem to play hard to get, with only a few open to the public, including the stately Royal Gardens reopened in 2019 after a five-year renovation. But most are private, visible only from greenery peeking out from behind high walls.

If you pause in front of the sixteenth-century Palazzo Soranzo Cappello, you might catch the scent of lemon trees, climbing roses and pomegranate flowers. They grow just over the long brick wall along the canal, where once the aristocratic families who inhabited the palazzo cultivated fresh vegetables and fruit. Now just for show, the garden is still cultivated, but the lemons, unharvested, are left to dry out on the branches.

Behind Soranzo Cappello is a larger secret garden of legendary fame that has been restored as a kind of palimpsest of what it was when abandoned. It's a garden which was described in Henry James' *The Aspern Papers.* Not so much beautiful as haunting and mysterious, the garden on the grey winter day I visited was the picture of Romantic decadence, with vines growing untamed over the ground, large leafy trees giving shade and shards of sculpted stone ruins artfully scattered among the leaves. "Shabby... with great capabilities" is how James depicted it, words that must have inspired landscape architect Giuseppe Rallo in his reconstruction.

The garden, where they actually shot *The Aspern Papers* film in 2017, is maintained by the local Cultural Heritage office, whose offices occupy the palazzo. It is accessible only with advance permission as are a number of other gardens: some are attached to monasteries, but most are now, alas, not open to the public.

Gardening in Venice is especially hard work — and costly. The very earth has to be brought in and garden waste transported out, and all by boat because you can't burn leaves and wood outside. The survival of this greenery, says Gregorin, author of a book on Venetian gardens, "stems from someone's willingness to care for them." But when things change, "when the palazzos are sold, no one knows what will happen. We can only hope for the best!" As the palazzos become hotels, as most of them are today, the attention to gardening fades.

It is said that Venice excels as an antidote to its own antiquity. Few people understand this better than Živa Kraus, a celebrated pastel painter whose work and life bring together main strands of contemporary art of Venice since the 1970s. Now she runs one of a dozen elite art galleries in the city.

We met one chilly December day in the narrow, brick-walled room of the ancient Ghetto building that houses her Ikona Gallery of photography, where she has worked over the years with scores of world-class photographers. She founded it in 1979 and moved to this site in 2003. She is also an accomplished painter, much admired by Alberto Moravia, one of the twentieth century's leading Italian novelists. He called her "a realist of the invisible." Kraus says few photographers succeed in creating a real artistic dialogue with the city, rather than just producing images which inspire exclamations of, "How beautiful." When the very best photographers succeed, "It's always an individual discourse because every person is different."

In 1973, after studies at the Academy of Art in her home city of Zagreb and then at the academy in Venice, Kraus worked as an assistant to Peggy Guggenheim at her renowned museum for twentieth-century European and American art. The American heiress started collecting from 1938 in London, Paris and New York, bringing to the fore previously unknown artists like Mark Rothko and Jackson Pollock. The Peggy Guggenheim Collection, which she set up in 1949 in the unfinished Palazzo Venier dei Leoni on the Grand Canal, exhibits key moments in the development of form and color — even if a number of the scribblier pictures make some visitors feel, "I could have done that!" Apparently, the museum was not greatly popular with the locals in the early years. "I saw few Venetians enter. Yet it was free!" Kraus says.

Kraus went on to work for the art Biennale in 1978, which she describes as a "meeting of art, culture and diplomacy at the highest level," bestowing honor on the selected artists who represent their countries.

Since the late 1990s, the Biennale has expanded enormously, both physically into the neighboring territory of the ancient Arsenal, and in popularity. Since 2017 there have been ninety pavilions attracting over 615,000 visitors.

I wanted to understand what it is about the city that has inspired the many artists she has known.

> Venice is an island, solitary and incomparable with any other city. Once, as a given, it offered a place to be alone, otium [a contemplative space], the thing that all artists must have: time to express themselves. I'm talking about forty, fifty years ago. Today with consumerism taking over the city at every level, it provokes greed and desire. It is as if Venice has become an obscure object of desire. Everyone wants to come to Venice, but the silence is much less evident than before. Artists choose to seek it just the same. Venice was built by men, but its harmony resides in the fact that it has been created with natural elements such as water, air, stone and light. Beauty means harmony, and Venice translates everything into such harmony and beauty.

What makes Venice a city of art, artisanship and artistry? Art that makes us marvel grows from rare and fragile traditions, from artists who by their work create a virtuous cycle of inspiring others to create and the succor of people who value what they do. When I go to places lacking these, where production and consumption trumps humanity and beauty, I appreciate Venice all the more.

MUSICIAN
THE PITURA FRESKA PHENOMENON
CRISTIANO VERARDO

Creativity is never straightforward, as I learned when I met Cristiano Verardo, who was a Venetian pop star in the late 1990s and early 2000s. Today he runs the only recording studio in Venice. I caught up with him early one evening in the brightly lit control room to get the inside story on the Venetian music scene. In a very unpresumptuous way, the crew-cutted, plainly dressed former guitarist told me a surprising story.

"Until about 2000, there was a great deal going on in music — many new bands and lots of singers — but all that has dissipated and we've not had a revival since, it seems to me. I was personally involved in the scene because I worked for a band for fifteen years, Pitura Freska, which was nationally successful doing music in Venetian dialect, so it was very Venetian. This all began in 1986 or '87, and lasted until 2003, and it was the start of an explosion of music in dialect that spread all over Italy. It turned out a lot of other bands and artists had the courage to do things in dialect. Before, music in dialect had always felt provincial. In Italy we have always been xenophiles, seeking to imitate the Anglo-Saxons, or we're working in Italian pop music, which, however, is very standardized. Dialect was taboo. Yet at a certain point, the dialect phenomenon exploded, also thanks to this band I worked in.

"You may wonder how this band got started. Before it was formed, I too played only English music or we did Italian pop, which was really like doing something 'old' for a youngster at the time. Or else we imitated the pop and rock from America and the UK. I was into playing reggae in English because it did not sound right in Italian. One day I met this person who wrote lyrics in Venetian dialect, and no one thought much of him, because he was a bit of a character. He went to bars and made a ruckus, he got drunk, all that sort of stuff, and we all thought, forget about him. He got booted out of bars for annoying girls. He played the guitar, but very badly.

"At a certain point he managed to get an engagement to play at a little theater in Marghera, near here. As he looked up to me because I played guitar in a recognized band, he asked me if I could help him out with the guitar. To tell the truth, I was embarrassed to appear on stage publicly with him. So, I got some other friends involved and we rehearsed his songs before the concert, on stage.

"Strangely this theater was packed! It might have been free, or maybe it cost a bit. But it was totally jammed. People had come because they thought they would make fun of this songwriter, right? We had arranged the songs quickly and when we opened the concert, something happened. He sang these songs he had written in dialect, and people understood! I had never heard that before. The audience were used to songs sung in English, where the public danced, but they had not been able to understand the words. Venetian is like a language for us. It is very direct — more so than Italian. Habitually, from when we were kids, we have always spoken in dialect. So, a really direct rapport was created with the public. They interacted with us! So this moment really struck me. I said to myself, 'Damn, this is important! Finally the audience is getting involved!' I got so into it that I said, 'Well, OK, let's do this right' and we continued, playing a lot of places, writing lots of songs together, and then we found a producer in Milan who believed in us at a time when we were really not in fashion, and he made us all the rage! And later we became, all at once, the hottest phenomenon.

But just before our first album came out in 1991, we went to this big motorcycle fair to play and we were all happy because our new album was about to be released. We played to an audience of teenagers, and after a few minutes they started to whistle at us, really whistle! Two thousand people whistling because they didn't like us. We were shocked. We played one song and ran off, so I recall thinking, 'Well, OK, our careers are over, but at least we did an album.' They didn't like the music and we were strange. Not fashionable. They didn't get it. After a couple of weeks, the producer in Milan called and said, 'We have a problem, the demand has exploded, everybody wants your album.' How can that be? They whistled us off stage the other day. But we were a hit. We returned to Milan that January to begin a year-long tour, two evenings in Milan, one at 9 p.m. and one at midnight because so many people wanted tickets. So, we sort of got our revenge, and after that things always went well, despite the difficult start.

The interest in dialect music petered out soon after the millennium, in part because of more noise restriction laws, while TV talent shows became all the rage, adding to the new use-and-throw-away consumerism and online streaming that continues to undermine live music culture.

"This [decline in interest] happened everywhere, not just in Venice," he reminded me. "But in Venice it's even harder, because, as you know, we are an island, isolated. Playing live is even harder here because we have a problem: every minor noise is heard more loudly than anywhere else. That's because we have no background noise," of traffic, he said. "So, music now has a bad reputation, because it disturbs people. The local places here get fines for noise, and a lot of places have thrown in the towel. I have friends who have local music venues, and at a certain point they got fed up with the fines for noise and gave up doing music, which obviously impoverishes culture."

11

ORIGINS
WHO IS VENETIAN?

We are Venetians, gone away this very morning
If you don't find us in the mountains,
You'll find us in the wine cellar.

We are more beautiful than the Paduans
We Venetians, so said the king
Who is no more, but will return. One never knows.

—FOLK SONG

Who is Venetian?

This is the story that has come down to us and is still retold in millions of guidebooks and texts, typically like this:

> *The once great Roman Empire ruled Europe and beyond until the fifth century when waves of barbarians began to descend on northern Italy, wreaking havoc. Venice's birth is a heroic tale of proud former Romans who refused to be subjugated by the various invaders, of hold-outs determined to protect the glorious past, who, to save themselves, migrated in waves to the safety of the harsh, wild lagoons on the Adriatic coast, then inhabited only by hardy fishermen. Thankfully, the difficulty of navigating the waters kept further attackers at bay, and these settlers eventually established Venice as part of Byzantium, the eastern sequel to the by then defunct Roman Empire, and came to consider themselves Byzantium's successors.*

Since about 2000, however, new archaeology and new thinking about these events have made clearer that this self-aggrandizing account is more a reflection of the Venetian Empire's vanity, a piece of myth-making that took place hundreds of years after the fact, than an accurate reflection of the past. The sanitized story about their origins was invented by the Venetians beginning in the eleventh and twelfth centuries and would become deeply ingrained in official state ideology by the fourteenth century. The story fits into the larger narrative they constructed, giving the aristocrats who ruled Venice divine and historical justifications for their newly fledged powers and a pretext for colonial expansion across the Mediterranean.

These tales survive mainly as historical lore, but today's Venetians, threatened by depopulation, have come up with a broader definition of themselves, one that allows the term "Venetian" to apply more widely than simply to those residents who've been living in the city for more than three generations. Instead, the residents tend to define themselves today more by historical traditions of openness, by a person's emotional attitudes and by their level of commitment to the community.

But they know the traditional version of history and have only recently begun to get used to a less edifying view of the origins of Venice that has been revealed by the new research, that the ancestors of the Venetians were not in fact Romans. Venice sprung from the local population's contact with so-called "barbarian" civilizations that the official narratives tried to write out of history. The lagoon settlements from which Venice emerged were in fact outgrowths of the political and economic landscape created by the ruling Carolingian Empire, made up of Germanic peoples known as Franks. Moreover, it is a fiction that the settlers set up Venice within the Byzantine Empire, which would have linked them directly to the Roman past. Finally, the lagoon settlements were not created by an exodus from bellicose invaders. The centuries-long migrations into the lagoon were motivated mainly by commerce — not by self-defense.

"None of the three elements of this history stands up to the archaeological evidence, not one," says Diego Calaon, archaeologist and professor of anthropology at Stanford University and Venice University, who is in charge of excavations including those on the island of Torcello, the oldest surviving lagoon settlement.

The following is the updated version of what happened.

In the official telling, the lagoon is painted as a forbidding location. In fact it was not so harsh, but a rather good place to live, easy to access by boat, full of fish and perfectly located as a port. The archaeological evidence makes it abundantly clear that the area had been inhabited and had been active in trade from well before Roman times.

As far as the "barbarians" are concerned, they get a bad rap from historians of the invaded areas. But in French and Germanic sources, they come off rather better, just as today we are accustomed to viewing those on our side as our freedom fighters and the other side as terrorists.

History records that Attila the Hun's "hordes" swept down from central Asia in the year 453, triggering the migrations to the lagoon. They were followed by the arrival in 568 of the Germanic Lombards, whose invasion is associated with a movement of "refugees" — from Padua, Aquileia, and Altino, all once Roman towns in the area — to lagoon settlements such as Malamocco, Chioggia, Torcello, Burano and Murano. In the eighth century the Frankish Carolingian dynasty arrived, coming to rule most of Europe until their kingdom split up at the end of the ninth century.

The new archaeology suggests that the lagoon was settled not by refugees, people seeking safety from the invaders, but more probably by communities in commercial partnerships with the dominant ruling group, the Franks. The ports and housing unearthed in the region could hardly have been built without close ties to these powers, for the settlers needed vast quantities of wood for building houses, ports, boats and for cooking. Excavations have shown these materials could only have come from the terraferma ruled by a people who have always been called the "barbarians."

The archaeology suggests that commerce in the lagoon over these centuries focused first on salt and fish, but expanded over time. By the year 800, the Carolingians designated the lagoon as their route to the East, and encouraged the traders already in the lagoon to act as middlemen, conferring on them noble titles. The lagoon ports became fundamental in connecting the area with Mediterranean trade, especially to Alexandria in Egypt. This trade became very profitable for the lagoon dwellers, and according to Harvard academic Michael McCormick, medieval historian of great renown, the lagoon traders brought silk, textiles, oil and spices back from Egypt, and traveled there to sell valuable cargoes supplied to them by the Franks: European slaves, who had been captured as loot in the Carolingian wars across Europe. At the end of the eighth and early ninth centuries, the quickly expanding Islamic world was hungry for slave labor for domestic and agricultural work.

The idea that trade was based on slavery, however, is completely removed from the accounts that Venetians wrote much later. Slaves only get a mention when one of them happened to become a saint and earned liberation. The Venetians whitewashed their own history in the same way that Holland, Belgium, France and others who traded slaves from 1600 to 1700 would do later. With their Christian faith outlawing trade of Christian slaves, it was something that later Venetians were eager to forget.

"What seems to have happened is that any source to do with slavery was completely removed from the narrative," says Calaon. "They exist in documents but not in the historical narration, because they are inconvenient."

By the time Venice began concocting its past in the eleventh and twelfth centuries, the city was truly Byzantine, drawing its art, ceremony and much of its trade from Byzantium, where the Orthodox form of Christianity was practiced. But they were already seeking to break free from the rule of Greek-speaking emperors in its capital, Constantinople, now modern Istanbul. In writing their own history, Venetian upstarts were anxious to show their claims to independence and their links to Roman ancestry. This comes out in the way they recall how lagoon settlements came to blows with their Frankish overlords in 810. Charlemagne's son, Pepin, led an army against them, capturing their capital Malamocco on Lido. The lagoon settlers managed to retreat into the lagoon, later re-establishing their capital on the *Rivoaltus*, or high bank, a scattering of islands later called Rialto, which was to become Venice.

Venetian historians described this strategic retreat in heroic terms, claiming Venice used superior knowledge of the lagoon to fend off the Frankish attack, when in fact the Franks arrived over water and land, suggesting the Venetians had no exclusive claim to lagoon know-how. They began to appreciate the defensive value of the lagoon only in retrospect.

The official histories claim the Venetians chose at that point to throw themselves in with Byzantium. But that's not chronologically possible. Byzantium had no political power in the western Mediterranean at that time. In Frankish history, in fact, the episode is recalled simply as a matter of putting down a rebellious Frankish duke. The conflict ended with the lagoon settlers suing for peace. The Franks granted them some independence, nominally as a Byzantine province, but only under the Carolingian Empire. The lagoon settlements still traded with the Franks and printed Frankish money. They issued coins stamped with the name "Ludovico il Pio," who was a Frankish king. Its system of leadership, an elected doge, was much more Carolingian than Byzantine. The first basilica, the one before the existing Byzantine structure of St. Mark's Basilica, is believed to have been built in Carolingian style. And last, but not least, the Arabs, who were among Venice's early trading partners and who called Venice *Al-Bunduqiyya*, knew that it was a place with many "*Al Funduq*" (merchant's warehouses) belonging to the Franks — they didn't say "of the Byzantines."

Only at the end of the ninth century, when the Carolingian Empire was fragmenting, did the lagoon settlers manage to set up their own state, giving the Venetian Republic a lifespan of some 900 years rather than the 1,000 more regularly claimed. At the same time, the Venetians made up for fading ties to Islamic Alexandria with reinvigorated links to Byzantium, where the Venetians had a trade colony and felt more at home culturally.

Venetians today resist the idea that Venice at birth was not Byzantine, and therefore not Roman. "When I say, 'Venice was not originally Byzantine by any means, it was Carolingian,' the tourist guides rebel! 'It can't be Carolingian,' they say. But it is!" says Calaon.

According to myth, the island of Torcello is where Venice began. In the thirteenth century a bustling island city with a population of 15,000, it is the site of the church of Santa Maria Assunta, where a hardly legible dedicatory stone from 639 identifies it as built on the site of the oldest church in the lagoon.

The story of Torcello's founding constitutes a main element in claim of a sudden migration. It describes how the citizens of the Roman city of Altinum, now Altino, close to the lagoon, were preparing to defend themselves against the Lombards in the fifth century. But when they saw nesting birds fleeing the city, they decided to follow the omen. The Bishop Paul heard a heavenly voice telling him to climb the city's tower and seek the stars. The bishop did so and saw before him the lagoon islands like the stars of the sky. Some followed the bishop to Torcello, and others settled on Murano, Burano and on other islands that have since disappeared. In these legends, Venice formally came into existence at the stroke of noon on the March 25, AD 421.

This is misleading for it is known that the lagoon was inhabited well before this time, with early Roman authors like Strebo writing of marshes managed by dykes and canals in 300 BC, even before the Romans had arrived. Recent archaeology suggests that rather than being the seed from which Venice was born, Torcello was just one of a number of lagoon settlements established in the fifth to eighth centuries. Lagoons lined the Adriatic coast from Ravenna to Grado in that era and towns like Comacchio, Jesolo and Grado, just like Torcello, produced and traded salt regionally. The other lagoons have long since silted up, been filled in or become open sea. Venice intervened to keep its lagoon alive, but could not save Torcello, which declined when falling water depths around the island obstructed navigation.

"Torcello is not the place where Venice originated. Torcello is another city that was born a bit before Venice, with similar characteristics... that later, Venice would acquire and incorporate," says Calaon.

Over on the Rialto islands, the Venetians did something in the eighth to ninth centuries that was unprecedented. Not only did they build boats for local use, as happened on Torcello and elsewhere, but they built up their own seagoing vessels. "From a technical point of view, they were the first to deploy a fleet, one that was also military," says Calaon. "What we see in our excavations, for example of Torcello, is a city that looks a lot like Rialto, but lacks this technological outburst. The technology is what really sets Venice apart."

What happened? Why did Venice burgeon? That's exactly what Calaon is trying to figure out next.

❧

After these early beginnings, the Venetians set a course for power and independence, pushing out into the Adriatic in the knowledge that growth lay in trade. By the year 1000 the Byzantine power over the Adriatic had begun to wane and the Venetians would stealthily encroach on its territory, establishing themselves along the shores of Dalmatia, on the opposite side of the Adriatic. At the same time they ingratiated themselves into the weakening Byzantium court, helping them fend off Norman war bands that were threatening Constantinople itself. With that, the Byzantine emperor rewarded the Venetians with the Golden Bull of 1082, a charter giving them rights to trade freely throughout the empire — forever. That gave Venice a huge advantage over its rivals in

Genoa, Pisa and Amalfi, allowing its merchants to establish a thriving trading colony in Constantinople.

Alongside Byzantium, the Venetians had taken part in the Crusades launched by Pope Urban II in 1095 to win the Holy Land for Christianity. Venice profited from these great movements of pilgrims and knights to the Levant, providing ferry services and enriching itself with loot gained in fighting and plundering Muslim lands and ships. By the beginning of the twelfth century, relations with Byzantium had soured after the emperor took the 12,000-strong Venetian trading colony in Constantinople hostage. When the incident had blown over, the special relationship was dead. Meanwhile, Venice was building its prestige diplomatically while it bolstered its naval power by enlarging an armed shipping fleet in the Arsenal. In the Fourth Crusade of 1202–04, as we shall see later in this book, this fleet would grab much of Byzantine's power, territory and mantle of legitimacy. This became the turning point that gave the Venetians undisputed preeminence in the eastern Mediterranean for centuries.

Venetians may stiffen when asked to give up old ideas about history, but they have no hesitation in saying who is Venetian today. The answer almost always comes back to love and commitment: "I can say a Venetian is one who loves Venice, but not in a romantic sense," says the poet and author Isabella Panfido. "It is not about saying, 'Ah, how beautiful is Venice, a city with the moon at night and gondolas.' No, a person has to really love Venice, they have to do something for the city. First of all, they must live here and fight for the city. That in a broad sense makes a Venetian."

But from this widely accepted definition, viewpoints diverge. For Panfido, being Venetian is also about character:

> A pure-blooded Venetian has an answer for everything, and generally knows everything. He criticizes continually. 'Why don't they put the ferry stop there? Why did they make me pay a tax?' An ordinary Venetian is very showy, and dresses flashily, with a lot of gold, a shirt open to the belly — as you see I have developed a comic view of my fellow citizens. As in the 1500s, the world comes to Venice, so we see showy people walking around in their underwear or wearing outrageously costly clothing;

> Venetians are homosexuals, bisexuals, trisexuals. Everything happens in Venice. Even the nobles became noble because they had money and, as merchants, they were clever people, astute, with flexible minds, able to adapt to any situation, welcoming but also opportunistic. Not all of this may have been passed down to the present generation, but I can tell you this: Venetians still presume to be the sons and daughters of the great Venice of the past. Just by dint of being Venetian, they expect the world to recognize their superiority because they are the successors of that Venice. I too, deep, deep down, have this feeling.

The historian and author Alberto Toso Fei, like Panfido, defines the Venetian as, "Fundamentally, one who loves, works and lives" in the city (because "a city cannot live without inhabitants"), and "who acts to the benefit of the city as is true for city dwellers anywhere in the world."

> There are Venetians by birth, those who are adopted and who adopt the city and there are Venetians of the heart, of the spirit. 'Venetian' is a very comprehensive definition: whoever is born in Venice is Venetian, naturally, but this fact does not exclude the others. History teaches us that Venetians came from somewhere else, because they were refugees from the mainland, and according to another legend, from Paphlagonia, on the Black Sea coast of Anatolia, in Turkey....
>
> Personally, when I hear a definition of a real Venetian, I feel a bit sick, as though I've got a rash. Real Venetians don't exist. What categories could you define? Take, for example, the Jews in the Ghetto where they had lived from 1516. After half a millennium they could be real Venetians, surely? But clearly they arrived from somewhere else. The real Venetians could be the nobles, who descended from antiquity. There are still lots of them: the Zorzis, Querinis, Foscaris, Marcellos.... But some years ago scientists did a DNA study of some of the old families, tracing the maternal lineages, and what did they find? It actually is a strong possibility that they came from Paphlagonia in Turkey, so you see that even these real Venetians come from elsewhere.
>
> If we try to reconstruct the notion of belonging based on birthright, the painter Tiziano Vecellio is no longer Venetian

> because he was from Pieve di Cadore. The sculptor Canova wasn't Venetian, either. He came from Possagno. The same applies to the architect Andrea Palladio. He came from Vicenza or Padua and so on, the same thing happening with architect Jacopo Sansovino and a thousand other artists [and artisans]. These are people whose names, works and lives are inseparable from Venice and the idea of Venice. So, it's pretty clear that people put down roots in Venice, got assimilated into the local culture and learned the language, because Venice had a very strong identity.
>
> If I look at the numbers in my address list of all my friends who live in Venice today, more than half were not born in Venice. They came to study or work or for lots of reasons, for love, for example, and they chose to live here; they came from a thousand places, many from other countries, not necessarily Italy — but they are all Venetians, even, in some cases, more Venetian than a lot of other people I know, who were born in the city but do less work for its benefit and are less attached to it.

Simone Venturini, a councilor on the side of the governing party of Mayor Brugnaro, likes the question "because it gets to the point," he says. For Venturini, it all comes down to falling in love.

> We are not among those who think there are real Venetians and second-class Venetians, that those who live in the countryside or in Marghera or San Marco can be more or less Venetian that those who live on Giudecca. In this respect, Venice is very provincial. Does a Venetian have to be someone who lives in Rialto? Why is a resident of Giudecca, Lido, Burano, Murano or the countryside of Mestre any less Venetian? There is no such thing as Venetian. Venetians are those who love Venice. There are lots of foreigners who came to live in Venice — English, French and American — who love the place more than lots of Venetians who have exploited it....
>
> In my view we need to bring to Venice people who love Venice and keep those who fall in love with Venice there. We are restoring housing for twenty-five- and twenty-six-year-old graduates. These are little, inexpensive apartments for couples which they can rent for four years, and, if they do fall in love with the city, they have

> time to find a house to live in. Only in this way will Venice be re-populated, because in every city and town, people are having fewer children.... So we have to bring in new people, like they are doing in Boston, where there is MIT, which attracts people who fall in love with that city and stay. So, the university is a great engine, and we have an alliance with the university, which must grow.

Just to be fair, I also asked opposition leader Monica Sambo. Both sides sort of agree.

> Anyone who's born here is no different from someone born in Rome or Milan. In another sense, we Venetians do have a different way of life; we live at a pace that sets us apart. But that's not what makes you different. What's different is the way we get around and go to work. It's slow and takes time. Sometimes there are difficulties. On some days we have acqua alta. We're not special. It's rather that whoever decides to live here is a romantic; you have to be, with all the challenges of life here, the cost etcetera. So, in the recent years all Venetians, both those born here and the newcomers, are acquiring anew a sense of belonging and pride. If you stay here, against all the odds, you must be a romantic.

12

INSPIRATION

WHAT THE CITY MEANS FOR WRITERS

> *"A hundred deep solitudes create together*
> *the image of Venice — this is her magic.*
> *An image for the men of the future."*
>
> —FRIEDRICH NIETZSCHE, 1880

As I sit in front of the proverbial blank page awaiting my own inspiration before telling the story of the writers of Venice, I think about all the others who have faced the same blankness, no doubt at some point sitting at a desk with quill in hand or in front of a computer, fingers poised over the keys.

I have a particular affection for Dante Alighieri, whose work was introduced to me as a student in Venice. The literature teacher at Liceo Marco Polo, whom I saw as very severe, had us memorize passages from Dante's and others' poetry, something one rarely did in my American school.

Dante came to Venice in the early 1300s, when he is believed to have visited the Arsenal, then a buzzing shipyard thick with production-line workers who could apparently turn out a galley in as little as a day. The author of the *Divina Commedia* (*The Divine Comedy*), an epic, allegorical poem describing a journey of the soul towards God, through Hell, Purgatory and Heaven, seems to have been inspired in part by what he saw in the factory-like compound, for he used it as a metaphor to describe the eighth circle of Hell where corrupt officials are punished.

This is the passage, in a particularly vivid translation of lines from Canto 21 by Belfast poet Ciaran Carson:

> As in the Arsenal of the Venetians
> they boil cauldrons full of pitch as thick
> as shit, for caulking ships of every nation —
>
> leaking hulks in dry dock, others slick
> with new paint, their planks patched and
> plugged with tow,

the climate odoriferous and toxic,

workmen hammering at stern and bow,
or slicing ropes, fixing oars, cutting wire,
boys with buckets dashing to and fro:

so, here, but heated by God-power, not fire,
tar glopped and sputtered into the ditch. This,
the dead black glue of the infernal mire,

I saw, except for all the boil and hiss
I couldn't see a thing, for nothing came
of it but bubbles, bursting as they kissed.

Dante at some point may also have seen the twelfth-century mosaics in Santa Maria Assunta church on Torcello, which depict, on a gilded background, the story of Universal Judgement — the ancient idea that one's fate in the afterlife is based on their deeds in life — and this, too, may have inspired his epic, one of the greatest works of world literature. If so, it is just one of innumerable examples of Venice empowering creativity. Venice even inspired many who had never seen it, such as William Shakespeare, who situated the *Merchant of Venice* and *Othello* in the city, or the nineteenth-century poet Alexander Pushkin, who dreamed of escaping the bounds of tsarist Russia to be in Venice.

What set the city apart right from the beginning as a source of inspiration was its cosmopolitan character and the relative freedom of its citizens. Dante himself was an exile from Florence, but was welcomed and feted in Venice, which had a long tradition of openness. From the time it had first begun trading across the Mediterranean at the turn of the first millennium,Venice was a crossroads for Turkish, Greek, Slav and German merchants, and then crusaders who traveled there on the way to fight for Christianity in Palestine. It became a refuge for those whose religion was threatened, from the Knights Templar to Benedictines, Jesuits and Jews. It earned a reputation for tolerance, hospitality and generosity, encouraging visitors to join its celebrations. With a form of democratic governance and a booming printing industry, Venice in its heyday bubbled with innovation, giving birth to banking and newspapers, inventing the practice of health quarantines — and continuously attracting writers, artists and thinkers.

Not all of them loved Venice when they got there. Quite the contrary. But something about the city inspires, bringing forth everything from a celebration of Venice as the "sole shelter in our days of liberty, justice and peace, the sole refuge of the good" from fourteenth-century poet Petrarch to the French thinker Régis Debray's 1995 polemic *Against Venice*, which reviles the very existence of Venice and the foreign "idiots of Venice" who swoon over the city. Since then, countless other books, films and even current-day social media posts have added outpourings about the city.

One of the most recent writers to have made a home in Venice is Spanish author Eugenia Rico.

"I came to Venice because there is a time when every writer has to come here. Proust was here, Lord Byron used to swim in the Grand Canal. I have been fascinated by the writers and intellectuals who came here," says the author of several award-winning novels, the most recent being *El camino del diablo* (*The Path of the Devil*), a surreal tale about a journey through space, time, places and cultures.

As I chat with this writer from Oviedo, Spain, at a café facing the lagoon, she points to San Michele, just visible over the water, resting place of many poets and authors. Rico lives with her family in Palazzo Contarini, in housing its owners have chosen to rent only to artists and writers, and she compares her neighborhood, Cannaregio, to the artists' quarter in Montmartre, Paris.

The raven-haired Rico, forty-six, breaks off to take calls from her ten-year-old daughter, the publisher of the Italian translation of her book, and her mother. In between, our conversation veers frequently to the burdens of tourism, "how hard life is" for the residents, she says, and how, speaking Italian with a Spanish accent, she is often treated like a tourist, although she has lived in Venice for three years.

But we get back on track. "I have published many novels, but not one about Venice," she says. But she has something underway. "The problem is that writing about Venice is like writing about love. Every important writer has to write about love." She thinks of Venice as a place "out of reality," a place where "man built a dream that has come true" and "the most beautiful city ever." It is a place saved in World War II by its beauty, where the enemies refrained from bombing, and one that gives artists freedom. "It is not possible for an artist not to be attracted to this city because it is unique. It's proof that human beings can do anything."

Among the younger writers of Venice is thirty-five-year-old Giovanni Montanaro, a native of the city and an attorney of international law by day, who published his first novel in 2007 at the age of twenty-four. His novels include an historical love story about the fifteenth-century Italian painter Raphael and another about the "missing" year in the biography of the Dutch Post-Impressionist Van Gogh. Montanaro's sixth work, published in 2019, *Le ultime lezioni* (*The Last Lessons*), is a coming-of-age story set in Venice.

The clean-cut Montanaro, who also attended Liceo Marco Polo, focused his first novels on Europe, with which he has a close affinity, rather than on his own life or local surroundings. But his relationship with Venice has always been important. "There is a sense of belonging to but also a sense of rejection from a city of such beauty and importance," he says. This comes out in the recent novel.

Le ultime lezioni was "the first time I have felt able to write about Venice, which I never thought I would be able to do," says Montanaro. In future he would like to write a great story about life in 1900s Venice, but says, "I am not sure I am up to it. Perhaps I am too young. I feel it's very complicated, being Venetian; it's almost easier to talk about Van Gogh than Venice, because I feel a sort of responsibility for Venice... because it is so important, so delicate, so precious that it is not simple to write about.... The view one often gets of Venice [in novels] is one completely wrong, almost always totally." People see Venice as "the most beautiful place ever made by man. But, in reality, nature is decisive in how Venice developed and affects the colors of the city," says Montanaro. He wants to write of a "Venice where you go to the pool for a swim or play football or basketball, the daily things we love, in normal Venice. At the same time, it's a dynamic city, because every feeling is multiplied by its beauty... it's normal but with a difference."

Venice has produced its own native writers in the past, most notably in the eighteenth century with comic playwright Carlo Goldoni and the womanizing adventures described in Giacomo Casanova's autobiography, which have become legendary. But these are distant echoes for a writer like Montanaro. "The Venice you had with Goldoni, the dynamic of the campo," the social life of the square, could have been updated with the "dynamic of the condominium," but instead has been supplanted among Venetians by a "strong tradition of fantasy, of escape," a trend that has been reinforced by the oppressive expectations that arose after the 1966 floods of Venice for the city's preservation at all costs. Montanaro feels spiritually closest to a twentieth-century tradition of Venetian literature of escapism represented by Hugo Pratt, the cosmopolitan cartoonist who created the adventures of seafaring hero *Corto Maltese*, which have been translated into fifteen languages; or Alberto Ongaro, who lived in Lido and wrote fantasy. This escapist tradition has "a nautical character, linked to the sea, sailors and adventure... which, in my small way, I have inherited," says Montanaro.

But he also sets himself apart from these writers, seeing contrasts between himself and his good friend Tiziano Scarpa, who is twenty years older, and who grew up in an 1980s generation that rejected in part the novel as a bourgeois form of literature. "We are more serious. We grew up with abundance, but not with the idea that abundance would be eternal" like the generation born after the war. "Our youth was more Twin Towers," marked by a world shaken by the terrorist attacks, "which makes a big difference; they had absolute freedom, literarily speaking."

Alberto Toso Fei is a writer who is known not for imagining stories so much as for retelling them. A journalist, age fifty-three, he grew up on Murano in the 1970s hearing old stories about Venice from older people. Fearful that this history might be lost, Toso Fei started to write them down.

The eventual result was the best seller *Legende Veneziane e Storie di Fantasmi* (*Venetian Legends and Ghost Stories*), based on his interviews with elderly residents.

"Some Venetian stories had beautiful parallels with stories in other traditions, north European, Arab, Hebrew, and so forth," he says, "because Venice became a place where everything meets and everything became profoundly Venetian." But what Toso Fei is most proud of having discovered is that these stories all featured places that still exist in Venice today. "You can tell the story in the actual places where the stories were born" so the book took on the form of a guide, linking each of the stories to locations in Venice. "When you scratch the surface, you find the stones have a soul."

In contrast, author Donna Leon, an American who grew up in New Jersey, came to Venice on a whim. In the late 1960s, after she'd seen Katharine Hepburn cavorting through Venice in the 1955 film *Summertime*, her curiosity was piqued. "I came as a tourist" for five days, Leon explains when we finally found a café quiet enough to chat in. She recounts how she ended up spending thirty years of her life in the city and writing a globally acclaimed crime thriller series set there. Leon met a couple during her first visit who owned a jewelry shop and she struck up a friendship with them. As at that time she lived a very peripatetic life, she would return year after year and look them up. In 1981, after getting fed up with teaching in Saudi Arabia, "I decided that that was it. That was the end. I wasn't going to be an academic mercenary anymore, so I came here with no job, with no future, with no money, nothing. I came because my friends were here and I knew that I had a place where I could stay until I found something to do," says the slight, plainly dressed, seventy-six-year-old author. That something turned out to be teaching English at an American university in Italy. Then, one day, on the off chance, she sent a story she had written to a competition, winning the top prize. She has never looked back.

She has authored twenty-six novels describing the crime-busting of her fictional hero, the erudite police commissioner and family man Guido Brunetti. Leon located her novels in Venice because that was "the only place I ever lived as a grown-up" and because she knew the city well enough to describe the geography confidently. Living with Venetians, she "observed and admired" the culture. Italians are "warm, friendly and *spiritosi*, and they love to laugh — Venetians perhaps a bit less, because they are more sober — but there's a kind attitude toward life."

Did the place not change the way she wrote? "No," she insists. Venice gave her the background for her stories because crime book plots "can be picked up and taken out of [any particular] place and walked off to lalaland and put down there.... Crime books are formulaic." What changes most in her stories is the scenery, characters and setting, for which Venice has been a rich source.

During her time in Venice she has collected a circle of close friends and has come to understand the ways of the Italians, of the Venetian nobles, of the shopkeepers and gondoliers, realizing that in these other worlds, she will never be completely accepted. Leon vacuums up stories and tittle-tattle for her books but has scrupulously disguised sources to make sure they are unrecognizable because, "One of my codes is don't betray people that you know. I've never done it." Her award-winning books have been translated into thirty-five languages, but she has never allowed them to be translated into Italian in order to defend herself, at least on her home soil, from the acidity of fame. She has watched people get famous. "It's never made anybody better, nicer or more interesting. Fame distorts a relationship.... When people treat me with respect or start to almost fear me because I'm famous, I flee. I don't want to be treated as a famous person here."

Leon has in fact now moved away from Venice and for over a decade has been resident in Zurich, Switzerland. However, she returns almost monthly to Venice to stay with friends. She left Venice to escape the mass tourism. "It makes me crazy," she says, lambasting the "ugly crap" in stalls, and highlighting how the crowds jostle and knock people down, which has happened to her, and mostly how the pressure of overcrowding poisons the normally humane instincts of Venetians. The tourism has made Venice "unlivable" in her view. She believes "hopelessness" burdens the city and is herself pessimistic. "It can only get worse," she remarks, apropos of the local and global outlook for the environment, a subject that concerns her increasingly. In 2017 she wrote the thriller *Earthly Remains*, one of her most ecologically themed books, which takes place in the lagoon.

In the beamed living room of Donata Grimani's palazzo, some thirty participants seated in a circle, some on chairs, others on the corner sofas, look around at each other expectantly. Who will go first? Everyone holds in their hands something to read aloud. A besuited professor of Chinese, sitting under the tall lamp at the end of the room, clears his throat and reads a tract from an Italian translation. Then, going round the room, others read passages from Italian authors, translations of works by Apollinaire, Flaubert, Nabokov or the American poet who wrote lyrically on Venice, Anthony Hecht. Some have chosen literature from India and other far-flung places. One reads from a book he has translated himself, another from photocopies. When those seated around the room like what they hear, they shout, "Bello! Bellissimo!" Beautiful! Really beautiful!

In doing the readings, each person was offering their choice to be put before the jury sitting among them who select the best. These will be read aloud in both the original language and Italian in a series of first-Tuesday-of-the-month events that have become a Venetian institution. Called Casa delle Parole, House of Words, the evenings are set up and are run by Venice University literature professor and author Enrico Palandri in the classy auditorium of Palazzo Grassi. Sometimes compèred by British poet and translator John Phillimore, from time to time they feature visiting writers, like Vikram Seth and Francesca Segal, who read their own work.

❧

"Many writers seem to talk about Venice as having somehow a transformational effect, [presenting it as] a place that changes people in mysterious ways," says Gregory Dowling, an English literature professor at Venice University. This emerges, he explains, in the work of American poet James Merrill, who visited Venice regularly and wrote the Pulitzer prize-winning 1976 book *Divine Comedies*, which includes Venetian sections in *The Book of Ephraim*.

A further example is British poet Lord Byron, who came to Venice in 1816 for three famously dissolute years in the city during which he wrote prolifically — letters, poems and plays. Regarded as one of the greatest British poets, Byron learned a new Italian form of rhyme — the eight stanza, a-b, a-b, a-b, c-c form — which he experimented with, moving away from the more restrictive heroic couplets he had known in England. "Venice was crucial to Byron's development as a poet," says Dowling. The young poet, remembered in Venice for swimming in the Grand Canal, wrote his humorous picaresque narrative poem *Don Juan*, now considered his masterpiece, in the new Italian form. "It was partly the influence of Venetian society as well as its openness that enabled him to express poetry in a way he hadn't before," in a new colloquial tone, Dowling says, noting that homosexuality was tolerated in Venice, whereas it was outlawed in England. "He found this new form of poetry that permitted him to use the same voice that he was using in his prose. This was a huge break for him," says the soft-spoken professor.

For other authors, Venice played different roles. For Henry James, whose *The Wings of the Dove* takes place in part there, the city served more as a vehicle, "a summation of what Europe represents both in its beauty and artistic wealth" and also its "corrupting power" on the innocence of America. Or take American poet Anthony Hecht, whose 1979 narrative poem *The Venetian Vespers* tells of an expatriate American who has come to Venice to expiate a crime that isn't actually of his own doing, where Venice stands for the way vile commercialism can be transformed into artistic beauty and wealth.

Dowling likes the chapters on Venice in Vikram Seth's novel *An Equal Music*, which describe what happens to a classical quartet of musicians when they perform in the city. Hemingway's *Across the River and into the Trees*, meanwhile, written as the author hunched over drinks in the now famous Harry's Bar, in part recounts the story of a soldier scarred by war. It is one of the novels that for many Venetians best captures the true nature of Venice, though Dowling finds it unconvincing.

Dowling, a Briton who has lived in Venice for thirty-six years, has himself written historical thrillers set in the eighteenth century, which follow his Venetian-English tour guide Alvise Marangon, a reluctant spy for La Serenissima. *Ascension*, which takes place on the feast day of Ascension, is built on a plot to overthrow the doge; *The Four Horsemen* is a backstory based on Venice's relationship with the Muslim world through Constantinople. The stories draw on Dowling's long familiarity with Venice, while the hero, as a tour guide, gives him a vehicle to explain the situation in centuries past. "I'm trying to write entertaining spy stories that happen to be set in the eighteenth century rather than the twenty-first century," says Dowling, who sees his own influences as writers like Raymond Chandler, whose character Philip Marlowe is portrayed as a wisecracking private eye.

Walking through the angular streets of Venice, author Tiziano Scarpa is in his element. He talks animatedly about what he loves best — giving readings. "Did you know that Charles Dickens gave readings of boiled-down versions of his novels?" remarks Scarpa, who wears a mustache and a flat cap.

Scarpa won the 2009 Strega Prize, the most prestigious Italian literary award, for *Stabat Mater*, a novel about the rebellion of an orphan girl trained in music by Antonio Vivaldi at the Ospedale della Pietà orphanage. The fifty-five-year-old Scarpa's oeuvre also encompasses opera, theater and poetry, but he is most known in the English-speaking world for his book *Venice is a Fish*, a "cultural guide" to the city. He was asked to write it and says he would never have written a guide on his own because he dislikes being pigeonholed, preferring iconoclasm and freshness.

Though initially reluctant to write about Venice, he has now come to terms with it. "It has antique scenery, and when you write something situated in Venice you have the impression that the readers see the background and not the characters of the story. If you want to do a story situated in the present, you really need asphalt roads and cars — in a word, an edgy city," he says. But he has come to see the antiquity of Venice or any city as simply analogous to our language, just another historic relic that we live with. In Italian and other Romance languages, unlike English, this baggage of history carries not only ideas in words from the past but in the masculine and feminine genders. "I speak in a 1,000-year-old language in a city invented by people now dead, and this observation set me at peace," says Scarpa. The realization enabled him to see the setting of a story in the city as equivalent to expressing oneself in an old language.

But he is also able to get around that to some extent in the same way that Ian McEwan did in his 1981 novel *The Comfort of Strangers*, which is not set in a named city, but suggests the location is Venice. In *Stabat Mater*, Scarpa never names Venice and never uses words like *calle*, *campiello* or gondola, substituting *strada* for *calle* (street), *piazza* for *campiello* (square) and *barca* (boat) for gondola. "This is a way to avoid making the presence of the city too heavy, to draw attention to the characters instead of the city," he says. He acknowledges that location does influence the way artists work, giving the example of how Venetian artists, on learning about oil paints, used them to paint huge canvases because, unlike frescoes, they stood up to humidity. But, in his view, "Art is about transcending oneself, not doing or expressing what one is. That's not art.... Art is not, I am a dog, and I say 'woof'. Art is 'I am a dog and I say 'meow'. It's about expressing something different from oneself."

13

NATURE

THE SHIFTING ENVIRONMENTAL COMPASS

> *"...threats to the inland waters of La Serenissima came not from the sky or sea, but from men."*
>
> —PIERO BEVILACQUA, *VENICE AND THE WATER: A MODEL FOR OUR PLANET*

It's spring 2019. With our gaff-rigged sailing boat *Pevarina* moored on a remote island in the southern lagoon, a place where teeming mullet make the water swirl around the wooden hull, I lie in my sleeping bag in the open hold and gaze up at the cloud-diffused glow of the moon. I listen to the birds chattering and wonder in passing about the tiny lights we had seen late in the night shuttling back and forth on the horizon. I nod off, only to be awakened abruptly at dawn with the answer.

"Bandits, bandits!" my companion Giampaolo Rinaldo shouts at barely 6 a.m., waking us up excitedly as the boat rocks violently with the wakes of speedboats racing by.

We now understand. The lights we had seen were fisherman in motorboats, tracking back and forth as they scraped the lagoon bottom for contraband: clams. These illegal raiders use up to 400-horsepower outboard engines to swirl mud in the shallows, washing valuable clams into a cage in a way that erodes the lagoon and stirs up pollution.

This early morning revelation took place while we were taking a grand loop through the southern lagoon in *Pevarina* to see how man and nature co-existed. We found lots of examples of benevolence in this otherwise natural world as we traced small streams through the marshes, passing an ordinary fisherman dipping a net from a pole, another using a hand rake to collect clams and others in waders scooping up sea worms for bait with their hands from the *velma*, the intertidal muddy bottom of the marsh. But the rude awakening by bandit fishermen provided a striking example of malevolent human industry, which unfortunately has a huge presence that is causing the lagoon to change close to irreversibly.

The lagoon has since time immemorial been a productive place, but since the end of the Republic, the equilibrium that prevailed has been lost. While a new drive to halt environmental degradation has had some results, such as improved water quality, the overall health of the lagoon is in sharp decline. The constant problem in the past, when rivers flowed directly into the lagoon, was canals filling in with sediments. Now it is exactly the opposite: erosion. The sediment-bearing river water is limited to twenty-three tiny inlets. Meanwhile, the dredging of the Canale dei Petroli cutting across the lagoon and the three openings to the sea allow a new rush of seawater to enter daily with the tides, and this has eaten the crater in the southern lagoon and is destroying natural arteriole channels that feed the lagoon ecosystem. Boat traffic — and illegal clamming — adds to erosion. As a result, the lagoon's bottom mud, which harbors sea life and builds the marshes, is being washed away. Several million cubic meters of sediments are washed out to sea annually, making the lagoon deeper, saltier and less a lagoon — in some areas, it's even sterile and unproductive.

Yet, much lagoon life thrives. As an internationally recognized ecosystem, one of the largest of its kind in existence, the lagoon salt marshes still harbor migratory birds, with 40,000 of them visiting annually and with many new bird species arriving. Sea life and plant life are adapting, with new varieties — including some invasive fauna and flora symptomatic of globalization — appearing. Some fish more often seen in saltier water are making inroads, replacing the old species in decline. Meanwhile, ways are being found to adapt humanity's presence in the lagoon, making it sustainable and giving hope for an alternative future.

We had made our way in our vessel by sail and motor from Venice following the 17-meter deep Canale dei Petroli, a shoreline-hugging channel dug as a waterway for shipping coming from the open sea to the refineries in Marghera. As straight and wide as an airport runway for most of its length, it is flanked by rows of towering lampposts that glow with eerie orange lights at night. Halfway down the lagoon, we curve around the unlovingly named Casse di Colmata, the "artificial landfill islands," B, D and E, formed in the 1960s with the industrially contaminated mud dredged from the Canale dei Petroli. Now overgrown wastelands, they represent the aborted industrial expansion into the lagoon that buried rare salt marshes — the *barene* — in an area twice the size of Gibraltar, but that was halted in 1969 in the face of an outcry against damage the landfills were causing to the lagoon. Passing all the industrial ugliness, we enter into one of the less disturbed areas of the lagoon, at the remote outpost of Cason Millecampi.

There, we spend the night with the kind permission of the caretakers of the newly built but unused lodge, and we dine on quite passable store-bought thick and hearty minestrone and bread with an apple tort for dessert as we celebrate my sixty-fifth with an embarrassing rendition of "Happy Birthday." This is sung by Rinaldo, a Venetian who has made boating his life after forsaking a career in computing, and Alessandro Corsi, an avid sailor and former hotelier, new to Venice, who are traveling with me. I couldn't have asked for a nicer way to celebrate.

All around us we are surrounded by barene, irregular-shaped flat tables of earth just knee-high above the water. They are covered with plants that over the seasons pass from dry wintry brown, to summer green dusted with flowers turning from violet to red. They have evolved to survive periodical immersion in salt water and, like desert plants, they conserve moisture. They include the tall-stemmed and wide-leaved *Limonium*, marsh rosemary, and also *Artemesia*, which have fluff on their leaves like the alpine edelweiss to protect against the harsh sun; along with the succulent flowering *Salicornia*, which are full of water and vitamin C. Sailors of yore, who knew nothing of vitamins, chewed them to prevent scurvy.

Below the tops of the salt marshes run the ghebi, the veins that allow the marshes to "breathe" tide water in and out twice daily. The tides rise by an average of 1.63 meters and then ebb away, exposing the vast glistening mudflats, the velma. The nutrient-rich mud hosts myriad sea worms, shellfish, clams, crabs and endless microorganisms that live in the space created by the one-meter rise and fall of the tide. Rinaldo remembers a fishing trip with his father when, due to miscalculation of tides, they ended up stranded in a boat on the intertidal mudflats overnight. He spent hours leaning over the sides, fascinated by the endless life crawling, poking up and slithering around on the mud just under the boat.

Beyond the tidal mudflats, where the tides do not expose the bottom, the shallow lagoon hosts a range of sea life and sea grasses. The lagoon is home to species of anemone and molluscs that live only in this fresh- and salt-water zone, which is characterized by freezing winters and sweltering summers.

As recently as the 1970s and '80s, more fish populated the lagoon because pollution from agricultural and industrial runoff into the lagoon made the water rich in nitrogen and phosphorus that fed the microcrustaceans that fish eat. With more food, fish proliferated. The dirtier water also came with algal blooms, fish die-offs and smells, a process called eutrophication that arises when water stagnates. European-supported improvements in water treatment inland have reduced the pollution and, now, with fewer nutrients, fewer fish thrive. Cleaner, and in many areas deeper and saltier water — more like the sea — has brought the return of marine life not seen in the lagoon since the eighteenth century, such as flying fish, tuna and sea turtles. The cleaner water has also been linked to the return of plant life and species such as the threatened *Pinna Nobilis*, the hand span-sized bivalve shells that stand vertically in shallow water. The lagoon is slowing turning into the sea.

The fishermen know best what's in the water. "Many species have disappeared but fortunately others are replacing them," says spokesman Luigi Vidal, who represents the San Marco Cooperative in Burano, the oldest cooperative in the lagoon, founded in 1896. Throughout the 1950s, fishermen used sail or oar and the same sorts of nets and boats that had been employed for centuries. Now they use motors to catch a lot of sea bass and bream, but there are fewer shrimp and flounder than in the old days.

He shows me around the two-story brick structure which houses the cooperative. There are offices upstairs and a white-tiled ground-floor area where the hundred cooperative fishermen sort fish and clams. Vidal paints a dark picture of a threatened profession. "In recent years, in the lagoon or in the sea, fishing has been diminishing" all over Europe as the methods of fishing change, especially for traditional small-scale fishing. The number of fishermen in the lagoon is declining.

Fishing had been tightly controlled under the Republic to prevent misuse of the lagoon, with rules against stringing nets where they might block canals and restrictions on fishing methods so as to preserve stock. But that regimentation slowly fell away after 1797, and administration has become ever more lax. The greatest upheaval took place in 1983 when the Philippine clam was introduced into the lagoon. By the 1990s, this fast-growing shellfish dominated fishing activity. Fishing on the lagoon was dramatically transformed from one of environmentally friendly seasonal fishing for fish, crab and squid to a monocultural clam gold rush. At its peak in 2003–04, some 1,000 men — many who had never fished before — were scouring the lagoon bottom for clams with methods that dispersed bottom sediments, accelerating flattening and disruption of the lagoon while destroying seagrass that acts as a nursery for young fish and filters the water.

Introducing the alien clams was "worse than an error, it was a criminal choice. They compromised completely the biodiversity of the lagoon bottom," simply because it was convenient to buy seed clams already produced elsewhere, says Lorenzo Bonometto, a leading lagoon scientist who studied the issue for the Ministry of the Environment. "If you change and stir the lagoon, if you whip it up and ruin it, to the Philippine clams that is an advantage. In these circumstances, they are more productive than our native clams," though the native clams make better quality food.

"There has already been a collapse of the Philippine clams. Why? Because after an initial huge success exploiting the organic components of the bottom sediments" this kind of fishing destroyed this fertile layer and "for this reason numerous zones that were once productive are now sterile," says Bonometto. "This is robbery-as-fishing that has destroyed the environment, causing the disappearance of the traditional fishing.... It was madness, absolute idiocy" allowed by the Veneto regional government in "blatant contradiction" to the special laws, even though an alternative long-term strategy was available. "In the short term it won votes, which is how things work in Italy."

At its height, the clam harvesting madness could earn a man more in a day than he earned in a month at ordinary jobs. Attempts to impose regulation sparked ferocious protests blocking the Grand Canal and causing bloody strife that ended in a murder. Lagoon bed destruction, including loss due to construction of a waste pipeline dug through the lagoon and dredging canals, have also reduced clam-rich areas. Despite regulation, some illegal fishing continues alongside the 200-odd boats using non-traditional approved methods to catch clams, while only a handful of fishermen, especially those with family traditions, have kept up more diversified, environmentally friendly seasonal fishing practices.

No one doubts the effect on the lagoon. "It could be that this activity leads to increased erosion of the sediments. It would be absurd to say that's not so," says association head Vidal. But, "Often, the troubles of the lagoon are all blamed on fishermen, perhaps to draw attention away from other, graver, problems that perhaps suggest that others are responsible for the slaughter of the lagoon." Sometimes fishermen's nets are said to be blocking the flow, causing it to stagnate, while at other times the nets are praised for acting as buffers to the wave action of boats. "Today, what is happening in the lagoon is not the fault of clam fishing, even if we could say that clam fishing got out of hand, becoming too big and too intense, causing environmental problems, because in the end the resources were also diminished."

"If you look at the morphology of the lagoon, that is to say the natural form — the salt marshes and the mudflats, and the increasing depth of the water — then the lagoon is not well," ecologist Alberto Barausse explains as we chat under spreading trees of the University of Padua. "But then you need to decide what you mean by that. Certain habitats are disappearing and others are being born. The problem is that the salt marshes, a protected habitat, and very rare, are disappearing." As deeper water replaces marshes it threatens the wildlife, such as the small fish who live in the shallow water. This threatens species survival and artisanal fishermen who fished for these fish lose their way of life.

Part of the effort to prevent the lagoon from turning into blue sea includes the placement of end-to-end, sausage-shaped plastic nets of stones along the edges of the remaining salt marshes, where the mud meets the water. These orange nets of rubble, visible along many of the busier channels in the lagoon, dampen the waves from passing boats that constantly bash the barene.

Elsewhere, strategically placed "artificial salt marshes" are being created. Some are city-block-long loops a few steps across that are filled with light grey mud and bounded by closely driven tree-trunk piles sticking knee-high out of the water. Others as big as swimming pools have bean-shaped outlines, more like real marshes. Some have the tubes of stones forming the perimeter. Much of the 16 square kilometers of these artificial barriers take the force of waves from open water, performing an anti-erosion function and supporting bird life.

The mud and sand used to make artificial salt marshes are dredged from the lagoon shipping channels. Without periodic dredging they would be filled in by the shifting sediments. But not all the dredgings can be reused because so much sediment has been polluted by the old industries at Marghera. For this reason, a system to dispose of or treat the toxic mud and sand has been developed, with the un-reusable polluted portion placed in a "sealed" depository at the built-for-purpose Tresse island, which happens to be nearing saturation.

"Decades ago they used to throw the dredgings into the sea. Now, they have decided against dumping back in the sea, as it would be a waste of sediments," says Barausse. "Therefore, the mud is used to make artificial marshes" to help conserve the lagoon.

But the artificial marshes are not real marshes. The interaction between plant, soil and water is very complex, beyond the capacity of men to recreate in short periods, so "what they turn into will never be like the original, or at least not for decades." Sometimes marsh plants grow on them, often they are bare — in part because the builders fail to make them exactly the 0.2 to 0.4 meters above the water that salt marshes require. Many I saw showed few signs of life.

Bonometto is not against the artificial salt marshes but blames the lagoon administration for indulging "the convenience of the builders" and the heavy machinery they use for ignoring better and more refined methods that would give long-term results. "They are lost opportunities," he says.

Barausse suggests resources would be better used in supporting existing salt marshes in a preventative way, as was the case with the European-funded LIFE VIMINE pilot project around Burano, Mazzorbo and Torcello islands, which used natural materials and provided employment for the fishermen. Supported by the Burano fishing cooperative, the three-year project used less environmentally impactful bundles of tree branches instead of bags of stone around the salt marshes. These could be handled by manual labor instead of machinery. The project worked to educate boaters, promoted sustainable tourism and engaged the local community. It got good results in conserving an area of 3.53 square kilometers of the lagoon, but its funding ended in 2017.

"The lagoon still has the capacity to function as a lagoon and it is capable of responding with a certain efficiency to variation," says Bonometto. The VIMINE project showed that, "If instead of impeding and going against natural processes, we help them along, supporting them, the lagoon can still respond in an extraordinary way. Only, it continues to go in the opposite direction."

However, just recently, since the 1970s, in the central lagoon where the Canale dei Petroli was dredged and a deep crater has opened, the lagoon has "completely collapsed... directly as a result of profoundly wrong human intervention... that has lost the culture of management under the Republic," he observes. The collapse, taking place in the same years that the special laws were passed to save Venice and its lagoon, "has caused the loss of extensive areas, nearly to the point of irreversibility in terms of the structure and function that has maintained the lagoon since its origins," Bonometto has written.

The salt marshes, the shallows, the reed beds and the dunes of the lagoon put brakes on disturbances from waves, wind and sea. They purify the water and like forests, absorb carbon. The marshes now cover 8 percent of the lagoon, or 47 square kilometers, a fraction of the 170 square kilometers they covered in 1900. This equates to a 70 percent loss due to erosion and land reclamation. Much of what is left is enclosed in the walled-off areas of the lagoon called valli da pesca. "If there are no salt marshes... the whole system will be in crisis," Bonometto says.

The outlook for the lagoon affects lives too. Very few fishermen remain who carry on age-old ways of fishing in the lagoon. Roberto Vianello is one of them, and has seen an upheaval in his lifetime. "I am part of a family of fishermen and market gardeners back to time immemorial. I am fifty-one years old and, with my brother Claudio, we carry the trade forward, but we may be the last because my nephew is not interested in fishing," says Vianello, whose tanned, weather-worn face betrays his line of work. He talked about his job enthusiastically as he showed me his boats in the canal at Malamocco:

> I have a boat from my grandfather, made over fifty years ago. They don't build these boats anymore due to a lack of young people who want to do that sort of arduous work. We fish in the sea and in the lagoon for crabs, like *moeche*, soft-shell crabs, for smelts and the whole variety of seafood in the lagoon and sea: squid, bream and mullet, that sort of local fish, using a *tremaglio* net, which has three parts. We try to go out on the water in good weather, avoiding storms and wind, but at times we go out anyway, putting our lives in danger. But it's all worth the trouble as long as we can earn something.

But things have changed since he began fishing with his father in the 1970s.

> The lagoon we see today is not the same as it was thirty years ago. The motorboats go faster, damaging the banks. The water then was less agitated. There used to be 200 or 300 boats doing traditional fishing. Now we have maybe seven or eight. Not so many types of fish live in the lagoon either. There used to be about twenty-fives types, with the shellfish. Now we find, at most, ten. You used to get oysters, the flat type, really good ones, big scallops and lots of kinds of local shrimp. They were delicacies that you got in the local trattorie that specialized in lagoon fish — not anymore.
>
> New clams were seeded in the lagoon [the Philippine variety, in 1983] and later we had a new market. I used to fish for them, but it got to be trouble, so I gave it up. There was such chaos. The fishing industry nowadays thinks more about the God of Money than saving their own environment. If you take something today, it won't be there tomorrow. The aggressiveness is not just about the fishing, it's about the whole lagoon, the boats and everything.
>
> When fishing for clams became practically illegal, a lot of fishermen said fishing wasn't worth the trouble. You just get fines, ruin and debt, and then they take everything and you end up in jail. I have continued to fish because I am a bit obsessed and hardheaded. I want to make sure everything is in order, that there will be something left for future generations. If we succeed in creating

something for them, and if they are willing to do it, there it is. I am willing to teach what I know. But there is no one following after me. It makes me a bit sad.

I am on the wooden viewing platform atop Cason da Pesca Val Dogà, a lodge at the northernmost point of the wildlife-rich northern lagoon, and from here we have a panoramic view. The blue-gray water lightly ruffled by the wind opens onto the light brown salt marshes and behind them we can just make out the distant church tower on Torcello with Venice faintly in the mists beyond. A big man in a gray sweater who is the lodge caretaker, Franco Bonigolo, who with his wife Anna has run the remote lodge for four years, is regaling us with the tales of raising fish, hosting bird hunters in season and of fending off fish marauders in the vast valle da pesca, a closed-off salt marsh, behind the lodge.

The lagoon has thirty-two such valli da pesca, taking up a sixth of the lagoon. They date back to the earliest days of Venice, when they also served as fishing and hunting reserves. Historically, they were seen as part of the common property of Venice, but have since come to be regarded as private property — despite attempts to change that in court. The matter became a focus of public interest because the valli da pesca control the water flowing from rivers into the lagoon and could be relevant to flood control. Valle Dogà has gates allowing lagoon water to enter, but most of these enclosed marshes are cut off.

Today twenty-four of the valli da pesca raise fish, and all but two also cater to the business of bird hunting, where a single shelter amid the salt marshes from which to shoot birds — incredibly — can cost about €100,000 a season. Inside the lodge, the hunters dine around big oak tables and rest on the high-backed lounge chairs in front of hearths and wood-burning stoves. Winter is hunting season, when a valle da pesca makes most of its income.

The much riskier and less lucrative fish-farming activities involve seeding with tiny fingerlings and then corralling the mature fish at the end of the growing season with methods used since Roman times. The return varies according to the weather and with other vagaries, but fish raised in such natural surroundings are of better quality than those farmed industrially, such as those produced industrially on the other coast of the Adriatic, where much of the fish eaten in Venice comes from. When the bream, eels, mullet, sea bass and other types of fish are harvested from October to January in a big square pond near the lodge, thieves sometimes come in the dead of night to dip their nets. When Bonigolo gives chase they run away, sometimes leaving behind paths of plastic sheeting laid to drag the heavy nets full of fish over land and dyke to a waiting boat.

The curious visit too, sometimes, during the summer for planned tours. "But they want to see it in an hour!" exclaims Anna. Valle Dogà covers an area almost as big as the city of Venice.

With journalist Silvio Testa shadowing us in his sail and motor *topo pontà*, his partner, nature guide Luana Castelli and I are touring the northern lagoon in a *cofano*, a low sliver of a boat designed for hunting birds in the salt marshes. It is an arduous trip that we will take wholly by oar over three days, looping from Venice all the way to the furthermost northern end of the lagoon and back.

Leaving Venice, we push through the worst of the roughed-up water into the open lagoon. Near Sant'Erasmo island, we take our cofano with its minimal draft into calmer water by leaving the channel and traversing shallows full of anemone, seagrass and tiny crabs. Then we cut through the Canale Pordelio, a channel paralleling the seafront, a route followed by travelers in the Middle Ages when roads were scarce.

Near sunset, with gray mullet jumping around the boat and duck, heron, tern and ibis swooping past and roosting in the reeds, we see over the marshes a line of flamingos on the horizon, perhaps a thousand of them, of the lightest shade of pink. These birds, along with ducks, sleek black cormorants, long-legged avocet waders, slender egrets and magnificent swan, are among the species populating the lagoon. Flamingos arrived around the millennium from Tunisia, and now some 6,000 to 7,000 winter in the remote lagoon. The ibis, though a native of Africa, arrived from France, where it had escaped from captivity. The yellow-legged gull also came in recent decades — in part due to the habitat loss elsewhere (a story with a Venetian footnote to be told later in this book). All these arrivals are signs of humanity's influence on the biological shape of the birds' global habitat.

Nature guide Luana Castelli shows the author the salt marshes in the lagoon.

The first day of rowing takes us as far as Cavallino, a rural town on the lip of the mainland that wraps around the lagoon. There, hosted by Castelli's mother, Bruna, we enjoy a feast of pasta with local asparagus and fried onions, and hard-boiled eggs and cheese. We move on the next day, rowing northeast through the maze of salt marshes and out into the Palude Maggiore, one of the numerous waist-deep lakes within the lagoon. After rowing hard against the wind and current and coming across massive houseboats using restricted canals despite warning signs, we reach our destination, Cason Montiron, a ramshackle brick hut originally used by fishermen on a little island all of its own. Silvio makes curly pasta for supper, while Castelli shows me the *Salicornia* growing at the water's edge and we talk politics until deep into the night under a moon-lit sky.

Castelli is a founder of the Limosa Cooperative, set up in 1987 and dedicated to "sustainable and responsible" natural and cultural tourism in the lagoon. She gives tours by bicycle, on foot and by traditional boat. When weather intervenes, the tours use public transport, causing less pollution than the standard, high-speed tourist trip in a motorboat. "In Venice the need to find a solution to mass tourism is urgent," she says.

"We try to travel and organize small groups, so they visit places a few at a time and not in a hurry, making use of a network of people who live in the lagoon and on the islands so that tourist spending is distributed all over the area. This is responsible tourism, while mass tourism is all about profit, with earnings all going to the same places."

Tour participants include school children as young as four and adults as old as ninety from all over Italy and abroad, with each group following a tailored program. Children love animals. The adolescents need to get involved. A challenge is posed by overprotective Italian families. "These families, typically, are afraid that the children will get cold, dirty or wet if it rains when the children go into nature, because they all live inside houses, at school or in a car. We especially need to work on the adults, because the kids have fun when it rains. But that's not what the Italian mammas want!"

The tours include visits to historical sites, like Lazzaretto Nuovo, an island once used for plague quarantines; to Burano for trips with fishermen; to the dunes and forests on the beachfront islands like Lido; to see the migrating birds in the valli da pesca; and to farms on Sant'Erasmo, where the tourists can buy vegetables, helping to support the islanders' way of life. "It's important that agriculture survives there because only people who live on the island and engage in agriculture know how to defend these places, for example, against acqua alta, and to maintain the canals and streets," she says, in contrast with mass tourism which is supported by shops selling souvenirs and fast food but has no real connection to the place.

"If lots of people visit with environmental objectives, the place can be saved," she says. Most of the people who tour the lagoon know only Venice. "When I open the map, 100 percent of the people who come with me to the lagoon, who may have visited Venice before, declare, 'Oh, I didn't know that there was this lagoon!'" So she first explains that, "Without the lagoon, there would be no Venice — and also the other way round."

POET
EVOKES THE MOODS OF THE LAGOON
ISABELLA PANFIDO

Few have captured the spirit of the lagoon like Isabella Panfido, a friend from my school days in Venice who became a poet, translator and writer. She is the author of Lagunario, *translated into English as* Venice Noir: The Dark History of the Lagoons. *As we drank espressos out of tiny cups in her living room, surrounded by family heirlooms and pictures of Venice, I asked her about the lagoon.*

"Perhaps I will disappoint you but my relationship to the lagoon is above all intellectual. All I write is an elaboration of trips with my family around the lagoon in a motorboat when I was a girl. All my memories of the lagoon are linked to my childhood, almost always on Sundays, in the daytime, between ten in the morning and four in the afternoon, usually in the spring, but also sometimes in winter.

"I remember some winter fogs; it was like being inside a glass of milk. You had no sense of orientation, not even the possibility of getting any. The motorboat had a compass, so you could orient the boat. But, in all this, I remember the odors of the lagoon so well. The odors of the lagoon were very strong and you sense that they vary according to the depth; when there's little water, there's a lot of odor; with a lot of water, you sense instead the odor changing, and it's the water that has an odor, or what I call the odor of water, which is an odor of moving water. There's also the odor of still water, the odor of water that moves slowly and the odor of water that moves quickly — and they are all different. Italian has no words to describe the differences — you have to add adjectives. For example, for still water, in Venetian, you say *da freschin*, which is the odor of fish. In Italian you use the word *mucido*, which means 'stagnant', for water that is standing. As to the other odors, I don't know. I'd say the odor of fast-running water is like the odor of wind, perhaps. However, for me, for my sense of smell, they are each olfactory categories, each very distinct and very different.

"In fact I think that anyone who knows any route through the lagoon could do it blindfolded, just going by smell. I think they could. There are classes of distinct odors. If you go slowly in a flat-bottomed rowboat, which can enter the salt marshes, in the little channels the odors are so strong and they are really different. I have more recent memories, bonds, with the lagoon.

"I have gone on trips to lagoon areas where you usually don't go, in the most northern parts, where you can go only when the water is high, because if you go at low tide, you can't move. You get lost. It's a real labyrinth. On the map you might see what looks like a salt marsh, but it's not there, or it's not there anymore, and perhaps the color of the water looks less deep, and you have to go on a hunch, so you try to make out the sandy margins. What I want to say is that the lagoon is a living organism made of living material.

"But it is also one of the more changeable environments that humans can experience, because so many different elements interact and intrude. First of all, there's the water, obviously, then the sky, and according to the temperature and any change of weather, the color of the sky changes, and in reflection, the color of the water too. So that even with the same tide levels, the effect of the refraction of the light completely changes, for example, if there are clouds, if the sky's background is grey or blue.

"Another very important element is the flora, or vegetation, which changes, not only according to the seas, but also with the contribution of the silt from the rivers, and how much is removed or how much excess moves towards the sea. Because the more sediment there is, the easier it is for the barena to be covered with vegetation. The less silt there is, the more water there is.

"So the environment is in constant metamorphosis. And it is truly hard to recognize. That is, even if you always do the same trip, you can get lost! Because the points of reference you need in order to orient yourself are changing. So, it's a hugely fascinating place, because it's such a small space that is so adapted by man; there are so many abandoned houses and inhabited islands within one of the most intensely inhabited parts of Italy, one of the most intensely inhabited countries in Europe, which is part of one of the most densely inhabited continents.

"And yet the lagoon is also a space with the atmosphere of a huge desert, where the weather can be aggressive. I've never seen aggression in the lagoon, but unfortunately it exists; there are tornadoes and very rapid changes. People have died in the lagoon. It is above all disorientating, not just physically, but also psychologically. So the lagoon is many, many things, and we've not even mentioned animals. It's dense with animals. And we've not talked about people, but of course people live in the lagoon, although fewer and fewer of them. There's a crab fisherman that I write about — OK, so he's invented — but I have known a painter who lived in a boat, and he lived alone and he lived off the lagoon, with its atmosphere, its isolation, in this desert, in this wonder of nature that is the lagoon."

14

WOMEN

THEY DON'T ALLOW FEET TO BE PUT ON THEIR HEADS

Spes et amor grato carcere nos retinent
Hope and love keep us in this pleasant prison

—ENGRAVED AT THE CONVENTO DELLE VERGINI,
CONVENT OF THE VIRGINS, DATED MAY 2, 1557

Corte del Milion, the ancient place where Marco Polo lived in Venice, makes a good starting point for the story of Venetian women, my guide, Tiziana Plebani, assures me.

This small square, with a white stone wellhead at its center and bounded by ancient façades, is where Marco Polo lived on returning to Venice. Twenty-four years earlier, in 1271, and then just seventeen years old, he had set out on an odyssey with his father and uncle that would take them overland across Asia to China, and to the dazzling court of Emperor Kublai Khan, and beyond. No European had ever been there before and come back to tell the tale. It was still an age when the earth was thought to be flat; Polo's book describing the journey, *The Description of the World*, seemed unbelievable to readers at the time, and many questioned its truth. After his epic journey, he returned to Venice to live a quiet life as a merchant, raising a family and dying at age sixty-nine, reportedly murmuring on his deathbed, "I have only told the half of what I saw."

Marco Polo claimed to have traveled thousands of miles by donkey, horse and camel, braving bandits and man-eating beasts and scaling mountain passes so high that no birds flew there "because of the height and the cold." He had become a trusted envoy of the emperor of China, who sent him round the empire to places where he saw black rocks that burned, paper as valuable as gold, snakes with legs — and met a king with 500 wives. We find these things less fantastical today — for we understand that thin air over the Himalayas prevents birds from flying so high; that the Mongol conqueror of China, a man with a harem of wives, did indeed exist; that the burning rocks were none other than coal; and that the invaluable paper was, in fact, the first paper money.

But questions followed Marco Polo to his grave. After twenty-four years away, he had been given up for dead. He came home in the winter of 1295 at forty-one years of age, his father and uncle by then being nearly seventy. At first, no one recognized the travelers in shabby clothing. But all was well after Polo, who had assembled all their relatives, ripped off his outer rags to reveal Venetian clothing and sliced open a hidden pocket with a knife, allowing diamonds and precious stones to spill out. These were valued at a million — in gold, presumably — but the name Corte del Milion probably comes from Emilione, an ancestral family nickname. He was yet to have one more adventure. Soon after he returned, he joined the Venetian sea battles against its rival Genoa, was captured, and then spent 1298 in a Genoese dungeon, where he met the writer Rustichello, who helped pen his book. And this brings us back to the other point about Marco Polo: his book, also called *The Travels of Marco Polo*, was passed from hand to hand, each copy a handwritten manuscript. The eventual existence of 150 different versions of his account, some with passages rendered even more dramatic by Rustichello, made it harder to quell doubts about his story's veracity. Even today, some scholars ask whether he really went as far as China, accusing him of just gathering stories from merchants in Constantinople. Polo always insisted he was telling the truth.

It is the skepticism he faced and the fortune he left that makes for the starting point of this story about women. I am led to Corte del Milion by Plebani, an historian who paints a picture of Venetian women enjoying greater freedom and being able to speak more freely than their contemporaries around Europe. In her words, "*non si fanno mettere i piedi in testa*," literally, "They don't allow feet to be put on their heads." Or, to put it another way, "They don't allow themselves to be pushed around."

This image of the strong character of Venetian women has deep roots. It goes back to the ancient *Veneti*, occupants of what is now the modern-day region of Veneto, around Venice. The women of this seafaring people managed their households for long periods of the year while the men went to sea in ships, trading with people on the other side of the Adriatic. According to Lorenzo Calvelli, a professor in ancient history at Venice University, pre-Roman artifacts from the settlements in Padua and Este show that, "They had stronger, more prominent and more independent roles than other women. This is different from other parts of the ancient world" and he says that the trend continued into Roman, medieval and later times. Evidence is found in Roman inscriptions that record women's property rights, their building of funerary monuments and taking important roles in the economy and in society. "I don't even know if this parallel has ever been drawn, but to me it really resembles the status women would have in Venice in the Middle Ages and later," he suggests.

But to return to Corte del Milion. Plebani, a bright-eyed, salt and pepper-haired retired Venice University professor and author of books on women's role in history and, most recently, on Marco Polo's final will and testament, explains that on his death, Polo, having no male heirs, left everything to his daughter Fantina. In the year 1336, Fantina's spouse's family, the Bragadin, attempted to seize the inheritance, but she stood her ground, taking the case to the magistrates. They ruled in her favor. "The customary rights of women got looked after and Fantina Polo is evidence that the state provided for women and that women had what we call 'agency,'" says Plebani. "That is, they were effective in demanding their rights... it wasn't the custom in many other parts of Italy and elsewhere."

And, like the *Veneti*, later Venetian women managed their family affairs while staying at home, and could borrow and loan money and even invest in ships up until Venice began to lose its network of sea trade toward the end of the Republic. A third of families were headed by women, due, in part, to the high mortality of men during sea travel and in war. When Venetian women were widowed, they had rights established in Roman times to keep the dowry that they had brought to the marriage, Plebani says. Lots of extraordinary wills have survived, detailing how these women allocated their belongings and how they wanted to be buried.

One of them is that of Fantina Polo. The actual house where the Polo family lived was burned down, and none of their physical possessions survived. But Plebani, who spent years researching the Polo legacy, says the inventory in her will lists among the goods passed down to her a gold *paiza*, or passport, given to Marco Polo by the Mongolian emperor, along with deer musk, rhubarb, the horn of an animal believed to have aphrodisiac qualities, and a Mongol headdress studded with jewels. "These are things that could only have come from China and they correspond to Marco Polo's own descriptions," says Plebani, exasperated by Polo doubters, who persist to the present day.

We move on to Castelletto, an area behind the market in Rialto and where is found the Ponte delle Tette, the Bridge of Tits, which for a century from the mid-1300s served as the city's officially sanctioned red-light district. As a port, Venice always supported a vibrant sex trade. The government, concerned at the time about the extent of homosexuality among men who spent long periods at sea, established this area for prostitutes. Dressed in red and yellow, the women would stand in windows and doorways, breasts uncovered and legs exposed, much as prostitutes do to this day in the red-light districts of Amsterdam and other cities. Later, prostitution became more dispersed throughout Venice.

From the 1500s, a higher class of prostitutes became a feature of Venetian life. These women, such as the poet Veronica Franco, were cultured courtesans who entertained their clients at dinner with music, song and by reciting poetry. The prostitutes created their own associations, *scuolette*, smaller versions of the great scuola welfare societies that attended to the needs of Venetians. They lived together in apartments and took care of one another. Prostitution, Plebani says, "could be a choice that was more like freedom than a marriage and, perhaps, allowed them to be with men they liked." She adds that although men and women did socialize in Venice at balls and festivals, possibly more than elsewhere, sexual freedom "was allowed for men before and after marriage, but not for women. No different from our age!"

Prostitution greatly expanded in the seventeenth and eighteenth centuries, in part in response to the demands of European Grand Tour visitors, many of whom came to the city as much for sex as for culture. This was so especially during the Carnival, the duration of which was extended to six months to encourage the growing trade. Thomas Coryat estimated in 1608 that "at least 20,000" prostitutes worked in Venice while Venetian diarist Marin Sanudo had noted a figure of 11,654 prostitutes in 1509, which would be about 10 percent of the population, similar to the number in Rome at the time. The trade was closely controlled and taxed by the authorities, for whom it became a key source of revenue, in part because of the decline in commerce as Venice's empire fell away after 1500.

In the seventeenth and eighteenth centuries the sex trade also attracted foreign men who wanted to escape oppressive laws against sodomy in places like Germany and England. Venice had a reputation for tolerance as well as licentiousness. As Charles Baldwyn wrote in 1712, "...their whole city may well be term'd the Brothell house of Europe, and I dare say virtue was never so out of countenance or vice so encouraged in any part of the World and I believe not in any age as at this time in Venice."

This reputation has stayed with Venice, even after the Republic ended in 1797, but Plebani debunks the focus that many guidebooks and accounts of the city place on the titillating aspects of the Venetian past. "But it was the same everywhere. Paris had a huge number, as did Rome. Prostitution was just one of women's occupations at the time."

"Come along to the Frari church. I want you to see a beautiful portrait by Paolo Veneziano, of the doge and the *dogaressa*, the wife of the doge, with the Virgin Mary," Plebani tells me.

We stand in a side chamber of the soaring fourteenth-century church, before an arch framing a medieval painting with a flat, gilded background. In the center, the Virgin, in a deep blue shawl, sits with a haloed baby Jesus on her lap. The chubby infant talks with the robed and crowned Doge Francesco Dandolo who is kneeling in prayer. Saint Francis of Assisi urges the doge on from behind. The Virgin herself looks toward the doge's wife, the Dogaressa Elisabetta Contarini, shown in the gown of a devotee. Contarini kneels before the Virgin in prayer, flanked by Saint Elizabeth of Hungary, symbol of charity.

This 1339 painting, using the symbols of the medieval cult of the Virgin Mary, shows that the state is represented not just by the doge, but the doge in alliance with his dogaressa, a relationship that strikingly illustrates her role at the heart of political power. Her position is nothing like that of the queens in England, but prominent in comparison to other states. Not only did the dogaressa have her own installation ceremony and her own contract with the state, she also served as patron of the scuola charities and was important in the family alliances behind the real power of the state.

Among the lower classes, marriage was seen primarily as a religiously sanctioned tie between man, wife and offspring. For aristocratic families, it also served to manage inheritances, patronage and political alliances. Particularly after the 1500s, with the decline of the seagoing empire, aristocrats used arranged marriage to concentrate inherited wealth, allowing only the first son to marry. Unmarried offspring, typically, were sent to convents and monasteries — not always voluntarily. By the 1600s, the city had more than fifty nunneries, many on lagoon islands, accommodating some 3,000 nuns, and they could be quite comfortable, even elegant places to live, like the aristocratic San Zaccaria. Women ran them. They were given some education, and managed the businesses of the convents, such as vineyards and salt works, while maintaining contact with the outside world and even putting on plays and concerts.

This was not to last. With the advent of Protestantism, nunneries in Venice suffered a backlash. The German priest Martin Luther, in his sixteenth-century revolt against the Catholic Church, saw all monasteries and convents as corrupt, and, in reaction, the Catholic Church cracked down, imposing a practice called "closure" that limited residents' access to books, outside contact and freedoms. Nunneries were supposed to be bastions of chastity and prayer, providing a counterbalance to the worldliness outside, but now, on any pretext, they were lambasted as bordellos where, as wrote diarist Girolamo Priuli, "the most grave sins of these whoring nuns" were bringing down God's wrath onto the declining Venetian state. In fact, cases of sexual transgressions were rare, but the accusations since that time have only served to heighten Venice's reputation for licentiousness.

In the tree-shaded Campiello dei Squelini, a small square with a bookstore in one corner and walled garden opposite, Plebani pauses to describe Venetian women who, along with a few other noted figures in England and France, became the first European voices of feminism.

Among the Venetian voices of the late sixteenth and early seventeenth centuries was Lucrezia Marinelli, who lived near the square. She penned polemical treatises against the reigning ideas of Aristotle, who saw women as imperfect men, and published *The Nobility and Excellence of Women* and *The Defects and Vices of Men*, along with her own epic poetry and plays around 1600. Meanwhile, the self-taught Arcangela Tarabotti opposed the ideas behind forced closure in nunneries. She entered the Sant'Anna nunnery at age ten and published posthumously *Paternal Tyranny*. And last but not least, there was Moderata Fonte, also known as Modesta Pozzo, who had been a child prodigy, and published *The Worth of Women*, along with plays and poetry. The

Jewish Sara Copia Sullam wrote poetry and invited to her home both Christian and Jewish intellectuals and artists.

Why were these voices heard in Venice? I ask Plebani.

"Women had it better [here] than elsewhere. But the mentality of the times was part medieval and part modern, so it was still patriarchal.... It was not easy going for women, but they had more chance to publish than elsewhere because Venice was a center for printing and the city protected, to some extent, heretics," who otherwise would have been burned at the stake had they gone to Rome, Plebani says.

That relative freedom in Venice also gave rise to opportunities for women as early as the 1500s when they worked in trades normally limited to men. Woman in street theater in that era were still considered prostitutes, but by 1600, as Venice became the first to commercialize drama and opera, performing plays and opera in theaters, the status of women rose. They could have well-paid careers — without the taint of prostitution — as did opera singer Anna Renzi and composers Barbara Strozzi and Antonia Padoani Bembo. In the eighteenth century, women began to work in the cafés and shops of the city.

They also became artists. Plebani takes our whirlwind journey through Venice's history of feminism to a last stop at the fourteenth-century San Pantalon church, a gem of a building behind a plain brick façade which inside holds a neck-craning, jaw-dropping, three-dimensional ceiling fresco of the life and martyrdom of Saint Pantalon by Gian Antonio Fumiani.

But we have come inside to look at a less imposing, but nevertheless intriguing, oil painting on the wall of the sacristy. It depicts Eliezer sitting in front of a well in Mesopotamia with curious camels in the background and a robed Rebecca accepting his gifts of jewels. This striking picture of the Bible story of the search for a wife for Isaac, painted by Elisabetta Lazzarini, is an example of the many works by female artists that have tended to be overlooked. Most of these women artists were sisters or daughters of noted artists. In this case, Elisabetta was the sister of the better known Gregorio Lazzarini, who trained Tiepolo. She is among the less celebrated but brilliant sixteenth- to eighteenth-century female painters such as Marietta Robusti, Giulia Lama and Rosalba Carriera.

Venetian women went on, in the centuries after the Republic, to break into new trades and industries. From the late eighteenth century they took part in art and education, even playing a role in Venice's abortive uprising of 1848. Later, in the 1930s and 1940s, they broke through entry barriers at the universities, got the vote in 1946, and went on to fight against violence against women and campaign for the environment. From medieval times, Venetian women competed in rowing races on an equal footing with men and won the same prizes, something unique in Europe, or the world — but not until 2010 did Giorgia Boscolo become the first woman to become a *gondoliera*!

I bid a grateful *arrivederci* to Plebani and picked up the contemporary story of Venetian women with Chiara Curto, a blonde with a broad smile, who wears a boater hat with a blue ribbon and the striped shirt of her profession as a *sandolista*, someone who rows a sandolo for the tourists. She was not eager at first to speak to me as I was yet another journalist interested in her because she is a rare female in a job dominated by men. But she relented when I said I only wanted to hear her experience in dealing with journalists.

> At the beginning of my career as a sandolista, I was happy to share my experience with the news media, because, anyway, naively, I thought only of telling about my experience, nothing else. In reality, I realized quickly that the various people who interviewed me had their own idea of what I should say. What I actually said was of little importance to them because my words were inserted into a narrative that already existed but which did not reflect, in the end, the reality of what I was saying. I was simply relating my experience, my enthusiasm, my passion for rowing, and so on. But my words were made part of the issue of gender equality, which was not the way I told the story.
>
> My experience, contrary to what I have understood the media wants me to express, is very positive. My colleagues have always been supportive. They help, teach and have patience with whoever begins a new job. Anyway, it was not easy the first day, not even the first month, or for that matter the first year. Not for anyone! And probably that's true for all my colleagues.

> The last time I was in the press was in an article a few months ago in which the journalist pointed to me as the only one wearing the striped shirt of a gondolier who had been downgraded to row a sandolo. The gondola is the symbol of Venice, and it's the more elaborate boat, but for me to row a sandolo is to be one of the gondoliers and I don't in any way feel downgraded. I didn't even try to get the authorization to operate a gondola. I took the test for the sandolo.
>
> They were looking for a heroine! They looked for someone who, against all the odds, took her own road. They wanted a superwoman. They looked for the exception. And that's not me at all. If you want to support a type of person in some kind of role, beyond whether they are male or female, there is no need to make them special. That is, you need to make them normal, integrated into society, as women are in reality. I am not portrayed in that way in the article. And that's not respectful in relation to my colleagues and the women who, in future, will do various jobs that are unusual for their sex. Equality means normality, not news.

Among other Venetian women breaking through glass ceilings is Monica Scarpa, who grew up in Venice and serves as CEO of SAVE, the company that runs the fast-growing Venice and Treviso airports. She has accomplished what many aspire to, having both a successful career and a family. She has two children. "Anyone who is a parent must reconcile work life with family life as best they can," she says in remarks to a university group. "Within the family, it is no longer the role of the woman to look after the children and the man to work, but more like a partnership, a 'joint venture,' in which each has to make a contribution." And if a woman should decide not to pursue a career, and stay with her children, that, she believes, is equally valid.

I ask her how the role of women at work and at home compared to those in other countries.

"Italian women continue to have, in some ways, little support. So, in terms of having structures in place to support women and families and enable them to undertake, with peace of mind, a regular job, we are much behind as a country. This is for sure," she says. In terms of parental leave for childbirth, UNICEF ranks Italy twenty-fourth among the rich countries, behind many of the northern European countries and Japan, but above the UK and the United States.

I also spoke with women from different generations who are long-time family friends: Alberta Basaglia, who grew up in the 1950s, and my assistant Sofia Bareato, born in the 1990s. Basaglia, a psychologist who once ran Venice's youth services and directed an advisory center for women, has long dealt with violence and discrimination against women. She is the daughter of Franco Basaglia, the reformer of Italy's mental institutions. Bareato, a recent graduate in Chinese language from Venice University, is now a high school teacher of Chinese. They had complementary things to say.

Bareato, who grew up in Padua, sees herself as following in the footsteps of generations who have experienced major change. She reeled off the story of some of the women in her family, starting with her housewife, stay-at-home grandmothers, as we made our way one day to the train station.

> For the generation of my own mother, who was born in 1954, things were already very different. She was twenty in 1974, the age of sexual liberation, of the mini-skirt. Most of the women of her generation worked and went to university.
>
> In my generation, in the north of Italy, it's rare now for women not to work. Many study. But problems remain. For example, we still lack the social safeguards around maternity, and in this sense we are discriminated against. Perhaps because of the legacy of Christian-Catholic thinking, we have the idea that the mother has to stay with her children. Abroad, people seem to believe Italian mothers are like hyper-protective hens looking after their brood. In Italy, mothers have lots more responsibilities within the family than the fathers do.
>
> As far as young single people are concerned, I don't see big differences in lifestyle, other than more personal freedom to go out in the evening. As for men my age, I have friends with brothers, and clearly there is a disparity in how they are treated. The girls at home are expected to do more housework, while parents are more permissive with boys, and sometimes really indulgent. Boys get more freedom to go out because they are seen as better able

> to defend themselves, and girls are more liable to be hurt. And then there's the matter of divorce. In my grandparents' generation, some would refuse to divorce, no matter how they suffered in marriage, and those that did divorce were seen as aliens by the society around them.
>
> It has to do with religion. The roots of the Catholic Church run deep, even today in a lot of people's minds. My grandma still watches the Mass in the Vatican on TV every Sunday, but among us young people — well, at least those who go to university — very few are believers. It's a real rarity to find someone who says, 'I believe and go to church.' And in the workplace, my friends have experienced job interviews in which they have been asked, 'Do you have a boyfriend?' If you have one, of course, you might have a baby, and go on maternity leave. So being women counts against us in employment when it is already hard to get a job. But in general, things have gotten better. Then there are incidents, up-skirting with a mobile phone, for instance. You really feel bad when that happens, and it's difficult to believe, but you have a sense of guilt, almost instinctive. Even when women are subjected to violence many never go to the police because they are ashamed, and they are asking themselves if their dress was too short. What did they do wrong?

Basaglia, a Venetian in her sixties, is also the co-author of a recent novel about two Venetian girls growing up in Venice. She told me:

> At present, the situation for Italians is difficult — or for people considered 'different,' in which I include women — these are hard times. The same things continue as ever. Women study more, do better, and then at work they are passed over for management jobs in favor of men, and when they have children they are pushed back. At the moment it's hard to separate the challenges of women from those of other people with differences, such as immigrants, and even among immigrants women come off worse. And they are talking about new laws, say on abortion, things that we thought had been settled. All family law, in a separation or for child protection, has been put back on the table, while childcare becomes ever more costly. When there's a crisis the most vulnerable suffer the consequences. It's an ugly situation, in general, all linked to politics.

The women's story in Venice continues, but as part of that of other Italian women. The only thing that might set Venice apart is the city itself, where the closeness to nature, especially to the rise and fall of the tides, heightens one's awareness.

In everyone's imagination, all the loves of us Venetian women have taken place on boats in the lagoon and going to the seaside at night. You only do these things in Venice, and, for sure, the sunsets in the lagoon are something, like Tintoretto pictures, so it's a city that feels romantic like a box of chocolates. It's a sweet city, a place open to helping you feel feelings, isn't it? When you walk on the street, you can hear your own footsteps and those of others, which doesn't happen so much elsewhere. You might even recognize someone from the sounds of their steps. Venice is beautiful. At the same time, it's part of another world and more down to earth. It's strange, beautiful and contradictory.

ARCHIVIST
BEHIND THE HONEST COURTESAN
ALESSANDRA SCHIAVON

My friend from school, Alessandra Schiavon, now works in the trove of priceless documents at the Venetian archives. She told me about how she rediscovered the inspirational story of Veronica Franco, a key figure in the history of women in Venice.

Like a sleuth, the twenty-two-year-old Venetian Alessandra Schiavon has searched long and hard through the voluminous archives of the Republic of Venice, tracing one lead after another, stepping closer and closer to her quarry. Now she had before her the packet of folders dated 1580 that she had been seeking, and, with her heart racing, she gingerly opened the handwritten parchment to find before her the treasure — the story of a woman who dared to fight for her freedom in a world of superstition and oppression.

It was 1976, and Schiavon, a whirlwind of energy, was then a graduate student. She had before her an account of an interrogation that would ultimately attract global attention to the Venetian courtesan-poet Veronica Franco. It was key to understanding how Franco stood up to accusations of heresy by the Catholic Inquisition and also gave a window into the thoughts and life of a woman who would forever after be recognized for her feminism, shrewdness in business, wit and erudition.

The document became the basis for the acclaimed 1992 book on Franco, Margaret Rosenthal's *The Honest Courtesan*, and Marshall Herskovitz's 1998 film *Dangerous Beauty*. No one had glimpsed those pages since the 1800s, when historian Giuseppe Tassini noted their existence. The rediscovery opened the public's eyes to the sixteenth-century world of Franco, giving Schiavon what she needed for her thesis and adding to Franco's published poetry and a collection of letters.

Schiavon was working at the Archives of the State, a brick-faced, three-story edifice that had begun as a Franciscan monastery in the thirteenth century, but had been taken over in 1815 as a storage place for the centuries of carefully preserved documents about Venice. "I was petrified when I entered. Students were treated with diffidence, and they had to work alone. In the archive, no one spoke in a loud voice. It was a place where everyone moved as if they were officiating at a religious rite," she says. Unfazed, she examined documents day after day that had to be brought to the reading area from the shelves in the archive, following traces of Franco's life from birth registrations to wills. And then she found the documents about the case made against Franco by the Catholic Inquisition.

The documents were a scribe's record of what was said at the 1580 tribunal at which Franco was tried for heresy, part of the Church's crackdown triggered by the advent of Protestantism. Franco's "maid servant, her son's teacher, told the tribunal that Franco disrespected the sacraments by not eating fish instead of meat on Friday, not going to church on Sunday and mixing with Germans — who were by definition Lutherans, that is to say, she was close to the world of heresy — which was a very dangerous accusation. In fact, she was very able in speaking out, and responded confidently," says Schiavon. Franco was able to explain that she ate meat when giving birth or unwell, which was allowed, and no, she did not cast spells, as she was not a witch, and in general she responded cleverly to the accusations. The prosecutors' questions and her answers were all duly written down by the unnamed scribe — and in the end she was let off.

All this went into the graduate thesis in which Schiavon told the story of Franco, who was born into a citizen, that is non-noble, family. She was listed in the era's official catalogue of Venetian courtesans, including her prices — two *scudi* — and lived most probably on Campo Santa Maria Formosa. Her clients included Henry III, the king of France, and many important personages and literati. What is thought to be her portrait, attributed to Jacopo Tintoretto, was painted in 1575. A volume of her poetry and a collection of letters was published five years later.

In some ways, Franco lived more freely than other Venetian women, but when asked by a mother if her daughter should follow in Franco's footsteps, Franco advised against it, saying that while many were forced by poverty into her profession, prostitution was "...to eat with another's mouth, sleep with another's eyes, move according to another's will...." She is thought to have built a refuge for retired and impoverished prostitutes.

For Schiavon, the story did not end with her thesis. She shared her research with Margaret Rosenthal and key parts of the film later based on Rosenthal's book showed the tribunal — albeit in dramatized form and with un-historical elements. As it happened, Schiavon got a position in the archives and has worked there ever since. She has put together many exhibitions of archival documents, including three on the conditions of women in Venice in the Middle Ages and Renaissance, and one in the Doge's Palace on the peace treaties of Europe. She rediscovered the last will and testament of Marco Polo and, recognizing its significance, brought it to light through her writing and presentations. Now, having passed thirty-nine years at the archives, she says she still gets up in the morning happy to go back. "This work is the most wonderful job in the world!"

15

TIDES

TROUBLED DAMS AGAINST A RISING SEA

> *"In the long term, if not the short, 'managed retreat' is our only option. The sea always wins in the end."*
>
> —HUGH ALDERSEY-WILLIAMS
> IN *TIDE: THE SCIENCE AND LORE OF THE GREATEST FORCE ON EARTH*

Some things happen unexpectedly and others take on contours in retrospect. So I found, when I looked back at my Venice diary of 2018, at a certain dark and stormy night in Venice:

> *1 October: Went home and cooked shrimps and pasta for supper. The storm was really blowing by the time I got to the flat, and inside the wind whistled from an invisible gap behind the radiator. The rain beat down against the window for hours. At night, however, no mosquitos attacked.*
>
> *2 October: Went to see Alvise Papa…* [head of Centro Maree, the tide monitoring center] *The nerve center resembled a B-movie control room, but in a palace, with people staring intently at an array of computer monitors. Papa mentioned that last night's wind coincided with a low 'astronomical' tide, that is the tide that is just due to the pull of the moon and sun. But the wind pushed up the actual tide by another 0.49 meters. He showed me a tide chart and pointed to a peak a week later, saying that if the wind had come at that point, with 'astronomical' tide at 0.81 meters, the extra 0.49 meters from the wind would have pushed the actual tide level up to 1.3 meters, triggering the acqua alta siren! It would have been a 'disaster,' he says. So much about acqua alta is happenstance!*
>
> *28 October: It happened today. The first big acqua alta of the year, with a siren at 09.17, followed by two steady tones. One tone is for 1.1 meters, two 1.2 meters, three 1.3 meters and four 1.4 meters or more. The tidal chart says the level should peak just after noon. At 12.30 I put on my green rubber boots. Stepping out along the canals, I found the water above my ankles and immediately had to re-learn how to walk. Walking at normal speed causes the water to splash over your*

boots and onto your legs. I slowed down, finding I also needed to watch out for little waves from the boats on the canal which rode up right over the submerged pavement.

Tourists used bin bags or fluorescent pink plastic booties over their shoes, walked barefoot or just got their shoes wet. Judging by the laughs and picture taking, high water looked fun, but not for the tourists who held heavy suitcases to their chests to keep them dry as they walked. One woman, who had given up, was dragging hers through the water. They looked really stressed. People carried small dogs and children while a man hefted an old woman onto one of the raised board walkways set up for pedestrians. Many shops are open, some with thigh-high 'flood' barriers at the door, even as clerks mop up, pushing water out with wiper blades on sticks or setting up pumps to spew water back out onto the street. In a pizzeria, waiters shuffling through the water served customers.

By the time I got to Piazza San Marco hip-booted policemen urged people on the walkways to move along and not to stop for selfies. The water in the square was too high for my boots, nearly knee high, so it spilled over the top and poured in. Cold. The crowd in the square seemed to be enjoying the spectacle, even when it started to rain. Someone chanted 'Mose! Mose!' and indeed the dam gates would have been raised for acqua alta this high.

29 October: As I lay in bed early in the morning I heard a siren and counted after it the following tones, one — two — three — four! That meant acqua alta today is higher than yesterday. Schools are closed. People are advised to stay home and hospitals are on alert. I had enough of traipsing around with cold feet yesterday (and my boots are still soaking wet) so will stay home, intrepid adventurer that I am. The water rose to 1.56 meters at 14.20, which is waist high in the worst affected areas. 75 percent of the city was flooded. As usual, after a few hours the tide receded and it all drained away. A friend sent a picture of someone swimming in Piazza San Marco, which had been closed off. Venice last had a peak over 1.4 meters in 2013. Today's was the fifth highest on record, 0.34 meters short of 1966.

Sadly, the postscript is worse. These events have now paled in the face of a new record flood recorded on November 12, 2019, of 1.87 meters, the highest in fifty years, flooding 85 percent of the city. Lesser record highs hit in the following days and the following month. The quick succession multiplied the shock, but most particularly the first acqua alta caused harm, with the St. Mark's Basilica damaged, a man who tried to restart a water pump killed by electrocution, and another found dead in his home. The mayor put the cost of the first and subsequent 2019 floods at over one billion euros, and other acque alte will come, as will exceptionally low tides, one of which occurred just two months later, leaving canals almost dry and crippling transport in the city. The extended flooding and tidal extremes have disheartened many among the city's depleted population.

People crossing Piazza San Marco on November 12, 2019, when the second highest acqua alta on record hit Venice.

"In Venice we have lived through a difficult period, one that has been dramatic for many people who have had acqua alta in their homes and shops. There was also damage in the islands of the lagoon and it will take a lot of time to repair everything," nature guide Luana Castelli wrote to me afterwards. "Some problems can't be resolved. When acqua alta invades for such long periods, the salt water permeates the walls of the houses and monuments. This experience has left a new feeling among many Venetians: that there is no future for Venice."

Puzzling over tides goes back to the dawn of science and, specifically, to the visit of physicist Galileo Galilei to Venice in 1592. With what he learned during his spring stay, he thought he had explained the tides — but he got it only partly right. In modern tide tables, between sixty to a hundred factors are considered, with the main ones being the gravitational pulls of the sun and moon. Yet in the twenty-first century we still struggle to master the tides and oceans, so it's helpful to keep in mind their vast complexity.

The 1966 tidal disaster that led to Italy's special laws for Venice launched decades of studies and planning that opened up a €13 billion tap of funding that would go into housing refurbishment, art restoration and a two-part program to save the lagoon. One part dealt with acqua alta up to 1.1 meters by bolstering the shock-absorbing effect of salt marshes and sea fronts while building smaller barriers and localized adaptations in Venice and on other islands. The other part, for flooding over 1.1 meters, when the sirens sound, envisioned massive dams at the three openings between the lagoon and the Adriatic Sea. These barriers were dubbed *Mose*, a strained acronym for *MO*dulo *S*perimentale *E*lettromeccanico (Experimental Electromechanical Module).

The word "experimental" was included in the barriers' name in a nod to the law's requirement that the solution be "gradual, experimental and reversible." This was because solutions to managing the lagoon have historically been found with an element of trial and error. In reality, however, the massive, bright yellow, semi-submerged barriers that are now under construction are built on a foundation of millions of tons of concrete fixed with enormous piles that have been driven into the sea floor, leaving no room for changing of minds. Mose also is thought of as referring to the biblical Moses who held back the tides in Egypt allowing the Jews to escape the Pharaoh — which sets expectations rather high. So, the naming has not been a great boon and already the €5.5 billion sea gates are decades behind the original schedule and three times over the estimated cost.

Announced in 1988 and actually started in 2003, the construction was set back after an enormous corruption scandal broke in 2014 — the largest in Italian history — and is only now stuttering forward toward an expected December 31, 2021 completion (though the dams may be used in emergencies before then). When the dams are ready, and a way to fund their €100 million annual maintenance bill is found, they then face their real test: whether they are up to the job and — while they were successfully deployed for the first time as an emergency measure on October 3, 2020, keeping the city dry in the face a 1.2 meter tide — serious doubts have been raised.

The record acque alte gave Venetians a scare.

The subject came up at dinner at the flat of my friends Andrea Pavanini and Francesca Paruzzolo. Over a glass of their Cabernet del Tocco, Francesca laughingly noted how people misunderstand the tide figures. "Even with 1.94 meters in 1966 the water only came to there," she says, gesturing to her midriff. The figure is measured not from street level but from the zero-tide mark found below street level at the base of the Punta della Dogana on the bacino. The depth figure makes it seem to come over the tops of heads. Andrea says Venetians feel other people don't understand how residents take acqua alta in stride. "Anything up to 1.40 meters is mainly an inconvenience and people can don their boots and get on with life."

By and large, in the aftermath of 1966, Venice removed anything that might be damaged by floods from the vulnerable ground floors. Habitation there is now restricted (though tourist rentals often flout the rules) and wiring and heating have been raised above flood levels. Now most acque alte cause very little damage. The "inconvenience" starts at 0.8 meters, when Piazza San Marco, one of the lowest points in the city, begins to flood. A gradual reduction of city services begins from 0.95 meters. Ambulances and fire boats can't get under certain bridges and have to be redistributed around the city to get to calls on time. The vaporetti have to change routes. Over 1.3 meters, many of the boardwalks have to be removed or they would float away.

"Above that, at 1.5 meters, is when it gets to be a disaster," says Andrea. "What made the other day [the record flood of October 28, 2018] spooky was that, as with the inundation in 1966, the water did not go down between the peaks of tide." The peak came on the second day, meaning wind had not allowed the first tide to ebb, so the second day was adding to the levels of the day before. That's just how the catastrophic record of 1.94 meters came about in 1966, flooding 96 percent of the city.

Consequences emerge both from the level of the water and from the frequency of these events — and both are rising.

This came across clearly when I poured over charts with Alvise Papa during my earlier visit to Centro Maree, set up in 1981 to provide a formal acqua alta warning system.

He answered the question that seems to have captured the public's attention worldwide: Is Venice sinking?

"Yes." Venice is definitely sinking, albeit very, very slowly, and it has been sinking for a long, long time, as far back as records go, which is 1872, and probably further.

Venice has subsided by 0.33 to 0.34 meters in the past 150 years. A small part of the drop is due to natural geological changes in the earth's surface. The greater part has been caused by man in the last century, and mostly from groundwater extraction from 6,000 wells used by industry and agriculture from the 1950s to 1970s. In the nearby Po River Delta, gas drilling from platforms on the Adriatic also caused subsidence. In 1971, most but not all wells were closed, and that slowed subsidence to two millimeters a year, but another force has picked up that is much more threatening: sea level rise.

This global phenomenon caused by the excess of greenhouse gases affects coastlines inhabited by a billion people worldwide. The average sea level rise predicted by the IPCC, the United Nations body for assessing climate change, is at 0.43 meters by the end of the century and it could be as high as a meter or more.

Although exceptional tides, even over two meters, have been reported as far back as the 15th century, the added effects of subsidence, climate change and canal digging over the last century or so are creating new, possibly unsustainable, stresses on the lagoon barriers and the coming Mose dam. Already, higher water levels progressively cause decay in Venice's aging walls, crumbling the bricks and rusting the ties that hold up the buildings. The effect of higher water is also aggravated by lagoon erosion — a single millimeter sea level rise can be related to erosion reaching up to a meter inland. While the tides took 1.5 to 2 hours to enter a century ago, now they enter in an hour. With the lagoon an average of 1.5 meters deep, twice what it was, the tides not only rise higher, they move faster and in greater volume on entering and leaving.

The instances of acque alte have also been rising since the last century; the number of floods over 1.1 meters has doubled since the 1960s due not only to subsidence and sea level rise, but because of increases in wind, waves and storm related to the climate crisis. Now Venice has acqua alta about sixty-six times a year over 0.8 meters, but by 2060 that will be 435, and events over 1.1 meters will rise from the current 5 to 65. But as with all nature, no simple predictions are possible. In 2009, Venice had 203 events of over 0.8 meters while in 2011, just 79 or 80. Such variations will continue.

The tide is what keeps the lagoon healthy. "Venice is in direct relation with the water because it's constructed in the middle of the water and for that reason the evolution of the tides has a much greater importance than in other coastal cities," says Papa. The Center makes predictions ten days into the future, sounds sirens three hours before the event and issues updates by text message as often as hourly.

It's easy to overlook the extensive preventative measures for minor flooding, below 1.1 meters, around the lagoon. To new eyes they fit right into the scenery.

Traveling along Lido and Pellestrina to Chioggia with family members during my 2018 visit, we focused on the fishing boats, the sun's rays sparkling on the lagoon's surface, and not least, some of the freshest fish, sea bass, sea bream, langoustine, mussels and clams I can ever remember enjoying — all caught that morning in the lagoon and sea. To people who come from landlocked places, such bounty is ever more rare. I did also notice, as we wandered through the picturesque streets of the ancient town of Malamocco on Lido and San Pietro in Volta on

Pellestrina, where new seawalls and raised walkways had been built for tides of up to 1.7 or 1.8 meters.

On Lido and Pellestrina, we sat at the seaside, looking over jetties and the tons of new sand added to create the 56 kilometers of beaches to resist Adriatic onslaughts. The beaches also promote tourism. Dunes have been reconstructed and fortified with dune grasses to defend against winds. At the Alberoni dunes on the southern end of Lido, we wandered for hours through fragrant pine trees, where the needles from the evergreens carpeted the path of the sandy ground, and we emerged at the far end at one of the long concrete walls of the Malamocco port opening. We looked out across the water and watched as, one after another, tankers and merchant ships, some stacked high with colorful container boxes, slowly entered and exited the lagoon on their way to Port Marghera.

In a canal in the fishing town of Chioggia, on the other side of the opening, we took pictures in front of a "baby Mose" barrier installed inconspicuously to prevent floods of up to 1.3 meters. These are among the minor works all over the lagoon, including Piazza San Marco where, under the paving, one-way flood prevention drains have been installed to hold back acqua alta of up to 1.1 meters.

But these defenses were already completed decades ago. Since then Mose has drawn all the attention and most of the money.

"The challenge," says Dario Berti, the lead mechanical plant engineer on Mose until 2017, "was this: to have a system that could intervene in the exchange between the sea and the lagoon with minimal impact, but only those over a certain level, because those below should be allowed to come and go" and the dams needed to have a minimal impact on the scenery at the ports and on the lagoon.

Solutions like ones in Rotterdam (two moveable storm-surge barriers, each a half-moon shape almost as big as the Eiffel Tower), and the Thames River Barrier (ten gates, each as high as a five-story building), both huge and visible, "would have too much environmental impact in this context," including destroying much of the natural dune reserves along the coastline, he says.

The solution for Venice, selected after decades of con-troversy from a number of interesting alternatives, would be of unprecedented design:

separate dams at the Lido, Malamocco and Chioggia port openings, each made of up to twenty rectangular floodgates, a total of seventy-eight individual gates over the three openings, each attached to the bottom on one edge by massive hinges. At the Lido opening an island would also be constructed in the middle of the channel as part of the dam structures. When required, the hollow steel barriers — each as big as six or seven boxcars laid side by side — are filled with air, causing them to float up to 45 degrees. Together they form a barrier that is designed to hold back the tide coming from the Adriatic for as long as needed and, when the tide subsides, the air is let out and they sink back onto the bottom, out of sight and allowing the flow of water and naval traffic to resume.

Mose consists of a series of floodgates built at the three openings between the lagoon and the Adriatic Sea. Normally, the hinged gates lay flat on the seabed. When the sea rises, the gates are filled with air, causing them to rise and form a long barrier across the opening.

"And there's another feature," says Berti, who worked on the installation of the 23,000-ton hardened concrete block foundations of the barrier and the air compressors and other control machinery installed in underwater maintenance tunnels. "These gates are in reality graduated... they can all be raised or some within a group can be raised," allowing for the management of the amount and rate of water flowing into the lagoon in high tide periods. Normal flow has also been slightly restricted by narrowing of the port openings. He dismisses the objections to the design, such as those from critics saying the barriers tilt the wrong way or that they could have been built at less cost without the maintenance tunnel.

Calling the landscape-sensitive design "courageous and innovative," Berti insists, "There is no magic solution. This is a good compromise uniting limited environmental impact and an efficient way to carry out" the variable requirements of controlling the lagoon tides.

Good though it may be, Mose may not be good enough.

"Mose is a costly, useless project with no guarantee that it will function well. It will require costly management and maintenance, is unsustainable for national finances and will be difficult to control," says Iuav University of Venice Professor Antonio Rusconi, a civil engineer, formerly of the Magistrato alle Acque and the National Hydrology Service. A long-time critic of Mose, he is not alone. Behind the numerous critics stand the 1998 rejection of Mose by the Ministry of the Environment's environmental impact commission, and doubts left by a very fraught, politicized design selection process.

The control challenge for the dams arises because acqua alta is never flat. When there is wind, and there is always wind, the surface is high here and low there, and it can even push water out one port opening and into another, says Rusconi. "The wind crams the water in places, pushing it up as much as 0.4 meters! Controlling this system will be controversial, with fights and legal issues. It will be impossible to manage, not just technically. This is where one finds all the defects and where things get unclear and unclean because this was a political choice, and we came to know that these choices got made because the big companies were paying." The waves will cause the raised barriers to flap, creating "multi-directional stress" that will cut the lifespan of the hinges, he says, while every storm will send sand, mud and debris into the wide grooves that are cradling barriers under the water, preventing them from re-closing.

The motive for building them under the water was to avoid sullying the landscape. This was a mistake, "because on the surface there will always be a huge yellow pontoon boat for maintenance, which is uglier even than the submerged yellow gates," says Rusconi. He believes that something visible but more easily managed, like what was done in London or Rotterdam, would have been better.

But most critically, sea level rise will make it necessary to close the barriers ever more often, eventually impeding shipping traffic and causing pollution as the water cannot be refreshed by the tides. Concerns also arise about how the barriers will deal with rain because in 1966, water falling on the lagoon and draining from the terraferma caused the water level in the lagoon to resurge. The wind could cause a sloshing bathtub effect, where the water shifts uncontrollably from one part of the lagoon to another, interfering with floodgate management, Rusconi says. "In short, the system is too complex!"

His conclusion: "Mose might work for small storms, lasting two or three hours, but if a very strong one comes, like in 1966, it will fail. The small storms were not the objective, the big ones were."

So why did the whole project go ahead?

"Incredibly, because the ministries were corrupt!" says Rusconi, with some anger and sadness in his voice. "Their judgements were bought! And, note, many times the corruption was not expressed in terms of money. Corruption also happens by means of, for example, promotions, career advancement, illegitimate awards... favors, jobs for the offspring of Ministry officials who were hired by Consorzio Venezia Nuova, the company responsible for Mose. In Italy we call it *parentopoli*, nepotism."

Mose suffered the largest outburst of corruption on record in Italy.

The scandal broke in June and July of 2014 with thirty-seven arrests of politicians, officials, magistrates, businessmen, professionals and technicians linked to Consorzio Venezia Nuova, which had from as far back as 2005 created slush funds, paying €21.5 million in bribes to politicians and magistrates to look the other way. The Minister of Public Works in Rome, the President of the Veneto Region, and state engineers that should have been checking on the work were among those caught for crimes including corruption, fiscal fraud and illegal financing of political parties.

The cases were based on eighty-eight investigations launched from 2010 by public prosecutor, Paola Tonini, and I sit in her modest office after a journey through labyrinthine security and police buildings at Piazzale Roma. Opposite, behind a big desk piled high with fat beige folders of judicial proceedings, sits the gentle-spoken, scholarly looking Tonini. I ask: What happened to allow these crimes to occur?

"The state's mechanisms of control on the management of the money were weak, and this allowed the robbery of state funds," says Tonini. That led to six convictions and thirty-four plea bargains with a total of eighty-three years and six months of jail time and over €50 million in funds and fines recovered. But why in this case — a massive state construction project — was such laxness possible? She blamed the setup of the Consorzio Venezia Nuova as a monopoly with nebulous management controls and lack of competitive bidding for jobs, adding, "Stealing from the state was probably part of the plan from the beginning."

Now the Consorzio is being run by a new administration under anti-corruption rules, but the theft from what is the costliest project ever undertaken by Italy drained funds that should have paid for other key local preservation projects. Damage has been exacerbated by the knock-on effect of delays caused by extreme caution under new commissioners appointed in 2014 to take over not just the financial but the technical management of the project. The setbacks have also caused technical malfunctions. For example, corrosion has damaged sensitive parts of the floodgate hinges inside the maintenance tunnels, exposing them to salt air for up to seven years, two or three times longer than anticipated. "It's not an insurmountable problem, but one that slowly gets worse as the construction time is extended," says Berti.

He believes Mose has also been slowed by the cumbersome administrative requirements of a state-mandated and controlled project. The delays have eaten away at funding, starving the company of money it needs to complete the work and for ongoing maintenance, which is expected to reach €100 million a year. Mose spokesman Antonio Gesualdi dismissed this issue, saying, "There is already money allocated to finish Mose. As regards maintenance, I don't believe a sum like €100 million will be a grave problem for Italy, the fifth or sixth economic power in the world." A commissioner has said publicly that the maintenance money should come from taxes on day-tripping tourists — a solution that suggests that Venice's other needs may go begging.

The tides have long baffled observers. Some thought of them as the breathing of the earth; others as caused by underground springs. The "unmoved mover", or God, caused them, according to Aristotelian theologian Thomas Aquinas. Galileo made the first scientific breakthrough on tides based on his experiments and discoveries in Venice in the summer of 1592.

During his visit, Galileo made an observation when crossing over to Venice on a boat, probably a barge carrying fresh water to Venice (which relied until 1884 on fresh water transported in to top up supplies provided by its rain-collecting wells). The water in the barge remained still when the boat was moving steadily. When it stopped or sped up the water would slop about, falling at the back end and pushing up at the front and vice versa, and then it would oscillate back and forth for some time, hinging at an unmoving halfway point.

Accepting the theories of Copernicus, who said the earth revolves around the sun, Galileo deduced that the whole Adriatic Sea might be similarly affected by an external force. He would publish these ideas forty years later, following trials and tribulations with the Church, in *Dialogue Concerning the Two Chief World Systems* (1632), a book showing Aristotle, Ptolemy and Copernicus on the cover in contemplation of the tides on the seashore. In it he states that the study of tides could prove that the earth revolves around the sun. He believed the daily rotation of the earth on its axis and its annual orbit around the sun produced complex patterns of planetary acceleration and deceleration.

Galileo explained that the tides worked in the Adriatic as water does in a slopping bath, with large tides at either end at Venice and Trieste in the north and Brindisi at the south, and very little at the "fulcrum" at Pescara and Ancona. He insisted on collecting data to make his point, and in doing so helped forge the basis of the scientific revolution, even if he got one glaring aspect of tide movement wrong: he left out the role of the moon. It would be in Cambridge in the 1680s that Isaac Newton, with his understanding of gravity, clarified the influence of the sun and the moon on tides.

But even today, with all modern technology, tide prediction is tricky. Accuracy is relatively good for minor tides. However, as Alvise Papa of the tide monitoring center says, "For incidents of over 1.1 meters, a lot of energy, wind and intense weather activity comes into play. With so many variables it's much harder to forecast." In short, the more violent the weather, and the higher the acqua alta, the harder it is to be precise — so a certain humility in the face of nature seems in order.

1966 FLOODS

MEMORIES

LUANA CASTELLI AND PAOLO PUPPA

Understanding Venice's battle with the tides begins with the floods of November 4, 1966, which hit not only historic central Venice, but the islands and the land bordering the lagoon at the same time as floods in Florence and the Arno River. They also affected the enduring psyche of Venetians. I talked to witnesses to the event.

Here is Luana Castelli, an environmental educator and guide, who at the time lived in a village in Cavallino, on the peninsula separating the lagoon from the Adriatic Sea.

"I have very precise memories. A great furor erupted. People were very upset about something. I was only five, but I remember they started to put sandbags in front of the door and I could see that salt water was pushing out of the drainage ditches onto the fields, where it should not be. Everyone was worried. Some people were crying. Others were saying, 'The sea is full,' because the high tide prevented water from leaving the canals... the water rose and rose and at a certain point they gave up on sandbags. 'There's nothing left to do. Let it go,' my father said, and they left the bags and the water, which went into the house, while we retreated to the upper floor, lifting above the water everything we could from the ground floor, where the kitchen was: furniture, the television....

"The water rose as high as the windows, more than a meter. I remember the farm animals, including thirteen pigs, squealing like children in their stalls. The cows could keep their heads above water. [Luana's mother Bruna Bozzato recalled: 'But for a while we didn't know if they would survive. We saved some of the pigs by carrying them through chest-high water. My husband sobbed because he thought we would starve without them. It was terrifying. The dirty water washed in bullfrogs, which I hate.'] In the end, the other animals saved themselves by swimming onto stacked bales of hay.

"My grandfather later rowed to our house right over the fields, which stayed flooded for three days. He brought milk for the children as we had nothing to eat. My little brother was crying because he was hungry. Everyone was desperate because the floods ruined everything — all the plants, trees and vines, all destroyed. The situation was really grave. We had no idea how long the floods would last. The farmers lost all the crops. I remember seeing my father crying. He was a strong, energetic man who was not afraid of anything. The experience really marked my childhood."

Paolo Puppa, retired professor of theater history, lives in historic Venice. He was twenty in 1966.

"It was a moment of terror because the water rose above the ground floor. I still lived in my ancestral home, which is very old, with Gothic columns. We stayed dry on the upper floor — and we came down the marble staircase to watch the water rise like a wild animal, rising and rising.

"You need to know that when there is acqua alta, the water normally flows in for six hours and ebbs for six hours. That time was terrible because the water did not ebb, so after twelve hours it began to rise again. The scirocco, winds from the southeast, had blocked the ebb. The water rose to a crazy level. We thought, 'What if this continues for yet another twelve hours?'

"I remember my mother's eyes filled with terror. There was this silence, this nauseating odor. You saw the floating dead bodies of the rats. It was a scene fitting the description of the *Death in Venice*. Now when acqua alta reaches a certain level, the siren goes off. It is almost like a wartime siren, so in a sense the acqua alta recalls the atavistic fear that remains in the minds of older Venetians.

"Then the wind died and the tide started to ebb. People went out on the street to see what the disaster had done. You have to understand that at that time at least a third of the people lived and slept on the ground floor.

“I do recall my mother’s crying, in part because the house was old and it had important, precious contents — all ruined — like the inlaid wood paneling that we had to throw away. The water stayed for twenty-four hours and then for months we smelled this rotten odor of dirty water, and on the ground floor there were *pantegane*, huge rats, all dead, that floated right into the house. It felt just like an apocalypse.”

16

SYNANTHROPES

MAKING PEACE WITH THE ANIMALS

> *"Synanthropes: from the Greek syn-, "together with" + anthropos, "man," meaning wild animals that have adapted to living in proximity to human beings and benefit from the association."*
>
> —WIKIPEDIA

From her rooftop lookout, thirty-four-year-old naturalist and environmental scientist Francesca Coccon scans the horizon with binoculars, searching for winged invaders. Her quarry is a gull with a man-sized wingspan of 120 to 144 centimeters, a white head and body, yellow legs and a yellow beak with a red spot on it. She rises at dawn to survey the urban landscape with her clipboard and pens in hand, noting the birds' locations, counting their numbers and observing their behaviors — all in order to learn how the creatures' increasingly troublesome habits are changing.

Since just before the millennium, growing numbers of this bird, the yellow-legged gull, have descended on Venice, as they have on many other cities around the world, seeking new sources of food. Until the 1990s, man could not come close to this gull, which would flee, but the gulls have since figured out that we are less fearsome than they had thought. In the city, gulls find food everywhere.

A gull can rip open plastic bags of kitchen waste left out for collection. In Venice, where so many people enjoy a meal *al fresco* at street-side cafés, the gull has learned to pluck sandwiches from the very hands and off the plates of startled diners. Failing that, it waits around with a pleading look until a softhearted human tosses over a morsel. These omnivorous birds have even been known to pick off the odd rat, sparrow, swift, swallow or pigeon. They spark exclamations of horror at dinner parties over extremely rare incidents where they have really made a meal of chihuahuas, puppies and kittens.

Something had to be done.

The response came in the form of a small army of men and women in lime-yellow and turquoise uniforms, equipped with aluminum pushcarts, who spread out through Venice at dawn. One by one, in early to mid-morning on all days but Sunday, they ring all the doorbells of the city, yelling "*Spazzino! Spazzino!*" Anyone still home at that hour, along with staff at hotels and restaurants and janitors at offices, on hearing the rallying cry, grabs the rubbish, hurries down the stairwell or opens the back door and hands over the smelly bags to the soldiers of hygiene with their square, two-wheeled aluminum mesh chariots, one for plastic and cans and, on alternative days, paper, and one for everything else.

The handing over of trash is usually met with mutual expressions of gratitude, pleasantries or sometimes a reminder that bags of refuse must never, never be left out on the street because the aggressors are ever-watchful, clever and determined. The yellow-legged gulls have added themselves to the wild animal population of rats, bats, pigeons and new and old bird residents plus all manner of insects who find a home in La Serenissima synanthropically, that is, near man so as to benefit from the association, along with domesticated cats and dogs. During the Covid-19 outbreak, when Venice was cleared of tourists and the traffic that had churned up the canals, Venetians also found their normally murky waterways blue and clean and filled with shoals of fish, scuttling crabs and plant life. Swans, cormorants and ducks fed and nested in the center. The gulls' arrival is adding a particularly interesting new chapter to Venice's long history of cohabitation. The birds gathered in the city after increasing destruction of their habitats around the world forced them to seek food elsewhere. Yet man's response in this case has shown how humans can adapt and how animals react to a measured intervention.

Before, Venetians did more or less what other urban residents do, leaving refuse out for collection. For years that had worked well enough. The new system was launched "because of the growth over the years of the excessive presence of gulls," Riccardo Seccarello, the spokesman for the refuse collectors, Veritas, says between frequent incoming phone calls. "The gulls found lots of food, breaking open the garbage bags. It was a disaster."

Keeping the waste away from gulls means allowing no bags or bins to clutter the streets, and any person unwise enough to leave refuse out can be heavily fined. Sweepers who work from 6 a.m. to 7:30 a.m. with long twig brooms also keep the streets pretty much clear of litter. If residents miss the collection — as the carts pause for not more than a minute at each address — a barge awaits in a nearby canal, at one of the fifty-three collection points around the city where people can deposit refuse directly all morning.

The lime-yellow and turquoise army also wends its way to these collection points, where a mechanical arm lifts the pushcarts from the waterside walkway and then releases their contents over the boat into chunky bins on board. About midday, the boats then make their way to Sacca San Biagio, a triangle at the end of the Giudecca where their contents are consolidated into even larger barges and taken away to Fusina, near the Marghera Port facilities. There, the city has one of the most advanced waste reprocessing plants in Europe — everything is recycled or burned to make electricity, without going to the landfill.

Venice produces 55,186 metric tons of waste a year, which works out to 2.4 kilograms per resident a day, which is twice that produced by people in other parts of Veneto. That's because garbage added by all those uncounted tourists bumps up the figures.

Seccarello, a tall, former journalist, ended his interview with me by giving the city a pat on the back. "We are happy.... The city is much cleaner and more livable."

Coccon turned up to our meeting with a laptop and presentation all ready.

"What did this new refuse collection system do?" she asks me in the manner of a thoughtful lecturer. "It created a substantial limitation of food sources that were previously available to the yellow-legged gulls who had found in Venice a fast-food restaurant under the open skies. As a result, what happened to the gull population? It grew exponentially." Globally the birds had moved inland away from their old ocean feeding grounds, at first finding food easily available in the open landfills. But some years ago, because of new European regulation, landfills were covered with earth, depriving the birds of this resource, and this triggered the move into cities, where again they found food in abundance. They also found, especially in Venice, places on the roofs, bell towers and churches to nest and reproduce, replacing their old nesting grounds along rivers and on the coasts.

The migration of the gulls to cities was observed as long ago as 1940 in England, and slowly, over the decades, it spread to Europe. It was noted in Rome in 1971. In the last twenty years, "the trend exploded, involving Naples, Trieste, Livorno, first coastal cities, then moving to colonization of cities further inland. The first nesting couple were observed in Venice in 2000," says Coccon. By 2005, twenty-four nests were counted. In her nine-month count in 2017, the population had risen to 456 couples and 2,500 individual birds, but she found that the new refuse collection "had a significant and negative effect on the presence and abundance of gulls." The greater the number of covered, street-side public waste bins, the fewer gulls were attracted to the streets, she also found.

When the new refuse collection system was fully rolled out in 2018, the number of gulls had dropped by around 30 percent, and gulls were now hatching fewer chicks. Some gulls have returned to nature, resuming fishing for cuttlefish and crabs or chasing fishing vessels for scraps, but the battle with the crafty birds continues. While fewer now frequent the neighborhoods, some have shifted to where food still abounds: the big squares, train and bus stations, all places with lots of people dropping morsels and where there are easy pigeon meals. Some shifted to lagoon islands, making themselves a nuisance for San Michele cemetery visitors. The gulls are but one of the new bird species of Venice among older residents like magpies, sparrows and swifts. Another new arrival, graceful cormorants, dive into the canals for fish to the delight of dwellers. But at lagoon fish farms, cormorants are seen as pests who can each eat their own weight in fish in a day. As a protected species they cannot be killed, so farms install automatic gas guns that "BOOM" to scare them away. Of course, birds aren't the only animals that Venice has to cope with.

Walking down the Fondamenta delle Cappuccine late one night, a tiny shadow scurried furtively across my path. I started in fear at the sight of a rat.

"Rats provoke an ancestral reaction, a bit like snakes and spiders, something very ancient, rooted deep in our primal minds; it's something about the way they move and their characteristics," observes Mauro Bon, head of research at the Natural History Museum. Bon, a Venetian and naturalist of long experience, says he, too, can be startled by these nocturnal mammals but is not afraid of them. Until recent centuries, people thought little of having rats at home, not realizing that they can host fleas whose bite transmits the bubonic plague or that the rodents transmit debilitating diseases like leptospirosis in their urine.

As urban environments go, Venice has fewer animals in its midst than some — most of the surfaces are bricked, paved or built on. Even the 500 gardens in the city provide relatively little space for wildlife. But it certainly has its share of rats. As counting them is impossible, it is unknown whether Venice has more rats than any other city, Bon tells me. But, anecdotally, and certainly in the local lore, they loom large. Everyone has a rat story. Bon recalls that in Venice after the Second World War, rats occasionally came up out of the toilet. In those days and going back centuries, rat numbers were kept down by cats. "Everyone had a cat at home. They were a great deterrent because they ate the young rats. Venice was full of cats at one time."

From the end of the thirteenth century, cats rode on Venice's galleys, their passage noted on logs, and a crew member was in charge of their care. In the city they were respected and loved as guardians against rats, but with the end of the Republic the stray cats were increasingly neglected. In 1969, touched by the sight of the emaciated cats in the city, the English poet and activist Helena Saunders, with Venetian Gina Scarpabolla, launched a cat care charity that today operates a sanctuary at Malamocco on Lido.

With few strays around anymore, Venice's cats today are mostly of the housebound mollycoddled sort. It is said that the decline of cats led to a rise in the rat population. The dominant rodent is the pantegana, as it is called in Venetian, the brown "sewer rat." With a 30 to 40 centimeter body, plus a lengthy tail, these aggressive, strong swimmers live all over Venice, especially on ground floors, and eat anything from dead animals to garbage. Less widespread and even rarer are the black rats, the historical carriers of the plague. They live in roof spaces and trees, while common mice find homes in walls.

"It's necessary not only to keep the city clean" and to remove food sources, but also "to have a continuous campaign against rats, an ongoing war in which there can never be a winner," says Bon. Venice targets rats with poison placed in black plastic boxes, each not much bigger than a pencil case, with a hole in either end. They are placed all around the city, often in the angle where buildings meet the street. Bait inside is laced with a blood anticoagulant that kills, but not until sometime later when the rats have moved on. Older poisons killed rats instantly, but the rodents, who are extremely intelligent, learn to avoid bait if they can link it with another rat's death.

Nobody loves rats, but pigeons get a lot more love. I can understand why. They have winning personalities, wandering closer and closer in a sort of dance of tentative bravado in the pursuit of crumbs. Shush them away and they come back. Sit still with legs extended on a step on a sunny day and a bold one will march across on your knee. They wander in and out of shop doorways, swoop down from cliff-like façades at the sight of a discarded bun and generally have no fear.

It has always been so. Poet Elizabeth Barrett Browning's toddler in May 1851, "made friends with the 'holy pigeons,'" in Piazza San Marco, "& they were surrounding him like a cloud today for the sake of his piece of bread," Browning wrote. Feeding the pigeons has always amused tourists — and the city has historically been reluctant to disappoint. It earned substantial sums by selling licenses to vendors who sold grain packets to visitors in the square — even when feeding was outlawed elsewhere in the city.

But the birds cause a mess, dropping their guano everywhere, reproducing at speed and posing a health risk. With few urban predators above them in the food chain — though the gulls have recently taken a toll — they quickly overpopulate and become diseased. So, after years of procrastination in the face of complaints about pigeon guano on windowsills and laundry, and after a decade of efforts by the city to reduce the population by feeding contraceptive grain and a program of netting and killing pigeons — the latter opposed by animal rights activists — Venice's authorities in 2008 finally did the obvious thing: stopped people from feeding the pigeons everywhere. It's now a fineable offense.

This seems to have caused a precipitous drop in the pigeon population. The numbers have stayed low, in line with the 23,000 birds counted in 2018, down from the 80,000 to 112,000 recorded in yearly counts dating back to 1996. From 2011, the controversial exterminations were paused.

From Coccon's perspective, these were steps in the right direction. She says the way to control pigeons, as with gulls, is to manage the availability of food. It is also possible to discourage pigeons from reproducing by placing mechanical devices like spikes on the ledges where they nest, a practice that is neither "cruel nor violent." In her view killing can be counterproductive because the remaining pigeon populations only reproduce faster to meet the continued availability of food.

Bon agrees, but speaks up for culling that gives animals a dignified death when necessary. "Some animals, obviously, create problems, but we need to manage these situations in... the correct scientific way. Many people have a very emotional attitude toward nature, and especially towards animals, placing more importance on the individual animal than on the species or the population." Urban over-populations occur, with pigeons for example, because of a lack of predators, something that never happens in nature. Elsewhere they stem from human lapses. A lagoon scheme, for example, traps and kill the nutria, a South American rodent as big as a small dog which was raised for its fur in northern Italy in the 1970s, but escaped and, since the 1980s, has become a liability, burrowing 5-meter holes that can weaken dykes. Bon notes that the animal rights protests in Venice have never targeted the poisoning of rats, "One of the few animals... that has few fans."

Venetians may vary in their affections for pigeons, some feeding them illicitly and others cursing them openly, but they have always doted on their dogs.

Public water fountains in the squares that trickle water all day long often have a plastic bowl underneath for the use of passing dogs. Leashed and muzzled dogs ride free on the water ferries and are welcome in many bars and shops. From big huskies to the tiniest chihuahuas, they are decked out with coats, carried in bags, pushed in buggies and cooed over by passersby.

Dogs pop up everywhere in Venetian painting and sculpture going back to the early Republic. In the Scuola Grande San Rocco, sculptor Girolamo Campagna depicts Saint Roch, the saint of dogs, who was saved from the bubonic plague by his dog licking his wounds and bringing him food. Paolo Caliari, known as "the Veronese," painted on the gilded ceiling of the Doge's Palace a big toga-draped woman with a dog at her knee, an allegory of faithfulness. A work by Carlo and Gabriele Caliari shows the Doge Marino Grimani on a throne meeting Shah Abbas the Great in 1603, with turbaned officials all round and a Persian greyhound and setter hound looking happy in the foreground. Most striking is Vittore Carpaccio's 1507 *Saint Augustine*, which portrays the saint in a capacious, sun-lit study with a small white German Spitz who is waiting patiently for his master, while Saint Augustine looks out of the window at an otherworldly vision. The position of honor afforded to dogs and cats in Venice was officially marked in 2018 with the launch of a new pet cemetery.

The affection shown to cats and dogs might be contrasted with the trophy rooms of the incredibly rich Natural History Museum of Venice.

After walking past a series of respectful exhibits of nineteenth- and twentieth-century explorers, visitors enter a high-ceilinged room where there are displays of trophy heads of a giraffe, hippos and antelope, as well as a stuffed ostrich, a skinned gorilla, stuffed alligators, tiger skins, elephant tusks, a stuffed elephant's foot as big as a barrel and an elephant-foot pool table — all collected by Venetian big-game hunter Count Giuseppe de Reali, who died in 1937.

A posted museum description says only that the Count contributed to the ethnographic and naturalist knowledge of Africa. Seen from the perspective of the twenty-first century, however, his trophy room looks more like a hall of horrors, for what was hailed in the past as a glorious triumph would now be condemned as a criminal activity.

The danger we pose to big mammals seems obvious enough these days, but finding a sustainable way to live with nature in all its forms can test the best of us.

Take mosquitoes. Coming out at dusk with the odd superpower of invisibility, they can drive you to distraction — which is why, perhaps, people don't deal with mosquitoes well, according to Dario Gallotti, of the Venice animal welfare department. Biocides should be used to kill mosquito larvae where they breed in standing water, which is what the city uses in street drains. The public needs to spray the standing water in gardens and other private areas. "But often people, perhaps thinking it's going to help, spray more dangerous insecticides into the air and these also kill beneficial insects, like butterflies and bees," Gallotti says with exasperation.

"We have a huge responsibility for what is happening," says Coccon, referring to the many animals making their way into Venice. "We cemented over too much, consumed too much, and what has been the result? Man has provoked, as a logical consequence, the increasing reduction of spaces for wildlife. In turn the birds, and in general all the animals who have lost their natural habitat, have been forced to move toward the city." Coccon speaks with conviction.

> I believe man has to learn to live with other species because the tendency is toward anthropocentrism. That is, man thinks he is the only one, alone simply due to the fact of being equipped with the greater intelligence and vision, and at times believing himself able to overcome his environment, nature, animals and all other living things. This is mistaken, and even though we have had this idea for centuries, now we have to reckon with the consequences and the real problems of today. So, my view is: Let's try to live together with nature, respecting other living beings, while trying to have as little an impact as possible on the ecosystem, which is the only one we have, and when its gone, we are all doomed.

17

ABANDONED

LAGOON STORIES OF REVIVAL AND OBLIVION

"...we will continue to dip our oars into these waters sacrificed to a civilization of plastic and detergents, as we are prisoners of a dream of finding again a small paradise lost, that archipelago known as Venice."

—ALFREDO BORSATO, PRESIDENTE ASSOCIAZIONE SETTEMARI,
IN THE PREFACE TO *ISOLE ABBANDONATE DELLA LAGUNA VENEZIANA, THE ABANDONED ISLANDS OF THE VENETIAN LAGOON,*
BY GIORGIO AND MAURIZIO CROVATO (FIRST EDITION,1978)

My rowing partner Luana Castelli tilted her oar, edging the cofano closer to a low, grassy outcropping amid the salt marshes, barely one hundred paces wide by thirty paces long. It didn't look like much, but this is part of what remains of the earliest inhabitation of the lagoon.

As with much of Venice, the excitement comes from seeing what's not there, what used to be, and standing at spots where history took an important turn. This is one of those places. It is the site of a lost civilization on the islands of Costanziaco, Ammiana, Ammianella and Centrica.

Rivers pouring fresh water and sediments into the lagoon engulfed these islands from as early as the year 600. But by the fifteenth century, they had been overrun by reeds, higher water levels and alluvial deposits that brought malaria and clogged up navigation, thus becoming unlivable and so the residents moved away, leaving churches and other buildings behind. Except for the surviving nearby islets of Santa Cristina, Ossario di Sant'Ariano — the former depository for bones interred on the cemetery island of San Michele — and this tiny patch on where we have stopped, Motta dei Cunicci, which means "little rabbit mound," the lagoon reclaimed them all.

Beyond the stiff vegetation, I can see stagnant, water-filled square pits where, in recent decades, archaeologists dug up relics and building foundations. All around this part of the lagoon, digs have yielded Roman amphora, coins, boats and tiled floors.

We row on toward Torcello, for the lagoon is full of island surprises, places where a past is revealed in glimpses, on little islands like Podo, for instance, where once a tiny fort stood, but now gulls nest in the green grass, or Ottagono Abbandonato, the "abandoned octagon," where nothing is left of a fortress but teetering shards of a red brick wall. Then there is the island of San Giorgio in Alga, Saint George in the Seaweed, named for the once-proliferating seagrass around it, fed by fresh waters from the nearby river mouth. As early as 1000 it was the site of a celebrated Benedictine monastery where Henry III, the king of France, and Pope Pius VI stayed. All of that was destroyed by time, by the military occupations of the Austrians and French, and by Second World War bombs. But fascination for the little islands survives, and new ways are sometimes found to preserve the lost islands.

When I hold the book *Isole abbandonate della laguna Veneziana* (*The Abandoned Islands of the Venetian Lagoon*), open to pages showing etchings of the ancient island of Poveglia, it makes me gasp. I see in the etchings from 1777 and 1806 a church with three windows set among trees next to a tall, thin bell tower, and a smaller house with tall chimneys. In the foreground, in the surrounding lagoon, boats are being rowed to and fro, while behind the island, sails on the masts of ships moored there fill with a breeze. At the time, arriving ships stopped at the island so that goods and people could be checked for infectious diseases. Tents of the sailors who were awaiting clearance are dotted all over the island, which was inhabited as early as the fifth century.

Some of the same buildings are recognizable a few pages later in an aerial photograph taken in the late 1970s, showing the island's triangular shape, neatly groomed fields, orchards at the wide end and a collection of buildings in a park-like setting near the apex. Although the island had already officially closed, having ended its life as an old people's home in 1968, habitation still looked recent; its buildings were mostly intact, windows shuttered, and the rows of vines still cared for.

In the fifty years after the last image was made, a startling neglect overtook this once attractive island. Except for one corner where a band of Venetians on a mission to save Poveglia had tried to tame them, the brambles and scrub trees had conquered the now truly dilapidated structures. Woody vines crawl over the façades; collapsed roofs clutter the floors with debris and let sunlight and rain fall into the rooms and corridors still painted in unappealing, institutional pea-green. No wonder novelists, film and TV producers and writers have adopted the island as a scene for films, spy novels and ghost documentaries.

In 1977, twin brothers Giorgio and Maurizio Crovato, then in their twenties, set out in a sandolo boat for a week-long circumnavigation of the lagoon. It would bring them to Poveglia and other islands in ruins, where vegetation had similarly invaded the crumbling hulks of old military buildings and once proud monasteries. They also visited "quarantine" islands whose long warehouses once received ships from around the Mediterranean. Armed with a camera and notebooks, the twins rowed for a week from island to island, sleeping in their boat, to document the state of these far-flung outposts, forgotten by a world too preoccupied to think about so much history fast being lost to the ravages of the weather, erosive tides and to looters who made off with everything from bricks and timbers to carved wellheads and paving stones.

In 1978, the pair organized an exhibition of the photographs and published *Isole abbandonate* with historic engravings depicting the islands as they had been next to contemporary accounts, and photographs to give a sort of before and after. "It jolted public opinion and all of the sudden people rediscovered this problem of the abandoned lagoon islands," says Giorgio Crovato, who forty years later is an historian. The publicity promoted a revival of interest that encouraged repurposing of some islands, efforts at preservation and a revival in concern, though most of the islands remain abandoned and continue to deteriorate, sometimes because of bureaucratic struggles over their fates, or simply because they are too small to bother about and no one knows what to do with them.

There are sixty-one islands outside the historic center of Venice, including the handful of inhabited islands: Murano, Burano, Torcello, a couple of monastery islands and a baker's dozen of privately owned islands (to be discussed in a later chapter). Beyond those, a score or more of the remaining islands are of historical interest, though not much is left to see. A number are tiny grassy knolls rising a few meters above the water, some with overgrown ruins or flooded archaeological digs, and others inhabited by seabirds or rats. Many islands have only recently been abandoned, as they were used by the military until 1965–68. A few islands had hospitals until they were decommissioned between 1970 and 2001. Behind each island lies a fascinating story, and many of them are examples of how the relics of the past can be brought back to life with new uses.

The island of Poveglia is slowly returning to the wild and has become a favorite location for horror and ghost films.

Another island with a past similar to that of Poveglia is reachable with a short ferry ride: San Servolo. Found just south of the historic center, near Lido, it has been a medieval monastery, site of secret diplomatic meetings and then a military hospital during the eighteenth-century war with the Turks. It remained a mental hospital until asylums all over Italy were ordered to close under the terms of the Mental Health Act of 1978, a law promoted by the Venetian doctor Franco Basaglia. The island itself was then idle before it won a new lease on life as an artisanal school and, since 1995, home of Venice International University, a consortium of a dozen universities from the United States, Spain, Germany, Italy, Israel, Holland, China and Japan.

The university is a lively place, but what's most intriguing about San Servolo is its service to mental patients, the first of whom arrived in 1716; before that they, and many who today would be classed as disabled persons, were locked up in the *fusta*, a decomissioned galley anchored in the main bacino. When Napoleon arrived in 1797, only paying patients were allowed to recover in hospital. He closed the *fusta* and moved the occupants to San Servolo, which is when it became an insane asylum, which accepted only men after 1870. Napoleon, declaring that health was a public benefit, opened up the hospitals to everyone at a time when the mentally unwell were first seen as sick, not criminal or possessed by demons.

Yet very little was understood about how to treat mental illness, and as a result, practices were adopted that by modern standards would be considered cruel. This is documented in the island's Insane Asylum Museum, opened in 2006. The museum and the archive are run by Luigi Armiato, a tall man with sparse white hair at his temples, who told me about the exhibits and tens of thousands of medical histories, photographs and other records kept on rows of towering shelves in rooms of the former asylum buildings:

> In the 1700s and 1800s, few cures were available. Instead, purges, bloodletting, mercury, and herbal treatments for the insane were routine, and when they did not work, restraints, handcuffs, straitjackets, and so forth, would be used. They tried cures with baths and showers — cold, hot and tepid, according to the illness — and then they had work therapies. The inmates worked in a bakery, a mill or at pastry-making, woodworking or gardening.

The photographs we have date to 1900, and you can see the fields they cultivated, and the dormitories with thirty people in a room. The ones who paid got better treatment. The hospital had some 700 or 800 patients. Many were admitted and then left after a while. Others stayed for thirty years.

At a certain point in the 1930s they started to use convulsion therapies, which used drugs or electric shock to induce painful epileptic crises thought to cure mental illness. Then the 1960s political movement against authority reached a climax in 1968, and within that battles were fought by Basaglia, which concluded with the closing of all the psychiatric hospitals. Basaglia's proposals met with resistance for the same reason that there are still insane asylums in the rest of the world — because people said, 'What's this? This person is mad and now he is free?' It is understandable. It's this idea that mad people are dangerous. In reality, very few are really dangerous. But someone who has been in a mental asylum, even if they get better or never had anything, can be stigmatized. The insane asylums were not at all protective of the sick; they were protecting society from the sick, to keep the sick apart and unseen.

Asylums do not cure. On the contrary, they create another sickness, what Basaglia called 'institutionalization', which means the sick person became completely stripped of his personality. What people saw was not the person, but the illness. And, at one point, people became part of the institution, like what happens with prisoners. The inmates lose an awareness of place and time, and, in the end, what remains is no longer a person, but a piece of the prison or asylum, so that they cannot have social relations, even among themselves. What did Basaglia want, in the end? That the treatment should be directed at the person — that is, at Mario, John or Maria — not at the schizophrenic, the depressive. It is freedom that cures. Not confinement.

A bit further on in the southern lagoon is the once-abandoned San Clemente, former site of an Augustinian convent and other monasteries. When Napoleon suppressed the religious orders, the island become a military garrison, and then, from 1855, the buildings housed an insane asylum for women, whose numbers included quite a few poor peasant women who normally ate little more than polenta. They came down with pellagra, a disease of vitamin deficiency that causes symptoms of "madness." Within a few weeks of a decent balanced diet such patients were deemed cured and sent home. The hospital continued to operate until 1992. Later, it and the neighboring island, Sacca Sessola, were purchased by investors, and this represented another trend in the use of Venice's islands — private, for-profit ownership.

After long delays and financial failures, San Clemente opened in 2016 as a Kempinski Hotels luxury resort, operating only in high season from April to October. Set among well-manicured lawns and shaded by tall palms, the former hospital block, now painted in vermillion, boasts 190 rooms. With a new conference center, several restaurants and a pool, the hotel attracts privacy-conscious international jet-setters who attend the annual Venice film festival, holiday makers and wedding celebrations, mainly from the US, England, France and Germany. "Guests greatly appreciate the peace they can find on the island which contrasts with the chaos in the historic center," says Erika Bello, the hotel publicist.

Nearly twice the size of San Clemente, as big as about twenty football pitches, Sacca Sessola — the name means "scoop-shaped" — was created from mud dug up from the Santa Marta Canal in 1870. From 1914 until 1980 it served mostly as a convalescent home for patients with infectious pulmonary disorders. I recall visiting a friend there in 1971 or '72, and that she had to stand thirty meters away on the hospital porch and shout to us. The island, unused after 1980, reopened in 2015 after a five-year restoration with a new name, Isola delle Rose, Island of Roses and a J.W. Marriot hotel that opens only seasonally for a similar clientele as the resort on San Clemente. All the restorations use the nineteen original institutional structures including a deconsecrated church. Even the walls of the roofless buildings have been preserved by building modern structures within the old walls. All around them is a parkland shaded by palms and willows, lime, horse chestnut and magnolia trees and an old olive orchard.

The rival hotels have some things in common; both are places where you also can hear birds sing and feel the breeze; both provide employment and preserve a heritage that otherwise would have been lost to time and the lagoon. And both generate a substantial amount of new lagoon traffic, as all of the guests get to and from the island by taxi or shuttle rides from Piazza San Marco.

Just north and west of Venice, the development of the island of Certosa has taken a completely different path — neither private or public. "In the case of Certosa, the aim is a middle path. The island remains a public regeneration project, but the money, the investment and the management are private," says the island's manager, the former Olympic sailor Alberto Sonino. In 2003, his Vento di Venezia group took over the island and is shepherding it towards a future as "a project of integration within the urban framework" which has its own vaporetto stop, restaurant and a 230 to 250 sailboat marina with naval services. When completed, the island of 0.22 square kilometers aims to become a "*quartiere* of the city" with gardens, a vineyard, a forested area and other attractions.

But it has been a long road to recovery. When Napoleon suppressed the monasteries, the fifteenth-century Carthusian and Augustinian monasteries were mostly demolished. The Italian military used the island to make explosives and for weapons testing, abandoning it in 1968. By the time recovery began in the 1980s, the island was covered with brambles and undergrowth. Apart from areas of archeological interest, there was little left.

"Unconditional growth is unsuitable for fragile places and... building planned new towns like those in China would be unworkable," comments Sonino. "Neither can we be too enamored with the principle of conservation. Often we would be conserving decay, conserving shit! For instance, when we arrived on Certosa, people talked of conservation. Conservation of what? The asbestos? The unexploded bombs? The refuse dumped on the island for decades? There was nothing to conserve. The little that is underground could preserve itself. The monks 500 years ago taught us to leave nothing to nature; they heavily took action to control nature around them, and then were at peace with the nature [environment].... So decay and abandonment cannot today be the basis of conservation... not here."

The fates of privately owned islands have varied. Santa Cristina in the north lagoon has been developed as a private resort by the heirs of Gernot Langes-Swarovski, of the global Swarovski brand. But money-making hopes for other islands have not always gone to plan. In the southern lagoon, La Grazia (also a former infectious disease hospital) and Santo Spirito sit idle, their surrounding brick walls slowly eroding, as is the case on Tessera and Carbonera, near Murano. The old lighthouse at Faro Spignon is up for sale as are others listed online by estate agents Macchione, who write with a chirpy sales pitch:

> *Small private island "Gemma"* [Crevan island, near Burano] *in an exclusive and fascinating position in the Venetian lagoon, twenty minutes from Venice, ... waterfront views... you can soak up an atmosphere of Venetian history and culture.... private landing, abundant trees, garden, green areas, orchard and vegetable garden. Small house in an old fort, transformed into a residence equipped with every comfort; 170 square meters, 3 bedrooms, 2 bathrooms, 5 rooms in all on 0.55 hectares* [about half a football pitch] — *Price: €9.5 million.*

When a project dubbed "Veniceland" was proposed in 2013 for Sacca San Biagio — the man-made garbage collection site and former incinerator island at the end of Giudecca — it comes as no surprise that Venetians feared their city was really turning into Disneyland. What happened was that the University of Venice collaborated with amusement park entrepreneur Antonio Zamperla for a year on the plan. They produced a pamphlet for the project that described it as a "future hub dedicated to culture, re-visualization of history and the ancient traditions of the lagoon, of entertainment and free time... a place for year-round Carnival." Zamperla declared it would have a 55-meter Ferris wheel, a rollercoaster and other rides and multimedia installations about the lagoon's ecosystem as well as animations of moments of Venetian history such as sea battles. There would be education centers for children, with the rides generating the income to pay for the cultural exhibitions. And he proposed to clean up the still-toxic site and create 500 jobs. All for €80 million.

The idea of more tourism attracted a lot of criticism and never took off, but it drew some support, too.

Historian Alberto Toso Fei was initially thoroughly against the idea, but not anymore. "There are lots of people who are not interested in seeing paintings by Tintoretto in the Doge's Palace," says Toso Fei. Let them see the "toy Venice" in an amusement park if it makes them happy.

"In modern terms, this is nothing more than what happened in the past, with the amplification of the myth." This project, he remarks, "is not what will make us a museum — Venice is that already." In the past Venice had a Carnival which ran for months "so it was already 'Veniceland' 400 years ago. So we don't need to renounce [this new Veniceland]. Our vocation is to be welcoming and fun [but not] lose our character in doing so! We need to remain faithful to ourselves."

Once abandoned islands that are not for sale include those with outstanding historical value: Lazzaretto Nuovo and Lazzaretto Vecchio, in the northern and southern lagoon respectively, which served as the first ever permanent quarantine hospitals. They were both set up under the Republic to control transmission of the bubonic plague and similar diseases.

The Black Death came to Europe for the first time from the Russian Steppes, transmitted via Mongols besieging Italian merchants in the Black Sea trading town of Kaffa (today Feodosiya) in the Crimea. In the autumn of 1346, the prolonged siege took an unexpected turn. A strange affliction began decimating the whole of the besieging army. It was the bubonic plague, which is spread by the bacterium *Yersinia pestis* carried by fleas that infest rodents, typically black rats. The plague spread to Kaffa, aided by the Mongols' catapulting dead bodies of the stricken into the fortified outpost. When spring arrived, the Venetian and Genoese traders manning the fort fled on their ships. The plague traveled with them, reaching Constantinople, Alexandria, Dubrovnik, Marseilles, Genoa and Venice, and then spreading across the continent. By 1353, the Black Death had killed 50 million people, 60 percent of Europe's entire population.

The plague hit Venice in 1348, killing possibly two-thirds of the population. A series of lesser epidemics struck during the next two centuries. In the sixteenth century the population of Venice rose to perhaps 150,000 before the next great plague of 1575–77, after which Venetians had Andrea Palladio build the Redentore church in gratitude for its ending; the end of the 1630–31 plague was commemorated by the building of La Salute church, designed by Baldassare Longhena. Each plague killed a third of all Venetian inhabitants. The deaths, inexplicable in an age before the concept of germs was understood, left people bewildered, many believing the outbreaks were punishments from God, and in their wake the piety movements became supercharged.

The word quarantine comes from *quaranta*, or forty, the number of days that those suspected of carrying the disease had to wait on the island before they could go to the city. Hooded plague doctors, with beaky black masks filled with herbs which they hoped would protect them, treated the disease by lancing the swellings, called *buboes* that appeared in the groin, armpits and neck. Alas, that only spread the bacterium, causing additional lung infections.

From 1423, anyone who showed signs of infection was sent to Lazzeretto Vecchio in the belief that those who survived might not have it. Most died, however, and excavations in 2004 found 1,500 skeletons stacked like logs in mass graves — probably only a small proportion of the victims. While the sufferers were still alive, friends and relatives were only allowed to approach only as far as shouting distance if they wanted to see their loved ones.

From 1468, Lazzaretto Nuovo was also used to quarantine residents who were sick with other diseases and also for ships, goods and sailors arriving in the lagoon. The brick warehouse and residences on the islands could house 4,000 people and 200 horses, along with vast amounts of cargo, which was "disinfected" with substances like vinegar, salt water and smoke. The copious graffiti of bored and frightened inmates as they waited for their forty days to expire is still visible.

After the fall of the Republic, both islands were used as military warehouses until 1975, after which vandals did a lot of damage. Some restoration has been completed and, with plans to make both islands part of a National Museum of Lagoon Archeology, they are now kept up by volunteers of the Archeoclub of Italy, who also give very fine tours.

The lagoon and its islands were also Venice's defense, but how exactly did they work? I asked Andrea Grigoletto, a lawyer who works with communities to renovate old military fortifications.

> Until the end of the fourteenth century, Venice's lagoon had no permanent military structures apart from wooden watch towers. So, how was the lagoon defended? Curiously, not by the water itself, in the way a moat protects a medieval castle, but through the secrecy of navigation [of the shifting channels

and shallow waters]. Today, navigation through its channels is easy because of the bricole, the wooden tripod-like channel markers and channels cleared by dredging. At the time of the Republic, there were no markers distinguishing navigable channels from the rest of the lagoon. Only the Republic's own pilots knew how to navigate from the Adriatic Sea openings to the bacino and islands, and, as employees of the Republic, they would accompany friendly ships on the passage. A hypothetical invader entering the lagoon, however, not knowing the navigable routes, would have immediately run aground on the shallows and so fallen victim to attack by citizen militias quickly converging in shallow-bottomed boats to kill the crew and tear the ship apart.

The Venetian lagoon was invaded over 1378–81 by the Genoese. The Genoese [having worked out the geography] made incursions into the Venetian lagoon. Greatly afraid, the Venetian defenders mustered all their economic might and best military forces to boot out the Genoese in 1381. But, having done so, they realized that the lagoon, as it was, was no longer secure. So they decided to build the first walled defenses of Venetian waters.

At the beginning of the 1500s, it was decided to restyle these fortifications to resist the heavy artillery of the period — basically cannons. This was accomplished with a different design, using not vertical stone [as in a castle] but sloping, 45-degree brick walls, with beaten earth inside and angular ramparts — in other words, proper, modern fortifications. In the 1600s and 1700s, the defenders built further fortifications, the octagonal forts, and also realized the terraferma side of the lagoon was open to attack by artillery — which, at that time, had a range of 3 to 3.5 kilometers — and so, they began to build a series of artificial battery islands on wooden piles between the land and the lagoon.

[After the fall of the Republic in 1797, first the French, then the Austrians each expanded the defenses.] The Italians built trench defenses around Mestre because of the First World War. After that, fortifications around Venice were mainly re-purposed, such as for munitions deposits, and with the fall of the Berlin Wall in 1989 the whole defensive structure was completely abandoned.

Taking a lagoon trip was the idea of my friend Mario Santi, who is a supporter of the movement to save Poveglia, the island that made me gasp when I realized how much it had deteriorated. So one Saturday I joined him and a dozen others, all supporters of Poveglia per Tutti, Poveglia for Everyone, for a lagoon outing one October weekend. We traveled in boats from Giudecca.

Sitting opposite me in the open skiff moving over the lagoon was the owner of a trattoria on Giudecca, Andrea Barina. When the Italian state announced that it would auction a ninety-nine year lease of Poveglia — which would remain state property — in the following month to raise revenue, Barina was the first to notice the announcement. "It seemed as though the government's real intention was property speculation yet again, and this time for a part of the lagoon that was very significant for many of us," he says, his hand guiding the outboard on the stern of the boat. "When we read this in the newspaper, we were all outraged," he adds.

In a trip to the southern lagoon, our topo, the Pevarina, pulls up at Ottagono Abbandonato, what remains of a seventeenth-century fortress.

Patrizia Veclani, who had come along too, soon joined in the campaign. Poveglia "is the only place where greenery, trees and a bit of serenity can be found in the middle of the lagoon," she says. "This bit of nature is necessary in a city of stone like Venice. It has become a symbol precisely because they have tried to take it away, to give it to a private investor to make money on any old project. Given the problems Venice has with hotels and tourism, the risk is that it would become yet another hotel." She blamed administrators who just see the islands as problems to be disposed of rather than as resources.

The supporters hatched a plan. As the auction set no minimum bid amount, they would try to buy the island themselves! The idea caught on and what started with a few friends snowballed into a "movement of the heart," says Barina, with an organization and a structure whose sole purpose was to defend this part of Venetian heritage from speculation. Unexpectedly, they raised about €488,000. The other bidder, who turned out to be Brugnaro, now mayor of Venice, offered €513,000, saying he would ensure its "public use" and invest €20 million to restore derelict buildings. However, the state decided in the end that all the bids were too low and took the island off the market "which is our great victory," says Barina. Poveglia per Tutti is now hoping to win the right to manage the island for a period of six years, during which time they could "create some synergies" to run the island as an urban park or perhaps a study center in collaboration with a university. They have numerous ideas, in fact, for not-for-profit use of the island "which is unique like all the islands in the lagoon," says Barina.

Councilor Simone Venturini, a spokesman for Mayor Brugnaro's office, insists that the outcome has been a missed opportunity. "It will take tens of millions to restore the island. Who has that kind of money? The bowling association? [a lawn ball sport club] What should we do — make it into a park? In Poveglia?... The reality is that some public assets today are only salvageable by private investors, who are not into charity. So, in the end, Poveglia will stay as it is because at the moment no one has the resources to get it in shape."

Even so, Barina hopes to see a place for children to play in, for families to use for picnics and for students to attend seminars, along with a restaurant for all the island users. "We need to think of something different, of something that is more closely related to the citizens because it is right that Venetians make use of their own heritage — and that includes the islands of the lagoon."

ISLAND CARETAKER
CASON MILLECAMPI IN ALL SEASONS
ERIKA ROTA

Every island has a unique story. Cason Millecampi, as big as three tennis courts side by side, in the southern lagoon was restored in 2015 when a new lodge was built there. But the Province of Padua, the owners, have kept the lodge closed under the care of Erika Rota and Giorgio Mineo.

"We are waiting for a decision as to when and how to use the big beautiful lodge. It should be used by the people who come by to visit, not as a luxury hotel, but a bed and breakfast — a refuge in the lagoon. It would be glorious to manage it for people who want to stay out here. We are here 365 days a year — summer, fall, winter and spring. No two days are the same, but we follow a slow rhythm, getting up early, but not too early, calmly making and enjoying breakfast, and then Giorgio does carpentry. Everything wooden here was made by him. I might work in the garden or kitchen. We have to keep up the machinery — the generators, the solar panels and the water filtration.

"We took the jobs as caretakers expecting to stay three months, but have been here four years, which must mean we feel happy. On arriving we were immediately covered by a thick fog, which is the worst. You see only white, not the sun or the sky, but when the wind picks up, it cleans it all away and all at once you are treated to insane sunsets that warm the heart.

"With spring, the green returns and the tamarisk explodes with perfumed flowers. Out come the white clouds and the sweet-smelling plants, the swallows and all the animals. Now and again great flocks of pink flamingos fly overhead. We see oystercatchers, hawks, and lots of small birds, which means we have to keep an eye on Leoni, our cat. We see sterna, which are the most annoying birds. They never stay quiet. The lagoon is full of beauty. It will be hard to go back to living in the city. Now we watch the seasons and note how the sunsets move, from here, to there, moving northwest. The same with sunrises. Since our first spring here, we have seen everything with new eyes; we hear the sounds and feel the warmth of the sun. Everything changes according to the time of day and the light, and also when it snows in winter and when the water is still. We continuously discover new things.

"There have been a few occasions when the lagoon has been demanding, with winds and high tides that came up over the lawns. Everything was under salt water and the winds pushed over the trees. It lasted a day. Sometimes in the summer you can see little tornadoes, which in theory should remain in the water. At the beginning we didn't know how to live here. But now we have learned about the winds, the currents and tides. We live inside this environment so we need to keep attentive.

"I've always liked looking around and observing, but now I notice little things more. Life has changed completely for me. I was an architect, which I don't do anymore. But I am happy, perhaps better off. I meet lots of people. You would have thought that the two of us living on an island with a cat would suffer from loneliness. But in fact lots of people come by in boats, more or less by chance, and we have a whole network of friendships with people who come back. We are open to meeting new people and, rather than being closed, perhaps out of necessity after spending the winters all alone, we need some company, and we have time to talk and get to know people. Nobody else is here. There's no television. Nothing to distract, so people chat.

"We have grown to appreciate nature. Our water comes from a 150-meter well and has to be purified, which means using all sorts of filters and chlorine. It seems a shame to use the water on the garden. So we collect rainwater, which reduces use of consumables, and use the washing machine when the sun's out to cut down on generator time. We are motivated now to maintain a more responsible attitude.

"So many people have little respect for the lagoon, zipping by at amazing speeds in ever-larger boats. Clearly, it does the salt marshes and wildlife no good. And then there's the mountain of refuse that washes up. Just behind us, on the salt marsh, we collect bags and bags of plastic of all kinds — baby shoes, children's toys, bottles. People just don't care. It's a shame."

18

WATER

THINKING THE UNTHINKABLE ABOUT THE FUTURE

> *"The heart is the city of Venice. The liver on the right hand is Chioggia. The lungs are Torcello, Mazzorbo and Burano. The veins are the canals inside the body of the lagoon. The flesh, bones and nerves are the different kinds of lagoon bottoms. If you want to keep this body alive, beautiful, healthy and robust, it is necessary to conserve it as a whole."*
>
> —CRISTOFORO SABBADINO, *OPINION O MODO DE SALVAR LA LAGUNA*, 1549

The year is 2060. This is an excerpt from the tourist guide to 'New Venice':

> *In the end the world faced up to its grief over losing this exquisite beauty. Defeat in the battle against rising seas was hard to admit for a place that for so long felt at ease in the water, but abandonment became inevitable for Venice and great swathes of the Adriatic coast. The city's attempts to stay the inexorable waters with dams around the lagoon and buildings on stilts had all failed. After years in denial, the authorities organized the withdrawal. The remaining tens of thousands of Venetians were resettled miles inland, to the much-debated new location (Las Vegas was never really a contender). Meanwhile, international funds poured in to save Old Venice's art, its great marble-fronted palazzi and mosaic-encrusted churches, which were hefted brick by brick, beam by beam, over water and land to New Venice, just as stone antiquities had been lifted from the path of water unleashed by Egypt's Aswan Dam a century ago.*

Outlandish fantasy or a possible future?

Venice, as everyone knows, is sinking, but in reality not very much. Its real challenge is sea level rise. And like everywhere else, the frightening consequences are something people would rather not think about — the ignored elephant in the room. While the Aswan Dam scenario is unimaginable today, the need to consider once unthinkable options is slowly dawning on Venice.

All the models for Venice show the sea will rise by the end of the century, with the IPCC, the United Nations body, putting the average predicted sea level rise at 0.43 meters, and it could be as high as a meter or more. The latter would put Venice and much of the Adriatic coast, from the Po River Delta and Ravenna in the south almost to Trieste in the north, under water by 2070. After 2100, the rise continues, pushing to 1.5 to 3.5 meters by 2200. The land area around Venice is among the low-lying coasts of the world which, like Holland, have been saved from the sea by man's efforts, utilizing dykes and pumps. Now from less than to 2 meters above to up to 2 meters below the mean sea level, Venice and the coastal lagoon area is very sensitive to climate change.

"The question is not whether we will really reach 0.5 meters, but when it will happen," says Georg Umgiesser, senior researcher in oceanography at the Institute of Marine Sciences (ISMAR). "It could happen in fifty years or eighty years, or even later, but I am sure that this will happen because we are not doing enough to control CO2 in the atmosphere. We are not doing enough to limit the increases in air and thus water temperature, which in the end causes the sea level to rise."

The threat, however, is actually much closer because of the way the city's defense against deluge is designed. The massive floating Mose dams can stand up to 0.6 meters of sea level rise, but well before that, at even half that level, they would put Venice in an impossible position.

"Mose will not help re-balance the lagoon," says Umgiesser, speaking to a room packed with Venetians eager for an update on the latest research. "When we talk about saving Venice, we once thought, 'We want to save the city and the lagoon.'" No one ever thought that these two things were distinct. Unfortunately, with sea level rise, this unity is over. "It means we have to decide what to save. Do we want to save the lagoon? Or Venice?... I am afraid that we must concentrate on saving Venice, the UNESCO World Heritage site. Mose is supposed to do this, but in my opinion it cannot. Why?... The number of times Mose will need to close due to sea level rise, say at 0.50 meters, will be 300 or 400 times a year." That means it will close about once a day to prevent the city from suffering acque alte over 1.1 meters. "That's not feasible."

With doubts raised even after the first emergency use of Mose on October 3, 2020 —the nine-hour closure excluding 14 ships was immediately decried by port authorities as long and costly — and overall usefulness possibly reduced by as early as 2040, Venice will have two options. One is to try to literally pump Venice up by injecting water underground back into the collapsed water table — which is like raising a pizza pie by blowing into the uneven inflatable mattress under it — a plan that is as uncertain as it is controversial. "If we don't want to raise Venice the only other possibility is to separate the lagoon from the Adriatic Sea," Umgiesser says.

The implications of this conclusion are staggering.

Shutting off the lagoon from the sea, ending the historic relationship between Venice and the lagoon, would be a monumental event, in cultural terms perhaps at least as significant as the moving of relics that were in the way of the Aswan Dam. Umgiesser is far from the only voice now raising this possibility. Apart from suggesting that the €5.5 billion Mose floodgates are likely to be pointless, the idea raises hard-to-foresee issues — for tourism, fishing, boating, and basic ecology. No one knows if blocking the port openings would turn the lagoon into a freshwater body or one governed by tides, and, if so, whether Venice would need the expensive, heretofore unaffordable sewage disposal system that it now lacks. Most of all, what would become of the city's port, an enormous economic mainstay for the region? Nonetheless, closing the lagoon has now become part of the thinking that is shaping Venice's future.

The conflict is really more than a matter of responding to sea level rise; it asks what nature is for. A balance had been struck for centuries, but that is now lost and a hard choice needs to be made. Is the lagoon a body of water to be exploited for economic gain by the port or by industry, or for fishing or tourism, regardless of the effect on its integrity? Or is Venice the lagoon's inseparable Siamese twin that only exists in a natural balance with this body of water husbanded by man over centuries?

The key actor in the fate of the lagoon — and of Venice — is the port.

To keep the port working, ships need unhindered access to the facilities at Marghera. To survive, the port authorities need desperately to keep re-dredging the Canale dei Petroli to keep the routes open for ships, and this activity is the chief cause of erosion of the lagoon, destroying its natural shape and life.

The head of the port "has not understood that the internal port, within ten or twenty years, will be unusable," according to Padua University lagoon hydrologist Luigi D'Alpaos. "Because either you choose to let ships enter the port, or you choose to defend Venice from acqua alta. This is the great contradiction Venice has always lived with. If I want to save the lagoon of Venice, I cannot, at the same time, protect the activity of the port because the interventions required for these two objectives are absolutely opposite."

But intermittent closure would not necessarily mean the end of the ports. "The industrial and touristic ports must be transferred outside the lagoon," says Umgiesser, raising a proposal that has been in play for years.

After the fall of the Republic, Venice muddled on as a goods port, but, by the late nineteenth century, it had already begun to introduce new industries. By the 1950s and '60s, Marghera had become an industrial port, and ships arrived laden with the basic materials, like petroleum to feed refineries. In the 1970s, it employed 35,000 people. But by the 1990s all that had changed. Market forces had mostly killed off heavy industry there, leaving tracts of Marghera as wastelands.

In their place, Marghera became a commercial port. Ships first brought grain and steel for trans-shipment to northeastern Italy, Germany, Austria and beyond. With privatization in 1994 the port grew more market-oriented, taking advantage of the explosion of Chinese exports of toys and motorbikes while expanding somewhat into the abandoned industrial lands.

At the same time, the old Maritime Terminal, once the commercial port, was until 2021 given over to tourist cruise ships.

"It's a port with many problems because it is inside a lagoon where canals have to be constantly dredged," says Venice University economist and geographer Stefano Soriani, who has written extensively about the port. He adds that conflicts over the perilous passage of cruise ships through the historic city added to the complexity of the port, which now employs 11,000 people.

Rather than go the radical route of moving the port entirely outside the lagoon, port authorities favored other lesser choices that allowed cruise ships to avoid passing through Venice. The one chosen in 2021 uses Canale dei Petroli, the channel from the Malamocco port opening to Marghera, allowing cruise ships to dock at Marghera instead of the Maritime Terminal. The option was originally modeled on Royal Albert Dock in Liverpool, Kop van Zuid in Rotterdam, the London Docklands and even Boston Harbor, becoming part of a grand "waterfront redevelopment," requiring a clean-up of the areas blighted by toxic industrial wastes. "Here there is a big conflict. What is the real problem to be solved?" says Soriani. "While these plans promote tourism, we risk dying of tourism!"

Another alternative is simpler, using the same route as far as Marghera, and then redirecting cruise ships from Marghera back to the Maritime Terminal along the Vittorio Emanuele canal, an existing but abandoned channel almost parallel with the rail and road bridges. Venice Mayor Brugnaro, among others, rallied to this option after the *MSC Opera* — a 275 meter-long cruise ship — collided with a dock and a tourist boat after losing control in the Giudecca Canal on June 3, 2019. The incident refocused attention on the need to deal with cruise ship routes.

Neither plan addresses the issue of sea level rise and both face vociferous opposition because they would require dredging of new canals, accelerating erosion of the lagoon and spreading pollution. The mud around the Vittorio Emanuele canal is particularly contaminated with toxins from Marghera industry. "These muds absolutely must not be moved because if they are, you whip up the poisons," says lagoon biologist Lorenzo Bonometto. "This is why I consider the idea to dredge Vittorio Emanuele insane and reckless." Apart from that, re-digging the canal would prevent tide diffusion, starving the area of oxygen. The smell there "would degenerate in the summer heat, making the entry ticket to Venice a horrible stink — not to mention that it would damage the ecology."

Oxford-trained environmental scientist Jane Da Mosto, who runs the think tank We Are Here Venice, believes the outside port misses the point.

The exception that allowed cruise ships to evade the ban on passing through the Giudecca Canal "seems the most absurd legislation I've ever come across," she says. "Because it's not up to Venice to provide solutions to the cruise ship sector. Venice should provide clear indications of how it is going to preserve itself and how it intends to protect the lagoon, and then it's up to the cruise ship providers to find solutions that enable them to carry on doing their business, profiting from the existence of Venice while the authorities ensure that they don't destroy it in the process."

Proposals have been put forward, not mainly by the cruise companies, for a new port just outside the lagoon on or near the coast with the Adriatic Sea that could involve just cruise ships, commercial shipping or both. It might emulate the Maasvlakte 2 project outside Rotterdam on the North Sea or the offshore, river delta container port at Shanghai. It could resolve the cruise ship paradox since a port outside the lagoon could eliminate the need for new dredging and avoid cruise ships traversing Venice. It also takes into account sea level rise issues.

"If we think that in ten, twenty, thirty or forty years a port inside the lagoon where Mose functions is a port that would be less efficient logistically in handling goods and passengers, then going outside could be a guarantee for the future," says Soriani. One idea, supported by environmental groups Ambiente Venezia and Comitato No Grandi Navi, among others, is to initially set up an outside port just for large cruise ships over 40,000 tons. Passengers would use environmentally friendly electric ferries to get from the vessels directly to Venice. "This means the port workers will continue to do what they do now at the Maritime Terminal where they now arrive", says spokesman Armando Danella. "So there would be no issue with employment."

The campaigners welcomed the 2021 launching of an ideas competition for an outside lagoon port. So proposals such as those put forward in 2017 and 2019 for docking facilities just outside the Mose dams at Lido or Chioggia, with passengers transported by eco-friendly ferry to Venice, may now be revived.

But the idea for an outside cruise ship port faces opposition from the beach communities nearby, especially Cavallino-Treporti, on the spit of land north of the Lido opening, an area popular with tourists, particularly Germans who come for the sun, for the campsites and for side trips to Venice. The main criticisms concern pollution, pressure on nature and logistics.

Corralling the cruise ships there only shifts their cancer-causing exhaust fumes. The prevailing south-easterly winds would blow the noxious gases right over the attractive dunes and cypress trees on the coast back to Venice. And as Venice is a transit port, not a get-off-look-around-get-back-on port, with cruise passengers tending to begin or end journeys in the city, traveling onward by train, plane or car, their connections could cause mind-boggling local transport issues. Up to seven or eight cruise ships can arrive in a day, each with 4,000 or more people who, with all their luggage, must be transferred to and from points in Venice and the airport. Apart from added vehicle pollution, the extra traffic could exacerbate existing congestion on the single road that runs along the peninsula which would be used to re-provision ships and transport passengers.

Many question why Venice needs to cater to the economic benefits of the cruise ship industry by building a new coastal port at all. Why not just exclude giant cruise ships in favor of environmentally friendlier alternatives, like a new ship from Finland that runs on liquified natural gas, which is much less polluting, or, even better, new 11,000-ton cruise ships — a quarter the size of mega cruisers, each carrying just 230 to 250 passengers — that turn off their engines at dock. They could pass through the lagoon via the Giudecca Canal to the Maritime Terminal without risk, thus making the disruption of a coastal port unnecessary. Three such smaller vessels are already being built at the Fincantieri shipyards in Port Marghera.

The original proposal to establish a commercial port outside the lagoon came in 2016 from Paolo Costa, head of the port of Venice from 2008–17, and mayor of Venice from 2000–2005. We met one fine October day at a café table on Campo Santo Stefano and drank spritz, while he recounted the story of the rise and fall of VOOPS, the Venice Offshore Onshore Port System, which he called "one of the many battles that I have lost."

Inspired in part by China's rhetoric about a new Silk Road connecting East and West, with a terminus in Venice, he recognized the city could be at the heart of Europe if it had a port built for the future that was compatible with Venice's needs. He got around the problems raised by building in the lagoon with a proposal for a port facility eight nautical miles offshore Venice in 20 meters of water, deep enough to accommodate the newest mega containers and other shipping. Protected by C-shaped seawalls, ships would be off-loaded there, and then batches of cargo container boxes would be transported back to Marghera in specially built low-impact ferries.

The project was ready to go. China was ready to finance the estimated €2.2 billion cost, and it could have been completed by 2018, but it didn't suit Italian competitors, who complained that if it went ahead, Venice would render other ports redundant. "It was a disruptive situation because the other ports would have not had much to do, even if I designed it so that all those in the north Adriatic would have benefited. But opposition also came from northern Europe, Rotterdam, Antwerp etcetera," Costa told me.

Timing was another problem. The Mose scandal was still fresh in people's minds and money was short. A protest group against cruise ships dismissed VOOPS as another Mose: useless, damaging and likely to serve only the big companies. "If it had been 1968, people probably would have said, 'Yes, go ahead,'" says Costa. "Today, Venice is one of the many problems of Europe and Italy. If you go to Parliament and say I want money for Venice, they say, 'Why Venice? What about Florence? Naples?'....We lost the moment." But in the 2021 cruise ship ban the government also called for proposals for a port for big container and transoceanic ships — so something like his idea might still see the light of day.

❧

The reality is that politicians are failing to take the initiative. "We need to invest, but here's the problem: We should have a strategic vision about what to do with Port Marghera which is the greatest problem that this territory has," concludes Soriani. Lack of focus has led to inaction. "Until now, no strategic plan has been developed. The economic and the socially minded experts have not agreed on anything — they have no shared ideas."

If things go on as they are, "Sooner or later it's going to be impossible to live here. The city will gradually shrink. It'll become a ghost city," says environmental scientist Da Mosto. "It means that it would be kind of the end of humanity as we know it which is why we have a phrase, 'Venice for the Venetians, Venice for the world,' because if we don't save Venice as a living city with a healthy resident population, we're not going to know how to deal with so many of these global issues."

Lidia Fersuoch, president of the Venice branch of Italia Nostra, the oldest and largest environmental group in Italy, believes sea level rise may force the public hand. When I met her she was frustrated with the political process and yet "not totally pessimistic" about saving the lagoon and Venice in the short term. She has "a little seed of optimism, and that optimism is a response to global warming," she says. "I hope that the sea level rises will be such that the lagoon will finally be closed. It's absurd to say this, but there is nothing else that will achieve useful action!

"When the closure of the port openings becomes inevitable — because, unfortunately, it will be," as global warming is already out of control, "in fifty years or twenty years, the lagoon will have to stay shut and then how will it function? We need to think about that, about how to create the system, the engineering, ways to activate the tides artificially. It won't be easy!" she says, adding that these questions should take precedence over Mose, "but I see no one talking about them."

Instead of the dystopia envisioned at this chapter's opening, it is possible to imagine another introduction to our tourist guide of the future Venice, but from a much earlier decade.

The year is 2030:

> *As it brought tourism to heel and repopulated, Venice began sorting out its environmental woes at a stroke: it banished the mega cruise ships, later adding a port for all shipping offshore in the Adriatic, ending the era of damage and risks. The tourists, meanwhile, found they preferred new fleets of the small, environmental cruise ships, and the big cruise ships are now increasingly mothballed. The new mini-liners bring passengers dedicated to living more in balance with the planet while new tide-regulating floodgates, which succeeded the Mose project, combined with ports restructured to connect with the offshore facilities, the end of dredging, electronic motors instead of outboards, and measures to support the salt marshes as a barrier to the sea, revived the age-old natural balances and kept the local economy going. Together they brought La Serenissima back from the brink, giving it new life. In excursions around the lagoon, expect to experience the return of glassy smoothness of the water, broken only by the occasional sailing boat, the mostly inaudible hum of the passing e-ferries and, with the new tranquility, the marvelous way the human voice once again carries over the water and across the canals.*

19

EMPIRE

WHY THE GOVERNMENT OUTLASTED ALL OTHERS

... Venice, the one and only
miracle and wonder of nature.
This high ruler of the sea,
lofty virgin, inviolate and pure,
without equivalent or peer in the world,
... where I, too, thank God, was born...

—CHAPTER XII OF THE *TERZE RIME* COLLECTION OF POEMS BY VERONICA FRANCO, 1575 (TRANSLATED BY ANN ROSALIND JONES AND MARGARET F. ROSENTHAL)

I could tell from the exhausted look on Alessandra Rizzi's face when I walked into her modest Venice University office at well past five in the afternoon: this was one hardworking professor. After waiting in the hallway, under the bulletin board, for her to finish earnest discussions with a series of students about arcane matters of Venice's medieval past, I took a seat opposite her. Were it not for the friendly twinkle in her eyes, I might have had second thoughts about imposing brain twisters so late in the day.

I wanted to hear her views, though, on the extent of democracy in the Venetian Republic — or was it the police state some called it? And, most of all, I wanted to know why the government had lasted so long? What kept it together for some 900 years, up to 1,100 if you count what came before, much longer than any other state before or since, longer than the 426 years-duration of the Han Dynasty of China and the 482 of a single government in the Roman Republic, longer even than the 874 years of its closest rival for longevity, the Byzantine Empire. No modern states come even close to its record.

When Rizzi looked me in the eye and smiles, saying, "Those are the million-dollar questions!" I was chuffed. But for me the questions are hugely pertinent. Despite trials that would befall it — invasions, setbacks in trade, plague and internal strife — Venice would always not only survive, but quickly return to its former strength. Even in its final era of so-called decadence before its demise in 1797, it was still functioning pretty well. The Venetians stayed loyal to the state, even in the face of hardships. How did that happen? It was more than luck. Luck does not last so long.

This becomes all the more intriguing when you learn, for example, that Venice never expected to become an empire, that passing vicissitudes of fortune — in particular the extraordinary events of July 17, 1203 — turned what was a mercantile city-state like Genoa or Pisa into an empire. What was different? In an age of feudalism, of arbitrary power, when elsewhere in Europe mighty families ruled by whim and self-interest, Venice had a limited democracy that, at the very least, kept power out of the hands of a tyrant. At its best it provided a deliberate and thoughtful approach to deciding the policies of state. What's more, its system of justice worked. No one was above the law. People could expect to get a fair hearing by the standards of the day and when a decision — or any legal agreement or contract — was made, it would be honored. This was the solid foundation on which Venice and its empire rested. Government may not have always been for, or by, all the people, but it certainly heeded the wider population, pursued the common good in many ways, and was at pains to muster plenty of popular support for its rule. This includes the building of self-serving stories — myth-making in the terms of that age — to explain its own origins and win the hearts and minds of its people (to be covered later in the chapter on myth).

It quickly becomes clear that Venice the state — the government, politics and military — and Venice the empire — the commerce, markets and merchants — were one and the same. It is impossible to talk about the one without the other because the remarkable fact about Venice is not so much that it grew to become an empire, but what gave it such tremendous resilience. Venice overcame its major trading partner — Byzantium — taking over its empire, and expanded for centuries despite deadly rivalry with the Genoese and the huge Ottoman Empire. Later, it held together despite trans-oceanic trade with the Americas. Venice even stayed the course through a territorial tug-of-war with Germany, the Papal states and France that finally brought its centuries-long decline to an abrupt end.

Rizzi's views are set out below. First, though, the story of the rise and fall of the empire needs telling.

The critical turning point that came on July 17, 1203 can be said to have stemmed from the moment two years earlier when some 10,000 Venetians gathered in the hulking expanse of the newly rebuilt St. Mark's. The crowd expected dramatic news. Enrico Dandolo, Venice's blind, ninety-four-year-old doge stood before them under the glimmering gold mosaics. He set out why he had gathered them together and asked for support for an attempt to recapture Jerusalem for Christendom.

A few weeks before the St. Mark's Basilica gathering, six French knights had arrived to negotiate with the leaders of Venice to acquire transport to carry an army of crusaders from across Europe. The scale of the operation was staggering. The French envoys wanted ships for 20,000 foot soldiers, 9,000 squires and 4,500 knights with their horses and provisions. Meeting this demand would require the largest fleet ever assembled since Roman times and severely stress Venice's economy.

The government agreed to the deal in exchange for a share of the booty and a big payment just before departure. As a last step, before sealing the accord, Dandolo spoke in St. Mark's and then introduced the envoys, asking the men dressed in knightly finery to address the crowd.

One of the knights, Geoffroi de Villehardouin of Champagne, who later wrote an account of the moment in Venice, stepped up, saying:

> My lords, the greatest and most powerful barons of all France have sent us to you. They have begged your mercy to take pity on Jerusalem, which is enslaved by the Turks, so that, for the love of God, you should be willing to help their expedition to avenge Jesus Christ's dishonor. And for this they have chosen you because there is no nation so powerful at sea as you.

According to this very partial re-telling of events, all six envoys fell weeping to the floor and knelt before the people of Venice. No sooner had they finished their appeal than a flood of emotion swept through the church. People raised their hands, crying and chanting: "We agree! We agree!" The French envoys rose joyfully as the crowd sang and cried.

This moment boosted the Fourth Crusade and the events that were to follow opened doors to the riches of the East for centuries to come for Venice. Though already strong in the upper Adriatic, now, via Palestine, Venice would become linked to trading routes that stretched all the way to China. It would help introduce to Europe items like Tibetan musk, cinnamon, pepper, nutmeg, cloves and camphor along with ivory from India and Africa, clear glass from Tyre, dates from Arabia and, via Beirut, indigo, incense and pearls. Its merchant ships would travel as far as England and northern Europe and, across the western Mediterranean, throughout the Adriatic and Aegean.

"Venice changed the world. Not alone, but as prime mover, it was an engine in the growth of global trade," wrote the modern chronicler Roger Crowley. As the link between Europe and the Orient, Venice efficiently facilitated long-range exchanges, exposing Europe to new tastes, ideas and influences, enriching it with new foods, words and visual concepts. In the end, Venice's role hastened the decline of the Middle East and fostered the rise of the West as the industries that had made the Levant wealthy — soap-making, glass-making, silk, paper and the production of sugar — were taken over or undermined by the Republic. "It was Europe's first colonial adventure," said Crowley. "It provided something of a model to its successors, notably Holland and Britain, as to the ability of small maritime states to gain global reach."

The knights then returned in summer 1202 with only a third of the promised soldiers and just over half the down payment. To save the crusade and prevent Venice from defaulting on debts incurred to build the fleet, the knights had to make a deal with Venice to loan them the money in exchange for using the crusader force to subdue Venice's enemy, Zara, along the Dalmatian coast, on the way to Palestine. Despite a papal threat of excommunication for attacking a Christian city, the 200-ship fleet subdued Zara in October and then faced a new dilemma: lack of money and low food supplies.

At this juncture, certain European leaders offered the crusaders a cash reward if they took another diversion, taking their forces to Constantinople to put the young pretender Alexius IV Angelus on the Byzantine throne. This was not Dandolo's idea — and would mean a huge gamble for Venice — but he went along. The crusaders also favored the plan, despite another papal warning, convinced that Alexius, son of a deposed emperor, had supporters who would throw open the gates of the walled city in welcome.

On June 23, 1203, the people of Constantinople stood on the city's castle walls looking at the extraordinary sight of the vast fleet of crusaders tacking north up the Bosphorus. They wondered why it was there. At the same time, looking up from their ships, crusaders gasped at the sight of a city many times larger and more populous than any other in Europe. The fleet headed to the opposite shore to await the supporters of Alexius. None came. The city showed no interest in him.

Disappointed, the crusaders prepared to do battle, launching their main assault on July 17, with battering rams and scaling ladders manned by the crusaders while the Venetians made a ship-borne attack at the point where the 21 kilometers of walls were at their lowest. The Venetians used improvised "flying bridges" suspended from the masts of their ships. These devices consisted of yardarms lashed together and topped with planks to create bridges wide enough for three men to walk abreast from the masts to the tops of the defensive walls. When the ships came within range, the Byzantines showered them with stones and arrows, keeping the vessels from pressing too close. The initial assault failed.

Then the old and blind Dandolo did something remarkable.

Following his orders, his own galley advanced with Dandolo standing "in the prow of his galley, fully armed and with the banner of Saint Mark set up in front of him," in the words of Villehardouin. When the galley ran aground under the walls, several men grabbed the standard and planted it on the shore. Dandolo's courage gave heart to the others to move forward and press the attack. The red and gold flag of Saint Mark was soon seen flying from one of the towers. The Byzantine defenders fled, leaving the Venetians to open the gates and rush into the city. Dandolo's act of bravado had turned the tide and saved the expedition. It became the single most iconic moment in Venetian history.

Soon the world's largest, wealthiest and most fortified city fell. The victors installed Alexius IV on the throne, but when he failed to produce all the promised pay-offs, infighting broke out, and fires were set that destroyed much of the city. The invaders decided to "pay themselves" by confiscating goods, and, starting in 1203–04 stripped churches and palazzos clean of their art and treasures, with the Venetians taking their share of Constantinople's booty including the four bronze horses, which would come to be known as the *Cavalli di San Marco* (The Triumphal Quadriga), still standing today in St. Mark's Basilica. The invaders soon deposed Alexius and divided up Byzantium's lands, with Venice taking three-eighths of Constantinople, plus western Greece, Corfu, and a scattering of bases in the Aegean Sea.

The transformation from a merchant power to a colonial one came unexpectedly, disrupting Venice's overseas trade through Byzantine ports, a change not initially appreciated back in Venice, which was forced to "expand into the chaotic ruins and build a new empire," wrote historian Thomas F. Madden. However, Dandolo and his successors would lose no time in projecting a new, more powerful self-image by displaying the booty in Piazza San Marco and taking the title of "Lord of a Quarter and Half a Quarter of the Roman Empire." All of this advanced the Venetian quest for an ancient and distinguished identity as they began to portray themselves as the new Byzantium, successors to the Roman empire.

Historian John Julius Norwich portrays the episode in darker shades. The sack of Constantinople in the thirteenth century destroyed "not just the greatest and wealthiest metropolis of the world, but also the most cultivated, both intellectually and artistically, and the chief repository of Europe's classical heritage, both Greek and Roman." Western civilization suffered "perhaps the most catastrophic loss in all its history." He blames Venice and Dandolo for the havoc.

Venice's fortunes rose and fell over the next 600 years, its empire consolidating and expanding before, eventually, geopolitics began to shift against it. Yet the city always seems to have had something in its favor, something that gave it resilience. That something is hard to define, but it certainly begins with its form of government. By the late thirteenth century, the independently minded Venetians of the lagoon had fully consolidated the rules of government, eschewing the factionalism and vendettas that they themselves had suffered until then and that always undermined feudal kingdoms and family-run city-states. It was the first empire since the halcyon days of Rome and Greece to be run using democratic forms, one that was so far ahead of its day that it would centuries later win the praise of reformers in England, and the mixed admiration of the revolutionaries in America who created the United States, whose later entreaties for diplomatic relations Venice studiously ignored. The Venetians doubted the new country would endure.

The set of procedures and interlinked governing bodies evolved by the Venetians grew from Byzantine models that were much more than a simple oligarchy — rule by the few — and under which power passed, nearly always, from one leader to the next without strife. They included, in the early twelfth century, direct election of the doge and even control by the *arengo*, the public at large, which could demand the appointment of leaders and creation of legislation.

But, in what by any measure is a remarkable transition, on May 27, 1172, public disappointment over a failed mission to save Venetian hostages in Constantinople led a mob to lynch Doge Vitale Michiel II after a confrontation in the Doge's Palace. It resolved nothing and in an act of mass remorse, the more experienced and levelheaded among the Venetians suggested that future governing might work better if doges were elected by a group of wise men. The volatile arengo was gradually supplanted by a rule-bound limited democracy dominated by patricians — a mix of aristocrats and merchant families. This step-change fostered stability and has echoes today.

Then, from 1297, the *Serrata*, or "closure," with brief exceptions slammed the door on entry into this ruling group, so only families who took part in governing at that moment in time could claim, and be guaranteed, permanent, hereditary spots in the government's ruling body. From 1315, the names of the nobles were inscribed in the *Libro d'Oro*, The Golden Book.

Government took place in the Doge's Palace and all the members came from the patrician group known as "nobles," who represented about 1 percent of the population — and, among them, only the males took part in the largest body, the Great Council. They voted on major issues and elected from among themselves those who would rotate through positions of power in the pyramid of higher-level bodies. The most powerful was typically the Senate, but passing measures always required overlapping approvals, which prevented one or another body from growing over-powerful, but also made government cumbersome.

Though the doge — the word comes from the Latin, *dux*, for leader — served for life, his power was more moral than political. The oath he had to take limited his travel, contacts and benefits. He could not accept a gift more substantial than a pot of herbs from any foreigner. The list of restrictions on his freedom grew to 200 pages by the sixteenth century. He had many ritual duties, but few prerogatives. To prevent the formation of parties and cliques, the process of the doge's election took a deliberately convoluted path. The Great Council typically selected thirty men by lot, who chose nine of their own number, who nominated forty candidates, of whom twelve were chosen by lot, and these men choose twenty-five representatives, who drew lots to choose nine, who named forty-five, of whom eleven chosen by lot selected forty-one — who actually voted. Everything militated against one-man domination.

While only nobles could vote or hold office, the opinions of the Venetian people mattered — as seen when the Fourth Crusade was launched. Without such popular support (or perhaps widespread coercion) no government can stand for long. Why did the Venetian rulers get that support, not just in the city of Venice but also in many of the places they colonized?

I put this question to Alessandra Rizzi and in her reply the word "pragmatic" kept coming up. Venice lacked a program, a set of values for export. "Pragmatism is what mattered in Venetian politics," she says. "Decisions were never a matter of principle. There was this need to let things be. When Venice conquered a city or territory, it would take a look at local institutions, laws and officials. If they functioned, they just kept them in place. They preferred mediation to rupture, and made extensive use of the pacts with local rulers and local laws to keep things ticking along."

The politicians were mostly merchants who saw problems in terms of time and money and were always ready to change if it would cost less and get results; they worked out issues by negotiating contracts. "'*Pacta sunt servanda*' the Venetians said, which means 'we need to maintain good faith in agreements', and not for moral reasons, but because keeping faith in agreements made the system work," says Rizzi. The words *pacta sunt servanda*, a term used in international law even today, are inscribed on the church at Rialto, the second oldest after St. Mark's.

Famously, Venice had its share of police, spies and anonymous denunciations with special postboxes to receive them, but this was common for the age. What distinguished Venice was a "highly refined" system of justice that acted quickly to "understand situations, to be pragmatic rather than act on principle.... The administration of justice was a foundation stone of Venice," Rizzi says. "It was an instrument of governance. And justice had to be fair. If you go to the many cities that were once part of Venetian territories, you will see the emblem of justice in one place or another. The officials arbitrated based on what they thought fair and what allowed them to have a clear conscience. They had to pay close attention because God was always watching."

The enormous trove of documents stored on 72 kilometers of shelves in the Venetian archives and dating to the time of the Republic bear ample testimony to the meticulous nature of agreements forged by the empire's diplomats and the care with which decisions were made by judges and commissions. All in all, these historic records leave in no doubt the paramount importance of justice and careful administrative deliberation in Venice.

During the rise of its empire, Venice had dangerous rivals, foremost among them the city-state of Genoa, where a fierce dedication to free enterprise existed without the backing of a stable government. The internal politics of the city were so fraught that the people repeatedly asked outsiders to take over.

Venice and Genoa fought over trading posts, preyed on one another's shipping and fought war after war for supremacy. The fourth war with Genoa was the most severe test of Venetian society. In what came to be known as the War of Chioggia, Venice was threatened on its own doorstep. In the conflict of August 1379, after a Venetian defeat at sea, Genoa and its allies Padua and Hungary had surrounded Venice itself, occupying the town of Chioggia in the southern lagoon along the Adriatic. The siege caused terror, weeping and shouting in Venice; it was feared conquest could come at any moment. Genoa's commander, Pietro Doria, ruled out compromise: "There will be no peace until we have first put a bridle on those horses of yours on the portico of St. Mark's... then we shall be at peace."

But Genoa's Doria failed to press home his victory at Chioggia, choosing instead to lay siege to Venice — which proved to be an error. His hesitation allowed the Venetians to regroup. They used their greater knowledge and mobility in the lagoon to block channels by sinking rock-filled ships in them, thus bottling up Doria's forces and ships at Chioggia and turning those laying siege into the besieged. This strategy also bought time until another fleet of Venetian ships returned from a successful raiding mission and, by June 1380, the 30,000 by then starving Genoese attackers surrendered. "Venice, merely by surviving with its spirit, its institutions, and its key colonies intact, had in fact won the long duel with Genoa," wrote historian Frederic Lane.

The Republican government remained rock solid even during this period of adversity, retaining the whole population's allegiance. The war bruised the Venetian economy, but it bounced back. The Genoese fared less well. Torn by factional civil wars, the city passed from one ruler to another; soon the Genoese merchants left the Adriatic to the Venetians. Even as the Ottoman Empire grew to superpower status on land, Venice led at sea, sweeping up ports from the disintegrating Byzantine Empire and establishing colonial rule over regions of the eastern Mediterranean, Greece and central Italy, creating what it called its *Stato da Mar*, the sea state. By the end of the fifteenth century, the Venetian naval empire had reached the apogee of its power, and this period generated the wealth that built Renaissance Venice, the face of the city that still draws visitors today.

Well before bullyboy Napoleon came along, however, Venice's economic decline was foretold. By the start of the sixteenth century, the Ottomans, who had taken Constantinople in 1453 for their capital, brought Venetian maritime superiority to an end, picking off their colonies one by one.

These Turkish victories alarmed the European powers who launched a new maritime crusade. Offshore from Lepanto in Greece on October 7, 1571, the two sides fought what would be the largest sea battle since antiquity. The confrontation involved 400 ships, with Venetians, Genoese, Neapolitans and Spanish forces eventually defeating the Turks in bloody hand-to-hand combat that left an estimated 10,000 Christians and 25,000 Turks dead. The action freed thousands of Christian slaves from the Turks, who had been used to row Turkish galleys. To Europeans, the victory seemed to mark a momentous turning point in the fortunes of Christendom, halting the Turkish advance. In the end, however, it was more of a moral victory. Within a year, Selim ordered the fleets rebuilt and had begun to reassert Turkish supremacy over the eastern Mediterranean. At the end of the seventeenth century the Turks made a last push into Europe, but it ended in their defeat and with them permanently ceding their European territory.

Venice withdrew to its traditional home in the Adriatic, gradually taking a more secondary role in sea trade as other European powers pushed into the Mediterranean. But the city remained prosperous, with its energetic development of industry making up for any maritime trade losses. Even at a competitive disadvantage, regional shipping stayed buoyant through the eighteenth century. This is the period when Venice is said to have fallen into decadence, more interested in Carnival than work. But as the historian Fernand Braudel has written, "Decadent Venice... is still the city that welcomed Tiziano, Tintoretto, the unforgettable Lorenzo Lotto... the music of Monteverdi... Venice is not dead, nothing has happened after it gradually lost the dazzling colors of its historical power. After all, the rest of the warrior has its attractions."

As the Stato da Mar was slipping away, Venice already had an inkling that the world of the Middle Ages would follow suit. When, in 1488, the Portuguese Bartolomeu Dias discovered a way to India around the Cape of Good Hope, the need for Venice as a trading crossroads was diminished. "This is more important to the Venetian State than the war with the Turks," and it will "rip the heart out of Venice" depriving it of its commercial income, wrote Venetian ambassador to Portugal, nobleman Girolamo Priuli. With the French, Spanish and English monarchies building powerful kingdoms dwarfing the scale of Venice, La Serenissima's nobles sought an insurance policy against decline by expanding the Venetian empire's dominion into the Italian mainland to offset losses at sea. Venice would know the new territory as its *Stato da Terra*, the land state.

The policy attracted criticism as a diversion from the main issue of maritime trade, on which the city's greatness had been founded, but many nobles shifted their attention to the new land, establishing estates and agricultural interests there. With the help of mercenary armies, Venice took control of much of northeastern Italy, only to aggravate the pope, France, Germany and other Europeans who formed the League of Cambrai and took the acquisitions away after the 1509 Battle of Agnadello. But thanks to European treachery and shifting alliances — and to local revolts against the harsh French and German rule (harsh compared to that of Venice) — by 1516, Venice had won back all its territory.

Venice soon adopted "neutrality" in order to hold its mainland territories which worked until Napoleon's forces marched across them in pursuit of the Austrians. In the mainland cities, the upper classes mouthed French revolutionary slogans, but commoners, furious at the requisitions and abuses by French soldiers, rose up and called out "Viva San Marco!" In Venice, a small number embraced the French democratic ideals and plotted against Venice's oligarchic government. By the time Napoleon had advanced to the edge of the lagoon, Venetian military commanders reported they had no means to mount a defense, even if the lower ranks seemed ready to fight. On the pretext of a deadly incident in the lagoon involving the French vessel *Le Libérateur d'Italie*, Napoleon railed against Venice, vowing to "destroy this ferocious and sanguinary government." He demanded that Venice abolish the Republic.

On Friday, May 12, 1797, the Great Council met for the last time. With tears streaming down his face as people outside shouted "Long live San Marco! Long live San Marco!" Doge Ludovico Manin proposed a motion to surrender authority to the French. Acting without a quorum, the Great Council voted in support by 512 to 20 with 5 abstentions, and the Republic of Venice was no more.

In 1802, William Wordsworth wrote as the last lines to "On The Extinction of the Venetian Republic":

> Once did She hold the gorgeous east in fee; ...
> Men are we, and must grieve when even the Shade
> Of that which once was great is passed away.

HISTORIAN
THE VENETIAN ANOMALY
GHERARDO ORTALLI

The biggest mystery about Venice is how it managed to survive so long. Medieval historian Gherardo Ortalli, president of the Veneto Institute of Science, Literature and Art, is one of the foremost thinkers about Venice's past.

"Venice has always said that to maintain credibility you cannot let down the relationship. It has been a constant principle. But what is a contract? It is a social pact — a pact of the Enlightened.

"The law, in Venice, was very similar to English law — and this is exceptional, not just in Italy but throughout Europe. In other countries, the law was based on a hierarchy of judicial sources. First, local laws are considered and then, if there is no precedent there, judges turn to general law and finally to great principles dictated by tradition. Venice did not have this hierarchy. Its law looked at local norms, then traditions, but if they were of no help then discretion was required. It seems aberrant today. Today discretion is seen as an arbitrary power. But discretion is actually impartial justice from a person who judges fairly. The reasoning is logical, and also very modern. They said, 'No matter how many laws you make or how much you educate the judges, the complexity of the world is such that no judge can ever succeed in prescribing everything.' At the point at which a nation no longer has local norms or tradition, what is left? Just fairness — justice. This is why Venice has a totally different history from other [European states].

"When Venice was growing, it conquered a wider territory on the terraferma by force. However, the formal arrangements for the colony were never a unilateral act by the victor, but always a pact. At a certain point, the Venetian authorities would arrive at the conquered community and announce to its people and their representatives: 'Pay attention, Venice is growing so fast that new agreements overlap with [existing law], so be careful what you say because promises must be respected.' This is the *pacta sunt servanda* principle. Although these were not equal negotiations, the new communities regarded these pacts and laws as guarantees of local autonomy that they could rely on. [This situation] is a total anomaly that historians struggle to understand. This is a structure inherited from Byzantium, and it is different from that common in the rest of Europe. Venice endured because it had a governmental structure with a weak ideological but strong contractual base. This is the logic of the merchant, who knows how to make pacts and contracts and that these must be respected.

"How did that play out? In my opinion it is clear. It is reflected in the rapport between the holders of power and the subjects. This was the miracle of Venice. Take, for example, the Spanish dramatist Leandro Fernández de De Moratín, who came to the Republic in the second half of the 1700s, when a crisis in Venice was already self-evident. Venice had lost the wars [with the Turks et al. over territory]. It was no longer the empire it had been, yet it was a rich city, where things worked. Venice's strength had been waning since 1500 and Venice was very cautious. So, when De Moratín came to Venice, he wrote about the city with all its defects, and he concluded along these lines: even though nothing was going well in this ancient state where the aristocracy ran things, with prostitution and gambling everywhere, still people enjoyed themselves, worked and were contented.

"De Moratín was puzzled by this state of affairs — by the capacity of Venice to make itself out to be a good government and to convince its people that the government was not the enemy. That's the Venetian anomaly. How did they convince the people that theirs was a good government? What *is* good government? God only knows. But in my view, the respect that Venetians had for contracts and for pacts was fundamental. People knew these agreements would endure."

20

ISLANDS

VANISHING SOLITUDE AMIDST THE MARSHES

"As fragile as a piece of lace, as unpredictable as the mood of an adolescent, as changeable as the sky in spring, the Lagoon once had a very different morphology from that we know today."

—*LAGUNARIO*, PUBLISHED IN TRANSLATION
AS *VENICE NOIR: THE DARK HISTORY OF THE LAGOONS*,
BY ISABELLA PANFIDO

Patrizia Zanella is waiting for me at the ferry stop on Sant'Erasmo island when I arrive on a cool Tuesday afternoon in December. A diminutive but strongly built woman of sixty-two in a lime-green quilted coat, with short hair and glasses perched on her head, she ushers me over to her three-wheeled car. This is an *ape*, a "bee," the working version of the Vespa scooter that is so popular in small Italian towns. On the island, it is the main form of transport, there being only one circular, paved road, lots of farm tracks and footpaths, but no car ferry.

I toss my knapsack in the cargo bed at the back and squeeze into the cab next to her. With a huge growl for such a tiny vehicle, the bee moves off. She is going to show me round the market garden island, second in size in the lagoon only to Venice.

"Life here is tranquil; it's serene, clearly," for the 650 residents, explains Zanella, a lifelong inhabitant of the island, former glass worker and then a nurse for thirty-eight years at Venice's hospital. With its church, a bar-trattoria and a supermarket that keeps traditional hours, closing for three hours at midday, Sant'Erasmo meets basic needs, even if things do cost a bit more. For other shopping, people go to Venice or to Treporti on the terraferma. Some commute to jobs in Venice or Murano. But now, "Half of us are over sixty and few remain who go to work. We are getting fewer year by year." With barely thirty children living on Sant'Erasmo, the small school struggles to stay open.

"We don't live in condominium flats. We live in houses. That's already a more human setup than condos where people who live in the same building sometimes don't even recognize each other on the stairs!" says Zanella. "Up to twenty years ago people used to commute to Murano where they had work in the glass factories. Today, they go to Venice and work in the hotels and offices. Those who remain on the island have been here for generations. If anyone buys a house here it is for vacations. Very few come to live."

We buzz by the fifty-bed Lato Azzurro, a tree-shaded villa painted in pale yellow, that is the island's only hotel. We push on past fields holding rough bouquets of the deep-green, prickly leaves of the violet artichoke. The mild micro-climate and salty soils created by ninteenth-century dredgings that were dumped on the Venice-facing side of the island give flavor to the succulent, edible flower heads, which mature from March to May when the island celebrates its artichoke festival. Other experimental agriculture, including hydroponics, is making headway in supplying the growing demand for vegetables from Venice. We drive down a track to what's left of the beach and a salt marsh that wraps around it. Sant'Erasmo was originally a coastal dune, like Lido, and it boasted a substantial sandy shore, the *Bacàn*. But that has been eroded by currents since the Mose dam project restructured the nearby lagoon opening to the Adriatic. Only a stubby strip of beach remains.

Zanella pulls up in front of a high-walled compound in the middle of fields. We leave the three-wheeler outside and enter a neatly kept cemetery no larger than a tennis court. Half a dozen older women stand among the closely set graves, each consisting of a rectangular, pale white slab with an engraved headstone. They are placing fresh flowers, adjusting the plastic blooms already there or chatting among themselves. One or two greet Zanella warmly. Many come regularly to the cemetery, and the visits have become a social time for widows and widowers on the island.

Sant'Erasmo is an example of how people live in the lagoon. Along with Sant'Erasmo, communities live on Murano, with 3,000 residents, Burano and Mazzorbo with 1,500 together, plus a few who inhabit Torcello, eleven at the last count, and Le Vignole — sixty-four. Add to that two monastery islands — San Francesco del Deserto and San Lazzaro degli Armeni — with even smaller inhabitant numbers. These history-rich communities preserve a way of life that exists only in the lagoon, one that is threatened by pressures similar to those faced by Venice as a whole — depopulation and, for some, out-of-control tourism.

Most afflicted by excessive tourism are Murano, Burano and Torcello. In season, long lines can grow to board vaporetti for these islands. Tour boat operators at Tronchetto, the parking lots at the end of the road bridge to Venice, also herd busloads of tourists 300 at a time onto boats for whirlwind island visits, bypassing public transport. This trade has been troubled by collusion between hotel desks and involvement of the Mafia in the boat transport to certain of Murano's glass sales showrooms, according to court cases. "It's tourism but one that leaves little to the city, while making profits for the operators. The problem is precisely that of tourism management in the hands of those who profit legally or illegally," according to Giovanni Andrea Martini, the elected official in charge of the islands.

At the same time, depopulation diminishes island life. Local government is trying to counteract these forces, says Martini, by bringing new residents to the area with new job opportunities, making use of the spaces for new projects, start-ups and businesses. But so far, they've not reversed the trend.

Located in the northern lagoon, a forty-minute ferry ride from Venice, Burano consists of single-family, two- or three-story homes along the canals, painted in a pastel palette ranging from pink to green and purple. The island — a ten-minute walk from end to end — is at heart simply a quiet rural village; no cars, open spaces and real serenity. Many people enjoy living there, but appearances are deceptive. What Burano is known for, what has always powered its existence, are the traditions of lace-making and fishing. Both are in mortal trouble, and tourism, which has overtaken both, is a Faustian bargain that leaves few happy.

Burano, whose name may come from the Boreana Gate of Roman Altinum nearby on the terraferma, was settled by the fifth century. The reputation for lace goes back to the sixteenth century, when across Europe, kings and commoners alike wanted the delicate needlework — used for collars and cuffs and decorations. The trade fell on hard times at the end of the Republic, and after a brief pre-First World War revival, was left only to women who could make lace to sell to tourists visiting the island.

Today the women who make lace are getting very old. Lace is still sold in shops on Burano and in Venice, but virtually all of it is machine-made from elsewhere. There are ten women who still make lace work inside the Museum of Lace on the island and do lace-making demonstrations from their wooden chairs in a brightly lit upper-floor room, "but, on the whole, there is no production," says island chief Martini. "We set up a project to relaunch a school but it never took off." The museum lacemakers nonetheless keep going, indefatigably. One of them is 102-year-old Emma Vidal. As a matter of daily routine, "she goes to the museum [to sew]and then steps out for a bite to eat or a pastry at a restaurant, then takes a nap before returning to the museum." But, sadly, Vidal died in 2019 and the living tradition will soon be no more.

Tourists buy the low-cost manufactured lace, but the growth of tourism has itself become a problem. "As many as 10,000 tourists arrive in a day in the summer," says Martini. "It's a siege, with boats bringing over 300 passengers at a time. We have always said that the number of tourists should not exceed the number of inhabitants, which is 1,500." But ironically, as Burano has no hotels, with the last ferry departing in late afternoon, the island is starved for business in the evening. The huge influx, with thousands arriving at the same time, seems not to have done much for neighboring Mazzorbo, an island reachable over a bridge with some modern housing, a hotel and vineyards.

Other sustenance comes from boatyards and from fishing. Even in the 1960s, fishing on Burano supported the population of 11,000. The number of fishermen is down in the whole lagoon, with a fraction using traditional methods. "Unfortunately, we don't see a very rosy future for fishing" in the lagoon due to changes in work practices and climate, says Luigi Vidal, who runs the Burano fishing cooperative.

Murano, settled at the same time as Burano and whose name commemorates another gate of Altinum, the Ammuranium, is a much bigger island at 1.17 square kilometers. Just ten minutes from Venice by ferry, the community enjoys its own elementary school, as well as rowing, boules and tennis clubs. Similar pressures of tourism and depopulation have taken a toll.

Every day thousands of visitors arrive, some to see the sights, such as the Veneto-Byzantine-style Basilica dei Santa Maria e Donato, one of the oldest in Venice, or the glass museum in Palazzo Giustinian, but the lion's share are there to see glassblowing demonstrations — one every thirty minutes or so — or to buy glass souvenirs ranging from trinkets to handmade drinking glasses for €60 each and mind-blowing sculptures with if-you-have-to-ask-you-can't-afford-it prices in shops.

The craft of glassblowing is what made Murano what it is. It was very much to its advantage that in 1291, Venice banned glassmaking in the city because of the risk of fire, issuing a decree that required the industry to go to Murano. The island, with its semi-autonomous government, would become famous all over Europe for beads, goblets, mirrors and chandeliers. Murano's population grew to 30,000 residents and noble villas, churches, convents and literary academies were constructed there by the fifteenth and sixteenth centuries. When Venice declined, Murano declined. Glassmaking carried on, even after the fall of the Republic, but today it faces what may be its greatest crisis.

In the early 1990s, the glassmaking industry still had 4,000 employees. In recent years it has "collapsed as if off a cliff edge" according to Martini, with numbers down from 200 furnaces thirty years ago to thirty-five today and only 500 workers at the last count. Whereas manufacturers once made all sorts of glass for general use, only the artisanal work remains.

This decline is linked to the competition in glass from other sources outside Murano, especially from Chinese goods passed off as Muranese — and much skulduggery has occurred with kickbacks to travel agencies steering Chinese tourists to the doors of certain outlets. It is also linked to the difficulties and costs that artisans face in respecting the European Union standards on management of fumes and materials. These outlaw use of highly toxic arsenic and cadmium, traditionally used to create red and yellow glass. The troubles are exacerbated by the old industry's many abandoned sites severely polluted with mercury and other toxic minerals, requiring expensive clean-ups, according to Martini.

Some of the heirs of the great historic glass firms have simply taken their businesses elsewhere. Those that remain have made efforts to boost locally made glass, aided by a Murano trademark created in the 1990s. The Abate Zanetti School of Glass continues for now on Murano, but recently Venice itself lost its Institute of Art which once trained artisans and designers, including the renowned Carlo Scarpa.

Author of the latest guide to Murano, Michela Scibilia, however, sounds an optimistic note. She believes the tribulations have led the younger generation of glassmakers to begin to forswear the rivalries of the past "and in a small measure they have learned to work as a team, something that was not happening ten years ago."

On San Lazzaro degli Armeni, a monastery island in the southern lagoon that is less than half the size of Burano, another world lives on. For the twenty-eight monks along with five novices, the monastic way of life continues there with little variation, as it has for over 300 years. When we pass through the dining hall, Levon, our tour guide, explains that, "The monks eat in silence, without talking, while up on the pulpit" — he motions to a carved wooden platform along one wall of the long room — "one of the novices reads in ancient Armenian, for fifteen minutes, and then they call him to come down, but if he makes too many errors or reads badly," he has to continue until it is right, and fifteen minutes becomes half an hour. "You see it's very severe. They have to work to read well, without errors."

Levon, an Armenian and lay believer, is quick to add that this regime has a purpose. The monks come from all over the world, from Argentina, France, Turkey, Egypt, Syria and Ethiopia, and each individual is part of the diaspora of 9 million Armenians. Less than 3 million Armenians live in modern Armenia. Monks from the island monastery go on missions — twelve of the twenty-eight are currently abroad — some dealing with destruction of ancient Armenian cemeteries and churches in Syria. They comfort the families and re-open church schools in places like Aleppo. "This kind of work is difficult.... Our Catholic Church is saying to the residents, 'We are here. We give hope where there is not much hope left.' So the monks must not make mistakes. They must learn to think and speak."

We follow along through the refectory and then to the fifteenth-century church, rebuilt in the 1880s in the neo-Gothic style, the library and the exhibits of Roman statuary from Aquileia. We glimpse, at a distance, the long hallway where the monks reside. Along the way, Levon recalls the genocide of the 1.5 million Armenians that began in 1915 under the

Ottoman Empire and only ended in 1921 when the Soviets occupied Armenia. "As our's [the story of our holocaust] was silenced, it made others easier," says Levon, referring to the 1940s Jewish Holocaust and others since. "Of this there is no doubt."

Armenians had suffered persecution before. The monastery itself was founded because a band of monks led by Marug di Pietro, also known as "Mechitar," had to flee the Ottoman Turks in the eighteenth century. They found refuge in La Serenissima's community of 5,000 Armenian traders and were welcomed by Doge Sebastiano Mocenigo. After the monks were given the island of San Lazzaro by the doge, Mechitar established the new monastery and set about preserving threatened Armenian culture. The monastery and the church, spared by Napoleon, and with its onion-domed bell tower, have grown to include a complex of buildings amid landscaped grounds, including a 150,000-book library with rare texts by Aristotle and Dante Alighieri as well as 4,500 rare manuscripts including a Gospel in Greek from 1300, a Koran in Arabic, dating from 1500, a Book of Esther in Hebrew from 1200 and many Armenian bibles. From 1750, the monastery translated and printed books in thirty-nine languages, including translations into Armenian of the world's greatest works of literature.

Among the monastery's admirers was the poet Lord Byron, who rowed or swam to the monastery for lessons in Armenian language, a task he set himself as a challenge. His desk, pen and letters are preserved in what is called the Byron Room. Fewer monks live in the monastery these days. In the 1950s, there were fifty in the order. The monks ceased printing books in 1989, but they have taken on the new task of digitizing the texts to make them available online, and have already completed some 200 volumes.

On the island of San Francesco del Deserto, in the northern lagoon, the yellow sign posted prominently at the dock outside the entrance says:

ZONA SACRA e di PREGHIERA

Zone of Holiness and Prayer. And to make clear that this spot, measuring some hundred paces across, is not meant to be disturbed, a tall chain-link fence runs along the water's edge all around the island to prevent access except from the dock, where a path leads to a heavy wooden door, which is kept firmly shut. The fence and the sign are recent additions aimed at deterring unwanted visitors.

But organized groups can visit. Some 25,000 visitors a year make the trip, including some for religious retreats, especially in the warm months when the island, with its well-kept lawn and gardens, is at its most beautiful. A special boat picks up the visitors from Burano, dropping them at the dock and, on arriving at the door and ringing the bell, a friar opens up, welcoming guests. On our visit, Friar Felice, a tall, graying man in a brown religious habit and a knitted cap, met us and, by way of introduction, he recounted the story of Francis of Assisi.

The saint-to-be stayed on the island for forty days in 1220 on his way back from Syria and Egypt. That's when "the miracle of birds" took place, the Friar says. "While Francis was praying with his traveling companion, the birds of the island gathered round and sang so loudly that they couldn't hear themselves pray. So, Francis said, 'Quiet! We are praying.'" The birds, respectfully, stayed quiet for the whole time the two men prayed. Saint Francis also is said to have stuck his walking stick into the ground at the monastery; from it grew a great pine. Interestingly, just such a tree still grows there.

Later, Francis resumed his journey to Assisi, where he died in 1226. He was canonized two years later, leaving behind the religious order that advocated a simple life, the practice of poverty and kindness to animals.

The gentle Friar Felice took us inside to an ancient cloister, explaining that the island's name, which means "of the desert," probably comes from the thirty-year abandonment at the end of the 1300s due to plague or malaria. But the friars returned in 1420, and they have remained ever since, barring an interval when the island was taken over by Napoleon's military forces, who also made off with much of the library's collections and columns of precious stone. Today, not including the few additional monks who come and go, the island has just five permanent residents. They spend their days in a set pattern of prayer, interspersed with gardening, household and office work. Friar Felice himself has lived on the island for twenty-three years.

He took us around the medieval cloister and through the chapel to see the focus of most of today's pilgrimages to the island, a stone engraved in Latin that states: *Hic est locus ubi oravit seraphicus pater Franciscus*, "This is the place where the angelic Father Francis prayed."

We walked out behind the ancient buildings, passing a new block with a hall and residence, and entering the landscaped half of the island. Taking a path shaded by tall cypress trees, we reached a lagoon overlook with a breathtaking view over a salt marsh where swans were nesting. Beyond was a silent panorama of the northern lagoon. We could see the low, flat, green profile of Torcello and the colors of Burano, and, further on, the ancient island of Sant'Ariano, which once served as a bone depository; Santa Cristina, now a private resort; La Cura, with its ruins; and La Salina, where once upon a time salt was produced. In the far distance on the horizon the snowy Alps rose over the lagoon, like a castle resting on the misted sky, a reminder of the eternal beauty of the lagoon that endures despite contemporary pressures.

21

CONSERVATION

"AS IT WAS, WHERE IT WAS" RECONSIDERED

"... the shade of melancholy upon its beauty which is rapidly increasing, and will increase, until the waves which have been the ministers of her majesty become her sepulcher."

—JOHN RUSKIN, MID 1800s

Giorgio Nubar Gianighian nods at a 400-year-old desk inherited from his father-in-law. "Material matters. Take the piece of wood making up that desktop. Dirty, old, broken, stained, with signs of woodworm. Maybe the top of that desk is more modern than the legs, but it is still beautiful. It is an important element of our past: it should be preserved as it is. It is not a renewal that is needed, it needs conservation," he says. Bad restoration, renewing it to make it look new, risks destroying it. "Like a good dentist, you need to keep the materials, the teeth along with the signs of age.... When you have a little stain he won't take out the tooth. He will remove the small rotten parts and gently replace them with something... to maintain the tooth's integrity."

Gianighian, a former professor of conservation architecture at Iuav University in Venice, had been explaining the principles behind the restoration of a five-story tenement in Campo Santa Margherita. Constructed in 1803, the residence provides a home for eight families. Its windows look out on a tree-shaded, stone-paved square, busy with residents and students. The windows overlook the fishmongers' stalls where gulls squawk and wait for discarded fish heads. But the staircase was in a poor state of repair, and the landlord — an association that owns some 500 properties donated to charity — wanted it replaced. The stairs had been propped up by scaffolding.

Gianighian had examined the staircase carefully and noticed that it was mostly structurally sound. So instead of replacing it, he devised an attractive steel "crutch," consisting of four red posts joined by crossbars, which rise up through the stairwell between the flights, preserving, rather than replacing, the original stairway. The repair, typical of what could be done in the "other" 90 percent of buildings in Venice — that is to say, everything other than the palazzos, churches and monuments — showed that restoration with a bit of skill can cost the same or less than a rebuild. "You can prove that restoration is not as expensive as you think," he says.

This view of preservation is by no means universal. Definitions vary, even among the countries of Europe. Some nations allow replacement of time-worn parts with new materials. Others, like Italy, emphasize preservation of the layers and patina. Conflict arises when experts disagree about what constitutes the "authentic" building and which parts are worth preserving.

Take the tenement by the school of San Rocco, says Gianighian. Originally four sturdy houses until 1548–50, the tenement was cut into eighteen apartments with many alterations in subsequent centuries. Over 450 years' worth of "layers" can be discerned. "And this is beautiful, if you are trained to understand that this is beautiful, that men and women are beautiful, even though they have wrinkles and signs of age. This is what we have to teach students and the people, which is not simple."

Some colleagues in the School of Architecture disagree, saying that restoration is "complicated and boring," he says. They ask, "Why should I lose time designing a crutch when I can destroy the staircase" and create an opportunity "to express my powerful skills in design? With this concept in Venice you are creating bad conservation architects because you don't teach the beauty of the past." A colleague has argued that all the buildings of Venice are "false" because they are all "altered." Gianighian counters, "This is not falsity. This is integrity. This is authenticity. All the layers are there and you can see them and they contribute to the beauty." Restoration is about keeping "beauty for you, for me, for your children, the children of your children. You have to do something because by itself, [a thing of beauty] doesn't last," he says.

Before the late modern era, monuments everywhere were seen primarily as symbols, and less as valuable material records of the past. Until the mid-nineteenth century, restoring a building meant intervening and substituting or renovating the aging parts or simply updating according to the newer styles of the time. This approach was exemplified in Venice by the restoration of the thirteenth-century Fondaco dei Turchi, the Grand Canal warehouse and living quarters for Turkish merchants which today houses the Natural History Museum. It was renovated, or rather reinvented, by Federico Berchet in the 1860s by returning it to what he believed to be its original or intended state. Well intentioned as he was, the project failed because what he'd thought of as original turned out to be a figment of his imagination based on poor information and wishful thinking. The Grand Canal façade today recalls a Disney remake of a castle.

Fondaco dei Turchi as renovated today by Federico Berchet in the 1860s. He returned it to what he believed it was meant to look like. The result has been criticized.

A similar approach had been applied earlier to St. Mark's Basilica by nineteenth-century architects and later decried by John Ruskin, author of the groundbreaking 1853 book *The Stones of Venice*. Ruskin discriminated between what he considered good and bad historical periods. He was fanatically attached to the Venetian Gothic, Byzantine and Islamic styles of architecture as applied up to the fourteenth century. The Renaissance marked "the knell of architecture, and of Venice itself," but for him everything Gothic in early Republican Venice had once been a triumph of art; he called the Doge's Palace "the central building of the world" and Piazza San Marco "a great Book of Common Prayer." So, he was particularly pained when the Austrian administration undertook "modern works" in the nineteenth century designed to "clean" St. Mark's Basilica. "Off go all the glorious old weather stains, the rich hues of the marble which nature, mighty as she is, has taken ten centuries to bestow — already the noblest corner... on which... the age of generations had dyed in gold, is reduced to the color of magnesia, the old marbles displaced and torn down." Fortunately, a campaign led by Ruskin and Venetian Alvise Zorzi led to a reconsideration of the standards of conservation.

Such views were reinforced in 1902 by the sudden collapse of the bell tower in Piazza San Marco, a structure that is as immediately recognizable internationally as Big Ben or the Eiffel Tower. Alarm was felt around the world. On the day of the collapse, the city government voted unanimously that it should be rebuilt, "*com'era, dov'era*," "as it was, where it was" — at least in terms of its look. It was copied down to the last detail externally (while the unseen internal construction was thoroughly modernized) but the trauma of that well-publicized moment reverberated for decades. The idea that a monument must stay "as it was, where it was" persists in many cases today. Mayor of Venice Massimo Cacciari used the same formula on the night after La Fenice theater burned to the ground in 1996. It was rebuilt and reopened in 2004.

Since the 1970s, the basic principles of conservation have been agreed upon and codified, according to Mario Piana, chief conservator of St. Mark's Basilica. "From the last decades of the nineteenth century and for all of the twentieth, the tendency has been to concentrate on conservation of the materials, that is, there is this idea that any product of man's genius, not just a monumental building, is unique, and should be respected as much as possible, and modified as little as possible." But the compromises involved in maintaining the old structures continually cause controversy.

Take the architectural renovation done on a later building, the sixteenth-century Fondaco dei Tedeschi, historical residence and warehouse for German traders in Venice. It was converted in 2008 after many years of disuse into a posh shopping mall. "It's appalling," says Gianighian, one of its many detractors. "They destroyed late fifteenth-century masonry to create... a half-round window" to show off the escalator. The Dutch architect Rem Koolhaas, who redesigned the space, "said everything is false. Everything is restored recently... so I will remove it," Gianighian says, adding that Koolhaas got away with changes that were not in the city's master plan because he is "an archi-star" and with a "very powerful and rich" client. The building was then owned by textile magnates, the Benetton family.

Others, like restorer Adriano Cincotto, are more forgiving. "That palazzo was already destroyed" by earlier alterations of the *fondaco* made at times when "there was no culture of conservation.... To me it seems that they preserved the place pretty well considering what they had to work with," he says, referring to pre-existing alterations made during the decades when the building served as a post office. "Who knows what would have happened to it otherwise. At least it was rescued."

"Theory is something for the powerful and the classroom," says the hefty Cincotto, who is clearly used to working with his hands. He once led a team that removed, repaired and remounted, using molten lead, the earthquake-cracked, 9-ton, 10-meter steeples rising over the towering Santi Giovanni e Paolo basilica in Venice. "What counts for us is the welfare of the artifact. This is why we have official certification. We decide according to the circumstances." A professional restoration charter in 1977 established the guidelines for what conservation workers can do. "I've never worked in England, but I know that... when you have a deteriorated decorative element, you remake it, albeit using the original techniques. In England, by now, no materials are original.... Here everything is worn out, but it is original! The Italian custom is to strengthen, but situations do arise when you need to change something. That is done so that the restoration is like the original, but you can see that it has been made new."

The need for restoration in Venice is unending. "Look around! Even on the outside of the buildings you can see the render falling away. A city in this condition is not in any shape for tourism," he says, adding that not only do the restorers need to keep up with maintenance, but for many years they have found that the old restorations are now in need of re-restoring. But it doesn't all get done, he says, because money coming into Venice is drained off to pay the multi-billion euro bill for the over-budget and corruption-riddled Mose dam.

The debonair Chief Conservator Mario Piana pinpoints, among all the threats to Venice's wealth of heritage, the tourism monoculture. The fact that Venice now lives substantially from tourism "has impoverished Venetian society," he says. "A city is not only the physical part — the stones, the brick and the wood — a city is also a complex society. A society that is no longer complex is no longer a city," he says, referring to how the many skills of the populace and varied commercial activity have been stripped away by mass tourism.

Piana looks after St. Mark's Basilica, which is visited by 5 million tourists a year. "Over twenty years that makes 100 million visits," he says. "But it's probable that in all the years preceding, from the time the Basilica was built to the middle of the last century, it had nowhere near 100 million visits, probably far fewer." For this reason, the church is subjected to an unprecedented level of wear and tear. To preserve it, tourists must be channeled through roped-off areas with mats protecting the mosaic of marble on the floors.

The mass of humanity shuffling counterclockwise through the 1,000-year-old Italo-Byzantine structure, gazing up at the expanses of gilded mosaics under the domes and on the walls, also raise the level of humidity to a damaging degree. Especially in springtime, the moisture from the collective breaths of so many people deposits as water droplets on the walls like those that form when you take a beer out of a fridge on a hot day. "The condensation by itself causes little degradation, but the water is a vehicle for polluting compounds, like sulfur, which is emitted into the air by industry, and in the region around Venice, a great volume of it is produced," he says, even after the industry at Marghera on the terraferma near Venice was downsized.

The mosaic tiles tend to detach over time, but techniques to keep them up have been developed. In the nineteenth century, says Piana,

> The tiles were taken down and the mosaic was reconstructed, usually respecting the iconography, that is, the original subject. For the depiction of the Baptism of Christ, for example, the artist re-created the mosaic, but in the style of the epoch. In the 1900s, the *proti*, overseers of the time — the architects in charge of restoration — removed the mosaics, pulling up the vaulted arches behind them, gluing the mosaics to paper or cloth to hold them in place and then re-building the ribbing and adding brickwork backing.
>
> Today we would not do that sort of thing. If detached and reapplied the mosaics tend to go flat and line up. But when they were first created each one tended to have its own slight angle. This is subtle but important if you think of the effect the angle has on a gilded background, with a sheet of gold between two layers of glass. The reflection of the light would change considerably as would the angles of all the other tiles.

In recent decades, he has helped develop new preservation methods that involve carefully mapping hollow spaces behind the tiles with a stethoscope or a tuning fork. Then the backing mortar is injected through a 1 or 2 millimeter hole with porous slaked lime sometimes mixed with 3 to 5 percent resin, after washing out salt crystals between the wall, the plaster and the mortar on which the mosaic tiles are mounted. "This extends the preservation of the artifact, but anything, living or not, will come to an end," says Piana. "The problem is to delay that as much as possible."

He does what he can for the Basilica, but the effects of the monocultural economy go further. It has contributed to a wider decline in the "culture of maintenance," a failure in the standards of day-to-day upkeep affecting ordinary, non-monumental buildings, says Piana. Often this is because houses have become second or third homes lived in for just a few months a year. Absent owners don't know when the roof leaks or a plumbing problem occurs, thereby allowing it to persist and cause damage. And many new inhabitants don't understand how to maintain the old houses.

Take the traditional floors made of terrazzo — crushed marble fragments mixed with mortar and then polished. These floors are adapted to Venetian buildings, which move on their mud foundations. Being very heavy, thick, and yet able to adapt to movement, terrazzo adds to a structure's stability. Terrazzo lasts for centuries. Tiny cracks and minor undulations form due to movement, but applying a plaster-linseed oil mixture every few years closes them. Those who misunderstand this have tried substituting cheaper, lighter, and shorter-lived modern materials. But instead of forming tiny fissures like terrazzo, wood deforms, tiles break and concrete fractures into big pieces — eventually causing major structural problems, Piana explains.

"It's a different mentality," he says. "People who see undulation in the terrazzo floors don't understand that it is normal and you just need to slip a wedge under the furniture leg if it does not sit level.... So it's a mindset, but not only that... the whole building sector is changing." The concept of construction has shifted — due to the fact that labor now costs more than materials — to labor-saving solutions. Often, architects or owners who misunderstand the role of terrazzo choose to replace it. "Gradually, you lose one room, then another above, and so forth, and the structure becomes more precarious. The loss of materials is permanent." A similar situation arises in palazzos converted into hotels, which require a bathroom for every room. Builders cut into the walls and floors to install plumbing and wiring, severely weakening the structure. "There are laws that should be changed, but there's a whole culture that does not accept the idea that floors must be preserved." The situation is made worse by the loss of artisans who specialize in terrazzo. Only two or three remain.

❦

The work of preservation is down to owners, and fewer and fewer take the trouble. An exception is the Countess Elisabetta Czarnocki-Lucheschi, whose home is Palazzo Nani-Bernardo on the Grand Canal. The door from the street — along a long narrow passageway that dead-ends at the Grand Canal — opens to a courtyard and one of the fine secret gardens of Venice. The countess shows me the gardens and the piano nobile, where we stand looking out the windows at the Grand Canal.

"Once a family occupied each palazzo. Over the years, they were divided among the sons, daughters and grandchildren. And it's very sad," she says. "When I was a little girl on the vaporetto with my mother, she would tell me, 'This house belongs to so and so, this one to another and that one another.' And now going down the Grand Canal the only *palazzi* that still are owned from top to bottom by families belong to the Berlingeri in Santa Maria del Giglio and at San Moise, us and the Volpis. Just three. The rest are hotels or divided into apartments. The community is gone. My childhood friends have also left Venice; they've gone away. So it's sad that only a few are left."

The countess, in her sixties, is now the sole resident at Nani-Bernardo, where she devotes herself to "keeping the sixteenth-century palazzo alive" for the future and for her daughter and granddaughter who now live in Paris. But when she grew up, the house was full of family, with generation after generation inhabiting the four-story, 2,400-square meter residence with seventy steps up a staircase to the top floor. In order to pay for the upkeep of Nani-Bernardo, she has moved her own lodgings upstairs and rents out the piano nobile and the nineteenth-century Renaissance-style walled garden at back for weddings, corporate events, concerts and as a film set. Parts of the 2005 film *Casanova* with Jeremy Irons were shot there. She even rents out some of the luxurious rooms to visitors. "I do my best. But with the garden, maintaining this and that, going up and down the stairs, it's hugely demanding economically because life in Venice is very expensive; there are not enough artisans. It gets very complicated" when something needs fixing. "Can you imagine what 600 meters per floor means?"

"It's a great joy to have a house like this, and I am most proud of the property, and with such a garden" — where she has planted roses. "It is so special and unique. I do it with great love. I try to hold on as best I can," she adds. And after that what will become of the palazzo? She rolls her eyes. "When I am no longer around, someone will provide for it."

Upkeep of palazzos call for skills ranging from blacksmiths and gold leaf appliers to specialist plasterers and scores of others, but with standardized certification of the trades across Europe, the older skills are sometimes lost. In the past fifteen years, for example, "The culture of bricklaying has been destroyed. Bricklayers don't know how to make mortar because they can get it already premixed in bags. How is it possible to call yourself a bricklayer without knowing how to make mortar?" restorer Cincotto fumes. "Otherwise you just become a work machine. Once bricklayers had a brilliant culture." Restorers need traditional lime mortars that allow moisture to pass through, not modern pre-mixed mortars containing polymers, which make mortar harder and prevent the passage of moisture. "Restorers have to make their own mortar these days," says Cincotto.

Many craftsmen involved in restoration and artisanal work struggle to find the right materials. Bell makers, for instance, who hang their bells from wooden joists made of larch or chestnut, require timber carefully selected for its ability to augment sound. Oar makers use beech. The Republic of Venice commandeered whole forests for its own use for ship building and construction. They would split the trunks in quarters so that the grain remained good and visible, and thus more useful to artisans. They cut trees to order and according to the lunar phase. The wood was then sun-dried and cured, for a year or more. Now wood merchants cut down whole tracts of forest, dry the logs in computerized ovens for fifteen days and then saw them into straight planks, which distorts the grain, changing its sound qualities and making the wood unsuitable for some traditional uses.

When as a seventeen-year-old I lived in Venice in 1971, contrasting my American home with Venice's abundance of history left me overawed. I was a bit shocked, for example, that my Italian brother, Giovanni Keller, used to play basketball in what I then believed to be a disused fourteenth-century church. Only on my return half a century later did I realize that the repurposing of this building, the Scuola Grande della Misericordia, which in fact had been a welfare society under the Republic, had nothing at all to do with cultural indifference. It was one of hundreds of buildings belonging to societies and religious organizations forcibly closed by Napoleon as part of his colonization of Venice. After its secularization, the Misericordia was used as military lodgings, a warehouse and from World War I to 1991, a basketball court and gymnastics stadium. It was converted to a meeting and exhibition hall in 2015. Other similar buildings closed by the Frenchman were just razed. One became a cinema. Another a prison.

For many reasons, repurposing of Venice's thousands of old buildings and monuments is a routine part of its urban life. Take, for example, the award-winning 2013 restoration and reopening of the early 1800s Porta

Nuova Tower, a ten-story brick structure originally built for winching masts into position on tall sailing ships. Inside it now, massive brick arches lead to an observation platform on the roof with a breathtaking view once reached by a vertiginous, zigzagging wooden staircase. The tower's European-funded restoration was part of an ongoing revivification of the ancient Arsenal. It is now used by the Biennale of Arts for exhibitions and offices. But a number of the Arsenal buildings still lie empty or in ruins.

"The problem is that heritage has to be saved from obsolescence. A dead thing is of no use. The idea is not to have beautiful dead bodies," says Paolo Baratta, head of the Biennale, to a recent gathering of renovators and artisans in one of the Arsenal meeting rooms once used by the military to store torpedoes. "Heritage means taking care of objects that don't have any use anymore, but which we still want to remember." The Biennale has generated €40 million over the past two decades for renovation, he continues, but the job is not just over because an old building has been made good again. "There should be an awareness of the difference between preserving an object and preserving a living entity. The first challenge requires money and technicians and an ability to do the work, and the second requires an inflow of new blood into empty spaces. If there is no new blood, restoration of those empty spaces is difficult to justify economically. Public money cannot be spent. Whoever has the energy *and* the money for restoration, please apply."

The latter comments were addressed obliquely to Alessandro Ervas, a blacksmith at the meeting who had brought to Baratta's attention that the Biennale rarely uses Arsenal spaces to meet the objectives of the broader community, rather than simply those of the exhibition. Ervas had asked about a self-supporting project that had used the old Arsenal forges briefly in 2004 for public demonstrations and education. The project, in support of artisanship, was never resumed despite many spaces in the Arsenal still going unused. The magnificent tower, for example, is mostly empty. Other buildings have become, many say, "sterilized," blank white spaces for the exclusive use of the Biennale. This is why it is not uncommon to hear the view among residents that the Biennale is like a "spaceship" that arrives in May, flies off in November, and leaves little behind for the residents.

Others have been disappointed that the Arsenal itself has not taken up the possibility of becoming a living naval museum, building on its historic past, showcasing the great sailboats and ships and the skills that went into them. "The world would come to see!" says one proponent, rowing champion Gianfranco "Crea" Vianello. But so far, such dreams have not found support.

There are many, many dreams for an abundance of Venice's historical structures — palazzos, tenements, industrial buildings, even a ten-story crane in the Arsenal bought by the Italian military in 1886 to lift big guns onto ships. It stands rusty, empty and boarded up, its future locked up in bureaucracy, funding shortages and politics. But much restoration and conservation gets done too.

Cincotto, among others, soldiers on, despite sometimes having to turn away young people seeking work in the field. He is repelled by those who would unscrupulously undermine the restoration trade and angry about people he believes "milk" Venice for gain. "Because, after all," he says:

> ...[Re]storation is a beautiful line of work. It never gets boring. You never do anything repetitive. You pass your days studying, too... I have lots of experience in all sorts of areas, and have learned a great deal, but I continually have to study materials and search for solutions, judging which way works best. You are working in beautiful places, you see beautiful things, you learn so many things... and when you overcome difficulties, it's like climbing a mountain.... Finally, you look behind you — like if you went up Mount Blanc — and when you're on top you are near God, you feel like God, don't you? This is the same sensation. When you overcome difficulties that are not easy, real ones, when you succeed, your heart is full.

The question often asked, however, is which Venice should be saved?

Venice has always been making decisions about how it should build and shape itself, whether to adhere to "*com'era, dov'era*," preserving Venice "as it was, where it was" or to create instead a Venice for the present and future, one focused more on its contemporary tastes and needs.

The foreigners, the donors, the tourists — even UNESCO itself — tend to fall on the side of preservation, of keeping Venice true to the past, to the Venice of the Republic, as a repository of history. Even some historians fail to appreciate that Venice has continued to evolve, giving short shrift, for instance, to the way its citizens in 1848 briefly reclaimed their independence, or to the early twentieth-century entrepreneurs who brought industrial growth, or how, since 1966, Venetians have powered an environmental movement to save the city. Venetians themselves can struggle to identify which Venice they want to preserve, the "victorious history" that glorifies the past, the one that is attractive to many outsiders, or the history that records "the crimes, follies and tragedies, the pomposity and greed, the bathos, the parochialism of humankind, together with the joys and successes," through to the present, in the words of historian R. J. B. Bosworth.

For Venetian novelist Giovanni Montanaro, the floods of 1966 were a watershed. "In 1966… the city was greatly transformed from what you might call a normal city, into an exceptional city," he says. "Before '66, the idea was to bring in more cars, to push it into modernity. After '66, people said, 'No, it's different.' And from that moment the vision created for Venice was so firmly set that it is hard now to create a different perception of the city." The changes since 1966 transformed Venice from being seen as a city "that had to run at the speed of the world to one that had to be saved." That effort has given Venice better sewers, transport and many restorations but also, according to Montanaro, "We have this idea of preserving everything from the past, which is important, but it has also become a bit of a weight.... A religious sensibility" that is blocking the growth of the city. "Our idea that 'the past is sacred,'" has consequences, adds Montanaro, as preservation trumps everything, so that even the little marble lions next to the St. Mark's Basilica that kids used to jump on is now fenced off.

"In reality, today's Venice is more influenced by the idea of decadence, the *Death in Venice*, the Romantic Venice," according to Shaul Bassi, professor of Shakespeare at the University of Venice. "Instead, we need to return to the idea of Venice as a contemporary and global city — that of Shakespeare. Shakespeare did not look at Venice as a city of the past. He saw it as a city of the present! He said, 'Ah, London could be like Venice, or should be like Venice.'" At a time when the existence of the British monarchy was being questioned, Venice attracted interest for, among other features, its government by aristocrats instead of by a king or queen. In the sixteenth century, Shakespeare understood that Venice, much more than Tudor London, was an international, cosmopolitan city.

In Bassi's view, "Venetians accept that they need to change the way they think or else they will succumb to nostalgia. Nostalgia can be paralyzing... if one only thinks of the Venice of the 1970s and reminisces about it, saying, 'Ah, how beautiful Venice was. There were schools, Venetians, palazzos and not so many hotels.' But we can't go back. However, now we have the thriving cultural life of a great city! For me, there's more stuff than in San Francisco." For the professor, who knows all about imaginary Venices, "This moment is highly schizophrenic for Venice because it is 'the best of times and the worst of times'. From a social perspective it's the worst ever, because our society becomes ever smaller and angrier. But from the cultural perspective it's a magic moment because every day there is a new museum, a new exhibition, a new spectacle. However, if everything becomes only tourism, we are a bit..." he says, trailing off, fighting off thoughts of a darker future. Personally, he says he strives to be an optimist because he believes there is still a chance of using culture to create employment which will bring Venetians back to live in the city and thereby maintain the community.

FORMER MAYOR
ON VENICE AND THE WORLD
PAOLO COSTA

Venice is the whole world's problem, or so it feels, according to the ultimate political insider, Paolo Costa. He draws on his varied career as a parliamentarian, his time as Venice University rector, experience as an EU and Italian minister and time as head of the port of Venice (2008–2017) and mayor of Venice (2000–2005).

"What does the world want from Venice? That Venice stays there, that it should not change, not even a little. It should not adapt or become a city of tomorrow, but rather stay a city of the past, physically, that one can visit. That's the global attitude and what the world wants.

"The problem is that Venice has this silent partner — the whole world. Among the people I meet there exists no one who doesn't tell me what I must do for Venice — even if I don't ask. When I was mayor I adopted this rhetorical expedient: I would say, to ambassadors and well-cultured people, 'Naturally, you know the expression [used when the original thirteen American colonies rose up against being taxed by the British Empire], "No taxation without representation," ... Well, here in Venice it's the other way around: "No representation without taxation"! Please don't come to me to say what I must do, because you don't pay! OK? If you pay, you may speak'. Everybody offers their advice in good conscience, and is convinced of being right, because Venice belongs to the world!

"There are places that culturally belong to the world.... But we are expected to bear the costs of keeping Venice for the world. But it's not just costs. They also expect me to do what they say! 'Don't you dare use Venice! Don't you dare make it live in a modern way. Don't risk building a transport system,' like the underground transport system I wanted. 'Continue to use only the vaporetti!' [which were introduced over a century ago].

“The cultural problem at the heart of this is complicated. The idea was ‘*com’era, dov’era*’. When La Fenice theater [burned down in 1996], it was like a wound that needed to be healed immediately. They wanted to build a theater with 1,050 seats, but economically that would not fly. If we had built a modern theater of 2,000 seats with all the amenities of today, it would be self-sustaining, but instead the theater we have has to be subsidized every day because it is too small. What distresses me is the fact that the greatest defender in cultural activities should be UNESCO, which does not understand these things.

“Surely you know of Williamsburg in the United States? [the ‘living history’ museum in Virginia, a reconstructed town where the inhabitants wear period dress of the eighteenth century]. I went to see it and I understood. I said, ‘This is Venice in ten years!’ It is not that Venice is dying. Venice has died fifty times in history, with the plague and so forth. Venice survives. We are the generation losing Venice. My generation is failing to maintain the equilibrium between the continuation of its history and modern life. You should read the 1913 invective of [Giovanni] Papini against Florence. He was a futurist and he said, ‘Soon Florence will become a city where we pay 100 lire to enter and where we are reduced to exploiting, like beggars, the glory of the nation and the curiosity of foreigners.’ Between 1995 and 1996, after having visited Williamsburg, I calculated the maximum number of tourists that Venice could support, but it was based on the capacity for transport, rates of flow etcetera. Today, that point of view, which everyone quotes, counts for nothing. Because what counts today is not how many people circulate on the streets, [but] that each of those houses, where people lived until recently will, in a short time, be inhabited by no one.

“We are no longer state of the art. And here in Venice, the city of Aldus Manutius [Aldo Manuzio, the fifteenth-century printer who invented small portable books], the city that experienced centuries of innovation globally, now we can’t do anything! You can’t touch anything… any of the physical structures. No one is dealing with that. With my idea to redesign the port [a proposal that was not taken up, but if it had been taken up] we could… again become a leader and return to the sense of the Venetian Republic!

“There is no longer any pride. Most Venetians are old, fat, and happy to live off their incomes. What can be done? We can do what Venetians did before. They brought in people from Albania, the Greeks, the Slovenians, the Croats, the poor Italians. That was the Republic of Venice. It was the first multicultural republic that existed in the world. What is Italy? Is it a country that has renounced innovation? Do we sit and watch and exploit what we have? No, for goodness sake! But it is difficult to convince someone who gets along very well, earning a lot of money without effort, to give that up for something different.”

22

MYTH

HOW TO "READ" PIAZZA SAN MARCO

> *Pax tibi, Marce, evangelista meus.*
> *Hic requiescet corpus tuum.*
>
> *Peace be with you, Mark, my evangelist.*
> *Here shall your body rest.*
>
> —THE PROPHECY THAT BECAME THE MOTTO OF THE VENETIAN STATE

My return route from some engagement, late one evening in the winter of 1971, had taken me across a deserted Piazza San Marco. I had been warned about what to expect. As I stepped through the darkness under the arches enclosing the far end of the vast open square, a short woman with bleached and permed blondish hair shouted at me gruffly, "*Vuoi fare l'amore?*" I looked down without responding and plowed on as she called out again, with a note of exasperation, "Do you want to make love?" As a shy seventeen-year-old I had never encountered a prostitute before and was a bit terrified by the thought. This lone lady of the night, with a coat wrapped over what might have been scanty clothing, looked to me, frankly, old and ugly, which had also been predicted. The Republic has a long and colorful history of prostitution, courtesans and sexual liberty. In the 1970s, at least, the few remaining practitioners had a reputation for being near retirement age. Yet, curiously, solicitation of this sort, perhaps with those same words, had always been practiced under the archways, right back to the early Republic. It was once one of the many sorts of activities that we might today expect to see in a scene of a medieval town center painted by Pieter Bruegel the Elder or in colorful depictions of a traditional Arab souk.

Piazza San Marco has today been sanitized, controlled and, more recently, mobbed by tourists, but at least until Napoleon came on the scene at the close of the eighteenth century, city life thrived there. It was not at all like the forecourt of Versailles whence he had come. It was filled with fish, meat and vegetable sellers, street theater acts, snake oil haranguers, tooth pullers, bread bakers and money changers, mountebanks and newssheet hawkers, all clamoring for the attention of Venetians along with pilgrims, traders and later, Grand Tour visitors. In Piazza San Marco, officials conducted gruesome tortures on criminals and executed traitors by hanging; processions of thousands from every part of Venetian society, led by blaring silver trumpets, snaked through the square some forty times a year to mark religious and political events.

The space served as the front door to Venice, the greeting point for emperors, popes, pilgrims and traders from all over the world. It was also the ritual, ceremonial and communal center of gravity of Venetian society, where La Serenissima asserted her identity and values for all to see. While the lively street and ceremonial life of the Republic now has to be left to the imagination, or as in my encounter, just glimpsed, the square itself still tells the stories that the Republic's government wanted its people and the outside world to be told. They can be read in the buildings, the art and the layout, in the decoration and the words inscribed in stone, cast in metal and painted on canvas.

This "front door" to Venice, contrary to the way most people see Piazza San Marco, opens onto the water, to the bacino — the harbor where ships once docked and where important people arrived and departed. It was the view that was created to show off Venice's power and dignity.

From out on the water, anyone on a passing vaporetto can see — as did the sailors of yore — the broad *molo*, the stone-paved quayside, and behind it the Piazzetta, a square nearly as big as the central arena in the Colosseum. A pair of red granite Roman-era columns stand like giant sentry guards either side of this great gateway, and, at the far end of the space, the Italo-Byzantine arches of St. Mark's Basilica point upward toward the church domes looming like mountains above. Opposite the church stands the sturdy ten-story bell tower, with the cottage-sized *Loggetta* covered with ornamental carvings at its base. Flanking the Piazzetta on the right with one side facing the bacino, the refined Gothic Doge's Palace rises three or so stories with its wide façade of repeated rows of pointed arches below rounded arches, all beneath the expansive pink and white Oriental tracery walls. On the left side, further along the quay, the white Istrian stone Biblioteca Nazionale Marciana, the library with its long row of Doric columns, gives a taste of classical revival as does the squat, imperial-looking Zecca, the Mint, adjacent, where once the Republic forged the gold ducat and silver *grosso* coins used all over Europe, the Middle East and beyond.

Just inside the "front door," if one walks over to the far side of the Piazzetta — the shorter leg of the "L"-shaped Piazza San Marco — the long leg of the "L" opens up into the breathtaking piazza itself. There, the great gilded façade of St. Mark's Basilica faces an area three times as big. Entering from the Piazzetta, one stands just under the first of the archways of the Basilica, each with a story in gilded mosaic over a doorway. One might think the five arches, five domes and many spires of the Basilica were designed to be seen from afar, perhaps from the other end of the square, which is bounded by covered arcades of the three-story buildings bordering it. From there, the perspectives formed by the repeated arches make the Basilica look even grander and give a clear view of the centerpiece: the four bronze horses on the church balcony. In fact, the visitor was expected to approach first from the Piazzetta. That is why the mosaics introducing the church recount from right to left the story that Venetians most wanted to tell, the one that explains who they are: the story of Saint Mark — and understanding the piazza built in his name and the ideas behind it begins with understanding what Saint Mark means to Venice.

Venice needed stories; it was a new city. Unlike virtually all its contemporaries it had no ties to Rome, which was the source of legitimacy for others, including Byzantium. In the early ninth century, the Doge's Palace was a simpler building, surrounded by thatched, wooden houses. The square was a field with a canal running through it. But Venice already had its driving ambition.

The elaborations of the story of Saint Mark — one of Christ's disciples who is said to have authored the Gospel of Mark and founded the church in Alexandria — were launched in all likelihood, according to historian Iain Fenlon, "in a piece of carefully crafted mythology, invented to meet political and ecclesiastical circumstances in the aftermath of the schism of 606," when the cities of Aquileia, Grado and Venice first came to blows over jurisdictional church matters. After that, from the eighth to the fourteenth century, the legend was further embroidered to tie the saint first to Aquileia and then directly to Venice, despite a complete lack of evidence that Mark ever visited the upper Adriatic.

The myth was told in a story called the *translatio*, telling how, fortuitously, Venetians who landed at Alexandria in 828 heard the Caliph planned to desecrate Saint Mark's tomb. The merchants secreted the body out in a basket covered with pork, which repelled the Muslim customs officers. By the thirteenth century, another part was added, the *praedestinatio*, recounting how in the first century during a journey to Rome, Mark landed on a small lagoon island where the St. Mark's Basilica was later to be built. He fell asleep and in his sleep an angel told him that was to be his resting place: *Pax tibi, Marce, evangelista meus. Hic requiescet corpus tuum,* Peace be with you, Mark, my evangelist. Here shall your body rest. The text appears in the symbol of Venice, an open book held by the winged lion of Saint Mark.

The relics of Saint Mark gave Venice a one-up on its rivals. In the Middle Ages, holy relics represented the spiritual link between man and God. Saint Mark was represented to the people as Venice's special protector, enabling the city to claim God-given rights to the sea and confirmation that the doge's authority was vested by God, like that of a medieval king.

Piazza San Marco, to become the foremost symbol of Venice, was the heart of the city's religious and civic geography and the embodiment of the myths. The extant church building today, begun in 1063 and finished thirty years later, replaces two earlier versions. The Doge's Palace we see today, replacing two earlier versions, was begun in 1341 and has since undergone many restorations due to fires in subsequent centuries. Works to make the square more dignified and scenic, as befitted an important state, were already underway in the twelfth century under Doge Sebastiano Ziani. The square was paved in an elaborate pattern and columns added in the Piazzetta, to recall imperial Roman models, with the statue of the *Winged Lion of Saint Mark* on one column recalling Roman traditions, and that of the rather sidelined Saint Theodore, patron before Saint Mark came along, recalling the Byzantium tradition, on the other. Venice styled itself as the new Byzantium, Rome and Jerusalem combined. It would continue to build the square through the seventeenth century.

Venice's ideological messages — propaganda, advertising or public relations in modern terms — were continually transmitted to the populace through the scores of religious and civic ceremonies centered on Piazza San Marco.

One of the most spectacular, the Andata, is depicted in the 1496 painting *Procession in Piazza San Marco* by Gentile Bellini, which shows the wide piazza in the foreground and the Basilica behind it. To the sound of chanting choirs, musicians strumming instruments, blaring trumpets and beating drums, and with eight swallow-tailed banners of Saint Mark flying, thousands of the city's VIPs — noblemen, citizens, and representatives of the scuole — walk through the square with the doge, dressed in gold cloth and wearing his camel-hump shaped cap, the *corno*. Under a canopy around him are displayed the symbolic objects of ducal privilege, including a folding ceremonial stool and six silver trumpets given to Ziani by Pope Alexander III in gratitude for hosting the 1177 visit of Frederick Barbarossa, the Holy Roman Emperor, who had agreed to back Alexander III over a rival. The gifted emblems of authority show the doge to be the equal of popes and emperors. From Piazza San Marco the procession snakes through the streets of Venice, symbolically uniting the city together through the ceremonial display of harmony and unity.

Among the gifts Pope Alexander III is said to have given Ziani in gratitude for his mediation was a golden ring. It became the basis of the symbolic Marriage of the Sea ritual during Festa della Sensa, which was celebrated annually on Ascension Day, the fortieth day after Easter. The doge would be rowed out from Piazza San Marco in his majestic, double-decker, forty-two oar galley, the *Bucintoro*, to the opening of the lagoon to the sea at Lido, accompanied by an armada of gondolas, sailing boats and the city's prettiest courtesans. He would say into the winds: "Grant, O Lord, that for us and all who sail thereon, the sea may be calm and quiet." The doge then took the golden wedding ring from his finger and tossed it into the depths with the time-honored words: "We wed thee, O Sea, in token of our true and perpetual domination over thee." This rite of spring, performed yearly for centuries, was probably co-opted by Venice into its political-religious mythology, perpetuating similar ceremonies that had long taken place around the Mediterranean to appease the gods at the opening of the fishing season.

❧

At other times, Piazza San Marco reverted to its usual function as a meeting place. Among other colorful events in the square were public celebrations at the end-of-Carnival Giovedì Grasso, or Fat Thursday, when pigs and a bull were released into the Piazzetta, remorselessly chased, captured and then butchered on the spot with the meat handed out to the crowd. This brutal spectacle was watched from stands on either side of the smaller square by the doge, foreign ambassadors and nobility.

❧

On a rainy November afternoon, I enter the Basilica, following a slow line of visitors as far as the cash register set up to get visitors to pay for a peek at the Pala d'Oro, the tenth- to twelfth-century altarpiece with gilded frame above Saint Mark's burial crypt. This is a shop window-sized box of wonders with 1,927 gems and a series of 187 enamel pictures, each as big as a biggish paperback book page. They include the earliest depiction of the Saint Mark story. In ten panels with gilded backgrounds, little snapshots of action show the saint going to Aquileia, to Alexandria and finally at his *translatio* reception in Venice when he was greeted by the bishop — not the doge. A little further on, in the Cappella San Clemente, a dome of glittering mosaics arches overhead, showing the same scenes but these were added at the end of the twelfth century. This time, the doge with five patricians, who are soon to form the Great Council, are shown among the greeting party — an urgent update, so to speak — as by then the politicians wanted to be front and center.

My peregrination takes me around the church to another cash register where there is an arrow on a stand, this one angled up a steep flight of steps to the balcony and museum, where I can get a closer look at the bronze horses. The ones outside, exposed to the weather and pollution as they stand there on eight short marble columns, are replicas. Inside, you see the original war trophies brought back from the Hippodrome in Constantinople. The originals would have looked striking in the sun in front of St. Mark's Basilica as they were then gilded and adorned with silver reins. Today, with some of the original gilding still visible, the animals gaze directly at you, radiating a nobility and strength that feels remarkably lifelike.

I go back down and then out through the circuitous side exit of the Basilica, passing quickly the north façade, the victim of overenthusiastic nineteenth-century restorers who wanted to "clean" it, heading to the opposite external wall, the one facing the Piazzetta. The best booty was placed here, facing the "front door" for maximum visibility. I stand for a moment to take in everyone's favorite: the Tetrarches, porphyry sculptures of two pairs of half-size men side by side at the corner, each with one hand on the hilt of their swords, heads almost cheek-to-cheek and with one of each pair throwing an arm around the other. Hacked off a column in Constantinople, these are the four kings who had once ruled parts of third-century Roman Emperor Diocletian's subdivided empire. Their abandonment to this not particularly dignified display makes me recall Percy Bysshe Shelley's poem "Ozymandias" about the dictator whose broken statue lies forgotten in the desert, only these lacked the "sneer of cold command" on the lips of the hubristic leaders. These guys' short reigns appear to have been positively jolly.

I note, too, the inconspicuousness of a squat porphyry stump a few steps away, the Pietra del Bando. It was used as a dais to make public announcements and display the severed heads of traitors.

The story of Venetian myth would not be complete without mention of the worship of the Virgin Mary.

Of the 541 neighborhood shrines dotting Venice's streets and squares, 217 are devoted to the Madonna. They are mostly little statues in niches, often with a light bulb in place of candles. The Virgin Mary takes center stage in some twenty churches, too, not least the oldest church, Santa Maria Assunta, in Torcello, and Santa Maria della Salute church, which gives thanks for the end of the plague.

As I continue to explore the square, I look up at the Doge's Palace. Around the Porta della Carta, the gate facing the Piazzetta, are a series of statues that are political allegories for good government — fortitude, prudence, and charity. But my attention is drawn to the roundel sculpture on the wall facing the Piazzetta which personifies Venetian justice. A characteristic often vaunted by the city's government, justice is shown as the robed female Venetia, symbol of the Republic itself, combined with touches of the Virgin Mary. She is crowned, holding a sword and seated on a Salomic throne of lions — a promise to the people that justice will be delivered. The sculpture highlights the role of the Virgin Mary in Venetian state ideology.

When I go inside the palace, the link to the Virgin is made even more explicit in the image by Tintoretto, *Paradise*, reputed to be the largest painting ever made on canvas, which shows the Virgin, representing Venice, at top where she is kneeling before Christ. It makes clear that in one of the longest-lasting republics in history, all important decisions would be made under the auspices of Christ and the Virgin, with inspiration from heavenly hosts. Directly above it, on the ceiling, the culminating image, the *Triumph of Venice* by Paolo Veronese, shows the queenly Venetia floating above a city representative of Rome, while a winged Victory offers her a crown and, below, the Virtues of Peace, Security, Felicity, Abundance and Liberty form her court on a cloud. Beneath them are shown the submissive Venetian provinces gratefully celebrating their protection by the Republic before the lion of Saint Mark.

The Virgin connection is neatly tied to myth, with the date of the foundation of Venice said to be noon on March 25, 421, thus placing the moment on the Feast of Annunciation, the day when the archangel Gabriel informed the Virgin Mary that she would be the mother of Jesus Christ. No matter that this founding date was established in the fourteenth century; the story reinforces the specialness of the Venetian state — unconquered, with her virginity unviolated by outside forces. The idea makes up part of the cult of the Madonna, furnishing a comforting image of security for people from all social classes, and one that is intimately connected to their faith in the state itself — one of the reasons, perhaps, that the Venetians in the time of the Republic remained so loyal over such a long time.

At the end of the fifteenth century, Piazza San Marco had an unfinished feel. More importantly perhaps, the city was feeling unloved. That is to say, it was nearly broke, having drained its treasury spending on a war with Naples, and to give its insolvency a brave face (as one does), the city launched into a building program. It splurged on the Torre dell'Orologio, intending to show the rest of Italy that Venice had not lost its verve. Over the entrance to the main commercial street, the Merceria, the clock tower features two mechanized wild men in bronze who ring the hour. But Venice's reputation was soon tarnished again. Defeat on the mainland at Agnadello in 1509 briefly deprived it of its Stato da Terra, leaving Venice weakened, such that diplomat and political philosopher Niccolò Machiavelli commented that, while Venice eventually won back the mainland territories, "They have never recovered their former renown or power, and they live at the discretion of others, as do all other Italian principalities."

But in an effort to polish its image and regain confidence in the city as an international entrepôt, Venice continued to add showy buildings to the square.

In the sixteenth century, it began by rebuilding the north side of the Piazza, called the Procuratie Vecchie, in a neo-Byzantine style, with repeated arches like those of Orthodox churches. Later, when Jacopo Sansovino took charge of the square under the guiding hand of Doge Andrea Gritti, classical Roman architecture popular in the Renaissance came with him. Raising the tone of Piazza San Marco, he pulled down a tavern and older houses in order to erect the Loggetta, a meeting place for officials at the foot of the bell tower. Sansovino also built the Biblioteca Nazionale Marciana (a belated home for a gift of Greek manuscripts left to Venice by Greek Bishop Basilios Bessarion), and the Zecca, the Mint, all of them along the molo, the quayside. The construction continued into the early seventeenth century — completing the building of Piazza San Marco under the Republic.

The process of establishing a fitting appearance for the remarkable city of Venice had taken the whole of its lifespan.

23

LEGACY

PURSUING THE "GREAT VENICE" DREAM

> *"In the Port Marghera industrial zone, sites will principally be found for those facilities that spread smoke, dust and fumes damaging to humans, or that discharge poisonous substances in the water or produce vibrations and noise."*
>
> —*REGULATORY GENERAL PLAN* OF THE COMMUNE OF VENICE, 1962

For Luciano Mazzolin, the story of his thirty years of work at the troubled petrochemical plants in Marghera illustrates ways the industrialization of Venice went badly wrong.

"The subject is quite hard to explain, because the story of Marghera began well before my time, way back in 1917," he says as we sit in a quiet café overlooking the lagoon.

From the mid-1970s he and others battled with management and a government that failed to acknowledge the danger posed to workers at the Marghera plants, especially those producing vinyl chloride, a substance widely used to make PVC for packaging, pipes, automotive parts, construction materials and furniture. For years, workers handled the highly carcinogenic substance without adequate protection, while the owners obfuscated, denied and prevaricated about deaths, illnesses and the harm to the environment that vinyl chloride was causing.

"They were out-and-out criminals, in short," says Mazzolin, with vehemence. "They knew all too well the damage they were doing. We were able to find documents from the 1960s in which the company recognized the risks," but they continued anyway. "The information was there, and they had it, but it cost too much to dispose of these materials properly." Yet it took another three decades of protest and legal action to bring the chapter to a close. But what embitters the mustachioed, white-haired union activist and, later, city councilor, is that the convictions eventually achieved by the state prosecutor were an exception. The industry just moved to other sites in the developing nations, where the processes continue. "These things happen everywhere; they have happened in all the industrial plants in Europe and around the world."

As Mazzolin noted, this final chapter forms part of a much longer story, one that began at least a century earlier. It began with a dream of renewed greatness for Venice, a dream that has now run its course. For some time, Venice has been looking for new beginnings.

At the turn of the twentieth century, the Venetian entrepreneur Giuseppe Volpi and his coalition of Venetian heirs and business magnates envisioned *la grande Venezia*, Great Venice, the capital of a commercial empire, a step towards making Venice a model of capitalism. He said the industrial port at Marghera would represent a "new city of work" to show Venetians the meaning of modernity.

The earliest steps toward Great Venice began with the resorts on Lido. Before and between the two world wars, Volpi championed investors who threw their weight behind making Lido the prestigious resort island that it would eventually become. In quick succession in 1908 and 1909, Venice saw the building of the Veneto-Byzantine-Moorish extravaganza that is the Grand Hotel Excelsior, but also the restrained, classical and discreet Grand Hotel des Bains. Lido, by the turn of the century, was attracting Belle Époque royalty, celebrities and wealthy folk from around Europe and from America who found in Venice and Lido the right combination of high culture, physical comfort and liberty. In 1932, Volpi launched the international film festival on Lido, the first of its kind before Cannes, to bring the world's attention to the island. Today the week-long festival continues to thrive. The Lido beach resorts, meanwhile, have fallen out of fashion. The elegant Hotel des Bains is boarded up, its fate uncertain, while the Excelsior struggles on, but most of its elite customers have long since bolted.

In 1917, during the First World War, the Marghera industrial area began construction by reclaiming lagoon next to the older village of Mestre. Part of a trend that saw the great port-building projects at Genoa, Naples, Marseille and Le Havre, Marghera would grow by the 1930s to become a showcase for the fascism of Benito Mussolini, covering an area three times that of historic Venice by the 1960s with granaries, refineries and petrochemical and metallurgy plants employing 33,000 workers. A 1926 Fascist decree brought Marghera, Mestre, Burano and Murano into the current unified Venice administration, adding to the sense of a "Great Venice." But, by the 1970s, de-industrialization in the West combined with the petroleum crisis and the rise of industry in the developing world, undermined its economic foundations. Scandals over massive toxic dumping, under-investment in the plants and machinery, plus deaths from bladder cancer due to chemical exposure hastened its end.

Today the workforce has dropped sharply to 3,000 and large expanses of the area are now industrial wasteland. The port is still going strong; new kinds of green industry are slowly coming in and most of the toxic factories have closed or been updated, but the poison left behind remains, putting the brakes on hopes of reusing the area.

"The idea of 'Great Venice' as conceived of by Volpi was perhaps a bit naive," according to Carlo Rubini, an expert on the city's industrial history. "It was incomplete as an idea, and would have needed a global strategy. They tried to create a great city, a metropolis, especially during the Fascist years," when they could do what they wanted without democratic interaction. "What remains is this disjointed reality, where Venice is ever more concentrated on tourism, Mestre is a residential location and industry in Marghera is in decline. In essence, they created three areas in crisis."

Volpi, born in 1877, and his generation faced a period of grave poverty for ordinary Venetians. His defenders point to the employment and economic rejuvenation he fostered. His detractors emphasize the environmental damage and human suffering the industries he launched ended up causing and his controversial roles in the Fascist government of the day. He led its brutal colonization of Libya in the 1930s (for which he later became "Count" Volpi) and served as finance minister under Mussolini, who brought Italy into World War II on the side of the Nazis and led Italy into its own civil conflagration. Either way, he remains central to the history of Venice.

Volpi was certainly not alone in seeking to make Venice "great" at the beginning of the twentieth century. Gabriele D'Annunzio in his 1900 novel, *Il Fuoco* (*The Fire*), glorified the city and its imperial past, and in his political activity laid a groundwork for fascism that would be carried forward by Mussolini. His view was part of a larger re-evaluation of the past that was taking place at that time, causing some to put their faith in applying new ideas in science, technology and nation-building to human life in extreme ways. Some of these ideologies were threatening, such as fascism, and others simply provocative, such as the views of the futurist Filippo Marinetti. He derided the cautious, nostalgic critics of these new ideas, writing in 1910 *Contro Venezia Passatista*, (*Against Past-Loving Venice*). In a bid for publicity, the poet and writer flung thousands of copies of this manifesto, as a call to arms, from the recently rebuilt St. Mark's bell tower:

> To hell with that Venice mooned over by tourists.... Let us prepare for the birth of an industrial and military might in Venice that'll ravish that great Italian lake, the Adriatic, once and for all. There's no time to lose. Fill in all the stinking little canals with the rubble of those crumbling, leprous palazzos. Burn all the gondolas, those rocking chairs for cretins.

These ideas flourished in part due to the crisis Venice faced after the fall of the Republic in 1797. For the first time, foreigners — not Venetians — were determining the direction of Venice. The Venetian identity under the French was systematically suppressed, images of the lion of Saint Mark literally chopped off the walls. In Piazza San Marco they burned the Libro d'Oro, The Golden Book, listing all the nobility. Even uttering "*Viva San Marco*," "Long Live Saint Mark", was punishable by death. The humiliation went much further.

The Carnival, the Sensa and other Venetian festivals were banned. The French introduced reforms that some supported, though the Venetians had never before felt the need to be liberated. As early as October 18, 1797, after Napoleon had signed the Treaty of Campoformio, handing all of Venetian lands over to the Austro-Hungarian Hapsburg's anti-liberal monarchy, even the supporters of Napoleon's democracy felt betrayed. Even worse, before the hand-over, the French had broken up priceless Venetian medieval art for its gold and precious stones. They confiscated paintings, including a vast canvas by Veronese, 500 rare manuscripts and the ancient winged lion perched on the column in the Piazzetta; they stripped bare the Arsenal shipyards, ripped the gilding off the doge's ceremonial galley, the *Bucintoro*, and burned it ostentatiously in the bacino. They made off with the Cavalli di San Marco that had adorned St. Mark's Basilica. The horses were shipped off to Paris, where they were installed on Napoleon's Arc de Triomphe du Carrousel, after being put on show separately with the declaration that, "They are at last in a free country!" thus rubbing in the fact of the French victory and Napoleon's view of Venice as an undeserving police state.

When the Austrians took over on January 18, 1798, they cosmetically restored Venetian legal codes, but did little for the economy. Six years later the French came back, without their earlier pretensions to democracy. Napoleon, who had declared himself emperor, treated Venice as one of the spoils of war and set about undermining the power of the Catholic Church because he felt threatened by it. Though a Catholic himself, he ordered nearly sixty monasteries and convents closed. Many scuole, the religious benevolent societies, and churches were closed, demolished or converted, their art shipped off to Milan or Paris.

Napoleon then organized a hero's welcome for himself to Venice in 1807, after which he declared the city undisciplined and characterless. He announced plans to reshape Venice in the image of Paris, where modern principles of urban planning dictated that cities be organized in regular shapes, with broad avenues and large parks. Buildings and churches were razed to clear the broad waterside walkway, Riva degli Schiavoni, while a poor neighborhood was cleared for the Public Gardens, now site of the Biennale, and the church at the west end of Piazza San Marco was replaced with a symmetrical structure for a royal palace with a grand staircase entranceway that is now the Correr Museum.

After Napoleon was defeated, the Austrians returned to Venice in April 1814, promising to replace what he had taken. They brought the bronze horses and lion back from Paris, restoring a bit of Venetian self-respect. Little else came back, though. Poverty was evident everywhere in the crumbling housing for the lower classes and in the fact that the patrician families were selling off art collections and villas or renting crumbling palazzos to foreigners. The Austrians acted to boost living standards, making Venice a free port, running in gas pipelines to light Piazza San Marco and, most controversially, building the railway bridge in 1846 mainly to link their industrial centers in Milan with the sea. This structure helped expose Venetians to other Italians and foreigners, feeding nationalistic feelings against the strict Austrians, whose spies and censorship rankled the Venetians. When uprisings around Europe broke out in 1848, Venice saw its chance.

Led by the modest, bespectacled lawyer, Daniele Manin, Venetians stormed the Arsenal on March 22, taking Austrian weapons and warships. The Austrians, facing defeats on other fronts, just evacuated Venice, and Manin declared the restoration of the Republic. People shouted the forbidden words: *Viva San Marco!* But it was not to last. The Austrians later laid siege and bombed, and on August 19, 1849, the Venetians surrendered. Manin and the other leaders fled. The Austrians returned to rule until October 19, 1886 when Venice joyfully welcomed troops of the new nation state of Italy.

From that time onward, being Venetian also meant being Italian, and Italians are people who, like Volpi, wanted to find a way to reclaim their pride.

Lido's deserted beaches, on a cold, windblown day in late November, looked more like they did before they became fashionable. Along one side bulldozers had pushed up a long, head-height mound of sand to prevent the winter squalls from washing away the beach huts and amusement parks. Without bathers, with the view of the pizza stands and hotels blocked by the sand barrier, one could begin to feel the solitude that this curving 16 kilometers of beach backed by dunes and ancient pine forests once afforded. On this long stretch, Venice's bowmen competed over the centuries in displays of prowess before foreign dignitaries. Forlorn Christian crusaders encamped as they waited for months in the summer of 1202 to board galleys to Palestine. In the nineteenth century, this still unpeopled shoreline was rediscovered by English literati like John Ruskin and Henry James, who unanimously pronounced its untamed expanses to be the perfect reflection of Romantic ideals. Byron rode along the beach on horseback in the years after 1818, alone or in the company of other expatriates, not least the poet Percy Bysshe Shelley, who wrote of the beaches:

> This ride was my delight. I love all waste
>
> And solitary places; where we taste
>
> The pleasure of believing what we see
>
> Is boundless, as we wish our souls to be....

But these foreigners lamented bitterly the arrival of others, of sightseers and bathers following a new craze for swimming in the sea. By the middle of the 1800s, the new arrivals ferried to Lido on the vaporetti had brought with them public bathing establishments, restaurants and huts in which to don bathing costumes. James declared Lido "spoiled," turned into "a little cockney village" replete with a "third-rate boulevard... bitumen walks and gas-lamps" from the ferry to the beach on the Adriatic. The elegant hotels, however, vied with the French Riviera. "In America, those who have visited Europe talk more of your Excelsior Palace than they do of the Doge's Palace," quipped the banker J.P. Morgan.

Lido hosted Thomas Mann who visited with his family in 1911, and who later made it the scene of *Death in Venice*. It was also frequented by Sergei Diaghilev, the ballet impresario, who was visited there by composer Igor Stravinsky, who played him the first draft of the *Danse des Adolescentes* (*The Rite of Spring*), on the ballroom piano in the Hotel des Bains.

With a pause for World War I, the popularity of Lido surged during the Roaring Twenties, bringing French fashion designer Coco Chanel and a burst of Americans such as Cole Porter, George Gershwin and John Barrymore, often attracted to the scene for the Venetians' tolerance toward experimentation with sex, drugs and, for the day, shockingly flirtatious dances like the tango. The Venetian modernizers opened a Luna Park like the one on Coney Island in 1945, initially to entertain American troops.

Nicelli Airport, a casino, a cinema palace, health spas and hospitals were built and, in 1928, after American car magnate Henry Ford arrived with his golf clubs to find Lido had no golf, Volpi built a course at Alberoni. The "third-rate boulevard" turned into the Gran Viale, which still today is a spacious tree-lined street flanked by restaurants, bars and shops. After the Second World War, Lido boomed, and most of the building of apartment blocks that now line the island from end to end were built in the economic miracle of the 1960s, and in further development in the '70s and '80s, with peak population of just under 25,000.

"Lido was and still is the beach of Venice," says Danny Carella, the municipal head of Lido and Pellestrina, one of the six subdivisions of the city of Venice. We talked in his office, a high-ceilinged room in an old villa a few minutes' walk from the ferry station. As for Pellestrina, the 3,000 inhabitants there have mostly left fishing for new jobs, such as running the vaporetti. The undeveloped beaches of Pellestrina, home to rare birds, have sparked visitors' interest.

Since the 1980s, "Things have changed, in the sense that Lido has come on hard times because of the development of nearby beaches easier to reach by car. Lido no longer has an economy only based on tourism. Lots of people commute to jobs elsewhere," Carella says.

The population has declined gradually, falling to 17,000, and Lido has the oldest average age and highest average income of anywhere in Venice. "Many Venetian families continue to come to Lido for the tranquility," he says. Lido also attracts older beachgoers who want comforts and services, in contrast to the competition at Jesolo and Sottomarina, locations on the lip of the terraferma just to the north and south of Lido and Pellestrina, where music, partying and entertainment have drawn younger beachgoers. Things pick up during the few weeks of autumn when the Venice Film Festival takes place on Lido, says Carella, but, "the problem is the rest of the other eleven months when the place is left empty."

Though Marghera and Mestre were heavily bombed in the Second World War, they bounced back in the 1950s and '60s. The dredging of the ill-fated petroleum canal in the 1960s expanded industrial capacity. Growth followed the Italian economic miracle of those years, with plans to expand further with a new third industrial zone on reclaimed lagoon. But the floods of 1966 and the attention they drew to the need to preserve the lagoon put an end to those ambitions. The expansion was cancelled and many suspected the canal had contributed to the flooding. A final reckoning of the "Great Venice" must include the 157 workers who died from handling vinyl chloride produced at chemical plants in the last decades of the twentieth century, the air pollution and the over five million tons of toxic industrial poisons discarded on land and in the water over a century, making it the biggest industrial wasteland in Italy. Outrage over these legacies in the age of environmentalism was further fed by chemical leaks, including a phosgene leak in 2002 that, uncontained, could have killed everyone for kilometers around, and in May 2020, when an industrial explosion caused casualties and triggered the chemical warning sirens.

Most of the dangerous industries have by now been closed or updated, but the wastes remain a chief concern for the head of Mestre, Gianfranco Bettin, a writer and sociologist born in Marghera. He tells me that growth is being held back. "People are not investing here even if it is very well served," as the third port of Italy with an airport and docks in a strategic position in the northeast. "Why do they hesitate to invest? Because they would have to clean up the land and this cost is unsustainable, so it's easier to go elsewhere." The state should pay the cost of the clean-up, as happened with the transformation of the Ruhr industrial belt in Germany. "State intervention would create the right conditions to allow for the repair of the industrial area," he says. Some things are being done in terms of improving the streets and he has hopes for new launches of green industries such as biofuel. "It's not that we have not done anything.... It would just help to get a very strong push from the state."

Some 230,000 people now call the terraferma of Venice home, including the suburban Chirignago, Zelarino, Campalto and Favaro, but over half of the population is concentrated in Mestre. The area has experienced a ten-fold increase in population since the 1950s due to migration out of historic Venice and the arrival of foreign immigrants. Mestre has become a sizeable city, with all the usual big city problems of drugs, high levels of heroin deaths and street prostitution. But the unity of the terraferma and island Venice is now a fact of life. Bettin describes the talk of separating historic Venice as "short-sighted." Pointing to a huge aerial map on the wall next to his desk, he says Venice has always controlled its terraferma, which it needed for resources — wood, water, food — and to control the rivers flowing into the lagoon. "In the 1900s this link got more important through the creation of the industrial zone, tourism, the film festival, the Biennale and the birth of Port Marghera. It is not possible to imagine a future of Venice without industry."

In an unexpected way the future is best glimpsed at the city's new museum, the emblematic M9 Museum of the 20th century.* Part of an urban-regeneration project for Mestre, it offers a multimedia experience whose self-proclaimed objective is to help "the Italian people get to

* M9 makes sense as a name because in Italian the twentieth century is '900', or *novecento*, which literally means nine-hundred, but refers to the 1900s. For the ninth century, Italians say *nono* or ninth century.

know the century that most contributed to forging their identity today." I was doubtful I would like it. But on wandering around inside, I found that, despite the complete absence of the collectables seen in ordinary museums, the exhibits succeeded brilliantly and entirely through ephemeral screen images, interaction via touch-responsive surfaces and sounds, words and music heard over earphones. The exhibits tell the twentieth-century history of Italians at work, at home and through their culture and politics. Though the subject matter is about the last century, the museum itself is also about the current century: a sort of overview of how the twenty-first century experiences reality — digitally. In a sense, the past is the present and the present is the past, which is perhaps just what the museum means to convey.

The M9 Museum of the 20th Century, opened in December 2018 in Mestre, houses a totally interactive, audio-visual historical exhibition.

JOURNALIST
MESTRE'S COMING OF AGE
FABIO BOZZATO

Fabio Bozzato, aged fifty, writer on culture and urban transformation, a foreign correspondent in Latin America, for ten years a consultant to the city of Venice and a long-time resident of Mestre, generously showed me around his city. We're in the Mestre urban center, with its modern glass and concrete shopping center, stores of all kinds, plus, the tram station and an open market. It's called Piazza Barche, Boat Square. A century ago, ferries departed from here to Venice.

"In the 1960s, Mestre was considered and thought of itself as a quarter peripheral to the 'city', which meant Venice. Today, instead, all the urban functions, the vitality, the economics, residence, finance and infrastructure of the city are here. Venice has, in comparison, a minor role, maybe because it has become a giant tourist attraction. But the Venetians still say that over the bridge the countryside begins. So, when I am asked, where do you live? and I answer 'Mestre', they say, 'Ah, in the countryside'. It's touching to think that they really believe they are the ones who live in the city. They don't even have food shops! Those of us who live in Mestre, though we are part of the city of Venice, have an entirely different perception of 'city' in mind.

"In the Second World War, Venice was not touched by bombing, whereas Mestre was, because the train station was an important rail terminal. What you see of old buildings today in Mestre is what was left after the bombs destroyed the former Liberty-style houses that it had early in the century, when Mestre had its own local charm and autonomy. A few old houses have survived a bit away from the station. Both the Germans and the Allies agreed not to bomb Venice. Even so, in the 1950s and '60s Venice was in total decline, very poor, and dilapidated, so people began to leave with a lot of sadness. The exodus picked up after the floods of 1966, and many Venetians made Mestre their new home."

As we pass the pedestrianized central zone, Fabio points out an old villa that was once the headquarters of an electric company, and the public library, always full of students. He walks me towards an area that was under reconstruction for years and is now a cultural center.

"The exodus of Venetians today is not like in the 1960s. Some come to Mestre, but others go outside, into the countryside perhaps or to other cities. But they do come here to shop because all the big shopping centers are here. Companies have moved here from Venice, too, like Rubelli, an historic textile maker. I also discovered a stringed-instrument maker who had moved to this area, into a street the Mestrini considered dangerous. But he told me, 'No problem! I lived for ten years in the Bronx!'"

We stop to admire the M9 Museum. The modernistic building by architects Matthias Sauerbruch and Louisa Hutton consists of separate blocks with the outer walls covered with rows and rows of rectangular tiles of different colors.

"The M9 may well be the most beautiful building that Mestre has. I asked, 'So, how did you choose those colors?' and the architects said, 'Well, we went around and mapped Mestre, and we discovered that Mestre has these colors,' shades of red, terracotta and mother-of-pearl. It really made me think. We are used to thinking of Mestre without colors. We imagine it as a city in black and white, while these two architects, one English and one German, discover that Mestre has colors! What does that mean? We must still think we are a city, like any Italian city. So we need to come to terms with this. We have an historic center. Maybe Venice is not our historic center, but Venice is an historic center and must think of itself as metropolitan — Is it? This is always the issue.

"That is to say, in Mestre we have a metropolis that is made of land and water, of history and even elements of the contemporary. We have thousands of foreigners who came to live here many years ago who have had Italian-speaking children, while their parents speak Bengali or another language. If we take them — plus all these families not born here, that by Italian law are not Italian citizens, and now all the mixed couples — as citizens of Mestre, then we have a chance to become a city.

"In Mestre there are people from Bangladesh, China and Africa. In some schools up to 80 percent of the children are foreigners, and at the same time, the government institutions have never before been so intensely racist. These people live in Mestre and provide the labor pool for Venice. Every morning and evening you can see them on the Number 4 buses, commuting to jobs in Venice to work as sales assistants. They ride in along with the students who can't find places to live in Venice, and the tourists! In the past three or four years alone, we have jumped from 3 million to 5 million tourist visits to Mestre a year. Five thousand new beds will be available in new hotels in spring 2019. Imagine what that means for the city's transport, the food and drink sector, entertainment and the parks! What can the city offer and what impact will that have? The rents are already going up due to the impact of [the online accommodation portal] Airbnb. You can't find a flat as it is. It is a big shock for Mestre, as the rental prices have been pushed up so high."

The stubble-bearded, electronic-cigarette-puffing Fabio leads me to the tram that will take just ten minutes to whisk me back to Venice just over the bridge.

"In the last eighteen to twenty years Venice has also become a capital of international contemporary art, thanks mainly to the work in the 1990s by the then Venice mayor, Massimo Cacciari. He helped make culture an engine of growth for the city. But what Venice has become is hard to define because little is left of the city community as it was. In my opinion, the vital urban functions are now minimal, like the very soft beating of a fading heart. You could say Venice is a park, but it gives me more the impression of a resort. If I had to define it, I would say it's a big urban resort."

24

INCOMERS
SLAVES, REFUGEES, MIGRANTS AND MINORITIES

"Most of the people are foreigners."

—PHILIPPE DE COMMYNES, FRENCH ENVOY TO VENICE, LATE FIFTEENTH CENTURY

"What the hell have you been doing?" demanded Hamed Ahmadi's friend in Afghanistan who telephoned him in Italy, where the twenty-five-year-old was presenting a film he had helped produce. The friend tells Ahmadi the film had angered the Taliban and that his life would be in danger were he to return home. That was the first time that the cinematographer Ahmadi heard about the reaction, sparked by news reports, and at that moment he realized he was a refugee and would have to leave his life and family in Afghanistan behind.

"I was afraid. I lost 13 kilograms," after the call, he says. His team's short film *The Grandmother* had been screened days before at the 2006 Venice Film Festival. The story of a nine-year-old girl who lives in an orphanage in Ahmadi's hometown, Bamyan, it tells how the orphan's grandmother falls ill, causing the girl to turn to her teacher at her Koranic school. He advises her to study the Koran and pray. She does, but on returning to the grandmother's house, she finds her dead. The film ends with her turning her back on the school and refusing to enter.

This was interpreted by extremists in Afghanistan as defaming Islam. "But it's not like that," says Ahmadi. "Islam, like in Catholicism, teaches, 'If you want something, first you must take action, then you can hope to be blessed.'" But in Afghanistan, the "film was seen as an invitation to Christianity, which is a load of rubbish."

Ahmadi told himself to think of his fate as "starting a new life, like going to university and learning a new language and culture. I told myself that I would become a more worldly person." He joined the Forte Rosarol refugee camp near Venice, eventually taking a menial job gardening, and was later put in charge of younger refugees. They organized an Asian food festival featuring dishes proposed by the young refugees, many of whom had encountered new foods during their often harrowing, years-long journeys to reach Italy. The food was so well received that in 2012 they launched "Orient Experience" at a former kebab restaurant in Venice, despite naysayers who said Italians only liked their own food. In 2018, when we spoke, Ahmadi, thirty-seven, was living in Venice, and running five cooperative outlets staffed by refugees. He had re-established his life, even brought his family to Italy from Afghanistan, and was helping others.

His story is but a recent example of how incomers to Venice cope. There have been waves of immigrants and refugees from the Middle East, Africa and Asia in recent decades, pushed out of their homes by turmoil and attracted by safety and economic opportunity in Italy, despite an increasingly hostile political environment in the country. They join the artists, students, carers, Venice-philes and retirees moving to the city in a tide mostly countercurrent to, though not making up fully for, the exodus of Venetians.

Venice has been receiving immigrants and refugees from its earliest days. It has taken in those fleeing wars on the mainland, absorbed slaves brought from afar and harbored Greek, Turkish, German and Jewish traders along with Arabs and Persians. Despite periodical outbursts of Roman Catholic intolerance, especially with regard to the Jews, who would be segregated in the Ghetto, its pragmatic government has always found ways to keep useful foreign communities within its fold. But the greatest force behind immigration was perhaps the need to replenish the population after the repeated, devastating plagues that hit Venice between 1348 and 1630.

Each time the city quickly recovered. Authorities offered incentives to newcomers, helping the population to swell, with mainland immigrants flocking to Venice to take up vacant jobs. Wars on the mainland and far-flung disruptions — the collapse of the Byzantine Empire in 1453, the expulsion of Jews from Spain in 1492 and the sack of Rome in 1527 — also drove people, often the most talented and educated elites, to the safety and prosperity of Venice. For all these reasons, the city's actual population ever since 1300 has remained remarkably stable, fluctuating mostly between 100,000 and 140,000. The similarity in magnitude of the current-day population decline, down two-thirds from a post-World War II peak, has led observers to look to the example of the city's resilience after the plague for hope about what may happen in the future.

"It is necessary to increase the number of Venetian residents, regardless of where in the world they are born and grow up. After all, it's always been like this, hasn't it? When the plague took away some 100,000 Venetians, the city opened its doors and invited in new people to make it their own again. Perhaps the times we live are less grave than those of the pestilence?" asks the author Alberto Toso Fei.

Many arrived as refugees and a number came against their will. These were the slaves: mostly Russian, Tatar, Mongol and Muslim women from the northwestern Caucasus. Non-Christian slaves were preferred, such as Bulgarians, but there were also some Roman Catholic slaves, such as Greeks from Crete or Candia, captured in war or through piracy, or Albanians escaping the Ottomans. Venetians still brought black slaves from Africa even after the market for such slaves declined in the late fifteenth century. Slaves worked as servants, valets, gondoliers, mistresses and chamber or kitchen maids, and, despite the unimaginable trauma of slavery, many servants became beloved members of a family — as is evidenced by servants' wills leaving tokens to their masters, who in turn left bequests providing for servants' dowries and old age.

Traders like the Germans came via the Brenner Pass in the eastern Alps to sell silver, copper, gold and textiles and sought desirable goods from the East, such as cotton, spices, and incense. They were forbidden from doing their own shipping, but that suited them well as Venice's naval and merchant fleets provided ample opportunity for trade. In 1228, Venice began to build for the Germans a wooden warehouse located on the Grand Canal next to the Rialto Bridge, the Fondaco dei Tedeschi. In the sixteenth century it was replaced by the massive stone building that today houses a luxury shopping mall, but it originally provided trading and storage in the great courtyard on the ground floor, offices on the first floor and living quarters for 160 traders on the upper two floors.

Venice benefited from foreigners, but always stopped short of being overrun. In 1192, high levels of immigration led Doge Enrico Dandolo to evict all foreigners who had lived in Venice for less than two years. Venice would henceforth only accept foreigners subject to restrictions; for example, laws were passed which required that the gates of the Fondaco were to stay closed until the sound of the Marangona, the great bell in the tower on Piazza San Marco that marked the beginning and end of the working day. Such restrictions were commonplace at the time for foreign residents, and Venetians themselves trading in places like Alexandria, Egypt, were similarly forbidden from going out during Muslim prayer hours.

Like the Germans, the Turks came to Venice to trade and were subject to special laws, but their presence in the city was notable because from the fifteenth century onwards Venice was regularly at war with the Ottoman Turks, Muslims whose expansion into much of the eastern Mediterranean, southeastern Europe and North Africa eventually contributed to the decline of the Venetian Empire. The status of the Turks in Venice changed according to the alternately serene and stormy relations with this increasingly powerful opponent. They were feared as a Trojan horse at times of war, and aroused greater mistrust than would the Jews. But even during war, they stayed put, showing the importance afforded to trade under the Republic. The Turks were also granted a fondaco on the Grand Canal in what today is the Natural History Museum, the Fondaco dei Turchi.

Unlike the trading nations, the Greeks came to Venice to escape the Muslim Ottoman Turks advancing up the Balkan Peninsula. The Greeks were accepted and posed less of a political threat than the others, but were greatly feared in religious quarters. They practiced Eastern Orthodox Christianity, which was in conflict with Roman Catholicism despite efforts to bridge differences. Even so, Greeks established their own community in Venice, though they were not allowed to build their own church or set up a school until the late fifteenth century. Eventually they became insiders, though not quite Venetians.

But among all the incomers to Venice, those with the most complicated relationship with Venice were the Jews. The first Jews may have arrived as early as the thirteenth century, and certainly by the fourteenth century, when they came in waves to the region, both from the north of Italy, seeking to escape persecution in the wake of the Black Death, and also from central and southern Italy, squeezed out by oppression in the Papal States of Italy, and in 1509 by League of Cambrai armies spreading over the Venetian terraferma.

They first engaged mainly in medicine and moneylending, as Catholics were forbidden by Christian doctrine to loan money for interest. But even as the Venetian rulers saw the advantage of having Jews provide this service, they struggled to accept the morality of the moneylending by these non-believers, regarded as obstinate deniers of the Christian truth. The political debate raged for centuries in the government, which needed money lenders to finance trade and provide capital for the poor, but also vacillated, allowing the Jews in for short periods and expelling them at others. On balance, although the authorities taxed Jews heavily, the Venetians practiced a certain benevolence towards them, protecting Jews and allowing them to practice their religion. It was this relative religious tolerance that attracted increasing numbers of Italian, German, Spanish and Levantine Jews to Venice over the centuries.

But Venice also instituted a series of repressive measures, such as requiring Jews to wear a yellow hat or badge. Jews were not allowed right of full-time residence until an edict of March 29, 1516 decreed that, "The Jews must all live together... in the Ghetto near San Girolamo" and that gates would be built "to prevent their roaming about at night" with guards at the gates paid for by the Jews.

The Jews would also have to pay for two boats that constantly patrolled the canals around the Ghetto and any Jew found outside the Ghetto at night could be fined or imprisoned. Sometimes the limited space in the Ghetto caused serious crowding, and so, to compensate, the residents built taller buildings with smaller rooms than elsewhere in Venice.

"The Ghetto, on the one hand, is a negative thing, because it aimed to keep people contained and controlled, but on the other hand it responded to a need of the Republic, which wanted security," says Riccardo Calimani, the foremost historian of the Venetian Ghetto. "Unlike the Ghetto of Rome, where the Jews were oppressed and under pressure to convert, the Ghetto of Venice then became, in the course of the years, a defense [for the Jews]... a means of protection... [in the sense that] the individual alone is weak, but the community as a group is stronger when cultural and social life is centralized."

In short, the several thousand-strong Jewish community flourished in the relative stability of the Venetian Ghetto, the oldest in Europe, and in subsequent centuries the Jews experienced a cultural blossoming, building their own synagogues and schools. They were to become increasingly involved in overseas trade and in publishing, editing and correcting texts printed by Venetian nobles. Excluded from the artisanal trades, the German Jews loaned money while those of the Levant and from Spain increasingly took to the seas as commercial representatives on seagoing vessels. They worked for the Venetian aristocracy, who, in the declining years of the Republic, tended to prefer the safety of their villas on the terraferma, according to Calimani, who comes from one of the ancient Jewish families of the Ghetto.

The confinement in the Ghetto ended with the Republic in 1797, when Napoleon commanded that the doors be removed. On July 7 of that year, they were hacked to pieces and burned, an action that was met with celebration. "As soon as the gates were brought to earth, people of both sexes, without distinction, wove joyful democratic dances in the midst of the Square," according to a French soldier.

Suffering the same poverty as other Venetians in the aftermath of the Republic, Jews mostly left the Ghetto for other parts of the city, and, except for the five ancient synagogues, the retirement home and a bakery, the Ghetto has been only nominally Jewish ever since. Today the community, which is well integrated into the larger population, come to the Ghetto mainly for religious occasions at the seventeenth-century Sephardic — that is, Spanish tradition — synagogue, where Orthodox Judaism is practiced.

Their spokesman, the clean-cut, businesslike Michael Calimani, a distant cousin of Riccardo, met me in the community office nearby.

Out of the 22,000 Jews in all of Italy today, the current Venetian community of about 450 Jews is fairly small, he explains. Before World War II, 40,000 Jews lived in Italy, but this was reduced largely by the 1943–45 Nazi-Fascist deportations to the concentration camps. Two hundred Jews were deported from Venice, and their deaths are commemorated by a memorial in Ghetto Nuovo, the larger of the Ghetto's two squares. Today's community does have concerns about anti-Semitism, says Calimani, but mainly as a side effect of growing xenophobia in the country. There have been no major incidents — and for many years armed soldiers have been posted in a guardhouse in the Ghetto Nuovo as a precaution. Like the rest of Venice, the community's more immediate concerns focus on the wider exodus of Venetian residents.

The foreign tourists, many of them of Jewish descent, who visit the Ghetto each year may get the impression that the Venetian Jewish community includes the followers of the Chabad-Lubavitch movement, who maintain a lively presence at their synagogue-school housed in glass-fronted ground-floor rooms near the bridge in Ghetto Nuovo. The shopfront is one of a thousand-odd outposts of the Brooklyn-based Messianic breakaway from mainstream Jewry whose members wear Hasidic dress, with men and boys in black coats and hats and their temple hair in locks, as Eastern European Jews did historically.

"The Chabad-Lubavitch are not part of the Venetian Jewish community," Michael Calimani states without my prompting. "They are a community unto themselves that arrived in the 1990s. They serve the Lubavitch movement, which is, let us say, not the principal movement."

The resident Chabad-Lubavitch, or simply "Chabad," mission consists of three couples sent to Venice to run the school, a restaurant and "outreach" programs, according to the leader, Rabbi Ramy Banin, an Italian Jew with a long bushy beard who was trained in New York and wears Hasidic clothing. Calling itself "Jewish Venice" on its website, the Chabad brings in youthful devotees who sign up to the year-long courses in Venice and who gather daily to pray, study or talk to passersby. Sometimes they wander the streets to strike up conversations about the Chabad.

Over the years the relations between the Chabad and the Venetian Jewish community have reached a stand-off as the two communities compete over the tourists. The Chabad opened its Gam Gam Jewish restaurant near one of the old gates to the Ghetto, and some years later, members of the Venetian Jewish community opened the Ghimel Garden on the square, at the opposite end. The Venetian Jews run the information center, museum and synagogue tours.

The two sides have clashed over some of the Chabad's activities, such as very publicly celebrating the Shabbat Jewish holidays in the square, but by and large they are "very friendly and did some projects together," says Banin. He explains the Chabad's aim as spreading Judaism, especially to those "unaffiliated" with the religion, and reviving the Ghetto as a place of Jewish life and residence. "In the eyes of many Jews, thirty or forty years ago the Ghetto was sort of over, it just happened to be that the synagogue stayed here," he says in an interview. The Chabad brought change to the Ghetto and, "I think many of them [other Jewish residents] appreciate it nowadays."

These Ghetto visitors represent an example of a third category of incomer to Venice, one that falls between resident and tourist. Known as "temporary citizens," "city users," "temporary communities," or "heritage communities," they come to Venice regularly for brief periods and include the range of people associated with the Biennale and the 25,000 or so university students, who hail from all over Italy and the world, most of whom live in dormitories or rented rooms. They stay for a few years or just a semester or to attend particular short-term educational programs. This category is growing, says Shaul Bassi, a Venice University professor who has organized a number of theatrical and scholarly exchanges.

"I think these people are an important presence for the city, because they help make Venice more international and give it a cultural and artistic life that is on par with bigger cities. These people live like residents, not tourists. They need to be more visible, discussed and involved," he says, because "the future of Venice will see a convergence of those who live in Venice permanently and those who love Venice, write about it and think about it from outside, and if these components unite there will be a future" beyond tourism.

Among the more prosperous of newcomers are the Chinese.

You'll sometimes find Leon Gao, aged twenty-nine, for example, in his family's tiny leather boutique, L's Chic. The interior is all done up in white in order to contrast with the display of colorful purses, wallets and handbags — from quality brands made in Tuscany, Veneto and Sicily, along with the shop's own artisan-made bags, customized to meet the tastes of the Chinese tourists.

Since coming to Venice from China, Gao's industrious family has also opened two other shops, two bars and a restaurant. Gao's sister, who arrived first in the 1990s and later married a Venetian, has learned to cook Italian foods and serves as a chef in the restaurant. Gao, when he arrived in 2007, spoke not a word of Italian, but after some years at university, he speaks it fluently and has many Italian friends. Sometimes, when crossing the Rialto Bridge, he says, "I look at the Grand Canal, take a deep breath and feel fortunate to live in such a beautiful city."

Many Chinese, along with immigrants from the other parts of Asia, the Middle East, and North Africa, have come to the city to buy or run businesses. However, more than other foreigners, Chinese are blamed for the predominance of cheap Chinese goods sold widely in Venice — by no means primarily by Chinese merchants. As it happens, unlike many of the innumerable bag shops in Venice, Gao's family shops sell no goods made in China. But Gao finds both Italian and foreign customers, after eyeing the merchandise through the shop window, will sometimes walk away when they see Chinese staff inside. It's disappointing, says Gao.

A number of new Venetians are Italians and foreigners who have retired or found second homes in the city.

Chris Wayman, seventy, and his Italian wife were looking for "a beautiful city where we didn't know anybody" to retire to after their sons grew up. Residents of the United Kingdom, where Wayman worked in finance, they had visited Venice as tourists, liked it and decided to return, initially on a see-how-it-goes basis. But after a while, they sold their UK home and moved permanently to a flat in Venice. Wayman has learned to speak good Italian, takes part in rowing, actively supports the city and jointly runs a small publishing house. "People get to know you when they know you're going to stay," he says. He's glad he came, but would not recommend Venice for people with mobility problems. He says his presence "contributes to the survival of Venice."

Lorenzo Bacelle, seventy-two, grew up in Padua, and with his British wife Jane Garner, later settled in London, where he worked as a Jungian psychoanalyst. They too looked around Italy for a place to retire, and Lorenzo had a revelation in a dream that the choice had to be Venice, which he had often visited as a youngster. In 1993, they found a place overlooking the lagoon that was a "complete and absolute ruin," says Garner, but it had a brilliant view. So, over a number of years they lovingly did it up, at great cost and trouble. They now spend three or four months a year in the flat, their efforts having created a splendid home, "with a view of the Venetian islands, an air of remoteness, a lot of silence and natural sounds of birds and wind," says Lorenzo. When in Venice they take in exhibitions, the Biennale, the restaurants, often meeting Italian friends or Bacelle's family from Padua. Living in Venice only intermittently, though, they have made few friends among Venetians.

"What about us?" one often hears from many younger Venetians, especially those who have had to leave for abroad and yet magnetically return to visit family and friends, sometimes in the hope of finding a life in the city. But they are often disappointed, because unless they want to work in tourism, the city has little to offer. Several I know trained in the humanities or in a profession. One, at thirty, described this tribe of exiles. His views may be strong, tinged with bitterness, but it is a view commonly heard.

> There are two types of Venetians: the first type are those who live in Venice and will die in Venice, who are umbilically tied to the place; there are fewer and fewer of them. I have friends who leave Venice only once or twice a year. All of the rest of the time, they stay here, among these islands. The grandmother of one of my friends has never left San Polo for the past thirty or forty years. In the neighborhoods, except San Marco, which has always been an exception, you find everything you need — stores that sell fruit, domestic appliances, bread.
>
> The other type are the Marco Polos, like me, who are on an external journey. For Venetians like us, who start to venture out of the city, it's unlikely that we will return. We are travelers. We are destined to go on journeys because Venice is an island. We have to leave Venice. I see no future for myself here in Italy and no chance of rescuing the situation. The future is grey or black. My close friends and I, except one, have all left Venice. We live in Marseille, Berlin, Paris, Brussels, Ghent or London. Each of us has found what suits him or her, but, as far as Venice goes, they all think like me.

He rages about Italians being in a "bad way" and how Venice has been "sold out" and Italy is hopelessly capitalistic, how people just want to make money and how everything is based "on the old system of patronage used since Roman times." But beneath it there is a certain sadness.

> Now I've come back to Venice. Everybody always returns to Venice! I have lived most of the last decade overseas. Why? Because I miss contact with nature in other places and I don't want to work in tourism. I have a profession and I want to learn more, and what I need to learn you can't learn here, not even at the university. So, I

need to study elsewhere in order to grow.... Probably I will return someday to Venice. I don't know. It could happen.

In contrast, many foreigners who come to Venice find low-paying jobs Italians would rather not do.

Maria Drumea, a Romanian in her fifties, sits in the warm and well-lit kitchen of a Venetian household, sips her orange-spiced tea and nibbles a sugar cookie during a break from her job taking care of a woman in her nineties. "I came here four years ago from Moldavia, to sacrifice for ill parents and husband," she says in passable Italian, her third language after Russian. A big woman with glasses and gold teeth, she was a nurse back home and now, like many other Eastern European women, she is a carer. Back home Drumea could earn €250 a month, but in Italy she gets €1000. Eastern Europeans constitute one of the largest immigrant groups, with men often working in the building trades.

Ashek Mia wanders the streets and squares of Venice with a bunch of what look like day-old roses. "People buy for girlfriends," he says, in very broken Italian. A cheerful small man of fifty with gray crew-cut hair, he can make €20 a day, less his costs. "I like Italy. Not crazy here. Very peaceful," he says. Mia arrived in 2004 from Bangladesh, originally working for the ship-building firm Fincantieri. He stayed on, sending money home to his wife, three children and two grandchildren. He talks to them by phone but has never returned. Does he want to go back? "No... I don't know," he says, with a bewildered look, as if the idea was beyond possibility.

Mia, like most other Bangladeshis who work in Venice, lives in Mestre. Early in the morning or late at night he commutes to the city on a bus. Many of his fellow countrymen are seen on the streets of Venice, selling selfie sticks or spinning toys with little blue lights, throwing them up in the air for hours on end to attract buyers; others man souvenir and fruit stalls or work as cooks and dishwashers. Many Bangladeshis who have been settled in Italy for decades and are now in their second and third generations have their own businesses and do other jobs.

They are part of the 8.7 percent of Italy's population of 60 million who are immigrants, including incomers from the EU — though only

533,000 of these are there illegally. In the harsh anti-immigrant climate of today's Italy, however, immigrants — especially the non-whites — are scapegoated by some politicians for all manner of national problems.

Among those daily commuters to this historic city are people like Victor Egbon, twenty-three, a Nigerian beggar. He has been commuting from Vicenza daily for several years and taking up a station near a supermarket, baseball cap in hand, for a take of about €15 or €20 a day. He tells a story about having to flee Nigeria because he was threatened for refusing to join a gang, and he says that he is a Christian who goes to church every Sunday. When he calls home to talk to his wife, she "makes him crazy" when she pleads for money for food to eat. He shows me a smartphone picture of his wife and daughter and a shop he once had. He left Nigeria in 2014, he tells me, traveling overland and then with eighty-five Nigerians on a rubber raft from Libya, which foundered halfway. Twenty-three on board drowned. A rescue ship picked up survivors, taking them to a detention camp where Egbon spent over two years.

Egbon's story is typical. Hundreds of beggars commute to Venice: from scarved Romani women who have long been seen on the city streets to the now more numerous recent arrivals, such as the Africans, particularly Nigerian men. Like Egbon, the young Nigerians stand on bridges and on the campi, sometimes silently with an upturned baseball cap, forlornly waiting; others facing the flow of the crowds to pick out subjects. Some pester those at open-air café tables to the point that café-goers burst out in anger — or tears. They came to Italy in hope of a better life promised by the criminal groups in Nigeria that encouraged them to go there — but in general end up in poverty.

"The Nigerians are brought to Italy by Nigerian and Libyan criminal organizations. When they arrive they have to pay off debts for their transportation to Italy. The women are forced into prostitution," to pay off debts €25,000 or more, "while the men sell drugs or beg," according to Paola Tonini, the Venice public prosecutor. She affirms that most of the African beggars seen in the streets of Venice "will have been organized by criminal organizations and proceeds certainly go to the organization." The prostitution takes place mostly in Mestre, Marghera and other parts of the terraferma, where the women are seen nightly on the streets asking €20 per client. Women are "actually bought as young as fifteen or sixteen years old for prostitution" and, like the men, may be locked into forms of slavery that can last for years while they repay their debts. Meanwhile, they live in fear that failure to cooperate would lead to reprisal against their families back home. Tonini recommends giving to charities that help these individuals rather than offering handouts.

Back at Ahmadi's Orient Experience restaurant in Campo Santa Margherita, the waiters feel incredibly lucky. They have jobs and a modicum of security — something they fought long for.

"We all have the same story," says Yosef Marufkhal, twenty-nine, the manager and an Afghan refugee:

> No one dreams of leaving his family and country. Nobody likes having to go to another country. Our country is not like Europe. We have problems in our countries. They are not like Europe. We don't even understand who wants to kill us there. Somebody wanted to kill me in the name of the Taliban, another in the name of Jihad, and a third for another reason. We don't understand. We are tired, having left our families to come here. I left in 2004; from Afghanistan I went to Pakistan, but it was even harder there. I went to Iran, then Turkey. I was locked in a room for eight months. I couldn't even see the sun. It was like being in jail, but I couldn't get out because I couldn't pay. My family ultimately had to sell a piece of land so that I could get to Greece. I worked from 4 a.m. to 10 p.m. I went to Macedonia, Serbia, Hungary, then Austria, where I remained for three years. They weren't interested in my story. They laughed at me. I arrived in Italy in 2012. I slept in the cold on the floor of the train station for forty-five days until the Caritas charity helped me and I got documents. Now I have worked here for some years. I have become a partner with Hamed Ahmadi. Lots of foreigners work with us. Because I am a foreigner, I understand them. I have seen this difficult life. But this story is not only mine. All the foreigners that come here share the same story. Now, thanks first to God, secondly to Italy, and to the Italians, I have been given a life.

In the break after lunch, I interviewed Pakistani waiter Harsalam Hamad, just sixteen, who hardly spoke Italian, and his Gambian colleague Zamin Sallah, and, indeed, their stories were of hardship and of finding a haven in the restaurant in Venice. Finally.

At the end of my interview with Ahmadi, I ask one final question: "Is there anything I didn't ask about that I should know?" He answers:

> The young Venetians themselves don't want to go down the path offered to them in Venice because it's not a city that offers much work other than that linked to tourism. So many leave. Someone needs to take their place. I believe that within twenty years Venice will be a much more racially mixed place for those living here. It's a question of time. Venice will be more a city of people of color because Venice is a bridge between East and West, between North and South. The mixing is not something just of the present; it existed in the past. And from the point of view of those coming from outside, obviously, we need to be aware that we find ourselves in a city where being Venetian comes with privileges, and I understand this. We understand that we are in a place that makes us fortunate. And sharing this privilege will give us a common basis for living together here in the future.

A FAMILY
MOVING FROM ROME TO VENICE
CATERINA FALOMO

I came across a remarkable series of books of interviews profiling Venetians. So in July 2018 I looked up the author, Caterina Falomo, in Rome, where she then lived, and I learned that she was about to move back to Venice, where she had grown up. A few weeks after we talked, she, her six-month-old daughter and six-year-old son, husband and cat left their fifth-floor Rome apartment to travel to Lido. Writing those books had changed her, she said. She fell in love with Venice again. I wanted to know why, at a time when many Venetians were leaving Venice, she was going in the opposite direction.*

"My husband and I have long debated leaving Rome, and we've considered all sorts of options, but in the end it always came back to Venice. After fourteen years in Rome, we've realized that the city has changed: it's dirtier, the traffic is worse, people are angrier. It's not safe for the children; life is so limited. There is no living outside: filth covers the sidewalks. You can't go out on the piazza, 200 meters away from our home, because the drunks take over at night, leaving bottles everywhere. They do tidy it up somewhat in the morning, but only a few children play there. We hardly get to visit our friends. They live far away, and they work even further away. For everyone it's an hour to get to work and an hour home. By the time they get back, spending time with the children is all they can manage. To travel to see friends or go to the beach outside Rome you end up crossing the city in a car, which is endlessly stressful — not at all like a pleasant country drive. In my opinion, life should be slower. Even stopping for a

* *Quando c'erano i Veneziani* (*When there were Venetians*), *Veneziani per scelta* (*Venetians by choice*), and *I nuovi Veneziani* (*The new Venetians*).

coffee in Rome is stressful, what with having to wait in long lines and all that deafening din of plates.

"What we are looking for is a reality that's human in scale. I'm looking forward to a calmer pace — which for me is priceless. I want to be able to drop by the bar for a chat or a coffee when I feel like it, with or without friends, and then leave feeling more tranquil than before. A gentler pace of life is an inexhaustible source of well-being. I want my kids to have time with friends; in Rome all the parents are always rushing off after picking up their kids. We'll have some of that in Venice too, but I hope to find people who want to be together. A community, that's what we're looking for, so our kids can have friends round to the house, and not just hang out together at school where there's a teacher in charge. That's what's lacking today.

"As a society we talk a lot about the big themes of immigration. But if our children grow up together they get to know each other; they learn how other families, of other nationalities, live. When you start talking to people you don't realize it but you're doing a service to society; it helps people get over their differences. It's what we need to create, an open society.

"Venice means freedom for me. You are free to think because you don't have to watch out for cars and stoplights. You can keep moving: walk up bridge steps and down, never stopping. As you move, your thoughts continue uninterrupted. You are free to meet people en route in a way that's not possible elsewhere. It's marvelous. I only realized that by living in another, more limiting city.

"A child in Venice can be free with a capital 'F'. As a kid there in the 1980s, I played in the campo freely, riding my tiny bicycle around the square and making chalk drawings on the stones with friends. My house was 500 meters from school and I said to my mother on the second day: 'Why do you need to take me to school again? I want to go alone.' Almost without knowing it, and at age six — probably too little to understand what I was saying — I yearned to be free, to be independent. And the city let me be free. At six, seven or eight I could stop at the pastry shop to buy a treat on the way to school. For me this was a huge achievement.

"Now, having tried the alternative with my own children in Rome, having to tell my six-year-old every minute to be careful, watch where you step, stay on the sidewalk, a car is coming, I know that it's nonstop and extremely tiring. It interrupts life. In Rome, day-to-day life makes us all a bit dazed, victims of fragmentary thinking. It's the opposite of freedom."

Interview on December 12, 2018 in Venice's Lido, just before a dinner of pasta con salsiccia, and chicory with bits of pumpkin, alongside hard goat's cheese, pork, ricotta, salad and peach sauce.

"I am even happier than I expected. We have made the right choice. We have chosen the right house. The sun shines in all day through the windows. The Lido is as beautiful as Venice without the disadvantages. Here they still believe in a community of people who all know one another. People say the Lido is gloomy in winter, but that's untrue. Here there are marvelous days. People are more tranquil.

"There are very few cars in the Lido. We go around on bicycles, which is impossible in Venice — or Rome. We ride along the lagoon and there's this view up to the mountains. My six-year-old likes school. He has only thirteen kids in his class. In Rome it was twenty-six. He already knows how to read!

"We still miss friends in Rome, and all the culture on offer, but apart from that, we have no regrets. We see Rome now on the TV, with its dirt and holes in the streets.... It's a beautiful city that's been treated badly. Venice seems like a paradise in comparison."

25

MONEY

THE PERFECT STORM OF CONTENDING INTERESTS

> *"If we are to have any hope of making the kind of civilizational leap required of this fateful decade, we will need to start believing, once again, that humanity is not hopelessly selfish and greedy — the image ceaselessly sold to us by everything from reality shows to neoclassical economics."*
>
> —NAOMI KLEIN, *THIS CHANGES EVERYTHING*

As a journalist in the last decade of the Cold War, I worked in a news office in Hong Kong, on one of the frontlines, so to speak, between the communist and capitalist countries. This ideological fault line was mirrored in the West, with the parties of the left favoring state intervention and closely allied with the trade unions, while the right looked to business for solutions, putting more faith in the cold logic of the marketplace. Some in the West had long feared the way the left was promoting what they saw as unworkable ideas similar to socialist central planning, and out of these views grew what has come to be called "neoliberalism," professed first as a governing philosophy by Margaret Thatcher and Ronald Reagan. It was meant to let the market manage resources on its own, removing government from the social equation in policies designed to deliver services and economic growth.

After the Berlin Wall fell in 1989, the left realized it needed a refresh, and jumped on the bandwagon. Among the first to do so was the UK government of Tony Blair, which came to power in 1997, abandoning many traditionally socialist ideas and, for ten years, pursuing the agenda of economic neoliberalism which had begun on the right. Some of these neoliberal reforms worked, delivering better services at less cost, but others went too far. Typically, when the private sector was given a task but failed to provide the hoped-for results, the taxpayers suffered the consequences — be they financial or detrimental to the environment, health or welfare. The financial crash of 2008, which undermined finances globally, exacerbated these losses, leaving governments scrabbling to pay their bills and provide health services, security, schools and other things people needed.

This same shift to neoliberalism happened elsewhere in Europe, including Italy. From December 1999 the country was under the rule of the center-left Italian government of President Massimo D'Alema. Though D'Alema's government lasted just 126 days, it opened the door to unbridled deregulation in Italy, a program which continued later as the torch of leadership passed on from left to right in the subsequent years. Since the end of the Second World War, Italy has had sixty-one governments.

Neoliberalizations gone wrong in Italy had much the same result as they had had elsewhere, eventually adding to debt and social costs that the country could ill afford. At the last reckoning, Italian economic growth was stagnant, with its GDP from 2008 to 2018 falling by 3 percent compared with a rise of 13 percent in Germany, 10 percent in France, 11 percent in the UK and 4 percent in Spain.* Unemployment in Italy, meanwhile, stubbornly stays around 10 percent, and is much higher for youth. Income growth has stalled and social mobility trails behind in the industrialized world.

Amidst these problems, Venice has faced a "perfect storm," says economist Giampietro Pizzo, a member of the citizens' advocacy group Venezia Cambia, whom I met one chilly evening before the group's meeting in Mestre. "On one hand, globalization has created the tourist problem, and the second factor is liberalization" launched by Minister of Industry Pier Luigi Bersani, which, under D'Alema's government, threw out regulations of business and housing in a move that turned out to have disastrous consequences for Venice.

"A market left to itself does not work. It needs rules," says Pizzo. "The rules are not about us not wanting tourists, but about tourism being a component of the Venetian economy along with other things. If tourism eats up everything else, making it all disappear into a tourism monoculture, it's clear that we end up with a dead city! Not just dead, but a city at risk. This has happened in other parts of the world: when they are hit by terrorism or a global crisis, tourism falls or collapses; you

* Gross Domestic Product, GDP, is the value of all the finished goods and services produced within a country's borders, which is taken as the main measure of economic vigor.

find you lose tourism and have nothing," he continues, referring to the fates of places like Tunisia and Egypt. Or, today, he might have added, closer to home. Tourists stayed away after the 2020 coronavirus and the record floods of November 12, 2019, which a hotel spokesman blamed on scare stories about acqua alta in the "foreign press." "It's clear that Venice, historically, has been a city founded on economic interests, on the capacity to develop commerce and international relations. All that is normal, but when the interests become speculative in financial terms, a matter of profit, with no eye on long-term sustainability, devouring the human, natural and cultural capital, cannibalizing everything and then going elsewhere, it's time to oppose these types of economic interests."

The call to abide by rules harks back to when the arengo, Venice's early, unregulated democracy — a populism of another age — led to regicide, spurring the commoners and the wealthy to share power, and gave rise to the rudiments of modern democracy in the year 1172. Perhaps history has lessons after all.

The reputation Venetians had — and continue to have — for being greedy, money-grubbing scoundrels, has roots that go back to their earliest years and troubled relations with the pope and the Muslims. It also comes back to a spotlight cast by Shakespeare's play *The Merchant of Venice*, written around 1597. Its main character is the Jewish lender Shylock, and while he is not the merchant in the play, his harsh behavior seems to have contributed to the historical stereotype of ruthless Venetians. The economic plight Venice faces today is still often written off as just Venetians doing what they have always done.

"When you speak of Venice you speak of the Venice that is the real Venice and an imaginary Venice, and these two are always in superimposed tension," according to Shakespeare scholar Shaul Bassi. Shylock, depicted in the play, on balance, in a bad — some contend outrightly anti-Semitic — light remains the most famous of all Jewish Venetians, among whom many have been distinguished intellectuals, doctors and philosophers. In 2016, Bassi organized the first production of *The Merchant of Venice* in front of the Holocaust memorial in Venice's Ghetto, where Jews were once confined, to "deal with the ghost of Shylock and see if the real Venice and imagined Venice could co-exist and learn from one another."

Staged by the Compagnia de' Colombari of New York, the play turned out to be "a very, very powerful" moment. Bassi pointed with pride to a frame on his office wall with the *New York Times* story about the event, which marked the 500th anniversary of the Ghetto and the 400th of the playwright and included a mock judicial appeal by Shylock presided over by former US Supreme Court Justice Ruth Bader Ginsberg. Shylock, portrayed in the play as a conniving moneylender insisting on "a pound of flesh" as recompense for a default on a loan, was, with four centuries delay, seen to have been hard done by, even if he was a bit overzealous in his gruesome demand. Ginsberg and the four other judges, after hearing arguments on behalf of Shylock and two other characters, unanimously ruled he should get his money back — nullifying the ruling within the play that he had conspired against Antonio, the merchant borrower, and should give up all his property and be forcibly converted to Christianity. The mock trial's judgment put Shylock — and perhaps Venice — in a new light.*

Money came to Venice, as it did to the rest of Europe, mostly in the eleventh century. Coins with names like *bezants* and *saraceni*, minted by Byzantium and the Muslim states, came to be used for monetary exchange, mainly in towns and cities. At that time wealth was based on agriculture and most Europeans worked the land, consuming what they produced or bartering goods like candles, wine, livestock and beer. The kings and nobles sat above, collecting surpluses to fund their medieval manors and warriors. But barter would not suffice for Venice, where livelihoods depended not on ploughing fields but on sailing the seas.

Profits that Venetians made from trading salt, in particular, enabled them to send ships around the Mediterranean carrying bagfuls of coins to trade for cargoes of spices they would resell in Europe at prices non-Venetian competitors could not match. The trouble was that coins

* Although the play treats Shylock unfairly in the end, he does give a remarkable soliloquy, including this passage:

> I am a Jew. Hath not a Jew eyes? Hath not a Jew hands, organs, dimensions, senses, affections, passions? Fed with the same food, hurt with the same weapons, subject to the same diseases, healed by the same means, warmed and cooled by the same winter and summer as a Christian is? If you prick us do we not bleed? If you tickle us do we not laugh? If you poison us do we not not die?

would vary in value as the issuing states cut corners, adding less and less silver to the mix of metals. This caused fluctuations in the coins' value that complicated and undermined trading.

The Venetian grosso, the first high-value coin in Western Europe for more than five centuries. Made of 98.5 percent silver, the image shows Enrico Dandolo with St. Mark on one side, with Christ enthroned on the back.

To set things right, Doge Enrico Dandolo, famous for his leadership of the Fourth Crusade, minted a new Venetian currency, giving La Serenissima much more control over its destiny. He minted low-value "token" coins — ones with no inherent metallic value — the first since Roman times, which served for small daily purchases. For international currency they used silver from the crusaders' payments to create the grosso, the first high-value coin in Western Europe for more than five centuries. Made of 98.5 percent silver, the design stamped on the coins imitated that of Byzantine coins, but showed Christ on one side and Dandolo with Saint Mark on the other. Later they issued the 24-carat gold *ducat*, a coin modeled on the Florentine *florin*. These made Venice a leading currency market for centuries — and its coinage was accepted as far away as India and China.

In the Middle Ages, money changers sorted out the differences in coin value, evaluating coins for soundness and then exchanging them for a common currency. During the eleventh and twelfth centuries in Venice, they sat on *bancherius*, benches, before small tables positioned under the portico of the San Giacomo church at the foot of the then wooden Rialto Bridge. Each money changer had a ledger, pen and ink, an assay scale, an abacus and a bag of coins. But as new ways to handle money were invented, these *bancherii*, as they were known, would become the first "bankers."

A trader would leave his coins with a "banker" at his table. Then after each purchase, the buyer and seller would instruct the banker in person that they had agreed upon a sale. The banker would comply simply by reassigning the amount agreed on their ledger books to the seller, who also had an account. No physical money would change hands. This came to be known as the *giro* system, from the word *girare*, to circulate.

The first deposit banks emerged from these transactions, and though debate persists about whether they appeared first in Florence or Venice, clearly Venice was an early adopter. Without deposit banks, today's economies could not function. Deposit banks enable the flow of money within an economy. They became so important that the government in Venice began to impose regulation, requiring the bankers to deposit a large sum with the state to pay off depositors if the bank failed.

Deposit banking greatly increased the amount of working capital available and thus the size of the economy, but only insofar as funds were loaned out at interest. This, however, posed a problem for Christians for whom charging of interest on loans was considered a sin of usury. For this reason, before the twelfth century, most moneylending was done by Jews, whose holy books also disapproved of lending but who were not subject to Church laws. It took the form of pawnbroking, where an item of property was held by the lender as collateral against a loan. The service was much in demand among ordinary Venetians. But from the twelfth century, the Church began to soften its objection to lending at reasonable rates, typically not over 10 percent, so investors went to banks where they tended to get better deals.

Venetian voyages were paid for through loans and partnerships called *colleganze*, which shared out the costs and the risks of losses to pirates, storms and shipwreck. As many as 100 investors would take shares, later including many smaller investors who hoped that goods purchased cheaply in the markets of Sparta or Corinth could be resold at sizeable mark-ups in Venice or Constantinople. Along with the spices, silks and luxuries from the East, slaves, especially from Tana — modern Azov in the Ukraine — were traded and this continued even after 1366 when Venice closed public slave sales on the island of San Giorgio and at Rialto.

Venice grew rich. Outsiders of the era often struggled to grasp how it managed this feat as a place free from feudalism but tightly run; without fields to plough, yet visibly abundant in material wealth; powerful militarily yet frail, with its heart in a city within a shifting lagoon.

Historian Roger Crowley recently wrote:

> It was, in a sense, the first virtual city: an offshore bonded warehouse with no visible means of support — almost shockingly modern... the city rested on an abstract. It was an empire of cash. The ducat... was the dollar of its day... the Republic's fierce concentration on fiscal management was centuries ahead of its time. It was the only state in the world that had government policies solely geared to economic ends. There was no gap between its political and merchant class. It was a Republic run by and for entrepreneurs and it regulated accordingly.

Much of the wealth of historical Venice has been passed down through the generations but now something new is happening.

Some now see in Venice the hand of international finance that is visiting New York, London, Hong Kong and Berlin, where rich speculators are buying up heritage properties to cash in later. Investors are buying up palazzos, islands and rights to use Venice as a background for luxury cars and jewelry advertising, colonizing the city to strip it of assets. In this view, passionately expressed to me by the Venetian lawyer and rowing activist Giorgio Suppiej one evening as we traveled by ferry down the Grand Canal, Venice is a pawn of finance. He pointed out palazzi that were traded like chips in a great financial game as we floated by them on our way down the canal — €750 million was passed between hands in 2019, more than any other Italian city. By early 2021, this trend had accelerated with the pandemic's economic pressures leading to sales of some 50 Venice hotels, including many small- and medium-sized and family-owned, while raising concerns over dirty money entering the property market.

Others see the change differently, as something that came about due to the 1990s renewal of Venice by then Mayor Massimo Cacciari, who took office in 1993, alongside his deputy Gianfranco Bettin. "Cacciari was the watershed because with Cacciari we began to hear talk of a pluralistic, metropolitan city and of culture as its engine... pulling out the best of the city's social energy," journalist and commentator Fabio Bozzato told me during our walk around Mestre. It was only with this regime that in the first years after 2000, even as population was diminishing, Venice began to be seen as a global center of contemporary art, with the Biennale of Art as a driving force, supported by money from the Bach Foundation, from Russia, from François Pinault — who restored Palazzo Grassi and Punta della Dogana — from the Cini Foundation and from the Guggenheim, which became the most visited private museum in Italy. "He gave the city such a push that movement has continued in successive years," and, not incidentally, opened the tap of international capital flows that Venetians have encouraged, some would say misused.

"The Venetians are involved in exploitation of the tourist-based city. I see all my friends who, after the death of a grandmother or another older relative, remain alone in palazzos with, I don't know how many apartments, renting them out not to residents, but as bed and breakfasts because they can earn four times a much," says Lidia Fersuoch, the energetic head of Venice Italia Nostra, a heritage and environmental organization. "So there's a mix of interests, rooted in the Venetian soul, which is resistant if the public interests are not upheld.... Historically, the Republic's government put public interest ahead of the private. Now it's the opposite. The social contract — a spirit of social cohesion — that the city had for 1,000 years, has been lost. A free hand is given to big speculators.... Cacciari is the one who unleashed the neoliberal genie. Cacciari agreed to let the private sector do what it wanted.... He spurred it into action, creating a wave that is unstoppable."

Others are more sanguine about the money flowing into property.

I am waiting in the corner office of Alessandra Bastianutto, just steps down from the Frari church, where she runs the Venetian branch of Wire International Realty. She invites me into her small but minimalist glass-enclosed office. "What property do they buy? The residents, at the moment, buy little.... They find it hard because prices are high, so there's a tendency now to buy outside Venice — many are moving to Lido," she says. Properties in the historic center "sell mainly to Italians from the region — Lombardy, Piedmont, Tuscany, Rome, and many foreigners. Many are French and English in recent years and now many Germans, Austrians and Swiss — but fewer Russians and Americans."

They buy second homes, sometimes for holiday flats, and "because Venice is a dream for so many people," especially those "in love with the city who want to live in a romantic, artistic way." Others buy for profit — to rent to tourists, "which has really become the business of the city," she says. Storefronts are particularly hot properties because of the profit they produce. "It's easier to find [Venetian] sellers because they are looking to leave the city... residents find living in Venice a bit hard." Prices continue to rise, but she welcomes the new buyers. "The palazzos are often run-down, and simply to fulfill their dream of having a house in Venice, the buyers care for these places. They are good for the city."

There are suspicions, too, that the Sicilian Mafia have been buying palazzos and hotels, which raises the ugly head of organized crime, and its distant cousin, the black economy, which have endlessly complicated every attempt at change. Reporter Giorgio Cecchetti has documented this tale in Venice for forty years, covering in the 1980s and '90s the gangsters led by Felice Maniero, who stood outside the casino on the Grand Canal, loaning money to gamblers and later went into supplying drugs, and controlling tourist transport from Tronchetto parking, taking a cut from private taxis and tourist launches. That gang was defeated by the state but others continue, he says.

"The Sicilian Mafia, and especially now the 'Ndrangheta of Calabria, is the most important criminal organization in the world, even more powerful than the Chinese and Colombians, because it is spread all over the globe. It's run by an extended family, so it's extremely difficult to crack," says Cecchetti. They began in Milan and then spread to Piedmont, Emilia-Romagna and Veneto, investing in legal businesses and acquiring failing companies by surreptitiously lending them drug money. "Initially the businesses don't know who they are dealing with but slowly they realize and then gradually face threats with a pistol. When the Mafia takes over they continue to use their methods, lowering prices, in order to take out the competition."

This differs from the extensive "black economy," when people work without paying taxes on earnings or business owners, like the hoteliers, hire staff who are paid without the government taking a contribution to a pension scheme and so forth. In Venice, the black economy operates in transport in the form of illegal taxis — those that lack a taxi number

— but most people don't know the difference. "For years the politicians have let these things slide to get votes. In the accommodation field hundreds and hundreds of unregistered bed and breakfasts rent to tourists. Finally, restaurants and hotels hire waiters, cooks, often foreigners, in the black economy," he says.

But the government is cracking down on fiscal evasion, he says. The underfunded court system struggles to keep up with Italians' litigious tendencies — Italy has four or five times as many cases as there are in France and Germany because citizens here can go to court over little things. Even so, "In doing certain things the courts do succeed — even quickly," says Cecchetti. "The Mose investigation and first judgements were reached after two years. Super fast, in other words."

The "perfect storm" that has hit Venice was a long time brewing. It began with the exodus that took place after the floods of 1966, and then, from the 1980s, price pressure from second-home buying gave the property market a boost. When new Veneto region legislation encouraged the use of homes for bed and breakfasts, the situation grew worse.

The law aimed to stimulate tourism where tourists are scarce, and it worked well enough in remote towns. But in Venice, with its surfeit of tourists, it caused buying of properties to turn them into bed and breakfasts, even when the basic terms — that the owner lived in the property — were not met. "This had an immediate effect on house values," says Pizzo. "Clearly if you can use your own house for economic gain, this worsens the position of those in need of residence, either through purchase or to rent."

When, soon after 2010, Airbnb and similar online portals encouraged renting to tourists, things got worse. Now landlords, many of them Venetians, could fill properties with tourists who pay multiples of the amounts that long-term residents could afford, so locals found even less housing available for rent or purchase.

"It's evident by now that Venice is an enormous, sprawling hotel that has escaped any kind of regulation," says Emanuele Dal Carlo, part of the "informal think tank" Reset Venezia, which studied the housing shortage. They found residences — not just rooms but whole apartments — removed from the market and from taxation by online tourist booking. The numbers of properties unavailable for residential use was vastly undercounted. Airbnb is supposed to be about independent owners renting out for limited periods, while Reset Venezia found scores of properties under a single manager — a few estate agents — like a dispersed hotel. This had helped push the number of tourist beds in Venice to about 30,000; that is one for every six Venetians, compared to more rule-based markets in places like Amsterdam, where that figure reaches only one for every 100 locals.

This not only affects homes. The actual hotels, including high-end places, are losing out to this competition; even the fourteenth-century Hotel Danieli went into bankruptcy at one point because of the drop in guests. The number of five-star tourists has fallen overall, putting pressure on high-end hotels and resorts because the surge in tourism has come mainly from those on a low budget.

The Airbnb phenomenon, in particular, has also hit businesses, such as Hostelsclub, a homegrown dot-com travel agency specializing in hostels and budget accommodation. Representing over 37,000 places worldwide, Hostelsclub is for people who don't want to pay for "a penguin at the reception desk" and all the unnecessary extras, while it gives travelers the chance to meet other travelers, which is part of the experience, says founder Andrea Mehanna. He started the company initially because his parent's hostel on Campo Santa Margherita could not be listed on the major sites. Today, with Airbnb, the private renter of a room escapes the taxation faced by hotels and hostels who must pay for the cost they impose on the city for such things as refuse collection. "With hostels you are not expelling someone from his house and his city," Mehanna says. Renting apartments through Airbnb, which operates in 220 countries, gives an unfair advantage. "Logically, it makes sense to level the competitive playing field."

If that weren't enough, another piece of deregulation in the early 2000s made it easier to open bars and restaurants, doing away with a previous approval system. "If a bar generates ten times the revenue of a bread shop, the owner will not hesitate to throw out the bread shop and get a bar to move in. This is the market mechanism that expelled all the services," explains economist Pizzo.

The change has been dramatic. "The whole commercial fabric has been bent toward tourism," says journalist Silvio Testa. "I don't like supermarkets, but fortunately we have some, otherwise you'd have to go to Mestre to shop. There's nothing left. Everywhere is becoming a bar, a restaurant, places that sell sandwiches, wine and.... It's something pathological." It has also changed the character of residents themselves. The new rich in Venice, those living off tourism, have little knowledge of culture and spend lavishly on yachts, entertainment and gold necklaces, he adds. "The flood of money affects the tone of the city... making everything vulgar."

All this has fed the most serious current threat to Venice: depopulation, which has had different causes over the years. In 1951 population hit a peak of 174,808 in the historic center, but this reflected a wartime immigration because Venice escaped bombing. The population numbers had dropped by over 35,000 by the early 1960s as people returned to the mainland and sought alternatives to Venice's working-class housing, which was in very poor condition, with some houses lacking basics, like toilets. The hardships of the 1966 floods, which most affected ground-floor habitations and made up to 5,000 people homeless, again accelerated the exodus. People took the chance to move to the terraferma, especially Mestre and Marghera, where new, more spacious modern housing was becoming available. By 1975 the population hit 104,000, which some consider the proper level for Venice. After that, new factors related to tourism, living costs, an aging population and, more recently, pressures from acqua alta came to the fore, with the population dropping in 2020.

Birthrates and inflows of new residents, such as academics and foreigners, have failed to counteract the decline.

❧

"The problem, therefore, is one of producing rules," for the market, says Pizzo, who was a 2015 candidate for mayor of Venice. That should be simple enough but, he contends, "the political will of this [mayoral] administration goes in favor of speculation and profit, instead of opposing these forces as they have done in other European cities" and he cited Amsterdam, New York and Barcelona as examples. The fundamental rules, he suggested, should make Airbnb a complementary activity, preventing rental occupancy of a property for more than ninety days in any year, which would provide a more reasonable balance of income, still giving owners the equivalent of an extra year's rent, but providing housing for residents. Airbnb issued a promise in 2020 to "make a positive contribution to society," yet it spends millions to fend off regulation around the world, from Barcelona to Berlin and Boston.

Venice's other need is to tax incomes from rentals and direct the money back into renovation of the some 5,000 empty housing units in Venice, of which 1,000 are unusable because they are in need of repairs. Pizzo believes European Investment Bank loans could be obtained to put these houses back on the market. He says the way forward in managing the tourist flow is to adjust high-season prices for services like transport and museums via flexi-price cards tourists would buy, rather than through an entry ticket. In 2018 the city government won approval for a sort of entry ticket, a €3 to €5 day-tripper fee going up at peak times to €6 or €8, with fines of €50 to €300 for failure to pay. Similar to the "landing tax" for visitors to Italy's tiny Aeolian islands and Capri, fee collection on transport and at entry points were scheduled to begin in 2020. Expected to raise €14 million a year for city cleaning and transport improvements, the tax is proving complex to apply without targeting the wrong people — those who are residents, students or others with non-touristic reasons for entering the city. So its effectiveness remains to be seen.

The city's hopes focus in part on Brugnaro. In a 2018 interview, Councilor Simone Venturini, on behalf of Brugnaro's office, says that the mayor has brought the city back to financial health, cutting the city's debt from €800 million to €740 million. "The city was on the brink of financial breakdown" but today it has a healthy bank balance, says the thirty-year-old, neatly groomed politician who was wearing a blue sport coat over a striped shirt. He adds that "the beauty of it is that there has been no cut in services." Opposition politicians, however, say the debt reduction has more to do with Rome's increasing its funding for local administrations than anything Brugnaro has done. They insist service cuts have occurred.

As for the other challenges, Venturini says, "The real problem, which no one has understood for decades, is that Venice needs more than extraordinary economic resources to maintain the city." With all the city's complex demands, "the mayor should have powers to intervene," says Venturini. "Stopping the renting out of apartments to tourists is the real drama, even more than hotels, because hotels don't take space from residents.... But a mayor does not have the power to regulate these activities. It would take an act of Parliament," he says, insisting the mayor has done what he could, such as blocking the conversion of buildings to new hotels in the city. Venturini says blame falls on the mayor because the public do not understand that his hands are tied and because it serves political opponents to blame him.

The commercial deregulation of the last twenty years has undermined Venice and other "cities of art," where "the rules of the market and competition lead to debasement," Venturini acknowledges. The mayor has tried to limit the negative effects, for example, by removing the automatic right of bars to put tables outside, and by limiting takeaways. But what he can do has run up against the expectations of the public, "who want artisanal shops and not stores selling tourist junk." But changes must come from national government and "in the last few years we don't have serious government in this country." The mayor does not lack "vision," Venturini insists. He wants the city to come back to life, for artisans to thrive and for work and jobs to come back to Venice. "We want a recovery."

Critics retort that the mayor has power to do more and demand more from Rome. The ban on hotels, they point out, has been repeatedly overridden through his own administration's granting of legislative "exceptions" and by the decision to build hotels with a total of 5,000 new beds just over the bridge in Mestre. But Brugnaro maintains more tourists are good. "Venice's problem is not hotels.... We must welcome tourists. The hotels represent urban regeneration and they bring work," he told a press conference. "Stop complaining."

Critics regard the mayor as acting on behalf of monied interests, saying that he is motivated by his ownership of local properties and businesses such as Reyer, his basketball team, whose need for a publicly funded stadium, which he would profit from, he famously defended with an emotional outburst at a televised council meeting, placing the team's trophy on his seat and walking out, refusing to answer questions. Venturini denies that the mayor is driven by self-interest, saying that he has placed his wealth in a "blind trust," an arrangement whereby his assets are handed over to trustees who manage them on his behalf without, theoretically, his knowledge or right to intervene. Opponents like Pizzo call this setup "a little trick."

"With the failure of traditional politics, a group of interests" — owners, investors and various stakeholders — "has somehow understood that they can occupy positions of power to facilitate their own interests," says Pizzo. "Brugnaro made some important property investments, clearly directly his or ones he is indirectly linked to, for example, at the airport, whose interests are served by boosting tourist numbers. He has land at the foot of the bridge in Mestre on which hotels could be built. The model is that these interest groups name a political representative to promote their aims. Brugnaro, who had no involvement in politics before 2015, rose to power on the back of a devastating campaign spending €2 million to pay for self-promotion — in this sense taking after Berlusconi who also used his personal fortune to pay for campaigning. In this way, Brugnaro got himself elected, promising to 'resolve Venice's problems and create work.' But, in reality, his main mission, and I believe he has said so explicitly, is to protect, defend and advance the interests of certain groups in the city."

What will it take to change, especially since 2020 when Brugnaro won five more years in office? That is the subject of the following chapters.

26

FUTURE

INNOVATING FOR THE REVIVAL OF THE CITY

> "*A* [Venetian] *government administration ... can still today stop and reverse the process of degradation threatening to undermine all the frameworks of civil society, whilst continuing to offer the rest of the world a unique and inimitable example of a life admired and envied by all.*"
>
> —ITALIA NOSTRA, "MANIFESTO FOR VENICE," 2020

No one in Venice can outdo the dinner parties of Mara Rumiz, who on this October night has brought a dozen friends together, mostly from the publishing world. After sipping flutes of prosecco in her high-ceilinged living room, where the bookshelves require a ladder to reach the upper tiers, we find the big square table in the next room elegantly set and soon, before each diner, is placed a fragrant bowl of tawny squash soup with a dollop of cream swirled on top. On ladling out, the ebullient Rumiz, a former Venetian legislator, discovers she has made too little, so she goes without.

But the rest of us, unable to resist, tuck in, and soon spoons clink on empty china. Spiced meatballs the size of ping-pong balls, and slender, meaty kebabs follow, served with fried string beans, eggplant and yellow and red peppers with slices of dark bread — and all the guests have a glass of ruby red wine to sip. Conversations swirl around, and among them the seemingly unending arguments over tourists and how to manage them bounces across the table. I talk with my neighbor, Patricia Chendi, a bright-eyed editor from Milan and a lover of books who is keen to have me learn about Aldo Manuzio, also known as Aldus Manutius, who came to Venice at the end of the fifteenth century.

Between the mains and the desserts — homemade almond biscuits, pungent slices of sweetened, sliced ginger and high-octane raisins soaked in grappa, a type of strong grape brandy — she recounts how Manutius saw a gap in the market for printing rare Greek classics. Venice was already the leading center for printing, having blossomed after Johannes

Gutenberg introduced standardized, movable typefaces in about 1450. Manutius is known to posterity as the inventor of italic fonts, a compressed typeface, and especially for pocket-sized "octavo" books. Before, books had to be printed in quarto and even folio sizes, each as big as a lap tray, but he cut books to a quarter of that size or less, reducing the cost to about one-eighth of what it had been. It sparked an explosion of publishing that has lasted into our age and is the precursor to the mass-market paperback.

Today, for Venetians, the name Aldo Manuzio represents the tradition of innovation that characterized Venice. He had a lot of company. Historical Venice never stopped modernizing, with advances in finance and trade, glass-making, navigation, map-making and efficiency of manufacturing and ship and cannon building even into the late eighteenth century. But the decline of Venice was also caused by those merchants sticking to a well-trodden path of success, trading along the old galley routes of the Mediterranean while entrepreneurs in other nations used seafaring galleons and new routes to find trade in the Americas, Asia and Africa. This shift would contribute to the economic decline of Venice.

"If you don't want to be caught by surprise, you have to recognize that the future will be different from the past," wrote Piero Formica in the *Harvard Business Review* about the fate of Venice. "One major move by a competitor, or one new technology, is sometimes all it takes to end an empire." He might have also said the opposite, that the Venice of today could just be one innovation away from finding a way forward. Many are those who have innovative ideas for projects that could be critical in the revival of Venice.

"Some of the most important architectural designs in Venice have never been realized," in the estimation of Sara Marini, a professor of urban architecture, recycling and design at Iuav University in Venice. For example, the "really modern" modular design of 1964 for the city hospital by Le Corbusier, who saw Venice as a sacred place that could meet modern needs with its human focus. Were it not for his untimely death, the structure would have been built. Even though unrealized, as were other projects by Louis Kahn, Frank Lloyd Wright and Peter Eisenman — all rejected by city officials — they "raised doubts about whether Venice could be modern" because they think about "the soul of Venice," she says.

A challenging project that did get built, however, was that of Spanish architect Santiago Calatrava, who designed the first new bridge in Venice for seventy years. Officially called the Ponte della Costituzione (Constitution Bridge), the structure opened in 2008, and he declared it to be "an act of love for Venice, and for Italian culture in general." But the sleek bridge, with its slippery-when-wet glass steps and non-functioning, disabled access contraption, has sparked ongoing controversy over its aesthetics and durability.

"These are the projects that caused a crisis and made us think about the idea of Venice," says Marini. "Those that succeeded in being built... were absorbed into the idea of Venice, while the others, perhaps, didn't really engage with the city and remain part of the ongoing argument."

Venice, she says, "has fought against modernity and impeded the 20th century, sometimes due to circumstantial causes." One might cite as an example the outcry against French fashion designer Pierre Cardin's 2012 plan for a futuristic skyscraper, with sixty-five floors, overlooking the lagoon on disused land in Marghera. "But, at the moment," she continues, "Venice, in many respects, embodies the contemporary city in the sense that nowadays all cities want to create pedestrianized areas" to have public spaces where people meet. "That's what it's like here already." People are democratically walking instead of being separated by cars with the varying messages of prestige that automobiles can convey, says Marini. "So it's a bit strange that Venice, by staying behind in some respects, does protect itself from over-rational Cartesian modernity, so to speak, and yet it has anticipated what's now the dream of every city — slowness. It's fine to build new architecture, but this is a city already very much advanced."

But how should Venice react when, for example, a monument crumbles or a new building is needed? Are we still in the era of *com'era, dov'era'* — constant rebuilding and copying of the past — such as happened after the St. Mark's bell tower collapse in 1902?

"For me a reconstruction in the most contemporary fashion possible would be totally fine," she insists, adding that she wants to preserve the old buildings as much as possible, too. Today most of the modern thinking goes into the internal restoration of historic buildings, such as was done at the Punta della Dogana, the old customs house on the bacino, and by Fondazione Prada at Ca' Corner della Regina along the Grand Canal. "But I believe that a new palazzo would not change the rules of the game. It's not a question of the language [styles and forms] of architecture."

What has been most powerful for Marini in recent years has been instances of temporary architecture, such as the floating stage built for the Pink Floyd concert in 1989. "Today we see the city as fixed, but in reality history has always been changing," remarks Marini, citing the sixteenth-century neo-classical structures of Palladio and his San Giorgio Maggiore and Redentore churches, which "seemed too revolutionary at the time." She envisages more projects on water. These could be restaurants built on temporary islands floated out at peak times, or perhaps moored next to Piazza San Marco to give the tourists a place to picnic and then towed away with all the refuse visitors leave behind. Other ideas include inhabitable machines that produce energy and support the lagoon ecology. Rather than expanding historical Venice, "The need is to respond to the natural cycles of the lagoon, the tides and acqua alta," she suggests. "Venice is a city of variable density. The city needs to link itself closely to the lagoon, with people living there in a different relationship to the environment."

The future is what concerns Gabriella Giaretta, seventy-nine, who has taken on a big new project: converting into a museum the empty Palazzetto in the Loggia, the structure that stands above the arches of the pescaria, the fish market, in Rialto. With the latest in multimedia displays, it will tell the story of Venice's place in international commerce. And in the old market below, now with fewer and fewer fresh fish sellers' stands than before, a new "street food" market will nourish the crowds.

It will be "a museum that recalls what this area was like, how it has been transformed and how the commerce has changed," she says, as we surveyed the open spaces around the building. Smiling and earnest, her blonde curly hair carefully tended to, she says she wants the museum to let the younger generations know how things have changed, how once the Rialto sizzled with money, news and trade of precious jewels, gold and spices during the Republic, and how, in her own lifetime, the shops used to sell drapes, silk, and food, "not all these ugly things for tourists!"

Giaretta ought to know. She was born in a flat on the other side of Rialto in the first months of the Second World War. Her father and grandfather sold cheese wholesale and her mother's family had a bar nearby. When her father died, no one else in the family knew the cheese business, so in the 1960s they began selling purses to the tourists. Later she became a teacher.

Everyone says Giaretta works tirelessly for Venice. But why?

"Because I want the city's inhabitants to know their city, as well as those who come to see it. And I want, if I can, to do something when things don't go well for the residents — and the shopkeepers! ... In my small way, I try to make life better for people who live and work here. I have united all the Rialto shopkeepers."

My former Liceo Classico Marco Polo classmate, lifelong activist Mario Santi, has asked me to come along to the seminar at which he is speaking. He sits forward on his chair to address twenty French urban scholars and officials who are sitting around him in a tightly packed circle in a café. He pauses after each sentence, stopping for the translator to turn his words into French, as the delegation listens intently to his experiences as part of what the delegation's French leader has called the "*résistance urbaine*," the urban resistance, in Venice.

These days Mario, who has been an activist and self-described militant since the 1970s, has a hand in two long-running campaigns: Comunità della Vida di Giacomo dell'Orio, known as *La Vida*, a fight to save the last unused historic building in a campo for use as a local community center and to prevent it from becoming yet another restaurant; and, separately, a drive to turn Poveglia, one of the long-abandoned islands in the lagoon, into a public park and facility for the people — rather than another hotel resort.

In both cases ordinary residents have taken charge to make their views heard. "What's fundamental is the community deciding to manage directly some part of the public heritage that otherwise would be sold to private interests," Mario tells me. "These places would be more valued if they were given back to the community for cultural uses."

A great portion of the Venetian community takes part in the plethora of forward-looking local associations. So many have blossomed that there's even a guidebook to "rebellious" Venice!

In the future, tourists will be an even bigger part of Venice. Professor Jan van der Borg has no doubt that the tourism flood is becoming a tsunami. It has been growing exponentially. Anywhere from 25 to 30 million tourists visited in 2019 (the actual number is unknown because only those who stay overnight can be accurately counted). That will grow, by some estimates, to 38 million by 2025. "Venice has always been in line with the global tourism markets… and is going to follow this trend. We will be getting into a situation that is not manageable anymore," he says from behind a desk at his Venice University office.

The Dutch researcher asserted that "many public policies are actually the opposite of what a sound strategy would be," emphasizing "quantity over quality." The last few mayors of Venice, for example, have been keen to outlaw new hotels — but that only caused more hotels to pop up outside, in Mestre and Padua. He questions the holding of cultural events in the summer months when the city is already jammed with tourists. The May to November Biennale of Art could be scheduled off-season, say, from October to May. The trend has been "increasing numbers of people who are less interested in what Venice has to offer culturally," he says, referring to people who treat Venice like a big shopping mall where you stop for a couple of hours. More than three times as many people visit the luxury shopping stores at Fondaco dei Tedeschi than go to the Biennale. "Abolish Carnival," he suggests. "Why do we have an event that is not being attended by the Venetians anymore?"

It comes down to a question of who tourism is for.

"Tourism only makes sense if it makes the place more livable and more useful for those who actually need to make a living," says Van der Borg. "It is not for the tourists. It's always for the locals. They are the priority." The idea is to offer "quality tourism to generate added value for the local population."

Lots of other cities have found ways to manage tourism and have created strategies setting out what they want tourism to achieve, he says. "Soft measures" include encouraging people to stay overnight by hosting evening initiatives, like the light festivals of England. Others have aimed to "de-seasonalize" tourism. Visitor centers can help redirect tourists, who can be encouraged to book visits at off-peak times to spread crowds more evenly over the year. Another idea is a congestion tax, now about to be realized as an "entry tax," but he has doubts about this. "If you say we have reached a maximum number of tourists and you start to ask for an entrance fee, for example, I think there's a real risk that Venice becomes a museum." But that can be avoided if those visiting off-peak were instead given some advantages. He estimates that half of the exceptionally busy days and lots of the localized crowding could be avoided with such measures.

But what Venice lacks most is a broad strategy.

"All respectable cities are implementing strategic plans with respect to what they want to be" in 2030 or 2040 and how tourism fits into that picture. London has a plan. So do Paris and Rotterdam. The plan is shared with stakeholders — city users, inhabitants and commuters — and it sets out what the city wants to be: a Disneyland like Orlando? A student city like Boston or Cambridge? A city with a port or with advanced chemical industries? The strategy provides a framework of objectives and goals. "If you have a strategy someone can hold you accountable for not realizing this strategy," he says. But the "politicians don't want to be held accountable." In Venice, they too often listen to lobbyists like the hotel owners, gondoliers and cruise ship companies, he says.

The advent of Airbnb, which encourages use of private residential property for tourist accommodation, has contributed to population decline by forcing up the cost of rent and reducing availability of residential living space. However, Reset Venezia has come up with a new approach: the Fairbnb.coop platform. Taken up by supporters in Amsterdam, Barcelona and other European cities, the cooperative's stated aim is "community-powered tourism," turning tourism into a force for the good of the residents.

"We are working to put the community and the concept of fair-sharing back at the center of Venetian life and to the spread of a new culture of traveling based on responsibility, participation and sustainability," says Emanuele Dal Carlo, a Venetian co-founder and president of the Fair Bnb network, Societa Cooperativa.

Fairbnb.coop, which launched in preliminary form in Valencia, Barcelona, Amsterdam, Genova, Bologna and Venice in November 2019, and opened to the public in 2020, works like Airbnb in that it is a booking portal that lists available accommodation in private apartments and houses for travelers in the destination city, but with the crucial difference that only qualified accommodation is listed and half of the 15 percent commission paid by the visitor, and 50 percent of Fairbnb.coop revenues, goes into a crowdfunding pot for the benefit of community projects. These projects, selected by the site users and local neighbors, could fund the upgrading of areas of urban decay, such as building a park in an area lacking greenery. The tourist gets to feel they are part of the renewal of the city by protecting residency and fighting gentrification instead of participating in the "extractive" economy typically applied to historic cities; that is, an economy which takes resources and capital from the community but does not replenish it. Fairbnb.coop is owned by the participating hosts, local business owners and neighbors who collectively decide how to run the platform.

Its hosts are residents who pay local taxes and have only one house in the tourist market. "In the end, being on the platform will become an emblem of sustainability, of social responsibility and ethics that will draw a line between" accommodation contributing or not contributing to the community, says Dal Carlo. "Here [in Venice] we see all the negative aspects of tourism, ten years in advance, but the city is also an open-air lab where we can experiment with solutions for a more sustainable tourism."

Venice may overflow with tourists, but residents are in demand. In her TEDx San Marco talk in 2019, the scholar, novelist and tourist guide Cristina Gregorin stands and looks at the camera.

> *"I'm here to speak about living in Venice and the high quality of life that we, as residents of this city, enjoy."*

She makes a pitch for new residents, setting out the pros and cons of life in Venice, the challenges of mass tourism and housing, and touching on the history of the Republic, asserting that:

> *"Venice has a never-ending hidden energy. The city has always been reborn, but perhaps in a different form."*

Turning to face a second camera, she lists the benefits of a Venetian life: lots of walking, which is good for health, lots of cultural activities, safety for children, life at a human pace. She concludes:

> *"We need pioneers who will join us in challenging the enormous commercial and tourist pressure. So if the reasons I've listed here*

match with your expectations of a good life, please move to Venice. We await you."

A futuristic glass and wood structure within a former Giudecca garment factory that was once a convent today produces innovation.

The Venice Project Center, set up in 1988, drives forward a mindboggling array of future and historically focused activities to do with everything from preserving bell towers to urban agriculture in underused spaces. The Center creates digital tools for tasks ranging from locating looted and destroyed artworks and checking in real time on the numbers of tourists to other types of software. Harnessing the power of minds of university students and entrepreneurs, the Center aims to think a way out of Venice's dilemmas — and not just study them.

"By creating products, especially ones that could solve some of Venice's problems, we want to create jobs that pay well enough" so that the employees can afford to live in Venice, says director and founder, Fabio Carrera, fifty-six, an MIT-educated information scientist and professor at Worcester Polytechnic Institute in Massachusetts, which sponsors the Center. For Carrera, employment is the overriding priority for Venice. "Without high-level jobs nothing is going to change," says Carrera, who has a stubble beard, T-shirt and casual techie look. "Until we repopulate there is very little we can do to address the problems."

In 2017 he and others set up and in part funded a corporation, with ethical guidelines and employee ownership schemes from which to spin off new and exportable businesses.

Jobs suited to Venice could come from any number of fields. Tourism, when under control, is not a bad industry, he says, but it can drain money from the city and pays too little to support living in historic Venice. "We want to move away from extractive business to productive ones," he says. There are other businesses such as firms based on culture and conservation, "but that's not the Center's skill set," says Carrera.

The Center gets ideas in part from an association with the university's center in Santa Fe, New Mexico, which Carrera also runs, where they get "technologies that are a few years ahead of what is in Italy right now." That and the data they collect "feeds our start-ups," he remarks. Only a small number of the ideas get "monetized" and, as of late 2018, the Center had already created start-ups financed through commissions on transactions or by subscription, such as a public transportation app and a jewelry virtual fair for small artisans. Other projects include hydroponic food production of vegetables in underutilized, abandoned buildings (including a bell tower with vertical fields and robotic lettuce leaf pickers), and a website to help young Venetians use tourist rents to pay for mortgages of residential properties.

He sees lots of places to look for solutions. Once those jobs are created, housing is needed; there is public housing, and expensive housing, but nothing for the middle class. The other important need is mobility — especially for businesses — who tend to leave the city when they get more customers because the customers won't take the time and trouble to get into Venice. A controversial solution might be an underground system, but he thinks many lesser solutions could address the need in the short term.

"Tourism is a great opportunity in addition to being a problem. We could still become world leaders in management of tourism — if we solve the Venice problem," says Carrera, showing off some of his data on tourist numbers, such as how far the number of tourists exceeds ideal, socially desirable and safety levels. "At some point we need to put a ceiling on this. Whether you like it or not, it has to happen. A rebalancing of residents and tourists is needed. Our contribution to the rebalancing is what we are doing here, creating jobs" for new residents, he asserts, adding that the tourist ceiling should be a one-to-one ratio between tourists and residents — about half of current levels. "There would be a lot of complaints because we've allowed people to create hotels and everything else. It's not going to be a popular decision. Some mayor with balls is going to have to do this at some point because it must be done."

27

POLITICS
THE HEART OF THE PROBLEM AND THE SOLUTION

"As leaders we have a responsibility to fully articulate the risks our people face. If the politicians are not favorable to speaking truthfully, then clearly we must devote more energy to changing the politics."

—MARLENE MOSES, AMBASSADOR TO THE UNITED NATIONS FOR NAURU, 2012

The email about an interview I hoped to arrange with Mayor Brugnaro puzzled me. It was from his aide: *Would you be so kind as to send the names of the persons you have interviewed so far? A thousand thanks.*

Politicians don't normally ask journalists who else they have spoken to before setting up an interview. I understood he was probably trying to find out if I had been influenced by speaking to critics of the mayor. I responded that I had at that point interviewed over 130 people in Venice from all walks of life, but didn't think it right to name them for the mayor's scrutiny.

With that, the line went dead, so to speak. The promised interview never happened.

But the story did not end there, in that I received explanation from an intermediary as to how this had happened, and in doing so light was shed on the politics of the city. I was told I had come with "Anglo-Saxon" expectations of "modern democracy," but that the "majority of Venetians are querulous, critical, negative and in short, resentful," and that "Latin Culture" had prevailed. "The Latin culture... always looks for the worst and ulterior motives. For this reason the mayor... must remain vigilant. If people saw Brugnaro dressed in white walking on water at Lake Tiberias in Palestine... they would [not marvel at this miracle] but accuse him of being unable to swim!"

The idea that a darker side drags down the Italian mindset has some validity, but I was not wholly convinced.

The mayor has turned away many others, including the award-winning Francesco Erbani, who asked to talk to him for his fine book of reportage, *Non è triste Venezia* (*Venice Is Not Sad*). Brugnaro has a reputation for avoiding questions. I was particularly impressed by what Venetian salt-of-the-earth neighborhood campaigner Gabriella Giaretta had to say about the mayor. She was unequivocal:

> The mayor does not want to meet us citizens. During the electoral campaign, I talked to him and the opposition candidates about some of the needs of the residents.... But afterwards, when he won the elections, he immediately became extremely closed. He doesn't want to hear from residents because he says we complain too much, that we find too many things that are not going well. I have had contact with councilors, but never with him, even if I have written to request meetings. He avoids everyone. He has changed all the managers in the city government, substituting people who are unfamiliar with the problems and don't know how to resolve them. You can tell he doesn't want to be contradicted. I sometimes go to the municipal council meetings, but you can see he wants to cut them short and to cut out anyone who does not think like him.... He only wants approval.

One is led to ask if this is just the way politics is done these days. In the UK, we see many politicians who show complete disdain for journalists — and also for the public. In particular, leaders with a sense of entitlement have found oppressive the idea of having to defend one's ideas openly. Wasn't this just another example of that? It resembles the behavior of UK Prime Minister Boris Johnson's choosing to "answer" questions he posed to himself on Facebook, or the Twitter barrage President Trump hid behind.

I might have concluded that such besieged, shut-down behavior may well have been Brugnaro's personal choice, but then I was surprised by the comments made by his administration's councilor Simone Venturini in what was otherwise a very satisfactory and wide-ranging interview.

"I see that some people you have talked to are on the left, and very politicized in some cases, so they have a negative view of this administration," he says at one point.

"And so I have come to talk to you," I responded, thinking of how hard it had been to get anyone at all in the government to open up.

Venturini also doesn't think much of the administration's critics, either, particularly the environmentalists. "They're always the same people," he says. "In Venice there's a group of people who do the anti-cruise ship, no-TAV (train), no-Poveglia, no-airport thing. Those 100 or 200 who are on the far left, running around with banners and getting in the way... it's not the city that is against Poveglia, it's those with journalist friends who call CNN and get their photos taken and get famous." This vocal minority talk is odd, particularly in the case of Poveglia, where thousands of Venetians joined a crowdfunding bid to buy the island. Brugnaro says similar things to the news media often, blasting people who "complain" and using the phrase "always the same 200." The inability of many politicians to listen to their critics is disturbing. So blinded are they by their own ideology, that they can only demean and dismiss opponents. If only they engaged with them, they might learn something.

I spent time listening to people in Venice, and while many of them did, indeed, complain bitterly about the mayor, he has his satisfied supporters, though mainly on the terraferma. Among those living in historical Venice, the majority voted against him in the 2020 election. But the Venetian political story is more than a story of the mayor's office. It's really about the way people think, local divisions and the national and international forces at play.

The story of political power in Venice tracks the history of modern Italy, but is also set apart.

Ever since the communist Giobatta Gianquinto was elected in 1946 as the first mayor of Venice after the Second World War, Venice has shown its progressive bent despite being within the conservative region of Veneto. Even during the 1950s and '60s, when the conservative Christian Democratic Party held sway there, the left had a moderating influence, refocusing local attention on social problems. The strong presence of the Communist Party, with its supporters among the workers of Marghera, the Venetian artisans and intellectuals, made sure of that. In 1975, going against the trend in Veneto, Venice elected Mario Rigo, a socialist, and from that time until the election of Brugnaro in 2015, the city voted in center-left administrations, especially after the laws changed to allow direct, rather than party, elections of mayors. The first to be directly elected in this way was the nationally known opposition leader and charismatic philosopher, Massimo Cacciari, in 1993.

After the fall of the Berlin Wall in 1989, all over the world ideologies lost their force, leading in Italy to the national collapse of the Communist Party, and thanks to the "Clean Hands" corruption scandal around 1992, the Christian Democrats also disappeared. Their vestiges eventually found a sort of home in Italy's new Democratic Party. In Venice, the center-left mayors (Cacciari, 1993–97 and 1997–00; Paolo Costa, 2000–05; Cacciari, 2005–10; and Giorgio Orsoni, 2010–14) increasingly lost the support of the left voters with their preoccupation with power and deregulation of property that paved the way for the explosion of hotels and Airbnbs transforming the city into what many call "Disneyland."

Voters were also displeased with other issues ranging from the hiving off of Cavallino-Treporti from the city administration and the approval of the Mose dam to lagoon traffic and cruise ship chaos, misuse of Special Law funds for Mestre and the decline of Marghera industries. The six attempts since 1979 to separate Venice and Mestre show the frustration these problems have fostered.

By the time Costa's government arrived just after the millennium, voters had already begun to move to the right in the name of pragmatism and efficiency. But the real break came with the victory of Cacciari in 2005, leading a centrist coalition that beat the left-supported candidate Felice Casson. By the time Orsoni came on the scene, he sold himself as a technocrat, and his 2014 arrest for Mose dam-related corruption (though his conviction was later set aside) represented the coup de grâce for the left that opened the door to center-right proponent Brugnaro. An independent who made his money with an employment agency and who would later reveal his prejudices against homosexuals and Moslems, he rode the wave of ascendency of the parties of the right and discontent all over Italy, beating Casson in a close race.

In the 2020 election, Brugnaro promised to relaunch tourism after Covid-19, resuming policies aimed at short-term profit. The divided opposition sought more sustainable tourism, but Brugnaro, was swept back into office, delighting those who felt threatened by the drop in tourism while bitterly disappointing most lagoon dwellers. To make quite clear where his sympathies lay, the re-elected mayor marked his victory in Mestre — not at the municipal offices in Ca' Farsetti on the Grand Canal — the first time a winner has ever done so.

Widespread disdain for the state, deep pessimism — what my source called "Latin culture" — or sometimes self-loathing, does burden Italy today.

The causes of this are many and go back as far as the origins of Italy in 1861, origins that created a nation with intractable divisions, and that were exacerbated by open wounds left by the Second World War, a legacy of fascism and the unstable political system to which it gave birth. All of these have added to the persistent economic crisis. Italians have been disappointed in politics for a long time, and that aspect of the national character shows no signs of going away at the moment.

It is not uncommon to have conversations like the one I had with Venetian restorer Adriano Cincotto in his workshop.

"At present, you know, when you don't believe in yourself, many times you do things because you have to do them, but without quality — that sort of attitude," says Cincotto.

"Who does not believe in themselves?" I ask.

"A bit, all of Italy," he says. "Because if not they would start doing something."

Italians had hope in the 1960s and '70s, when protest movements demanded change, he believes, but those ideas have been poisoned since the 1980s, a period of fear and terrorism, and replaced by Berlusconi's "air of hedonism," when people adopted his get-rich role model. "People lost the sense of empathy.... To the point that now in this moment of crisis, people have woken up a bit, but can't manage — they don't have the defenses." Instead, he feels disillusioned.

"I find myself now, at almost sixty, working twelve hours a day for at least six days a week. I live with this contradiction, with a bit of anxiety, but not for me, because I am nearly finishing my work life," he says, "but for the generations coming behind me. We have not succeeded in giving them any of what we had hoped for; on the contrary they have, in many cases, much less. I don't understand how these youths of thirty will manage. They work four or five months a year on hunger wages, living with their parents. It is not a good life."

I heard similar, if more mixed, expressions from the Giudecca artist Serena Nono, who has worked on a series of portraits of female figures in the pale light of a lantern they hold far from their faces. "Perhaps I have begun this to explore loneliness, pain, and the fact of not understanding today's society. All my pictures are like that.... Italy is changing quickly, due to immigration, the economic crisis, lots of real problems, and people are reacting in an insane way. There is this new government, which has tones of fascism. What strikes me hard is seeing the majority of people — fearful for what is happening... agreeing with these behaviors." But she tries to stay positive. "There are lots of people trying to do something. It's very hard. But what can you do? One feels very impotent."

The general malaise contrasts with a somewhat feistier attitude toward the local political battles.

"Venice is not dead; it still has inhabitants, public institutions and sustaining economic activities. The politicians generally must understand that they have to maintain this life and this city," insists Felice Casson when we meet for an interview in late 2018. A gangly, bespectacled, scholarly looking former prosecuting magistrate, senator in the national government and twice candidate for Venice's mayor and an opposition Democratic Party councilor in Venice until 2020, he sits with me at a long, wooden conference table in the high-ceilinged Ca' Farsetti, the palazzo that belonged to descendants of Doge Enrico Dandolo and which has been the administrative center of Venice since 1826.

"Venice must be a living city, with people who work and live within it. That means we need to find an equilibrium between work, commerce, tourism and the life of citizens.... It is not acceptable for Venice to become a Disneyland and exist only for tourism," he says, speaking a bit like an attorney but with passion. To prevent this fate, the youth need jobs and housing, the possibility of "staying here and becoming citizens of Venice," he says. But how? I ask. He gives what he terms a "provocative" comparison. "Venetians who want to live and work in Venice should be treated as the World Wildlife Foundation treats animals like the panda," he suggests. "They need to be conserved, protected and helped." And if not, what then? "Venice will become a museum — and Venice cannot become a museum." If the hotels and restaurants take over everything, "at a certain point you will find no more Venetians, you'll find only sales clerks from Bangladesh, China and Africa — and I have nothing against them — but it will no longer be Venice!"

Casson charges the government — at all its levels — with "not only not resolving but making worse" all the major issues it faces.

"There is no perspective; no one looks at the future," says Casson. "What we have are politicians who think only about their term of office, about the next three to four years. Meanwhile all the cities, especially the big ones, and even more for complicated cities like Venice, need to take at least a medium-term perspective, if not a long-term one. We need to know what will happen to the port in Venice in twenty to thirty years time, what industry will be in Port Marghera, what will happen to Mose, to the lagoon, to the protection of Venice, to Mestre and what will become of its suburbs — but no one has any idea. There are no current projects planned. So we live, day to day, on the money that comes in from tourism and from the special law."

The Mose dam has been "a wellhead of corruption" and it will cost some €100 million yearly in maintenance that no one — not the city, region nor the state — has any intention of paying, he says. A commission should be set up to verify whether Mose will work or not and who will pay to maintain it. "If the answers are negative, enough! Shut it down."

As to the cruise ships, they could not continue to pass through the city's canals — and everywhere else in the world people do not expect to arrive in the city centers, he tells me. Since the 1980s, people have demanded the ships stay outside the lagoon, a solution that he favors. "Venice must demand to be respected!" But the problem remained unresolved, he adds, "because money is made from cruises to Venice and elsewhere, so continually making no decision" allowed the cruise ships' visits to go on.

The rerouting of cruise ships to Marghera in 2021 was seen by opposition as a flawed step forward. Within weeks, regional government had already announced cruise ships would still pass through the Giudecca Canal until the new facilities were ready, which was, they said, "imminent," but could take two years. Apart from the risk of jamming up the Canale dei Petroli, injuring the port economically, the arrangemment lacked any certainty that the outside port would ever be built. Thus they feared the Marghera cruise ship facilities would end up like the "temporary" 1933

Academia Bridge, as a permanent solution — or worse — Brugnaro might find a way revive his environmentally risky plans for renewed use of the old cruise ship port, Stazione Marittima, at the eastern end of Venice. He has continued to call for that solution and to speak against plans for an outside port.

Meanwhile, Port Marghera "has been allowed to slide toward destruction," Casson says. Whatever happens, expanding the port by digging new canals "must absolutely be avoided" because the zone is badly polluted. "It is totally impossible to control the spread of poisons in the lagoon" and new canals would aggravate the ruinous erosion already created by the Canale dei Petroli, the main shipping channel in the lagoon.

Casson criticized the Brugnaro administration in particular for a litany of omissions, inaction and failures: lack of long-term planning for the future; failing to pursue support needed from the national parliament — even though the government's party, the Lega, holds considerable power there; inability to think innovatively about the problems of the Mose dam, tourism and the port; cutting social services; undermining local democracy by weakening the six local area administrations and last but not least, proposing to move urban and regional institutions of Venice to Mestre — including Ca' Farsetti.

I raise my head from my note-taking at this remark. "There's a proposal to close Ca' Farsetti?" It felt to me like turning Westminster into a bingo hall or the White House into a bed and breakfast.

That's the idea, he confirmed, to move the municipal activities to Mestre, leaving only representative offices. "This can't be done... because this gives exactly the wrong impression — that you want to close the city and make it a museum! Keeping them open means the city lives, along with people and institutions. This choice costs more, that we know; we know Venice is complicated and needs money. But it's the job of politicians, with financiers and economists, to do things in a way that ensures this complicated, difficult city continues to stay alive. It's a challenge, but it's necessary...."

One of the sources of political stasis is that the islands and terraferma are like squabbling siblings.

Since 1926 the city of Venice has contained Mestre, Marghera and the other towns on the terraferma — once "countryside" — and Venice with its islands, was the urban center. Now, for all practical purposes, at least in terms of the population, commercial and political epicenters, the roles have been reversed. Within the city of Venice, the terraferma commands more power today because four-fifths of the 280,000 residents of Venice live there. Island Venice is the "historic quarter" and, in the eyes of many, including many Venetians, it has lost its urban-center status. The mayor of Venice does not really need to listen to the island Venetians, many believe. His fate — his re-election — is determined on the terraferma.

Politically, this change has made Venetians, especially under Brugnaro, feel ignored and forgotten. Referendums on dividing historic Venice and its lagoon islands from the terraferma have always failed because, while the terraferma and islands share vital organs — tourism, the port and, not least, the lagoon — their lifestyles and outlook could hardly be more different. The most recent vote on December 1, 2019 ended in a defeat for those in favor of separation — as clearly through apathy or rejection, voters were not interested in the option.

Mestre and the terraferma have only begun to deal with their own needs, aspirations and identity. The islanders often say the terraferma residents fail to understand the water and how life is lived in a city on a lagoon. But they don't get much of a hearing, in part because, for a long time, the people of the land have been treated as poor cousins and live with the consequences of Marghera's industrial legacy.

In addition to these divisions, authority in the lagoon territory is subdivided among a half dozen or more regulatory bodies. This has slowed and complicated any kind of overall development and change, as any proposal has to go through so many levels of permission.

No government is without strains. No country is condemned to victimhood, forever at the mercy of forces that afflict it. There is certainly nothing inherently flawed in Italian political DNA. Politics change. People power movements and unexpected crises like Covid-19 can unexpectedly change the course of history. Failed politics have left Italy struggling, but politics can resolve its problems.

For Casson, changing politics for the better demands nurturing the political culture, which "must come from the ground up, not so much from institutions, but from the schools and families. That's where awareness needs to change. I always come back to the question of the environment, which for our area remains the principal and fundamental issue. If we do not teach the young, the children, the university students to respect the environment and think from a different perspective, we won't succeed in changing things."

Of all the advocates for Venice, none are more pessimistic than Lidia Fersuoch, head of the Venice Italia Nostra, part of the national environmental and heritage organization, who sees around her "a project to break up the city." She expects the city's population to reach 30,000 or less in the next twenty years and declares herself to be "totally negative" about the prospects for the future of Venice.

But a light shines through her frustration.

"There's a solution for everything," she says. "I am not pessimistic in the sense of giving up hope... my pessimism is not about what can be done in Venice, *mamma mia!* You can change the fate of Venice, if you want. But the will is lacking! The problem is only political. If the politicians so choose, we can have funding, we can have a new law...." In fact, she sees potential everywhere in Venice, in a project that could transform the Arsenal and revivify artisanship, taking back control of the Biennale so that it works more for Venice — instead of its current "colonial attitude" towards the city — establishing a new museum of Venice and the lagoon, and other ideas to improve the quality of life. "I begin with the blackest of pessimism, but then, if there is the will, we can open up great new horizons for Venice because, as Corbusier said, it is the city of the future — if there is the will."

28

PROTEST
BEGIN WITH A VISION OF THE FUTURE

We resist.

We resist like the citizens of this city and we would like to share their dreams. We offer them lives of debris, fragments of beauty, plant wonders.
From below, there where we are, we give to those who pay attention to us the courage and hope to believe in a Venice made not only of stone, not only of voracious and hasty looks but a place to live, linger, grow and maybe, one day, become trees.

—"THE WEEDS OF VENICE: LITTLE STORIES OF PLANT AND HUMAN RESISTANCE," BY TIZIANA PLEBANI (TRANSLATED BY DANIELE PIO BUENZA)

On the top deck of the cruise ship floating along the Giudecca channel, the passengers have gathered along the railings. From there, at the height of the tallest bell towers, looking down at La Serenissima below, they see the landscape of terracotta tile roofs, the etching of canals and bug-sized people. The same passengers, looked at from the Zattere, the shoreline walkways along the broad channel, appear to be a dotted line of colored flecks flanking the skyscraper on its side, a moving, white wedding cake decorated with bright orange life rafts, picture windows and balconies. The giant is being pulled by tugboats out to sea, something that happens several times a day on weekends, but on this day scores of little boats are swarming forth as it approaches, carrying protesters who wave banners and chant slogans at the giant. "*No Grandi Navi!*" ("No cruise ships!"), "*Vergogna*" ("Shame"), and "*Fuori le grandi navi dalla laguna*" ("Cruise ships get out of the lagoon"). A thousand demonstrators on the water and pavements rail against the danger posed by the ships, which on rare occasions have lost control and careened into the quay. With police boats and jet skis zipping among the waterborne demonstrators to make sure they don't actually impede the ship's progress, the shouts of protest rise to a fever pitch in the minutes when the ship lumbers past. With passengers on its back, it moves by without stopping or slowing, with only the barely perceptible waves of a few passengers from on high. Perhaps they were too far away to read the signs or hear the words or maybe they understood no Italian. The ship passes. The protesters head home.

Protest is Venice's best hope, but it needs some support. Novelist Tiziano Scarpa had good reason to express concern. He said many initiatives have been championed by Venetian associations, "Yet the Venetians are so few. Don't let us face this alone." His point is well taken. With a declining, aging population, Venice finds it harder and harder to make its voice heard, even as its needs become more urgent. Protests have yielded many a small victory for Venice, but, on the major issues, change has been frustrated. The powers that be have had their way, and, as in the demonstration against the cruise ships, the problem is, in part, that those who might play a role and exert pressure, not least the millions of tourists who actually pass through Venice, struggle to appreciate, or even hear, the messages that protesters for the city want to convey to them. Nor does the news typically convey the full story, tending to describe Venice's challenges piecemeal and one-dimensionally, when they are more accurately seen as part of a wider failure of democracy, of government meant to serve the greater good hijacked by self-serving economic interests.

So, after years of strife, one is led to ask, What is the matter? Why do the changes Venice needs slip away? It was in 2014 that commentator Salvatore Settis set out a formula in his book *If Venice Dies*: "Saving the historic city in Venice (and elsewhere) won't simply happen by reviving memories of the city's past or indulging in the pleasures of the present. Even protesting won't be enough: the only effective move will be re-energizing the active practice of citizenship and exercising the right to the city." That "right to the city" is the opposite of marketization of the city. It is contrary to the forces of neoliberalism which would sell off heritage and demean the role of the culture and social relationships.

In the years since Settis made this call, the money juggernaut devouring Venice has sadly only gained momentum, but then, in these last few years, it also seems that something has changed the balance. Social media and public consciousness have moved forward, generating phenomena such as the Extinction Rebellion, amplifying the voices of causes that seemed to be lost. Are not Venice and other cities fighting for their rights and becoming part of this movement, and does not that fact open up new doors to encourage change?

The floods of 1966 launched Venice into the global consciousness, with mostly positive consequences in the form of decades of work to save the city and the lagoon. Now it's time to save the city from the impact of human beings.

Some fifty boats took part in the September 30, 2018 anti-cruise ship protest, swarming out to the passing ship, shouting, blowing hornsand waving banners.

"We find ourselves confronted by a grave situation," in the words of the demonstration organizer Marco Baravalle, an academic who has lived in Venice for decades and who is a leader of the No Grandi Navi committee, established in 2012. It's a week before the big demonstration and we sit on benches in the pescaria, the covered fish market at Rialto. As supporters assembled for his pep talk, the tall, dark-haired Baravalle explains that the coming protests rail against "turning Venice into a theme park" and are part of a wider movement formed of some fifty associations and committees from across Italy, representing a growing push for environmental justice, "for greater democracy and against corruption," he asserts.

"You can't separate environmentalism from a general critique of society and of politics," he says, adding, "The Venice demonstrations show this because the lagoon IS the city and fighting for the lagoon is fighting for nature. If the lagoon disappears, if the ecosystem disappears, Venice is transformed, and most probably wouldn't die, but it would not be the same unique city. I believe Venice is the symbol of how the environmentalist fight is equally a fight for the right to the city — about cities as public spaces that unite people — and so a political fight, and a critique of the whole model of development.... If we win against cruise ships, the idea of the city also wins, and for me the latter is more important."

His words echo what Settis has said. "The future of the historical city is a vast topic being played out not just in Venice or Italy, but in the rest of the world, too, and Venice... can be taken as its supreme symbol." I feel the same, that all of our fates are bound up with the fate of Venice. If it is destroyed, a precedent is set that will everywhere make more vulnerable cultural beauty, the communities that bind us and the future of the human values that make cities livable.

Some politicians seem to be indifferent or resigned to population loss in Venice. But tourists and holiday residents do not make Venice, Venice. People who live in Venice and particularly those with long ties to life there make Venice, Venice. In fact, they are all that stands between Venice surviving and its becoming a touristed ghost town. Venetians maintain more than just the centuries-old spiritual and cultural life of Venice with their social activities, sports clubs, save-

Venice associations, book clubs, schools and communal memories, language and knowledge. They safeguard the physical Venice, literally maintaining the know-how and structures as places that are living and viable. They protect the lagoon and the city's longevity because they know and love the place as no one else can.

All of us — or at least anyone who has ever been or expects to be a tourist in Venice — plays an equal part. Tourism is a facet of international and local consumption, like energy or water. Excessive tourism afflicts many of the most beautiful parts of the world while it brings needed economic support. But it is ultimately controlled by tourists who are, collectively, a mighty force. A consumer movement could demand authorities urgently manage the visitor numbers, support the local community and take action on cruise ship issues. This force needs to be harnessed.

In fact it may already be in play. They were surely part of why the Italian government banned cruise ships from the Giudecca Canal in 2021and probably motivated the August 2020 MSC line to announce its ships would not visit Venice at least through 2021, stopping instead at nearby Trieste.

Individual tourists also need to play an active role. They need to get used to additional planning when they visit places like Venice. Do you want to stay a few days? Chances are that there will be opportunities year-round. Do you want to pop over for a day in the middle of the high season or a busy weekend? Then be ready to accept you might pay more for the privilege. Tourists will be ready to accept such things if they are educated to understand the need, if they realize that Venice lives, that it is still a city and not a museum. After all, they too want to save Venice, and they want to visit a Venice that is not overcrowded, one they can enjoy and one where the residents welcome them.

Here, then, comes the really hard part: giving Venice a future means stepping back from high-volume mass tourism, and that means changing economic expectations, reducing profit for some — such as for apartment owners cashing in on rentals — and this may cause job losses and business closures. That is why a winding-down plan needs to cushion the economic pain, incentivize business to adapt, attract more non-tourist based jobs and rebuild the endangered Venetian community. People and business can accept change, if they have alternatives, reasonable support and clear rules.

Some, who regard themselves as political realists, don't believe a rollback is possible. But a step-change can happen. It has happened in the past in Italy, the country that against all expectations changed its divorce laws, that rose from poverty with the economic miracle of the 1950s and '60s, that has made inroads against organized crime, and that has gone a long way since 1966 in saving Venice and its lagoon — even if the job is far from done. What's more, Venetians are heroically campaigning to keep their city alive — and they won't give up.

A hope that many hold out for is the long-delayed action by UNESCO. The threats to Venice listed by this organization have been growing year by year. In 1990 it enumerated several "impacts of tourism." In 2014 threats from erosion, marine transport and water were added and, by 2019, they added threats arising from legal and management planning. Plans were agreed with Venice authorities for a solution, but those goals have repeatedly not been met by the Italian government.

The list is "designed to inform the international community of conditions, which threaten the very characteristics for which a property was inscribed on the World Heritage List and to encourage joint corrective actions," UNESCO Director Dr. Mechtild Rössler said in response to my written questions. "In many cases, it led to considerable support for the sites, including financial support whether national or international. The List of World Heritage in Danger is sometimes not fully understood by national and local authorities as it was intended by the [1972 World Heritage] Convention, so reactions are not really predictable." That may be so, but what Venice most needs now is the pressure of international opinion, and a UNESCO decision to put Venice on the endangered list might well give it the needed push.

Though the Covid-19 virus left Venice devoid of tourists and on its knees economically, it may have a silver lining. The drop in tourism has forced thousands of housing units given over to tourist and Airbnb rentals back into the residential market, lowering accommodation costs and encouraging Venetians to return. But the reverberations could be broader. "This could be the occasion that pushes us to begin reflecting on possible alternative paths to take, clearly not rejecting the resource of tourism, but managing it seriously," wrote journalist Claudio Madricardo. At the height of the pandemic even Mayor Brugnaro, normally a tenacious defender of the tourist economy, said, "It's clear that the model needs rethinking." He suggested high-speed internet cables newly installed in the city could be a basis for a revised form of development.

In 2018, Cristiano Dorigo and Elisabetta Triveron asked twenty-six Venetians from all walks of life to look ahead and describe in an essay, a poem or an image the Venice they each hoped for, the Venice they would like to live in, and they published them in a book by that name, *La Venezia che vorrei*. The contributors ranged from those born abroad to those who grew up in Venice, from inhabitants of the lagoon to scions of the terraferma. They reminisced and looked around them.

Journalist Gianni Favarato recounted the misadventures that have affected Port Marghera, where in 1925 at its launch, forecasters saw "a fable" in the making, but where "in the many years since, it has been transformed into an immense human, environmental, health, economic and social tragedy." Attempts to set this right have fallen short and he declares, "The Venice I want and that I believe many Venetians want is not this one!"

Historian Gilda Zazzara had a list: "I want politics that are not only local but begin from the local, that have the courage to say that consigning Venice to 'the spontaneous forces of the market' is a crime, that recognize that Venice is an example of how wild capitalism can be devastating not only in so-called developing countries, but also where it was born and triumphed. I want a politics that is capable of opposing the primacy of profit in the development of society. I am not crazy. It says so in Article 42 of our constitution." The Constitution recognizes free enterprise, on condition it does not damage the common good.

Poet and musician Maddalena Lotter, twenty-seven, born in Venice in 1990 and still a resident, speaks for a generation who have tended to leave the city for their work, and she wanted to emphasize what Venice has to offer and can build on. She eschews the tendency to see Venice as a "romantic cadaver," preferring to think of it more realistically as a "living being" that needs us to adapt our definitions of pleasure so that it can be treated with respect. To do that, tourists and residents must learn that the very slowness of Venice "teaches us that speed of movements (by metro, for example) does not guarantee the enjoyment of going to places, on the contrary, it often deadens pleasure." For her, this lesson is the key to securing a future for Venice.

This view that attitudes need to change, that people need to behave differently — and not that Venice itself is flawed —speaks to the heart of the matter. Venice is an ancient place and — without destroying what it is — cannot be other than an ancient place with its own characteristics. That people need to slow down to live in and, indeed, to appreciate Venice is one of its virtues, but oddly the very feature that is most under attack. What is happening to Venice is like a gold rush, and oddly has some parallels to what happened when gold was discovered in 1848 at Sutter's Mill in what was then a fairly deserted California. The unbridled greed that gripped the world in that era — making prospectors rich at the cost of genocide and starvation of the Native American population — has come again: Venice is one of the pots of gold where the legend of King Midas is unfolding.

Today the unbridled markets wreaking havoc in Venice are meeting resistance there, but those protests are running out of time. A passage in *La Venezia che vorrei* from Federico Gnech, a writer and Venetian by adoption, addresses the strain on Venetians.

Everyone in Venice believes they know what the problems are and how to resolve them, he says, "but we conclude every remark with a sigh, a moan or a curse — because, we say, the political will is lacking" to face up to the special interests.

> [W]e must be optimists because the miracle is already there — the city of Venice has existed for a millennium....We must take it back, a piece at a time, one by one and as a group.... Saving the public spaces, of course, but saving, before anything else, the mental space that Venetians have given up out of cynicism borne of present miseries.
>
> Let's conserve the marvelous architecture, for sure, but let us also recover, learning anew, the capacity to stay fascinated with it. Every political action — because that must be where we go when the moment comes — must begin with a vision of the future, from the extraordinary power of imagination of those who founded Venice, and from the utopia whose drive was exhausted during the centuries of money making. Start with resilience.... At that point it will be much easier to respond to the residents of other cities because we will be an example for them. We can say,

yes, we have wanted a house in Venice because we are selfish and we live beyond our stations, but we did it all for you. We have succeeded in saving Venice; we can save the whole world.

MY STORY

RETRACING THE FOOTSTEPS OF HISTORY

"[...] People don't take trips — trips take people."

—*TRAVELS WITH CHARLEY* BY JOHN STEINBECK

On my second-to-last day in Venice we were sailing over the lagoon in the dark of a cool spring night, well past midnight, with only the cloud-obscured moon above, the lights of Tronchetto, Lido and Pellestrina behind and those of Port Marghera ahead. Our *vela al terzo*, a gaff-rigged, open sanpieròta glided in silence over the black water, using the power of the light winds filling the cotton sail. We were on a trip from Venice that would take us up the 'old' Brenta river, the one that existed before the main river was diverted away from the lagoon in the sixteenth century. The trip was supposed to take place by day, but schedules had conspired to push the launch back. That was okay by my guides. Confident in their knowledge of the lagoon, with only lamps strapped to our foreheads to see by, we set out in the black of night.

Nicolà Ebner manned the tiller and Emiliano Simon and I took turns standing at the bow, dipping an oar rhythmically to supplement the meager winds. We could hear only sounds of the wind rippling the sails, the splash of the oar and the faint thrum of the refineries in Marghera ahead. We were heading to Fusina, further along the shoreline where, for centuries, visitors to Venice would arrive by river or land to board a boat for the final leg of their journey over the lagoon to Venice, from there clearly visible over the water.

It would take us almost three hours to get to Fusina, where we overnighted, sleeping in the boat, and then passed through the first of three locks the next morning to motor — this time we did use an outboard engine — upstream through the meadows and farmland as far as Villa Pisani. Also known as "La Nazionale," the 114-room, eighteenth-century country mansion of a doge had played host to Napoleon, Byron, King Victor Emmanuel II, Mussolini and Hitler. I had always wanted to see it, but what I most desired was to go back down the Brenta to get a feeling for what kings, popes and commoners must have felt as they approached Venice along the river.

The next day we rowed back towards Venice, going downstream for an hour or so, passing nesting swans, river turtles and fishermen along the banks, probably taking in a view not unlike that which travelers in centuries past would have had. When we tired of rowing and had run short of time, we switched the outboard back on, a luxury unavailable to those of previous ages. We passed back through the three locks and under the towering refuse-processing plants at Fusina by late afternoon, re-entering the lagoon under a pale blue sky. The winds had freshened, so we shut off the motor and hoisted the sail.

I took the helm, and, with the wind behind us, we headed for Venice, its profile looming on the horizon. For the hour it took to sail back to Venice, I kept thinking that for centuries until the rail bridge was built in 1846, most of those coming to Venice arrived just this way, by wooden boat, perhaps propelled by rowers when the wind dropped, or perhaps by sail; perhaps late in the day after a long tiring journey, then arriving with great anticipation, joy and the thrill of reaching a city unique in the world. Can we step into the shoes of others who lived in a place centuries before we arrived? Is not all of Venice a place so rich in history that in every corner we can relive the past which made us who we are? I felt I could, at that moment, and that history had come alive. For me a dream had been fulfilled and, finally, I had a story to tell.

Near the end of my stay we sit down to supper, seven of us, around a long wooden table in the kitchen with a log fire burning in the ample hearth. We are celebrating nothing in particular, just celebrating, as one often does when dining with Italians. Sofia has invited me to join her family and friends around a table with a red-checkered tablecloth in a country villa marooned in the suburbs of Mestre.

On plates before us we behold steaming hot, red chicory lasagna with smoked provolone cheese next to generous dollops of spinach risotto, big spoonfuls of potato puree and hefty slices of polenta, a dish of yellow cornmeal that our host has poured out, cooled and sliced just before we sit down to eat. All this is accompanied by steamed *malcotto* bread made with lard, good red and white wines from local vineyards, and followed by sheep's cheese, soft, fatty taleggio, and a chocolate torte and banana cake. We finished off with two kinds of grappa, one flavored with gentian and one with the herb rue. It was one of the finest meals I have ever had the pleasure to enjoy.

Somehow, all is right with the world when there's good food and good company. In months of traipsing around Venice, I had rediscovered old friends after so many decades away. I had added many other new friends, people who shared with me their opinions and fears for Venice, people who helped me in so many ways. In all the ways that mattered, the venture had succeeded. As the poet Dante says, *Noi non potemo avere perfetta vita senza amici* — We cannot have a perfect life without friends.

ACKNOWLEDGMENTS

I have tried to give my sources a fair and honest voice, but in the end, of course, this book sees Venice through the filter of my own eyes. Naturally, any errors, oversights or mistakes that appear, having escaped my best efforts to eliminate them, remain wholly the responsibility of the author.

I want to thank the love of my life, my wife Susan Daruvala, who has supported me always, as have my children, Joel and Anna, my sister Ruth Robbins and brother-in-law Jim Daruvala whose visit was most heartening. I wish to express my heartfelt gratitude to the Keller family, Giovanni, Ursula, Anna and Marta, my Italian brother and sisters whose cooperation and support made this book possible. Equally, I am greatly indebted to my good Venetian friends Stefania Senigaglia, Alessandra Schiavon, Laura Mangini, Isabella Panfido, Mario Santi and Checco Turio-Bohm, and, in Ancona, Fabio Spegne and Maria Pia. The book would not have been possible without their support, friendship and contributions.

I thank AFS International Programs ("Intercultura" in Italy) for originally giving me the opportunity to go to Venice from 1971–72. For providing a *pied-à-terre* over the months I worked in Venice in late 2018 I thank Elena Pollachi most warmly. Sofia Bareato, my research assistant, worked diligently and the final product would have been much diminished were it not for her enthusiasm. I am greatly indebted, too, to the indefatigable Luana Castelli and Silvio Testa for taking me on an unforgettable trip through the northern lagoon, for invaluable feedback on various chapters, and for advice and materials on the history of recent Venetian politics. I am grateful to Tiziana Plebani for her enlightening tour, Mariagrazia Dammicco for the visit to the Palazzo Nanni-Bernado garden, to Anna Messinis and Andreina Zitelli for the political insights, to Cristina Gregorin for an exacting read of the manuscript and to Giampietro Pizzo and Jan van der Borg for checking sections. Thanks to Emiliano Simon and Nicolà Ebner, rowing teachers par excellence, for their kind support at Venice On Board, and to Patrizia Zanella, for an insider's view of Sant'Erasmo island. I am grateful to John Francis Phillimore, who became a friend ready to share his droll observations. Thanks also to Luciano Baroni, Giovanni Caniato, Jenny Condie, Paola Lanaro, Vittore Pecchini, Paolo Peretti and Giuliano Zano for their valuable thoughts.

Thanks also to Mara Rumiz for guidance on politics and wonderful meals, and to Michela Scibilia for her expertise on Murano, hospitality and not least the maps, and to Lorenzo Bacelle and Jane Garner, for allowing me to make a base camp in their flat in Venice during April 2019. I want to thank most especially Caterina Falomo, who took a chance on helping a complete stranger, and my sailing partner Alessandro Corsi.

Thanks to my fine editors Sue Poulsen, Iain Maloney and Maria Scala; graphic designer Sarah Beaudin, proofreader Madeleine Curry and marketer Elizabeth Psaltis and for tips from Jean Daruvala, Ann Garvey, Anne Mariager, Clare McPhee, Becky Allen, Deborah Howard, Gioia Filocamo, Jennie Condie, oral historians Becky Porter and Sarah Lowry and finally, Kiran Nagarkar, who is now sadly no longer with us.

Parts of the environmental chapters first appeared in *The Guardian* in December 2019.

Over the years I have had the privilege of studying Italian with a number of superb teachers, startingwith Rosalba Francina, Rosario Maffei, Rosalba Silvestro and Daniele Pio Buenza in Cambridge, and Angela Galvan in Budapest and Federica Testaverde in Rome via Verbling.com. *Grazie molte!*

Finally, I am indebted to everyone who took the time to share with me their thoughts on matters Venetian, not all of whom are actually quoted in the text.

GLOSSARY

barena	salt marshes (as a whole)
bricole	tripod-shaped channel markers in the lagoon
calle	street in Venice
fondaco	warehouse
fondamenta	street parallel to a canal
forcola	oarlock for rowing Venetian style
ghebi	vein-like creeks in salt marsh mudflats where tide water enters and exits
palazzo	variously any big old building, but in the context of Venice an ornate multi-floored noble house
piano nobile	the floor or floors in a palazzo with a large central hall and radiating reception or living areas
portego	the large central hall on the piano nobile. The portego has large windows and typically overlooks a canal
sandolo	a traditional boat for two rowers now used for fishing, pleasure and races
sestiere	a district of historic Venice, of which there are six: San Marco, Cannaregio, Castello, San Polo, Dorsodoro and Santa Croce
spritz	prosecco with bitter Campari liqueur and sparkling water
terraferma	what the Venetians traditionally call their land territories, once much of northern Italy. Now, the name applies to Mestre, Marghera and nearby areas of Venice
terrazzo	floors made of a compressed and then polished mixture of chipped marble and lime mortar
traghetto	special gondola that ferries standing passengers across the Grand Canal
vaporetto	a ferry boat in Venice
velma	intertidal muddy bottom of the salt marshes

SELECTED BIBLIOGRAPHY

Aldersey-Williams, Hugh. *Tide: The Science and Lore of the Greatest Force on Earth*. London: Viking, 2016.

Belloni, Gianni and Antonio Vesco. *Come pesci nell'acqua: Mafie, impresa e politica in Veneto*. Rome: Donzelli Editore, 2018.

Bevilacqua, Piero. *Venice and the Water: A Model for Our Planet*. Trans. Charles A. Ferguson. Solon, Maine: Polar Bear & Co., 2009. First published as *Venezia e le acque*. Rome: Donzelli Editore, 1995, rev. 1998.

Benatelli, Nicoletta, Anthony Candiello and Gianni Favarato. *Laboratorio Marghera: Tra Venezia e il Nord Est*. Portogruaro, VE: Nuova Dimensione, 2006.

Bosworth, R.J.B. *Italian Venice: A History*. New Haven and London: Yale University Press, 2014.

Braudel, Fernand. *Venezia*. Bologna: il Mulino, 2013. First published as *Venise*. Paris: Flammarion,1984.

Brodskij, Iosif, Denis Cosgrove, Pierre George and Eugenio Turri. *La Laguna di Venezia*. Verona: Cierre edizioni, 2012.

Brown, Patricia Fortini. *The Renaissance in Venice: A World Apart*. London: Weidenfeld & Nicolson, 1997.

Burke, E. C. *The Greeks of Venice, 1498–1600, Immigration, Settlement, and Integration*. Turnhout: Brepols Publishers, 2016.

Calimani, Riccardo. *The Ghetto of Venice*. Trans. Katherine Silberblatt Wolfthal. Milan: Oscar Mondadori, 1995.

Caniato, Giovanni, Eugenio Turri and Michele Zanetti. *La Laguna di Venezia*. Verona: Cierre edizioni, 1995.

Casson, Felice. *Le fabbriche dei veleni*. Venice: La Toletta, 2015.

Cerasi, Laura. *Perdonare Marghera: La città del lavoro nella memoria post-industriale*. Milan: FrancoAngeli, 2007.

Chambers, David and Brian Pullan (eds). *Venice: A Documentary History, 1450–1630*. (Renaissance Society of America reprint). Toronto: University of Toronto Press, 2001.

Crouzet-Pavan, Elisabeth. *Venice Triumphant: The Horizons of a Myth*. Trans. Lydia G. Cochrane. Baltimore and London: The Johns Hopkins University Press, 2002.

Crovato, Giorgio and Maurizio Crovato. *Isole abbandonate della laguna: com'erano e come sono/The abandoned islands of the Venetian Lagoon: how they were and how they are now*. Republished bilingual edition. Teddington, Middlesex: San Marco Press, 2008. Originally published Venice, 1978.

Crowley, Roger. *City of Fortune: How Venice Won and Lost a Naval Empire*. London: Faber and Faber, 2011.

D'Alpaos, Luigi. *Fatti e misfatti di idraulica lagunare: La laguna di Venezia dalla diversione dei fiumi alle nuove opere alle bocche di porto*. Venice: Istituto Veneto di Scienze, Lettere ed Arti, 2010.

Davies, Robert C. and Garry R. Marvin. *Venice: The Tourism Maze: A Cultural Critique of the World's Most Touristed City*. Berkeley and LA: University of California Press, 2004.

Dorigo, Cristiano and Elisabetta Tiveron. *La Venezia che vorrei: Parole e pratiche per una città felice*. Spinea, VE: Helvetia Editrice, 2018.

Erbani, Francesco. *Non è triste Venezia: pietre, acque, persone. Reportage narrativo da una città che deve ricominciare*. San Cesario di Lecce: Piero Manni s.r.l., 2018.

Falomo, Caterina. *Quando c'erano i Veneziani: Racconti, visioni, passioni e speranze*. Venice: La Toletta, 2010.

________, (ed.), *I Nuovi Veneziani: Racconti, visioni, passioni e speranze*. Venice: La Toletta, 2013.

________, and Manuela Pivato, (ed). *Veneziani per scelta: i racconti di chi ha deciso di vivere in laguna*, Venice: La Toletta, 2012.

Fenlon, Iain. *Piazza San Marco*. Wonders of the World series. Cambridge, MA: Harvard University Press, 2009.

Ferraro, Joanne M. *Venice: History of the Floating City*. Cambridge, UK: Cambridge University Press, 2012.

Fortibuoni, T., O. Giovanardi and S. Raicevich. *Un altro mare: La pesca in Alto Adriatico e Laguna di Venezia dalla caduta della Serenissima ad oggi: Un'analisi storica ed ecologica*. Edizioni Associazione "Tegnue di Chioggia." Chioggia: 2009.

Freedman, Russell. *The Adventures of Marco Polo*. Illus. Bagram Ibatoulline. New York: Arthur A. Levine Books, 2006.

Gianighian, Giorgio and Paola Pavanini. Illus. Giorgio Del Pedros. *Venice: The Basics*. Venice: Gambier & Keller, 2010.

Gleeson-White, Jane. *Double Entry: How the Merchants of Venice Created Modern Finance*. New York: W.W. Norton & Company, 2011.

Goy, Richard J. *Venice: An Architectural Guide*. New Haven and London: Yale University Press, 2010.

Gransard, Marie-José. *Venice: A Literary Guide for Travellers*. London & New York: I. B. Tauris, 2016.

Howard, Deborah. *The Architectural History of Venice*. Rev. and enlarged edition. New Haven and London: Yale University Press, 2002.

Hughes, Hetty Meyric, (ed.). *Venice: A Collection of the Poetry of Place*. London: Eland Publishing, 2006.

Jones, Ann Rosalind and Margaret F. Rosenthal. *Veronica Franco: Poems and Selected Letters*. Chicago: The University of Chicago Press, 1998.

Jones, Tobias. *The Dark Heart of Italy*. Faber and Faber, Limited. (First ed. 2003). London: 2013.

Landon, H. C. Robbins and John Julius Norwich. *Five Centuries of Music in Venice*. London: Thames and Hudson, 1991.

Lane, Frederic C. *Venice: A Maritime Republic*. Baltimore and London: The Johns Hopkins University Press, 1973.

Laven, Mary. *Virgins of Venice: Broken Vows and Cloistered Lives in the Renaissance Convent*. London: Viking Penguin, 2002.

Lovric, Michelle. *Venice: Tales of the City*. London: Abacus, 2005.

Madden, Thomas F. *Venice: A New History*. London: Viking Penguin, 2012.

________. *Enrico Dandolo and the Rise of Venice*. Baltimore and London: The Johns Hopkins University Press, 2003.

Morris, Jan. *Venice*. London: Faber and Faber, 1993. 3rd ed. (First published as *World of Venice*, by James Morris), 1960.

Norwich, John Julius. *A History of Venice*. London: Penguin Books, 1977.

________. *Venice: A Traveller's Reader*. London: Robinson imprint of Little, Brown Book Group, 2002.

Panfido, Isabella. *Lagunario*. 2nd ed. Treviso: Santi Quaranta, 2017, trans. into English by Christine Donougher as *Venice Noir: The Dark History of the Lagoons.* Sawtry: Dedalus Ltd., 2021.

Pertot, Gianfranco. *Venice: Extraordinary Maintenance: A history of the restoration, conservation, destruction and adulteration of the fabric of the city from the Fall of the Republic to the present*. London: Paul Holberton Publishing, 2004.

Plant, Margaret. *Venice, Fragile City*. New Haven and London: Yale University Press, 2002.

Plebani, Tiziana. *Storia di Venezia città delle donne: guida ai tempi, luoghi e presenze femminili.* Venice: Marsilio Editori, 2008.

Rubini, Carlo. *La grande Venezia nel secolo breve. Guida alla topografia di una metropoli incompiuta (1917-1993).* Verona: Cierre edizioni, 2016.

Saikia, Robin. *The Venice Lido*. A Blue Guide Travel Monograph. London: Somerset Books, 2010.

Scandellari, Armando. *Leggende di Venezia*. Venice: Helvetica Editrice, 1984.

Scarpa, Tiziano. *Venezia è un pesce*. Milan: Feltrinelli, 2000. Trans. Shaun Whiteside, *Venice is a Fish: A Cultural Guide*. London: Serpent's Tail, 2008.

_________. *Dream of Venice in Black and White*, ed. JoAnn Locktov. Bella Figura Publications, 2018, bellafigurapublications.com

Scibilia, Michela. *Comprehensive guide to the island of Murano + San Michele Island*. Venice: Venice Photo Books, 2018.

Semi, Antonio Alberto. *Venezia in fumo 1797-1997*. Milan: Raffaello Cortina Editore, 1996.

Settis, Salvatore. *If Venice Dies*. Trans. André Naffis-Sahely. New York: New Vessel Press, 2015. First published as *Se Venezia muore*, 2014.

Testa, Silvio. *Tradizioni e regate della vela al terzo*. Illus. by Alex Pagnacco. Venice: Mare de Carta, 2011.

Toso Fei, Alberto. *Leggende veneziane e storie di fantasmi: Guida ai luoghi misteriosi di Venezia*. Treviso: Editrice Elzeviro, 2002.

Zanetti, Michele; Corinna Marcolin, Lorenzo Bonometto, and Valentina Niccolucci. *La Laguna di Venezia: ambiente, naturalità, uomo*. Portogruaro, VE: Nuova Dimensione, 2007.

NOTES

Direct quotes are in quote marks; indirect references are indicated in italics. Interviews by the author are not listed here, but are described in the text. They all took place between 2018 and 2020, mainly in Venice.

1 LETTERS

p. 5 *I still have the clipping from the...* Highland Park News, August 19, 1971.

p. 7 "astonished" at the very... Robert C. Davies et al., *Venice: The Tourist Maze*, p. 15.

p. 8 "momentary surprise which gives..." John Julius Norwich, *A Traveller's Reader*, p. 45.

p. 8 "Beyond the fancy of..." John Julius Norwich, *A Traveller's Reader*, p. 48.

p. 8 "Streets Full of Water. Please..." Jan Morris, *Venice*, p. 108.

2 FRIENDS

p. 19 *Venice, the city itself...* Tiziano Scarpa, *Venice is a Fish*, p. 1.

3 SCENES

p. 34 *There's been a steady exodus...* 52,996 as of December 30, 2018 according to City of Venice figures, but other reports gave the population as 52,000. Angel Giuffrida, "Inhabitants ebb out of Venice as city is flooded with water and tourists," *The Guardian*, January 10, 2020.

4 LIVING

p. 38 "the Venetian was bound to..." Deborah Howard, *The Architectural History of Venice*, p. 3.

p. 40 "There is no noise there save..." Henry James, *Italian Hours*, p. 12.

p. 45 *They marry less and later....* Peter S. Goodman, "Global Growth Cools, Leaving Scars of '08 Unhealed," *New York Times*, December 1, 2018.

p. 48 *For her, the real problems...* Pollution has been linked to respiratory illnesses, allergies, asthma and tumors all over Italy, which has an elevated incidence of these diseases. They cause one death in three nationally, and Venice, even without automobiles, has not escaped the trend, a Medicina Democratica report stated in January 2020, citing emissions from cruise ships, and Marghera and Po valley industry among the sources of emissions.

5 DYING

p. 50 "One day, perhaps, it will end..." excerpt from the poem "Lines", in *My Name on the Wind: Selected Poems of Diego Valeri*, translated by Michael Palma, Princeton University Press, 1989.

p. 50 *At heart, it is not...* Thomas F. Madden, *Venice: A New History*, p. 401.

p. 53 *In 1894, American writer Constance...* R.J.B. Bosworth, *Italian Venice: A History*, p. 56.

p. 53 "make death in Venice a virtual..." Margaret Plant, *Venice, Fragile City*, p. 196.

p. 53 "the most beautiful of tombs..." Tobias Jones, *The Dark Heart of Italy*, p. 248.

p. 54 "The rate at which Venice..." R.J.B. Bosworth, *Italian Venice: A History*, p. xii.

p. 57 *Venice as Disneyland...* John Russell, *New York Times*, August 2, 2017.

p. 57 *But the Disneyland trope...* Gregory Dowling, "Venice, not only Disneyland." https://www.tripfiction.com/venice-not-only-disneyland/, tripfiction.com, September 7, 2017.

p. 57 *Venetian psychoanalyst...* Antonio Alberto Semi, *Venezia in fumo* 1797–1997, p. 95.

p. 58 *Venetian doges had to swear ...* Thomas F. Madden, *Venice: A New History*, p. 427.

p. 58 *The population has shrunk and now...* For information on aging and demographics see http://www.venipedia.org/wiki/index.php?title=Demographics

6 CITIES

p. 61 "Every time I describe a city..." Italo Calvino, *Invisible Cities*, p. 78.

p. 64 "But luckily they did..." The metropolitan dream has returned repeatedly. Nicolò Spada, one of the early twentieth-century hotel developers, envisioned a double-lane tunnel under the lagoon to speed visitors' arrival. See R.J.B. Bosworth, *Italian Venice: A History*, p. 62.

p. 65 "had perfected a system of double-entry..." Jane Gleeson-White, *Double-Entry: How the Merchants of Venice Created Modern Finance*, pp. 8–9, 27.

p. 67 *The ideology, called neoliberalism...* For a useful explanation of this concept, see Stephen Metcalf, "Neoliberalism: the idea that swallowed the world", T*he Guardian*, August 18, 2017.

p. 67 *A single minibus full of the...* Aditya Chakrabortty. "Panic is on the agenda at Davos – but it's too little, too late," *The Guardian*, January 23, 2019.

p.68 "Do we really want the..." Salvatore Settis, lecture delivered at Ateneo Veneto, Venice, Italy, October 31, 2018.

7 ROWING

p. 80 "the historical memory of..." Massimo Gin, video at https://www.ilnuovotrionfo.org/video/, 2017.

p. 85 "I learned rowing alla veneta..." Cristina Gregorin, in comments to El Felze artisans' association, November 22, 2018.

8 TOURISTS

p. 87 *By the end of the 1990s...* Margaret Plant, *Venice: Fragile City*, p. 422.

p. 88 "about which so much has already been..." Robert Davies et al., *Venice: The Tourist Maze*. I am indebted to this book for much of the summary of tourist history.

p. 89 *The new Italian state...* The accounts of Venice after the Republic are largely based on R.J.B. Bosworth, *Italian Venice: A History*.

p. 90 *It was the first time...* The 200,000 figure is also used by R.J.B. Bosworth, *Italian Venice: A History*, p. xviii.

p. 91 *At present, on any...* The estimate of 40,000 commuters is from Fabio Carrera, interview with the author, November 2, 2018.

p. 91 *They follow a leader...* Relaxed requirements for training have allowed virtually anyone to lead tours, a loophole used by mainly foreign tour groups whose guides have been overheard spouting nonsense, such as "the Fondaco dei Tedeschi was an office of the Gestapo" or that 'Venetians die at forty to forty-five years of age due to the humidity." "Venezia le guide false e le leggende che contribuiscono a creare," *Industria del Turismo*, March 20, 2012.

p. 93 "Today is my first day here..." Tiziano Scarpa, *Dream of Venice in Black and White*, p. 6.

p. 95 *The boats carry some 1.6 million...* Eugenio Pendolini, "Venezia, la crocieristica macina record. Estate e weekend numeri da primato," *La Nuova*, February 4, 2020.

p. 95 *Tending to arrive on the busiest...* Anna Somers Cocks, "The coming death of Venice," *New York Review of Books*, June 10, 2013.

p. 95 *They generate terrible air pollution...* Until 2020, international shipping could freely burn fuel that is extremely high in cancer-causing sulfur but a 2020 International Maritime Organization rule requires the use of more expensive, low-sulfur content fuel or installation of a "scrubber" that cuts emissions by 70 percent. However, the fuel remains high in other pollutants and many vessels may try to dodge the new rules, unable to afford the cost of scrubbers and reluctant to pay the premium for cleaner fuel. See "New rules on ship emissions herald sea change for oil market," *Thomson Reuters Research*, May 17, 2018.

p. 96 *But the crisis unexpectedly...* "Venezia, il decreto del Consiglio dei ministri: 'Via le grandi navi dalla laguna'", *La Repubblica*, March 31, 2021.

p. 95 *Even at dockside, each...* "Luxury cruise giant emits 10 times more air pollution (SOx) than all of Europe's cars – study," by the Brussels-based, sustainable transport group Transport & Environment, June 4, 2019.

p. 96 *Cruise ship passenger numbers...* Kate Connolly, "Soaring number of cruise ships puts Arctic at risk, polar explorer warns," *The Guardian*, August 14, 2019.

p. 96 *Directly or indirectly creating...* Anna Somers Cocks, "The coming death of Venice," *New York Review of Books*, June 10, 2013.

p. 99 *In 2019, 1,092 people had left the...* "Venetian Exodus: Residents opting to flee inundations of tides and tourists," *The Guardian*, January 10, 2020.

p. 99 *It has been predicted that...* "Why are the Venetians fleeing Venice," *Newsweek*, January 1, 2009. Also, Jan van der Borg suggested 2050, interview with author, October 3, 2018.

9 LAGOON

p. 103 "The water 'beyond a limit...'" Michele Zanetti et al., *La Laguna di Venezia: ambiente, naturalità, uomo*, p. 181.

p. 103 "Seven fishermen out on the..." The author's translation draws on Armando Scandellari, *Leggende di Venezia*, pp. 99–104.

p. 104 *They resembled the jagged...* The play *Al Barenon... anime in guerra*, by Doria's grandson, Meme Pandin, about what happened there was performed in Venice in 2018.

p. 106 "A political and social organization ..." Elisabeth Crouzet-Pavan, *Venice Triumphant: The Horizons of a Myth*, p. 45.

p. 106 *Humble thatched houses...* I am indebted to Giorgio Gianighian, *Venice: The Basics*, for the account of early Venice.

p. 106 "Rich and poor live together in equality..." Mark Kurlansky, *Salt: A World History*, p. 81.

p. 107 *Gradually paved over with stone...* Joanne M. Ferraro, *Venice: History of the Floating City*, p. 8.

p. 107 *Any beaten earth path leading...* http://www.venipedia.org/wiki/index.php?title=Bridges (or that address with =Streets or =Canals for =Bridges)

p. 110 *Even so, water remained a scarce...* Elisabeth Crouzet-Pavan, *Venice Triumphant: The Horizons of a Myth*, pp. 1–17; Joanne M. Ferraro, *Venice: History of the Floating City*, p. 28; Giorgio Gianighian, *Venice: The Basics*, p. 33.

p. 110 *The demands of the lagoon are...* Elisabeth Crouzet-Pavan, *Venice Triumphant*, pp. 26–36.

p. 110 *Everyone — from rich to poor...* Piero Bevilacqua, *Venice and the Water: A Model for our Planet*, pp. 56–57.

p. 110 *Trial and error governed...* Michele Zanetti et al., *La Laguna di Venezia: ambiente, naturalità, uomo*, p. 187.

p. 111 "aquis pro muro munitur..." These words of the humanist Giovambattista Cipelli, known as L'Egnazio (1473–1553) are also on the wall of the Naval Museum of Venice.

p. 112 *The city tried to safeguard...* Piero Bevilacqua, *Venice and the Water*, p. 69.

p. 113 *Land reclamation from the nineteenth century...* Piero Bevilacqua, *Venice and the Water*, p. 77.

p. 113 *The petrochemical plants have...* Eight kilometers of metal piles driven in around the banks of the industrial area are meant to prevent further poisoning but 200 meters of the walls remained unfinished as of 2019.

p. 113 *To make way for bigger...* Michele Zanetti et al., *La Laguna di Venezia: ambiente, naturalità, uomo*, pp. 200, 202, 210.

p. 113 A study has shown the digging... "Venezia, Canale dei Petroli e scavi del Mose cause dell'aumento di acque alte," *La Nuova*, January 23, 2020. This study by Vincenzo Di Tella and Paolo Vielmo has reignited the debate about alternatives to reduce tidal flooding, such as the reopening the valle da pesca, discussed in 13 NATURE.

p. 113 *The true environmental costs...* R.J.B. Bosworth, *Italian Venice: A History*, p. 203.

p. 113 *The event sparked an outcry...* Michele Zanetti et al., *La Laguna di Venezia: ambiente, naturalità, uomo*, p. 197.

10 CREATIVITY

p. 116 "the actual stillness — one..." H. C. Robbins Landon et al., *Five Centuries of Music in Venice*, p. 175.

12 INSPIRATION

p.145 "A hundred deep solitudes create..." Marie-José Gransard, *Venice: A Literary Guide for Travellers*, p. 6.

p. 149 *Hugo Pratt, the cosmopolitan...* Among contemporaries important to the Venetian literary tradition Giovanni Montanaro also lists Pier Maria Pasinetti, Daniele Del Giudice, Roberto Ferrucci, Paolo Barbaro, Tiziano Scarpa, poet Diego Valeri and writer Carlo Della Corte. Scarpa himself said the writer who had understood Venice best was Barbaro.

13 NATURE

p. 155 "threats to the inland waters..." Piero Bevilacqua, *Venice and the Water*, pp. 21–22.

p. 156 *Now it is exactly the opposite...* Lecture by Luca Mizzan, head of the Venice Natural History Museum. I am indebted to him for the description of the lagoon, which draws on his remarks on November 9, 2018 at Compagnia della Vela.

p. 159 *At its height, the clam harvesting...* Fortibuoni et al., Un altro mare, p.153 and Michele Zanetti et al., *La Laguna di Venezia*, p. 209.

p. 161 *Barausse suggests resources....* VIMINE, an acronym for "Venice Integrated Management of Intertidal Environments."

p. 162 "has caused the loss of extensive areas..." Michele Zanetti et al., *La Laguna di Venezia: ambiente, naturalità, uomo*, p. 299.

p. 166 *Castelli is a founder...* Luana Castelli, Giampaolo Rinaldo and others have created 'Slow Venice', a brand that brings together a number of groups who want to bring an ethical approach to tourism itself. A spinoff has been the Associazione operatori del turismo sostenibile (OTS), the Association of Operators of Sustainable Tourism, whose manifesto sets out what 'sustainable and responsible' tourism is within the natural setting and how it can be delivered.

14 WOMEN

p. 171 "Spes et amor grato..." Tiziana Plebani, *Storia di Venezia città delle donne*, p. 198.

p. 171 *Marco Polo claimed to have traveled...* Russell Freedman, *The Adventures of Marco Polo*, pp. 5–7.

p. 174 *Thomas Coryat estimated in 1608...* Corriere della sera, May 19, 2019. See also http://www.enciclopediadelledonne.it/biografie/veronica-franco/

p. 175 "their whole city may well be..." Marie-José Gransard, *Venice: A Literary Guide for Travellers*, p. 18.

p. 176 *Nunneries were supposed to be bastions of chastity...* Mary Laven, *Virgins of Venice*, pp. xxiv–xxv.

p. 177 *The Jewish Sara Copia Sullam...* It is also recorded that Piscopia Corner became the first female university graduate in the 1670s, but Plebani has doubts over the claim as Corner never actually attended the university and was preceded by female graduates in Spain. A number of verifiable female graduates completed university studies in Italy in the 1700s.

p. 179 "Anyone who is a parent must..." Monica Scarpa, public talk at "Aula Baratto," Venice University, September 25, 2018.

p. 181 *Basaglia, a Venetian in...* The novel she co-authored is: *Alberta Basaglia and Giulietta Raccanelli, I rintocchi della Marangona, Baldini & Castoldi*, 2018.

p. 185 "to eat with another's mouth, sleep..." Veronica Franco, *Veronica Franco: Poems and selected letters*, p. 39.

15 TIDES

p. 186 "In the long term, if not the..." Hugh Aldersey-Williams, in *Tide: the Science and Lore*, p. 366.

p. 189 *Puzzling over tides goes back...* I am indebted for this information and the story of Galileo to Hugh Aldersey-Williams, *Tide: the Science and Lore*.

p. 196 *Mose suffered the largest outburst...* Gianni Belloni et al., *Come pesci in acqua*, p. 163.

p. 198 *A commissioner has said publicly...* "Mose, 100 milioni l'anno per la manutenzione. Pagheranno i turisti," *La Nuova*, May 8, 2019.

16 SYNANTHROPES

p. 204 *During the Covid-19 outbreak...* John Brunton, "Marine life flourishes in calmer waters in absence of tourists," The Guardian, March 21, 2020.

p. 205 *Coccon turned up to...* Francesca Coccon did the 2017 study with Lucio Panzarin and in collaboration with Veritas and CORILA.

p. 207 *In 1969, touched by the sight of...* It was called "Gruppo anglo-veneziano per la difesa degli animali randagi, Dingo" (Anglo-Venetian group for the defense of stray animals, Dingo), later just Dingo https://www.dingovenezia.it/

p.208 *Poet Elizabeth Barrett Browning's toddler...* John Julius Norwich, *Venice: A Traveller's Reader*, p. 138.

p. 209 *This seems to have caused a...* The figures provided by Francesca Coccon and Dario Gallotti, of the Venice animal welfare section, differed in detail but both told the same story. According to "gross estimates" provided by Gallotti, the pigeon count in 2009 dropped to 27,650 and to 23,041 in May 2018. No counts were made in 2007–08. In 2006 the number was 80,171, while in 1996, it was 112,276, with the figures diminishing in between. Rather than give a precise number in the text and risk giving the impression that this was the actual number, I have rounded, as the numbers are only gross estimates.

p. 210 *The position of honor...* To see some of these images, see research by Luisella Romeo on http://www.seevenice.it/en/dogs-venetian-art-museums/ and Erla Zwingle on https://iamnotmakingthisup.net/12855/venice-goes-to-the-dogs/

17 ABANDONED

p. 220 "Small private island 'Gemma'..." ... Notices abbreviated from http://www.immobilidipregioinvendita.com

p. 220 "future hub dedicated to..." Citing booklet at https://issuu.com/carattiepoletto/docs/saccasanbiagio_brochure-200x200-def

p. 221 *The Black Death came to Europe...* Ole Benedictow, "The Black Death: the greatest catastrophe ever," *History Today*, vol. 55: 3, March 2005.

p. 221 *The plague hit Venice in 1348...* Roger Crowley, *City of Fortune*, p. 172.

p. 221 *A series of lesser epidemics...* Joanne M. Ferraro, *Venice: History of the Floating City*, p. 75.

p. 223 *In the 1600s and 1700s, the defenders...* For more on lagoon military fortifications see, Il Piano di attacco austriaco contro Venezia, Venice, Marsilio: 2001, edited by Pierandrea Moro, with an introduction by Andrea Grigoletto.

18 WATER

p. 230 *All the models for Venice show....* For IPCC figures see https://www.ipcc.ch/srocc/chapter/summary-for-policymakers/

p. 230 "It could happen in fifty years..." Georg Umgiesser, Venezia Cambia public lecture at Sala San Leonardo, November 26, 2018. He cited similar figures to those of the IPCC, reflecting the fact that the predictions are in fact ranges.

p. 230 *With doubts raised even...*, Gianni Favarato, "Attività bloccate nove ore con le paratoie su, la conca di navigazione è ora il cruccio dei portuali," *La Nuova*, Oct. 4, 2020.

p. 231 *Possibly reduced by as early as 2040*... The prediction of 2040 comes from a lecture by Professor Luigi D'Alpaos on December 12, 2018 at Compagnia della Vela. He also calculates that with as little as a 0.3 meter of sea level increase, the Mose floodgates, designed to open and close twenty or thirty times a year, would have to close for sixty to eighty hours a month, and at 0.5 meters the rate of closures would hit 166 hours a month, enough to significantly obstruct shipping movement and undermine refreshment of the lagoon by the twice-daily tides.

p. 231 *No one knows if blocking* ... For some further information on a sewage system for Venice, see Robert Davies et al., V*enice: The Tourist Maze*, pp. 183–184.

p. 236 *The project was ready to go*.... For details see L'Agenzia Dire, May 23, 2016 https://www.dire.it/23-05-2016/55525-il-porto-di-venezia-aspetta-il-voops-e-marghera-sara-la-manhattan-italiana/

p. 236 *A protest group against cruise*... See "appello alle associazioni e ai cittadini del veneto per una grande manifestazione per l'estromissione delle grandi navi dalla laguna e contro le grandi opere inutili ed imposte,il 25 Settembre!" August 20, 2016, http://www.centrosocialerivolta.org/grandi-navi-a-venezia-storia-e-presa-in-giro-infinita-o-prossima-vittoria-per-la-citta-per-lambiente-e-loccupazione/

19 EMPIRE

p. 238 *Venice, the one and only*.... Veronica Franco, *Veronica Franco, Poems and selected letters*, pp. 126–127.

p. 240 "My lords, the greatest and most..." Roger Crowley, *City of Fortune*, pp. 33–34.

p. 243 "expand into the chaotic ruins..." Thomas F. Madden, *Venice: A New History*, p. 150.

p. 243 "not just the greatest and..." John Julius Norwich, *A History of Venice*, p. 142.

p. 243 *It was the first empire*... Thomas F. Madden, *Venice: A New History*, pp. 358–362.

p. 244 *The set of procedures and*... Thomas F. Madden, *Enrico Dandolo*, p. 57.

p. 247 "Venice, merely by surviving with its..." Frederic Lane, *Venice: A Maritime Republic*, p. 196.

p. 248 "Decadent Venice... is still the..." Fernand Braudel, *Venezia*, p. 73.

p. 248 "This is more important to the Venetian..." Thomas F. Madden, *Venice: A New History*, p. 294.

p. 249 *On the pretext of a deadly incident*... Thomas F. Madden, *Venice: A New History*, p. 368.

20 ISLANDS

p. 252 "As fragile as a piece..." Isabelle Panfido, *Venice Noir: The Dark History of the Lagoons*, p. 79.

p. 253 *Along with Sant'Erasmo*... 2011 census for Vignole. The other figures are from Giovanni Andrea Martini, president of the municipality.

p. 256 *This decline is linked to the*... "Accordi tra vetrerie e agenzie turistiche cinesi. Trovato il 'nero,'" *La Nuova*, September 27, 2019.

21 CONSERVATION

p. 263 *It was renovated, or rather reinvented*... Gianfranco Pertot, *Venice: Extraordinary Maintenance*, p. 58.

p. 264 "Off go all the glorious old weather stains, the..." Gianfranco Pertot, *Venice: Extraordinary Maintenance*, p. 222.

p. 264 *Mayor of Venice Massimo Cacciari used…* Iain Fenlon, *Piazza San Marco*, p. 145.

p. 270 *Only on my return half a century…* R.J.B. Bosworth, Italian *Venice: A History*, p. 6.

p. 271 "The problem is that heritage has…" Paolo Baratta, comments to visiting delegation, September 23, 2018.

p. 273 *Venetians themselves can struggle…* R.J.B. Bosworth, Italian *Venice: A History*, p. 248.

22 MYTH

p. 280 *In fact, the visitor was…* I am indebted to Iain Fenlon for his concise explanation of the mythical origins in *Piazza San Marco*, pp. xiii–xxi and pp. 1–145.

p. 284 *Of the 541 neighborhood shrines…* Marie-José Gransard, *Venice: A Literary Guide for Travellers*, p. 182.

p. 286 "They have never recovered…" Iain Fenlon, *Piazza San Marco*, p. 62.

23 LEGACY

p. 287 "In the Port Marghera industrial…" Cristiano Dorigo et al., *La Venezia che vorrei*, p. 54.

p. 288 *At the turn of the twentieth century…* R.J.B Bosworth, *Italian Venice: A History*, p. 103, p. 123.

p. 290 "To hell with that Venice…" Robin Saikia, *The Venice Lido*, p. 83.

p. 290 *These ideas flourished in part due…* I am indebted for much information on nineteenth-century Venice to Thomas F. Madden, *Venice: A New History*, pp. 372–392.

p. 292 "This ride was my delight…" Robin Saikia, *The Venice Lido*, p. 42.

p. 293 "In America, those who have…" R.J.B. Bosworth, *Italian Venice: A History*, p. 59.

p. 293 *Nicelli Airport, a casino…* The pioneers of aviation originally used hydroplanes due to the lack of proper terrestrial landing strips and the relative safety of water landings. One of the first such water runways was created at Sant'Andrea, and then later Nicelli airport was built. If landing at Lido today, the old water runway, on the left, and land runway, on the right, are still visible.

p. 293 *After the Second World War, Lido…* Carlo Rubini, *La Grande Venezia nel secolo breve*, pp. 208–211.

p. 294 *The population has declined…* Proposals to turn the Hotel des Bains into exclusive flats remain uncertain, but the tide of tourism in Venice has had some spill-over. Entrepreneur Teodoro Russo has done up and reopened the vintage 1907 Grande Albergo Ausonia & Hungaria, adding to its spaciousness and comforts. "The only possibility of growth in Lido, and I would say also for Venice, is to aim for quality," the developer said. "L'unica possibilità di crescita per il Lido, ma direi anche per Venezia, è puntare sulla qualità," *La Nuova*, August 13, 2017.

p. 294 *A final reckoning of…* Laura Cerasi, Perdonare Marghera, pp.15–27.

p 294 *Part of an urban-regeneration…* Description of M9 on its website, https://www.m9digital.it/it/il-museo

24 INCOMERS

p. 300 "Most of the people are…" David Chambers, et al., *Venice: A Documentary History*, 1450–1630, p. 325.

p. 301 *For all these reasons, the city's…* Deborah Howard, *Architectural History of Venice*, p. 56.

p. 302 "It is necessary to increase..." Caterina Falomo, ed., *I nuovi veneziani*, p. 111.

p. 302 *Slaves worked as servants, valets...* Joanne M. Ferraro, *Venice: History of the Floating City*, p. 78.

p. 302 *In 1228, Venice began to build...* Frederic Lane, *Venice: A Maritime Republic*, p. 61.

p. 302 *Venice benefited from...* Thomas F. Madden, *Venice: A New History*, p. 426.

p. 303 *Even so, Greeks established their...* E.C. Burke, *The Greeks of Venice*, 1498–1600.

p. 304 *It was this relative religious tolerance...* Richard Calimani, *The Ghetto of Venice*, pp. 10–11.

p. 304 "The Jews must all live together..." Richard Calimani, *The Ghetto of Venice*, p. 33.

p. 305 "As soon as the gates were..." Richard Calimani, *The Ghetto of Venice*, p. 251.

p. 310 *They are part of the 8.7 percent...* ISTAT, National Institute of Statistics, quoted by Roberto Savino, "Italians must wake up to this democratic emergency," *The Guardian*, March 19, 2019.

25 MONEY

p. 317 "If we are to have..." Naomi Klein, *This Changes Everything*, p. 461.

p. 319 *Or, today, he might have added...* Manuela Pivato, "Venezia, un milione in spot e comunicazione per riprendersi i turisti," La Nuova, January 5, 2020. See also: "Coronavirus, l'allarme degli albergatori di Venezia: 'Hotel semideserti, disdette continue'" *La Nuova*, February 5, 2020.

p. 321 *In the Middle Ages, money...* I am indebted for the information about currency, banking and lending to Thomas F. Madden, *Venice: A New History*, pp. 259–269.

p. 323 "It was, in a sense, the first virtual city..." Roger Crowley, *City of Fortune*, p. 373.

p. 323 *He pointed out palazzi that were...* In 2019 Venice led Italy with more than €750 million transacted in buying and selling of luxury hotels, 23 percent of the €3.3 billion total, Francesco Furlan, "Hotel di lusso, record di compravendite a Venezia. Nel 2019 affari per 750 milioni di euro," *La Nuova*, January 28, 2020.

p. 323 *By early 2021, this...* Alberto Zorzi, "Venezia, Luna Baglioni comprato per cento milioni. In vendita 50 hotel," *Corriere del Veneto, February 3, 2021.*

p. 328 *By 1975 the population hit 104,000...* Francesco Erbani, *Non è triste Venezia*, p.78.

p. 328 *Airbnb issued a promise in 2020...* Natalie Sherman & Michelle Fleury, "Has Airbnb grown a conscience," *BBC Online*, February 8, 2020.

p. 329 In 2018 the city government won... "Imposta di sbarco a Venezia, il Comune lancia l'appalto sui controlli," *La Nuova*, February 3, 2020.

p. 330 "Venice's problem is not hotels..." Alberto Vitucci, "Gli alberghi portano lavoro a Venezia, basta lamentele," *La Nuova*, December 4, 2018.

26 FUTURE

p. 333 *Historical Venice never stopped...* For more about innovations, see Frederic C. Lane's *Venice: A Maritime Republic*, pp. 255–257.

p. 333 "If you don't want to be caught by surprise..." Piero Formica, "Why Innovators Should Study the Rise and Fall of The Venetian Empire," *Harvard Business Review*, January 17, 2017.

p. 333 *Were it not for his untimely...* Other projects planned but ultimately never built include Frank Lloyd Wright's 1953 design for the Masieri Memorial, a Grand Canal palace; Louis Kahn's 1972 plans for a Palazzo dei Congressi in the Arsenal and Peter Eisenman's 1978 Cannaregio town square.

p. 334 *Officially called the Ponte della...* Michael Day, "Lawsuit gives rise to new bridge of sighs in Venice," *Independent Online*, January 12, 2014.

p. 334 *One might cite as an example...* Other less-celebrated examples include the ring of skyscrapers around the city, an idea floated by JDS Architects in 2010, and proposals for the homogenization of Venice with other urban conurbations involving motorways over the lagoon and "gateways" from the airport to facilitate access to "old Venice."

p. 336 *So many have blossomed...* These groups are described in *Guida alla Venezia ribelle* (*Guide to rebellious Venice*) by Beatrice Barzaghi and Maria Fiano, Volant Edizioni, 2015.

p. 337 *That will grow, by some...* Gian Antonio Stella, "Tuffi dal ponte, sesso all'aperto: A San Marco per fare picnic," *Corriere della domenica*, May 19, 2019.

p. 338 "We are working to put the community..." Emanuele Dal Carlo, quoted in 2017 in Monica Zornetta's blog, www.monicazornetta.it and also found on https://fairbnb.coop/emanuele-dal-carlo/

p. 339 "I'm here to speak about living in Venice..." Cristina Gregorin, TEDx San Marco talk, March 7, 2019.

27 POLITICS

p. 342 "As leaders we have a responsibility..." Naomi Klein, *This Changes Everything*, p. 64.

p. 342 "Would you be so kind..." email to author on December 10, 2018.

p. 342 *I was told I had come...* email to author on December 10, 2018.

p. 344 *Brugnaro says similar things....* Alberto Vitucci, "Gli alberghi portano lavoro a Venezia, basta lamentele," *La Nuova*, December 4, 2018.

p. 344 *Ever since the communist Giobatta Gianquinto...* I am indebted to Silvio Testa for this potted recent political history.

p. 345 *An independent who made...* Brugnaro has attracted controversy for banning from schools forty-nine books about discrimination or homosexuality, verbal bouts with Venice homeowner Elton John and, in 2017, ordering police to shoot on sight anyone who shouts "*Allāhu akbar*".

p. 348 *Within weeks regional...* Alberto Vitucci, "Grandi navi, tornano le Msc In Marittima e a Marghera," *La Nuova*, April 15, 2021.

p. 349 *He has continued to call...* E. T., "Il sindaco Brugnaro "affonda" sul nascere il nuovo scalo in mare," *La Nuova*, April 4, 2021.

p. 350 *The most recent vote on...* The 2019 vote fell short of the 50 percent quorum, so was invalidated, even though among those who voted the result was 66.1 percent for separation, with most of the 'no' votes on the terraferma and 'yes' votes in historic Venice.

p. 350 *In addition to these divisions...* The special laws passed in the 1970s and 1980s foresaw some kind of concentration of these powers, but this reorganization has yet to come to pass, despite efforts to amend the laws in

Parliament. The log-jam at the national level undermines everything further down the line.

p. 350 *No country is condemned...* Conversely, countries which have long enjoyed effective government can backslide. "Britain and Italy are the terrible twins of Europe," *The Guardian*, August 22, 2019.

28 PROTEST

p. 352 "We resist..." Tiziana Plebani, *Le erbe matte di Venezia: piccola storia di resistenza vegetale e umana*. The full text and translation is available on www.localsecrets.com until further notice.

p. 353 *Novelist Tiziano Scarpa had good...* Reprinted in Venezia che vorrei from *Corriere della sera*, February 22, 2018.

p. 353 "Saving the historic city in..." Salvadore Settis, *If Venice Dies*, p. 176.

p. 356 *They were surely part...* Eugenio Pendolini, "Grandi navi. Msc rinuncia a Venezia per tutto il 2020, Costa attende il via libera del governo," *La Nuova*, August 3, 2020.

p. 357 "designed to inform the..." Mechtild Rössler in an email response to the author's written questions, November 20, 2018.

p. 357 *That may be so, but what Venice...* At the request of the Italian government, a final decision was put off until the UNESCO expected to take place in 2021.

p. 357 *Though the 2020 Covid-19 virus...* Claudio Madricardo, "Coronavirus. The crisis that can save Venice", *Ytali* online magazine, March 7, 2020. https://ytali.com/2020/03/07/coronavirus-the-crisis-that-can-save-venice/

p. 357 "It's clear that the model needs..." Gianni Moriani, "Oltre il Coronavirus: idee per la Venezia del terzo dopoguerra," *La Nuova*, March 27, 2020.

p. 357 *Though the Covid-19...* Chris Allnutt, "Can Venice reinvent itself? With the tourists gone, residents are being lured back to the city," *Financial Times*, February 26, 2021.

p. 358 *In 2018 Cristiano Dorigo and...* Cristiano Dorigo, et al., *La Venezia che vorrei*: Gianni Favarato, p. 53, Maddalena Lotter, p. 93, Gilda Zazzara, p. 155, Federico Gnech, p. 81.

CODA

p. 361 "People don't take trips..." John Steinbeck, *Travels with Charley*, p. 208.

INDEX